A sociology of modernity

Confusion reigns in sociological accounts of the current condition of modernity. The story lines reach from the 'end of the subject' to 'a new individualism', from the 'dissolution of society' to the reemergence of 'civil society', and from the 'end of modernity' to 'another modernity' and 'neo-modernization'.

This book offers a sociology of modernity in terms of an historical account of social transformations over the past two centuries, focusing on Western Europe, but also looking at the USA and at Soviet socialism as distinct variants of modernity. A fundamental ambivalence of modernity is captured by the twin notions of liberty and discipline and examined in three major dimensions: the relations between individual liberty and political community, between agency and structure, and between locally situated human lives and widely extended social institutions.

Two major historical transformations of modernity are distinguished, the first one beginning in the late nineteenth century and leading to a social formation that can be called 'organized modernity', and the second being the one that dissolves organized modernity.

It is this current transformation which revives some key concerns of the 'modern project', ideas of liberty, plurality and individual autonomy. But it imperils others, especially the creation of social identities as ties between human beings that allow the meaningful and socially viable development of individual autonomy, and the possibility of politics as communicative interaction and collaborative deliberation about what human beings have in common. *A Sociology of Modernity* will be of interest to students of Sociology, Political Science and Cultural Studies.

Peter Wagner is Research Fellow at the Wissenschaftszentrum Berlin für Sozialforschung.

A sociology of modernity

Liberty and discipline

Peter Wagner

London and New York

First published 1994
by Routledge
11 New Fetter Lane, London EC4P 4EE

Simultaneously published in the USA and Canada
by Routledge
29 West 35th Street, New York, NY 10001

Typeset in Times by
NWL Editorial Services, Langport, Somerset

Printed and bound in Great Britain by
Mackays of Chatham PLC, Chatham, Kent

British Library Cataloguing in Publication Data
A catalogue record for this book is available from the British Library.

Library of Congress Cataloging in Publication Data
Wagner, Peter, 1956–
A sociology of modernity: liberty and discipline/Peter Wagner.
p. cm.
Includes bibliographical references and index.
1. Sociology–Philosophy. I. Title. II. Title: Modernity.
HM24.W183 1993 93-7382
301′.01-dc20 CIP

ISBN 0-415-08185-8 (hbk)
ISBN 0-415-08186-6 (pbk)

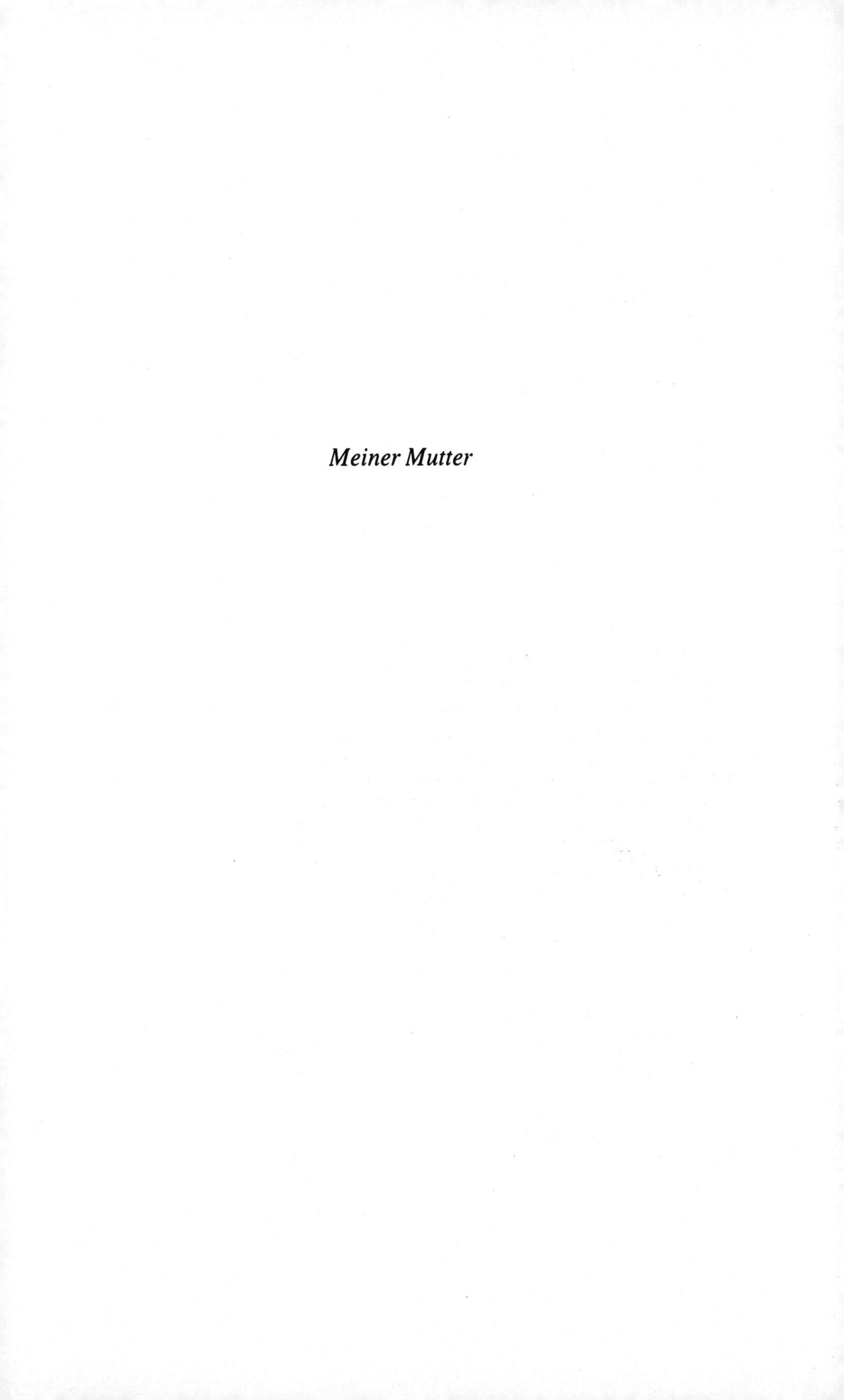

Meiner Mutter

Contents

Part V Towards extended liberal modernity?

Prologue

A SOCIOLOGY OF MODERNITY?

To propose a sociology of modernity seems tautological at best. What else is sociology, if not the systematic attempt to come to an understanding of modern society? At worst, a sociology of modernity could seem an impossible project. If sociology grew with modernity, as its mode of self-monitoring, then it could never achieve the distance to the object that every analytical endeavour requires.

Indeed, any attempt at a sociology of modernity risks falling prey to the problematic of its being enmeshed with the social world it tries to understand. Nevertheless, I think there is an important, if largely empty, space between tautology and impossibility. It seems worth trying to take a step back and gain some perspective on modernity, though it is still around us.[1] To look at modernity from a distance should be more easily possible in times of doubt and questioning. Indeed, the 'classical' sociologists, Max Weber and Emile Durkheim among others, were writing in such a period. And, among other signs, the debate on postmodernity indicates that we do so, too.[2]

There are good reasons for assuming that this is a particularly appropriate moment for trying such an assessment of the modern condition. Even below the level of the postmodernist discourse, contemporary Western societies have for the past two decades been widely seen to be undergoing a major restructuring. Most accounts of this have been in terms of crisis of one or the other core aspect of these societies: the governability crisis of mass democracy; the crisis of Keynesian-style demand management; the crisis of the social democratic welfare state; the environmental crisis of industrial technology; the relativist and post-positivist challenge to science; and so on.

In response to diagnoses of crises, concepts have proliferated that try to advance an understanding of the emerging features of the societies in transformation. The first, and probably still the most common of these concepts, was that of post-industrial society, proposed as early as the 1960s and in many respects a pre-crisis concept. Since then, notions like consumer society, knowledge society, information society, risk society, neo-liberalism, or new individualism have entered into the discussions. The notion of postmodern society is only the most fashionable of these new labels, equally vague and encompassing.

If there is widespread, though not unanimous, agreement on the existence of a major social transformation, there is also strong disagreement, even diverging views about its nature. The story-lines of accounts reach from the 'end of the subject' to the 'new individualism', from the 'dissolution of society' to the re-emergence of 'civil society', from the 'end of modernity' to an 'other modernity' to 'neo-modernization'. Confusion reigns, or so it seems.

To some extent, this confusion reflects the inability of sociologists to capture what I will call the ambiguity of modernity. Some aspects of social changes are emphasized at the expense of other, inverse ones. Furthermore, a basic rule for the analysis of social change is often disregarded. Authors describe a new social state and the process towards it in terms of comparison to an earlier state, but they hardly pay any attention to the adequacy and consistency of the concepts and terminology used to characterize the earlier state. A closer look reveals that most claims to novelty in the writings on 'new', 'other' or 'post' states evaporate. What is supposed to be new is very often a common feature of modernity.

This is one reason why I think that an attempt to understand the current state needs to be built on a historical redescription of modernity. Some may argue that a redescription is unnecessary given that sociology has already provided such an account over the years of its observation of modern society, from Weber and Durkheim to Parsons and beyond. However, the sociological canon cannot easily and directly be put to such use, exactly because sociologists were enmeshed in the modern project and modern practices they were trying to describe. While this inevitable fact does not make their work useless, it limits its use. This is the other reason why I think that a historical redescription, including a redescription of sociology, is necessary. My proposal is that sociological practices should be analysed and reflected like all other social practices of modernity. Re-reading modernist sociology will contribute to a current sociology of modernity, but rather as a source of interpretation than as a conceptual cornerstone.

THE OBJECT OF INQUIRY AND THE THESIS

The core argument of this reassessment of modernity is developed, in historical-empirical terms, for Western Europe. A practical reason for this focus is that I am most familiar with these societies, both from earlier research and from personal experience. An analytical reason is that this region is considered the birthplace of modernity, that its practices and discourses have provided the reference point in the construction of modern societies. I will, however, not refrain from looking beyond the boundaries of this region. From the turn of the eighteenth century, it was the United States of America and, after the beginning of the twentieth century, it was Soviet socialism that provided distinct variants of modernity. A contrasting look at these societies can enhance the understanding of the dynamics of modern social configurations.

Historically, the analysis will go back to the age of the democratic and industrial revolutions, that is, to the turn of the eighteenth century, a point in time which in some, though not all, respects can be taken to mark the beginning of modernity. A review of the two centuries since then will allow us to grasp the different forms the social configurations of modernity have taken, not only spatially but also temporally. An inventory of these forms is the precondition for understanding the changes that modernity is now undergoing.

It will emerge that the currently observable changes in social practices should indeed be regarded as a major social restructuring. They cannot be understood by merely seeing them as the continuation of certain trends of modernity, of 'modernization'. But they fall short of anything like 'the end of modernity', 'the end of history', or 'the end of the subject' (though meaning can be restored to these ideas). The latter notions imply the emergence of a social configuration that would be at odds with the constitutive ideas of human and social life as they developed between the sixteenth and eighteenth centuries. I think it can be shown that this is not the case. (While I will not attempt to demonstrate this explicitly, it can be implicitly understood from my reasoning.)

Rather, the current changes should be likened in scope and form to the transformation that set in towards the end of the nineteenth century and led, at that time, to a new social configuration, soon to be called 'mass society' and 'industrial society'. I shall portray that configuration as 'organized modernity'. The current changes amount to an end of that configuration, the end of organized modernity. The now emerging configuration, the contours of which are not yet fully and clearly visible, shares certain features with the nineteenth-century societies that preceded organized modernity, ones that I shall call 'restricted liberal modernity'. But it also shows features that are historically unprecedented.

Significantly, these latter features make it difficult to socially reappropriate the normative concerns of the Enlightenment, concerns which were highly alive during restricted liberal modernity, but tended to get lost or suppressed during organized modernity. Among those concerns that are most endangered are the creation of social identities as ties between human beings that allow the meaningful and socially viable development of individual autonomy, and the possibility of politics as communicative interaction and collaborative deliberation about what human beings have in common.

LIBERTY VERSUS DISCIPLINE?

This essay should be considered as an attempt to link an argument in terms of *social theory* to an informed *historico-sociological account*, and both of these to the problematics of *normative political theory*. The foremost task of social theorizing is to advance our understanding of *human agency*. To come to an understanding of *modernity*, is to me the most honourable ambition of contemporary history and social research. And the question of *liberty* can without doubt be regarded as the key problematic of normative political theory. Now, it seems to me that in order to come to terms with these key issues they have to be linked up to each other and brought to mutually inform each other. Otherwise argumentation will run empty, and masses of information and data will be heaped up without adding significantly to an understanding of the problematic.[3]

The double notion of liberty and discipline provides such a linkage. It captures the ambivalence of modernity in three major dimensions, namely the relations between individual liberty and community, between agency and structure, and between locally situated human lives and widely extended social rules.

The modern condition, it is often held, is characterized by freedom and democracy, and it is safeguarded by institutions that are based on the same principle of free aggregation. The most important of these institutions are the democratic polity, the market economy and the autonomous pursuit of truth, called science. While this has been the master discourse of modernity, an alternative, critical interpretation quickly emerged, counterposing the image of disciplinization by modern institutions to that of liberation. The entire history of modernity was characterized by the co-existence of these two discourses, but mostly they were segregated. Observers chose one or the other image, and they usually also chose between an endorsement and a condemnation of modernity. Only very few writers, such as Karl Marx or Max Weber, expressed a fundamental ambiguity in their reading of modernity and an equally fundamental ambivalence in their own attitude to the modern condition.

Accounts of modernity even seem to have become increasingly one-sided over time. Intellectuals of the late nineteenth century were more inclined to see a tragic double nature in modernity, combining unalienable gains and unacceptable losses. In more recent writings on 'modern societies', the achievements of the Western world are mostly either fully praised and its values whole-heartedly embraced, or its shortcomings emphasized and the loss of moral orientations condemned.[4] The current controversy over postmodernity – the very existence of a 'beyond' to modernity and its evaluation – is only the latest instance of such a polarization. The title of this book is meant to emphasize the need, analytically as well as normatively, to maintain the ambiguity and ambivalence which, in my view, are inherent in the modern project.

Although modernity emphasizes autonomy, the right and obligation to self-rule, it does not offer any guidance as to how one should design one's own rules, nor does it provide any criterion with which one should engage in rule deliberation.[5] The idea of liberty as autonomy was fundamental to modernity. Historically, however, the social context of the emergence of modernity provided material out of which boundaries for self-rule would be formed, for good reasons maybe but without sustainable universal criteria. The present condition of modernity can be characterized by a rapid, though not historically new, erosion of these boundaries, laying bare the absence of criteria.

Virtually all the present major political disputes focus on the individual right to self-define one's situation and possibilities for action, and on the definition of the boundaries and rights of the collective one is associated with. Issues ranging from abortion and genetic engineering to migration, citizenship and social rights, to the redefinition of polities in Western Europe and in the formerly socialist countries are a current focus of uncertainties and anxieties. These spring directly from the basic belief that human beings under modern conditions are not only enabled, but obliged to self-create their rules of life.

The historicity of human social life is the general form and context of self-rule. Nobody ever creates rules from nothing, in an empty space. As Karl Marx once put it: 'Human beings make their history themselves, but they do not do so voluntarily, not under circumstances of their own choosing, rather under immediately found, given and transmitted circumstances'.[6] As important as the idea of autonomy and self-realization was and is, the institutions that were historically erected – more or less – in its name had their specific features, interrelations and effects on individual and collective human action. It is with such a perspective that I shall try to analyse the building and the transformation of the institutions of modernity with a view to understanding their present configuration and its impact on the living conditions in modernity. Almost a decade ago, Anthony Giddens characterized his major book *The Constitution of Society* as an extensive discussion of Marx's above-quoted sentence.[7] Giddens himself arrived at the conclusion that institutions should be thought of as relatively durable sets of rules and resources that may have a wide spatio-temporal extension. Far from merely constraining human activity, channelling it into prestructured corridors, they also enable it by allowing human beings to draw on their rules and resources. In this sense, this entire book is one prolonged reflection about Giddens' notion of 'enablement and constraint by modern institutions', trying to spell out exactly who and what kind of activity is enabled and who and what is constrained.

If the major institutions of modernity can be regarded as durable sets of rules and resources, one characteristic trend in the history of modernity is the increasing extension of these institutions in both time and space. Sociological modernization theory, among other kinds of discourse, has taken this feature to denote a tendency towards universalization, a tendency viewed positively by modernization theorists. More modestly, I shall just note as evident that it is becoming less possible for individuals or groups of human beings to escape the reach of modern institutions. At the same time, everybody who makes successful use of these institutions can expect to extend his or, more rarely, her reach. Two issues are of key relevance here.

First, every member of modern societies, willing or not, is involved in the reproduction and change of these institutions by virtue of his or her own everyday activities. However, the capability of individuals and groups is, while constantly changing, highly stratified with regard to making use of these rules and resources or, even more so, with regard to reshaping them. For those who are less capable, but nevertheless forcibly exposed, the normatively underpinned promises of modernity may easily turn out to be 'blackmail' (Michel Foucault), an 'offer one cannot resist'.

Second, the wide extension of modern institutions enhances the tension between individual human life, which is bodily defined in time and space, and the chains of interaction in which any human being is engaged. The dislocation of human beings from ascribed spaces in local communities to much less pre-defined positions in large-scale societies is a common, possibly even the constitutive theme of sociology. In most of the sociological writings, however, strong preconceptions impede the recognition of the real issue. The misunderstandings extend in two directions. By overlooking the ways in which people link actively to institutional rules in their everyday lives, sociologists have tended to exaggerate the extent to which social practices are indeed delocalized, or 'modernized'. The social permeation of modern rules was historically much lower than sociologists often thought. In contrast, by over-emphasizing the coherence and functionality of modern society, sociologists have tended to neglect the active work human beings had to undertake to define and redefine their locations and identities in society, once they were indeed questioned.

Historical transformations of modernity involve major efforts by society's individuals to redefine their social places, with the outcome of these efforts always being uncertain. The need for such efforts is related to the historical extensions of institutions and to the uprooting of social identities which such extensions entail. These processes should not be condemned out of hand, as they may open up new opportunities as well. However, the reconstruction of social identities will be jeopardized if the new institutional rules are found to be inflexible and obscure by those who enact them in their daily lives.

If modern institutions do not merely enhance liberty but offer a specific relation of enablement and constraint, the substance and the distribution of enablements and constraints become important.[8] The history of modernity cannot simply be written in terms of increasing autonomy and democracy, but rather in terms of changing notions of the substantive foundations of self-realization and of shifting emphases between individualized enablements and public/collective capabilities. In this regard, my analysis leads me to diagnose problematic asymmetries.

The transformation of the human self during modernity should be seen as a parallel, and dramatic, process of both liberation and disciplinization. It makes certain types of self-realization much easier to achieve, but tends to prevent others. Among those other types is the possibility of a communicative relationship to a relevant collective of many others with a view to determining one's own fate. This may be called a tendency towards the self-cancellation of (political) agency (of liberalism, the liberal utopia) as an unintended consequence of *the process* of its pursuit *by* its actors and historical proponents.

THE APPROACH

The idea and perspective for this book grew out of earlier research on the historical development of the social sciences. Then, I tried to analyse the historical construction of those discourses that have come to be known as social sciences, their formalization and the setting of conventions for the practice of social science, and, in substantive terms, the interweaving of those discourses with other social practices. That research provided the two basic ideas that stand behind this book.

First, in theoretical terms, it supported a perspective in historical sociology that would look at the major social institutions as the building and conventionalization of social practices, rather than as systemic spheres of abstract, supra-historical entities. Second, in substantive historical terms, the analysis of social science lent itself to identifying a long formative period of conventions and habits, stretching from the late 1800s to the 1960s, followed by a period of loosened conventions and disoriented practices. Given that the discourses of social science were closely interwoven with the other social practices that they were meant to observe, not the least of which were states and markets, it seemed plausible to ask whether a similar sequence of conventionalization and de-conventionalization occurred throughout the entire social configuration. It is basically the image that such an examination provides which I elaborate upon in the following.

This book itself is a social science text, which is inscribed in the tradition of social science – though it tries to be less modernist and more reflective than the majority of other social science texts – and it is an attempt at self-understanding, of understanding one's own position in the present, with all the epistemological obstacles one may encounter. For this purpose, this text moves back and forth between giving an account of historical social reality and reflecting upon ways that accounts of this reality have been given. It treats its brethren, other social science texts, in a double way. It uses them as a source for the understanding of society, and it takes them as indicators of ways of seeing society at the time in which their authors wrote them.

There is, of course, no deprecatory intent in the latter practice, no implication of superior knowledge – apart from, maybe, hindsight. This practice merely reflects the inevitable status of social science, namely being part of the society it looks at and drawing its evidence as well as concepts from this social world. As this is true for every text I looked at, it is true for mine, too, which then may be viewed in a similar perspective. Since there is no Archimedean point, all that can be done is to weigh the evidence as carefully as possible and to be as self-reflective as possible.

I consider this text a work in historical-comparative social analysis, but I am aware of the objection, certain to be raised by specialists both in historical and in comparative study, that the analysis is far too sweeping and gives too little room for detail and difference to have a claim to that label. As widely as I try to search, the result will clearly remain insufficient in many respects. Obviously then, I cannot consider this book conclusive in any regard. It may raise many more questions than it answers, and some of its suggestions will certainly be found too preliminary and tentative. There is a risk in disregarding the boundaries of disciplines, and readers will have to judge whether it was worth taking.

Berlin – Uppsala – Princeton, December 1992

Acknowledgements

The ideas for this book were developed and most of the text was written in the environments provided by the Wissenschaftszentrum Berlin für Sozialforschung, the Institute for Advanced Study in Princeton and the Swedish Collegium for Advanced Study in the Social Sciences in Uppsala. I would like to express my thanks to all those in these three places who offered me their support and criticism, in particular Meinolf Dierkes in Berlin, Michael Walzer in Princeton and Björn Wittrock in Uppsala. Meinolf Dierkes, Heidrun Friese, Jeanette Hofmann, Hans Joas and Lutz Marz have accepted the burden of reading through all of the manuscript, and I would like to thank them for their comments and suggestions, which I have tried to heed as well as I could. And in a different way I want to thank Heidrun, too – for sharing the feeling for the ambivalence of modernity.

Part I

Principles of modernity

Chapter 1

Modes of narrating modernity

THE MODERN RUPTURE

For several decades, the term 'modern society' has rather unquestioningly been applied to the social formations of the Northwestern quarter of the world during the past few centuries. It relies on a basic distinction between these social formations and 'traditional' societies.[1] However, it has been immensely difficult to both exactly define the characteristics of modern societies and to show when they actually broke with traditional social formations.

Often, processes of urbanization, industrialization, democratization, the emergence of an empirical-analytical approach to knowledge are referred to.[2] All of these processes, however, extend over long periods of time, they do not always occur simultaneously, and some of them can be traced to regions and times quite distant from the so-called modern world and era. More specifically then, the so-called industrial and democratic revolutions are sometimes seen as the social phenomena constituting modernity.[3]

Even these revolutions are fairly extended and uneven phenomena in time and space. But if one starts with the political changes in seventeenth-century England and the economic transformations in the late eighteenth century, some demarcation is achieved. Furthermore, it can be argued that these developments had impacts, even if only gradually, on the rest of the world by changing the general conditions for phrasing political ideas and organizing economic practices. The close co-incidence of the American and French Revolutions then seemed to provide a sufficiently short period that could be seen as the beginning of political modernity.[4] During the nineteenth century, periods of industrial take-off in a number of European countries and in the US have come to be seen as marking a similar economic rupture.[5]

To many observers, these transformations lay so far apart and were so little connected that serious doubts could be raised on whether they constituted a major social transition. Social historical and anthropological research, in particular, could show that very little had changed in the orientations and practices of most human beings during and after these supposedly revolutionary events. If modernity was to mark a 'condition' or an 'experience',[6] then the qualifications required to show its existence were largely absent in the allegedly modern societies during the nineteenth century, and for a still fairly large number of people during the first half of the twentieth century.[7]

Some recent research, though, has re-emphasized the idea of the modern rupture, and a critical look at this research may help to clarify the issue. Michel Foucault sees the late eighteenth and early nineteenth centuries as a period in which new discursive formations emerged in the humanities, namely the tripartite set of discourses of biology, political economy and linguistics. From a perspective of the history of concepts, Reinhart Koselleck speaks of a major turn in the development of key philosophical and political ideas. Partly following Koselleck, Jürgen Habermas identifies the emergence of a self-reflective philosophy of modernity and the opening of the time horizon. The beginning of a social time of history marks the possibility of a view of history as a project. Inversely, Wolf Lepenies identifies the end of natural history. These analyses would indeed locate the beginning of modernity at the turn to the nineteenth century.[8]

I generally concur with this perspective, but one of its features needs to be emphasized. Broadly understood, all of these works are contributions to a history of concepts and of philosophy. Hardly any similarly clear ruptures occurred in terms of economic, social and political practices throughout society.[9] In such terms, the prevailing view seems to be that the revolutions were much less revolutionary, that is, pronounced ruptures during a short time-span, than the discourses about the revolutions. In as much as the studies by Foucault, Koselleck and others are about practices, they are about those of the very small minorities in a given society who were directly involved in the production of these discourses, namely about (proto-) intellectuals and (proto-) professionals.[10]

If these findings are reliable, one can understand the difficult relation between the judgement and the analysis of modernity, which haunts our thinking, in sociohistorical terms. It is the relation of affinity, but non-identity between ideas and institutions of modernity that is at the root of most of the problems in analysing the history of modernity.[11] The normative issue, that is, the *project* of modernity, may then possibly be more or less neatly identified historically and theoretically, even with all its internal tensions. However, this project has never translated into similarly neat and pure institutions.

To pursue an analysis of modernity, then, requires a distinction between the discourse on the modern project (itself ambiguous and amenable to a sociology of knowledge as well as subject to historical transformations), and the practices and institutions of modern society. Far from trying to erect some idealistic – normative and suprahistorical – notion of modernity, this merely acknowledges, *sociologically* and *historically*, that some break in the discourses on human beings and society occurred more than two centuries ago. This discursive rupture brought about the establishment of the modern ideas as new imaginary significations for both individuals and society and, as such, it instituted new kinds of social and political issues and conflicts.[12]

TWO PORTRAITS OF MODERNITY

The discourse of modernity is based most firmly on the idea of freedom and autonomy. Historically, it was used to interpret and reinterpret observable social practices in the light of this imaginary signification. By way of an introduction, I shall briefly sketch the main cognitive opposition that emerged in this process, the opposition between the realization of liberty and the undermining of liberty. Thus, two very common, but incompatible, portraits of modernity will appear. These are two opposed narratives, one of which may be called the discourse of liberation, the other the discourse of disciplinization. This sketch does not aspire to intellectual historiography, rather it is meant to generate the issues that a sociology of modernity will have to pay attention to.

The *discourse of liberation* stood at the very origins of modern times.[13] It goes back to the quest for autonomy for scientific pursuits during the so-called scientific revolution, to the demand for self-determination in the political revolutions – the model cases of which were the American and French ones – and to the liberation of economic activities from the supervision and regulation of an absolutist state.

In each of these cases freedom was seen as a basic – 'unalienable', 'self-evident' – human right. But it was also argued for with the collective outcome of liberations in mind, namely the enhancement of the striving for truth, the building of a polity to whose rules everybody had contributed and in which, thus, violence was no longer a legitimate means of action, and the increase of 'the wealth of nations'. In both ways – the establishment of individual rights and the collective justification for the use of these rights – the discourse of liberation was and is of major importance as a means of self-interpretation of and for 'modern' societies.

Throughout the past two centuries, however, the adequacy of this discourse has not remained unquestioned. It had not only an intellectual genealogy, but also a particular social location. It was pursued only by some groups, and it was socially conditioned. An early critique focused on the contrast between the discourse and the practices of the social groups that were supporting it.

A particularly strong version of such a 'critique of ideology' was launched by Karl Marx. He held that the allegedly universalist and scientific theories of political economy merely masked the interests of the emerging bourgeoisie. Rather than discarding them completely, however, he tried to separate their real insights into the workings of the economy from their ideological elements. Thus, he indeed subscribed to a notion of the need for liberating the productive forces; it was rather the social context in which such a project was to be carried out that had to be revolutionized so that all humankind could benefit from this liberation.

Quite regardless of whether one concurs with Marx's particular analysis, nineteenth-century European societies displayed, to almost any observer, striking contradictions between a universalist rhetoric and the strong boundaries between social groups as to the availability of liberties. The opportunities of entrepreneurship, of expressing one's views and interests within political institutions, of participating in the academic search for truth, were limited to a very small part of the population and the barriers erected were often formal (like the restriction of the suffrage), or at least formidable. In fact, the idea of *containing the liberal utopia* within certain limits, of creating boundaries against the consequences of its own claims is crucial to any understanding of modernity, as shall be shown throughout this book.

Still, from a twentieth-century perspective, it may appear as if the power of the idea of liberty ultimately overcame these boundaries. Not only were formal rules of exclusion lifted, but social mobility also increased. Related to such social transformations, the discourse of liberation itself changed its form. The functionality of social arrangements in 'modern' society was itself regarded as liberating human beings. The higher performance of economy, politics and science would set the individual free from many of the concerns of 'traditional' societies. It was recognized that the new arrangements also put new strains on the individuals who would have to comply with multiple role expectations according to their status in different spheres of society. But in many of the analyses put forward during the 1950s and 1960s, for instance, the gains in terms of liberty were seen as far superior to the losses.

The most sophisticated, and far from uncritical, version of such a discourse is put forward by Jürgen Habermas. While praising the performance of modern institutions and accepting their historical inevitability, he fully recognizes their liberty-constraining effects. He reconciles this ambiguous finding with the attempt to safeguard the 'project of modernity' by counterposing those institutions against a 'life-world' in which authentic, unmediated communication is possible and from which renewals of an emphatic understanding of modernity may always re-emerge.[14]

During the past two decades, such views of a functionally ordered society, be they generally affirmative or critical, have lost their persuasive power. From within this intellectual tradition some observers saw a gradual dissolution of the order; moreover, empirical findings on pluralization and disintegration of both institutional arrangements and social life-styles were reported, which were difficult to accommodate in mere terms of functionality. In this current phase, the emphasis on order is relaxed, and the discourse of liberation takes the form of a praise of individualization.

Ultimately, then, modernity is about the increase of individualism and individuality. In an early phase, few may have benefited at the expense of many. In a second era, differentiation may have occurred group- and role-wise, but not really on the level of the individual. Nowadays, however, modernity's achievements allow the development of a great plurality and variety of individual life-styles and life-projects, available to the great majority of the population of Western societies.

If such a discourse of liberation, all modifications notwithstanding, shows a continuity through more than two centuries of modernity, it is plausible to assume that it reflects important features of these societies. However, it has never been without a critical counterpart, the *discourse of disciplinization*.

A starting-point for the latter was the observation that liberation actually never occurred the way it was conceived in the liberal ideas. European revolutionary societies between 1750 and 1850 were marked by continuities, and the most important continuity was the centrality of the state apparatus. If we look at the Enlightenment writings, we shall see that the state, while feudal and absolutist in historical origins, was often regarded as the means to make Enlightenment social practices possible. One major argument focused on the necessity of the state for social order, another saw in the state a social incarnation of Reason, raised as a universal entity above the particularistic society.[15] In both cases, its nature as an effective and legitimate boundary to the potential infinity of possible autonomous social practices becomes evident. The *state form* as the container – safeguard and limit – of modernity is another major issue throughout this book.

The idea of the state as container of modernity, as an instrument to restrict practices and to discipline individuals, drew on an existing social institution. A second, and historically later, variant of the theory of disciplinization postulated the unintended self-limitation of modernity as the outcome of modern practices. Far from fulfilling the bourgeois-humanist promise of human self-realization through autonomy, so the argument goes, modern practices, once started, would transform human beings in both idea and reality so that the very notion of realizing a self becomes untenable.

Elements of such a discourse can be found in Marx's writings about alienation and fetishization as a result of the exposure of human beings to the market. Analogously, Weber argues that the achievements of the workings of bureaucratic and market rationalities transform the 'life destiny' of human beings and rob human life of some of its important qualities. Modern scientific practices, even if they were begun in its name, would turn out to be unable to maintain the quest for truth. And according to Nietzsche, the moral-religious project of a Christianity that was focused on the individual undermined its own foundations and cancelled any possibility of morality from social life. The argumentative figure of the *self-cancellation of modernity* in and through its own practices is a further theme that needs to be explored in this socio-historical account of modernity.

Such portraits were drawn from the experience of a modernity that had begun to unfold its full powers, powers that were seen as residing in the multitude of morally, economically, politically and intellectually freed individuals. While the societal effects of the interactions of these individuals were the problem at the heart of these analyses, the dynamic itself was seen as being unleashed by the freeing of the individuals.

The experience of twentieth-century modernity tended to alter the portrait of disciplinization again, with Weber already marking a different tone. However, a full new narrative of modernity, focusing on the subjection and disciplinization of individuals, only came into being with fascism, the Second World War and the massive material transformations of the modern societyscape between the 1930s and the 1960s. Theodor W. Adorno, Max Horkheimer and Herbert Marcuse as well as Michel Foucault identified a disciplining alliance of instrumental reason and will to power in the organized, administered societies of that time. Under the almighty coalition of knowledge and power, the question of resistance or compliance hardly seemed to pose itself any longer.

With plurality and difference apparently reemerging during the past two decades, images of instrumentality and one-dimensionality have lost their appeal. Still, the discourse of disciplinization has not given way to a new and unquestioned hegemony of the discourse of liberation. At least one strand of the postmodernist debate interprets pluralization not as a condition of the self-realization of the individual but as the expression of a fragmentation of selfhood, and sees the subject finally completely vanishing, disappearing even from the utopian point from which claims for societal alternatives could be made. Such kinds of arguments point to the possibility of a *historical transformation of the self* and to the conditions for, and understanding of, self-realization.

These two portraits of modernity were always in co-existence and, as I have tried to indicate, they even underwent analogous transformations over time. They were not always as completely separate as I described them. The most sensitive observers of modernity, such as Marx and Weber, contributed to both images. However, the gallery of modernity is full of pictures that emphasize either one or the other side. What we may conclude from this is, first, that the authors have indeed caught some relevant and crucial aspects of modern times. It is unlikely that they have all failed to see clearly. Apparently liberty and discipline are key features of modernity. The real task though seems to be to paint, so to speak, both sides of modernity simultaneously, to conclude on an irreducibly double nature of modernity. A more adequate portrait, then, would have to merge the two existing perspectives into one which maintains the ambiguity.

AMBIGUITIES OF THE ENLIGHTENMENT

We shall reconsider the Enlightenment and, with it, the modern project, as being haunted by a fundamental ambiguity. There is a number of ways of formulating this ambiguity. One side is fairly clear – there is the idea of self-rule, the rejection of any external, superior being or principle that could impose maxims for action. This is the very foundation of liberty as autonomy. By its very nature, it is without limits and boundaries. A radically modern conception allows no actor or instance to provide criteria or rules for setting boundaries to self-determination.

On the other side, most social philosophies in the realm of modernity do not rely exclusively on such a conception. The discourses of modernity reject the *imposition* of a substantive notion of good and right, as ordained by a God, but many of them accept the idea of the *recognition* of worldly values and rules, existing before and beyond the individual, to be discovered, known and followed by human beings. There are varieties of such conceptions, which I will not discuss in detail here.[16] Just three different basic ideas shall be mentioned, which can be found in various combinations. First, there is the idea of human *nature* as an anthropological frame for liberty. It may not only involve the concept of natural, unalienable rights of the individual, but also views on natural social orders, such as, for instance, the family and the public representation of the family by the man as head of the household. Second, there is the idea of *reason*. Reason was seen as some supra-individual and, maybe, supra-human category that, while it could be specified in different ways, would be invoked as a reference-point to which the strivings of free individuals would lead. Third, the idea of the need to consider the *common good*, beyond the right to individual autonomy, was a collectivist notion which could not be unequivocally derived from individual wills. The idea of the common good relates to the question of the foundation of the polity on liberal principles. It entails a distinction, in Isaiah Berlin's famous terms, of negative and positive liberty, liberty from constraints and liberty to achieve substantive goals, together with others, in community.[17] In different ways, all of these concepts (re-)introduced some 'other' criterion that could potentially be in conflict with the volition of individual, living human beings.

Two questions are important in this context. First, (a) how is the potential conflict between the two basic criteria of modernity handled? And second, (b) how is the 'other side' to the criterion of individual autonomy exactly determined?[18]

(a) The potential conflict between two criteria, if they were independent of each other, was well recognized. The most intriguing solution to the problem of the modern double-sidedness was the identification of the two sides. Free and knowledgeable subjects would strive towards the realization of their nature, of reason, and of common well-being. This Enlightenment faith, however, was soon shaken – though it still lives on, for instance, in the claim, upheld in neoclassical economics, that an economic order with a multitude of independent actors would regulate itself toward achieving a stable optimum position.

A way of upholding the optimistic proposition while taking real-world deviations into account was to argue that the individuals were not as free and knowledgeable as they were supposed to be. Education and/or exclusion were to be the means of dealing with the problems they posed. Such a view presupposes that some know better than others what is natural, reasonable or good. They may lead others towards this insight, but until that stage is reached, it is only they who have full membership rights to modernity.[19]

Put in these terms, we may distinguish two co-existing, though conflicting strands of Enlightenment thought, the regulating one and the self-guiding one.[20] It is important to note that the strengthening of one strand at the expense of the other, while dealing with some problems, tends to suppress or neglect basic features of modernity. The regulating strand suppresses the right to individual autonomy of those who are classified as unfit for modernity. The self-guiding strand, while underlining the idea of individual autonomy, neglects the questions of what the substantive aspects of human life are and how they can be identified and approached.[21] It is to this issue that I now turn.

(b) The idea of autonomy seems fairly unproblematic as long as we take it to refer to a single individual. Modernity, then, is about the possibility (opportunity and capability) of an individual subject's self-realization. Now, hardly anybody is ready to argue – though a few are – that it could make sense to speak of individual self-realization without any reference to a substantive goal and to social relations to other human beings. If asked about their understanding of a good life, most people would either give answers that refer to others directly or indicate objectives that need to be socially conceived. References to social *substance* and to *collectivity*, that is, to the fact that some values may be upheld only by collective arrangement, enter into the modern condition. They do so obviously empirically, and it can also be argued that they are inevitable in terms of principles of justification. From the point onwards that individual autonomy and liberty were thought of, their various complements co-existed with them. Both substance and collectivity set boundaries to the practice of individual autonomy. The ideas of individual autonomy and liberty neither could nor did exist intellectually or socially unbound. Controversies are rather about how substance and collectivity are determined. To advance the argument, I shall introduce a very crude distinction at this point.[22]

Early modernists argue that there are some cultural ascriptions that precede any practice of individual autonomy, both in terms of substance and of collectivity. Human beings, for instance, are born into a cultural-linguistic formation which gives form and sets boundaries to individual strivings. However an individual may define herself, she will draw on these forms and will relate to the community inside the boundaries as well as contribute to the historical path of this collective. Of course, this is the reasoning that stands behind the idea of the nation-state as the modern polity, and I shall discuss its relevance to the history of modernity later (see Chapter 3).

Classical modernists tend to turn from those substantive foundations to more procedural ones.[23] They put forward the idea of various separate conceptualizations of basic spheres of society, as realms of economics, politics, science and culture. The construction of these spheres and their relations to each other as a new kind of naturally interlocking order is largely the result of attempts to link individual autonomy to social outcomes. The power of the revolutions of modernity – the scientific, industrial and bourgeois ones – resided not least in the establishment of such new sets of assumptions about the conditions for the beneficial cohabitation of human beings. In all of these conceptualizations, the complement to the idea of individual autonomy is one of rationality, actually of specific rationalities in each realm. Then the argument is developed that human beings as rational agents will follow these rationalities, if they are free to do so. If everyone does so, then the interaction of all human beings will both advance their individual objectives and be of benefit to all. Thus, a means of reconciliation of the duality of individual autonomy and its 'other' has been provided.[24] Far from actually identifying and describing real social practices, these conceptualizations remained largely fictitious. Rather than reality, they described the 'project of modernity'. Knowing well that they were a fiction, the modernizers' optimistic assumption was that they would realize themselves once the appropriate social conditions were created.

Late modernists dwell on this fictitious character of the conceptual order of high modernism. They argue that even the idea of procedural rationalities makes too many assumptions and cannot be upheld for any general analysis, or as a basis for politics. In their view, everything – language, self and community, to use Richard Rorty's terms[25] – is contingent. I do not want to discuss here such anti-foundationalism in philosophical terms, but I want to point to some political implications (on sociological implications see Chapter 9).

Politically, anti-foundationalism opens the way for a critical analysis of the modernist ideology. At the same time, it is a strong assertion of the idea of individual autonomy, since, in a contingent world, every individual decides for herself who she wants to be and to which collective she wants to belong. In terms of political theory, it is a call for a radical liberalism, based on what we may call an individualistic political ontology. Indeed, we may accept as a historical fact that the transformation of the modern ideas into social practices occurred – and, as a complete set, possibly could only occur – in the guise of liberalism. 'Actually existing liberalisms', though, often included substantivistic and collectivistic theories – such as, most prominently, in the fusion of liberalism and nationalism in the nineteenth century.

Still, the organization of allocative and authoritative practices relied heavily on the idea of an autonomous individual, capable of goal-directed action, as the basic unit of social organization – as is most evident in the rules of law and political participation. Law is the institution *par excellence* that creates, in the view of the relevant others, autonomous individuals responsible for their actions. If this is the case, then a sort of imbalance is inscribed in the modern ambiguity, a shift towards individual autonomy. In rights-based liberalism, however incomplete, the individual is the only category that need not, often in fact, cannot, be debated. The individual is simply there, whereas what human nature is or how the collective good should be determined needs to be argued about. Substantive aspects of human interaction are subject to communication and consensus. And, to make the issue even more complicated, with whom one should enter into communication (that is, the boundaries of the community) is itself not given, but subject to agreement.

At this stage of the argument, I only want to take note of two very general points. First, this bias that is inscribed into the modern ambiguity may well allow for a gradual shift to a hegemony of individual autonomy, aligned only with a disengaged, instrumental concept of reason, in the historically dominant conceptions of modernity. Second, the shift in conceptions of modernity – from 'early' to 'classical' to 'late', though it is not linear and far from unequivocal – may be a first indicator of historical processes of de-substantivization and de-collectivization of the foundations of modernity.[26] Both points are not conclusions of any sort, but elements of a guiding hypothesis for a historical sociology of modernity.

Such a sociology then needs to search for the boundaries which are *actually* taken for granted in social practices and do in fact limit the range of individual self-rule, and for the kinds of activities which are *actually* considered as within the realm of possible self-realization. While there is obviously a great range of ways in which individual human beings make use of the available rules and resources for self-realization, there are also distinct historical forms of the construction of social identities. Such questions cannot be posed in purely individualistic terms since the nature of the boundaries depends on how present and relevant others see them. While they are not fixed by any supra-human will, neither can they be created or destroyed by individual will. One needs to transform the issue of contingency into a question for a historical sociology – as an issue of actual, rather than principled contingency.

FROM THE PHILOSOPHY TO A HISTORICAL SOCIOLOGY OF MODERNITY

The ambiguity of modernity takes on varied forms at different times and in different places. Some authors have observed that the double nature of modernity may be due to the specificities of its *intellectual genealogy*, at least in continental Europe. While the main substantive argument was one of commitment to self-rule, it pointed historically towards a rethinking of the prevailing religious notion of the heteronomy of the human condition as being determined by God. To present its argument, Enlightenment thought thus had to link up to the predominant rhetoric form and was phrased as a 'secularized religion' with Reason taking the place of God and History the place of Providence.[27] In tension with the substance of the proposition that should entail an emphasis on openness, liberation, plurality and individuality, the historical form emphasized the advent of a new order that was universal and total and demanded conformity and discipline rather than anything else.

The issue of how to supersede an old order was posed with regard to *social practices* as much as with regard to intellectual modes of reasoning. Again, the conditions of the historical advent of modernity, at least in (continental) Europe, entailed a bias towards an 'organized' or 'imposed' transition rather than an open one in which the outcome would be left to the free workings of a plural society. Pronounced differences in the sociopolitical backgrounds against which the modern project was proposed and developed distinguish the European experience markedly from the North American one. One of the specificities of the French Revolution was that there was a centralized state, endowed with the idea of sovereignty and a bureaucracy to practice it. It seemed quite natural merely to re-interpret this state, then seize it and put it to different uses, if one wanted to transform society. In the absence of such well-established institutions, the situation of the American revolutionaries at the time of their struggle for independence was quite different.

While the main argument of this book is focused on European developments, I shall also repeatedly refer to the North American part of the history of modernity. Apart from helping to understand '*American exceptionalism*', this comparison offers opportunities for a more profound understanding of the dynamics of modernity.

In Europe, the social movements that advanced the 'project of modernity' were well aware of the fact that the liberations they were striving for could not be obtained without conflicting with organized adversaries, not the least of which were the absolutist state and the aristocratic and religious elites of the late feudal period.[28] While they deemed themselves certain of promoting a progress that was inevitable in the long run, they also saw a need to impose it against still-powerful opponents. Among these adversaries were those who faced the threat of losing power, wealth and status. The case against them could easily be argued in terms of modern principles. However, there were also those who would ultimately gain, but who apparently did not yet have insight into the advantages to them. While they could and should be educated, the (temporary) imposition of the reasonable was seen as necessary to avoid risks to liberation. In this respect, the view of some bourgeois revolutionaries on a society, the majority of which was against them, shows analogies to that of Communist revolutionaries in the early Soviet Union and in East European societies after the Second World War.[29]

In the Soviet Union, the issue was phrased as the problem of 'socialism in one country'. This formulation refers very directly to the question of setting boundaries and imposing (a superior) order. Far from presenting a derailment of the modern project or the emergence of some kind of anti-modernity, Soviet socialism emphasizes certain features of modernity, though obviously at the expense of others. Just as American exceptionalism can be regarded as the epitome of one kind of modernity, so should socialism be seen as the epitome of another kind. The *modernity of Soviet socialism*, then, is a second issue for discussion by which I shall compare the West European experience to others, with a view to more firmly grasping the modern ambiguity.

With the help of this *spatial comparison* it is easier to understand why it is so fallacious when major parts of the present debates counterpose a notion of 'postmodernity' to one of modernity. The current distinction of modernity and postmodernity throws light (or casts shadows) on the modern double-sidedness, on the two sides of the modern ambiguity itself. Social phenomena that are labelled postmodern point to one relatively extreme social instantiation of modernity, whereas socialism finds itself close to the other extreme. Both social formations, however, move within the same sociohistorical space, the one created by, as Castoriadis would say, the double imaginary signification of modernity.

The spatial comparison demonstrates that there are varieties of 'actually existing modernities' – with the societies of the United States, Western Europe and the Soviet Union as three major twentieth-century types. It does not yet allow anything to be said about an inherent movement of modernity. On its own, the spatial comparison may, at worst, achieve nothing more than a somewhat more sociologically informed restatement of the dichotomy of liberation and disciplinization. To assess the validity of the hypothesis of de-substantivization and de-collectivization and, eventually, to demonstrate how such processes may come about, the spatial comparison of social formations along the lines of their expression of the modern ambiguity needs to be complemented by a *historical comparison*.

The historical construction of these social formations, as well as their transformations and – partly – demise, may be used to investigate the dynamics inherent to the overall modern project. De-substantivization and de-collectivization of modernity, if they occur, are not self-propelled trends but historical processes, of which there are also partial reversals, created by interacting human beings. For further analysis, the crucial issues are how, when and what kinds of shifts between the foundational imaginary significations occur. All this amounts to a quest for a historical analysis of the transformations of modernity. Such an analysis will begin with the modern rupture, that is, with the emergence of the master discourse of 'classical' modernity.

Historically, this fiction generated its own problems – problems that we can derive from the master discourse and can use for identifying the analytical issues for a sociology of modernity. As pointed out above, modern reasonings on the constitution of society suffer from the aporia of having to link the normative idea of liberty, as a procedurally *unlimitable* right and obligation to self-rule and self-realization, to a notion of collective good, be it merely in terms of a minimal livable order or be it in terms of substantive objectives of humankind, such as wealth, democracy or truth. Even if one held the idea, as probably some seventeenth- and eighteenth-century thinkers did, that a social contract and its rules of implementation could be signed once and for all, the philosophical problematic was troubling enough.

To complicate things, though, each of the reasonings laid foundations for a *historical increase of liberties* and, it seemed, greater substantive achievements if contrasted with the 'pre-modern' regimes. Compared to the late feudal and absolutist regimes with their ascriptive hierarchies and their detailed regulation of all aspects of everyday life, these ideas were no doubt liberating in the sense of setting free a dynamic of human-made change. In their theoretical stringency, they even developed a liberating momentum that has still not exhausted its potential and keeps providing justifications for claims which are valid and unfulfilled today. This is the incomplete character of the project of modernity that Habermas keeps emphasizing.

Here we can also identify the basic tension that characterizes this notion of liberty as part of a socially ambiguous double concept. We may consider 'rational mastery' (Castoriadis) or 'disengaged, instrumental reason' (Taylor) as expressions for the tendency towards an increase of opportunities, an extension of social institutions into time and space, a growth of enablements. This tendency is itself set free by the individual right and obligation to 'autonomy'. In social practice, those liberations tended to alter the kinds of substantive goals human beings were able to accomplish – by extending the reach of human-made institutions. Then, the question of the *collective determination of the substantive objectives of human strivings* (including the question of how far these objectives should in fact be collectively determined), which is an essential element of modernity, became ever more problematic, in at least three respects.

First, the achievable mode of life became a moving target itself. If scientific activities increased knowledge and economic activities increased wealth, changes in the conditions for collective self-determination would arise that would constantly have to be taken into consideration.[30] The agreement over substantive aspects of modes of social life, which was a formidable problem in the absence of pre-given criteria anyhow, would then be a *continuous* task in *continuously changing* circumstances.

Second, even if liberated scientific and economic practices indeed entailed a rather steady increase of human capabilities, it cannot be taken for granted that enablements would not be, at least temporarily, accompanied by constraints, or that both would be evenly distributed socially, spatially and temporally. From the nineteenth-century 'valley of tears' of 'primitive accumulation' to the twentieth-century concepts of 'deferred gratifications' as well as of 'modernization' and 'development', much of modern socioeconomic debate has centred on this problematic. The more uneven the distribution of enablements and constraints is, the harder one may expect collective self-determination under conditions of comprehensive participation (that is, the full development of political liberty) to be.

Third, beyond more or less directly perceivable, and perhaps even measurable, social distributions of enablements and constraints, the use and diffusion of all kinds of modern achievements will penetrate society and transform all of it to such an extent that certain values and practices will be impossible to uphold. Members of a society could be forced into a situation in which they will have to forfeit crucial identity-constituting practices, elements of their lives that they would not want to trade against anything else.[31] The self-determination of a collective, of whether achievements may be used, becomes fraught with imponderable contradictions and conflicts in such a situation.

The master discourse of liberal modernity denies the fundamental relevance of all of these issues. In its view, the normative potential of revolutionary liberal theorizing resided in a notion of the autonomy of the economic, political, scientific and cultural spheres from each other, and in their capability of self-steering if left to the free interaction of the participating individuals. The differentiation of these spheres, as in functionalist theorizing, is then the guarantor of liberty. For the past two centuries, much of 'modernist' social theory has relied far too much on such assumptions without really scrutinizing them. A redescription of modernity may possibly re-open the debate.

REPROPOSING A NARRATIVE OF MODERNITY[32]

I began my considerations above with the two concepts of liberation and disciplinization, as they can be found in narratives of modernity. In a second step, I have tried to transform this dichotomy into an ambiguity which is characteristic of modernity. This ambiguity resides in the double imaginary signification of modernity as individual autonomy and its substantive or collective other. I have argued that only a comparative-historical analysis can come closer to understanding this ambiguity, since there is no general principle combining these significations. The next task, then, is to transfer the concept of a double imaginary signification into the language and tradition of social science.

Whereas modernist social science tends to take the existence of self-regulated sets of institutions, such as the market, the state or scientific institutions, for granted and sees them as supra-human entities having causal effects on individuals, the kinds of institutions and their modes of working both have to be made problematic. I shall base my approach on a concept of 'duality of structure', as cast by Anthony Giddens, which sees institutions as simultaneously enabling and constraining human action, and as being reproduced through human action. A sociohistorical analysis will then have to spell out exactly who and what kind of activity is enabled and who and what is constrained. For this purpose, a distinction between different kinds of social practices shall be introduced (Chapter 2). I shall, for my own objectives, refer to only three kinds of practices: of allocation, of domination, and of signification and symbolic representation. The historical ways of habitualizing such practices and, thereby, extending them over time and space and making them into social institutions, shall be the key object of my analysis of modernity.

The historical analysis itself will start with a brief portrait of early post-revolutionary social configurations, that is, societies in the Europe of the first half of the nineteenth century. In a sense, this era was the heyday of liberal ideology, with the bourgeoisie in the ascendancy to power, as it has often been portrayed. While such a view is not invalid, I shall emphasize that the applicability of ideas of autonomy was effectively contained. With a number of institutional devices, not least the inherited state, boundaries were set to the modern project. This contained form of the bourgeois utopia, which was far from encompassing all members of a society, shall be labelled *restricted liberal modernity* (Chapter 3).

A certain self-confidence of the bourgeois elites with regard to the feasibility of their project was indeed temporarily achieved. However, from as early as the French Revolution onwards, restrictions could no longer be justified, and were increasingly contested. Also, the dynamics of liberation itself, the extension of mastery of the world and its impact on social orders, tended to upset those same orders. Often, the year 1848 is conveniently marked as the historical point after which major transformations of the restricted liberal social configuration and its self-understanding commenced. By the turn of the century, so many of the boundaries were shaken or even broken; so many people had been, often traumatically, *disembedded* from their social, cultural and economic contexts that one can speak of a *first crisis of modernity*, as a consequence of which societal developments were set on a different path (see Chapter 4).

One effect of the upsetting of social orders during the nineteenth century was that far greater parts of the population of a territory had come under the reach of modern practices. Consequently, they also had to be formally included into modern institutions. Of course, the most important of such social groups were the workers. With hindsight at least, the workers' movement and the formation of trade unions and labour parties can be seen as a major collective action towards the full inclusion of a hitherto barred part of the population into modern practices and institutions and their achievements. The obvious example is the granting of universal and equal suffrage; however, I also want to refer to participation in such modern practices as consumption of industrial commodities, the shaping of societal self-understandings in cultural production or to the extension of reachable space by means of technologies.

We may speak of this process as an extension of modernity, an increase of the permeation of society by modernity. The process of extension was one of the breaking of boundaries. As such, it was accompanied, at least among the elites, by strong feelings about the lack of both manageability and intelligibility of 'modern society'. This perception is an important background, if not the basis, of the cultural-intellectual crisis of modernity around the turn to the twentieth century. At that time, however, social transformations had already started that were to change the nature of modern institutions along with their expansion. These transformations entailed a *reembedding* of society's individuals into a new order – to be achieved by means of an increasing formalization of practices, their conventionalization and homogenization. As the extension was reached and the social access widened, practices were standardized and new constraints as to the types of permissible activities introduced.

These transformations occurred, *mutatis mutandis*, in all major kinds of social practices. I shall first sketch the practices of allocation, where they included the building of technical-organizational systems that were operated society-wide, as well as the conventionalization of work statuses and the standardization of consumption (Chapter 5). The emergence of the mass party and its restriction to electoral politics channelled the modes of political participation. The extension of policies of social support, later to be known as the welfare state, considerably reduced material uncertainties; at the same time it extended disciplining and homogenizing practices of domination into the realm of family lives (Chapter 6). Under the impetus of establishing cognitive mastery over society, new techniques, classifications and concepts were developed in the social sciences, establishing a new mode of representation of society. One of its features is a tendency to reify major social institutions (Chapter 7).

Taken together, these sets of social practices have almost been all-inclusive with regard to members of a society. However, these practices have been highly organized. Ascriptive roles do not exist under modern conditions, of course. But for a given position in society and a given activity, these practices have prescribed a very limited set of modes of action. I shall propose to describe the social configuration that has been characterized by such practices as *organized modernity*, and the transformations that led to it as a *closure of modernity*. It is the crisis of this organized modernity that postmodernist writings refer to when proclaiming the 'end of modernity'. It seems indeed appropriate to characterize some of the institutional changes in Western societies during the past two decades as a (partial) breakdown of established arrangements and as a re-opening of 'closed' practices.

If and in as far as these changes amount to a major social transformation, though, one should see this as a *second major crisis of modernity*, rather than the end of modernity. It includes strong trends towards de-conventionalization and pluralization of practices, not least the loss of a working understanding of collective agency that once stood behind societywide organized practices (Chapter 8). This loss of collective agency obviously entails a loss of manageability, the disappearance of any actor who is legitimate, powerful and knowledgeable enough to steer interventions into social practices. As such, the disorganization of practices of allocation and domination is directly linked to a 'crisis of representation' of society, in social science as well as in other intellectual practices. Quite a number of the assumptions of modernist social science do not survive this situation unscathed. However, the question of the intelligibility of, at least, parts of the social world remains on the agenda even in an era of 'crisis of representation' and alleged 'end of social science'. The main objective of social science, as I see it, namely to contribute to our own understanding of the social world in which we live, may seem more ambitious than ever, but it is by no means superseded (Chapter 9).

Quite certainly, these crises do not spell the end of modernity as a social configuration. They mark a transition to a new historical era of it. Some intellectual doubts notwithstanding, the double imaginary signification of modernity – autonomy and rational mastery – seems widely untouched and fully intact. An optimistic interpreter of present changes may want to term this new phase *extended liberal modernity*. Under conditions of the full inclusion of all members of society, the organizing and disciplining institutions are dismantled and respective practices relaxed. Difference and plurality, sociality and solidarity could be the key words of the future, as some argue. At the same time, the building of social identities has become a more open and more precarious process, and the erosion of once-reliable boundaries has rephrased the issue of exclusion and inclusion. The decrease of certainties may entail opportunities, but also introduces new constraints and anxieties (Chapter 10).

Thus, I tend to be much more sceptical, in the face of the building of more widely extended institutions (such as global technical and economic arrangements) and of the emergence of new kinds of boundaries inside such a more intensely globalized society. These transformations may entail a new process of social disembedding, of possibly unprecedented dimensions. During the building of the social formation of organized modernity, many violent and oppressive attempts at different kinds of reembedding were started and often violently interrupted. Similar processes may occur again; at the very least, the questions of social identity and political community are badly in need of new answers (Chapter 11).

Chapter 2

Enablement and constraint

Understanding modern institutions

SOCIAL INSTITUTIONS AS SETS OF RULES AND CONVENTIONS

The modernist view on contemporary society, as I have briefly portrayed it in the preceding chapter, emphasizes the autonomy of individual action, occurring in separately organized spheres of interaction each guided by its own norms. Claiming the beneficial, even optimum, outcome of social interactions in such a setting, justification precedes analysis in the master discourse of modernity. Such a perspective is not totally unfounded, since clearly human beings try to justify their actions and the social order to which those actions contribute. Imaginary significations have an impact on the organization of social practices. However, just as myths need to be placed in context in anthropological analysis, a social analysis of modernity needs to start with the actual social practices of human beings and to relate the modern myths to the organization of these practices.[1]

Social institutions are here understood as relatively durable sets of rules and resources, which human beings draw on in their actions. Institutions may pre-exist any actual living human being, but they are created by human action and only continue to exist by being continuously recreated. They are habitualized practices, the knowledge about them being transmitted in interaction, most strongly in socialization and education, but also in any other everyday practice. If we say that such kinds of human activity are routinized, we mean that they are part of the practical consciousness, of knowing 'how to go on', rather than of a discursive consciousness in which reasons and intentions are provided. However, human beings are in principle capable of giving reasons for their actions and of altering them. They are capable of continuous creative activities, of working with the rules and resources of institutions and thereby transforming them.[2]

It has been argued that theories of the constitution of society exaggerate the knowledgeability and capability of human beings with regard to the social order.[3] However, an understanding of social institutions in terms of a duality of structure does not preclude the identification of constraints on human action. Actions are situated in contexts in which the individual applies her own 'historical' knowledge (as traces in her memory) of rules and their meaning, of their concrete applicability and the likely outcome of their application or alteration, and is faced with the varying interpretations of the same or even other rules by other individuals. The judgement of 'applicability', both in the sense of possibility and of necessity, implies a view, by the agent, on the durability and solidity of the rules, that is a judgement on whether modifications will have adverse consequences, will be rejected, will be indifferently received, or may even induce a positive process of rule change.[4] In terms of their relative durability and solidity, it may be said that institutions also shape and re-shape the individuals, that they imply 'certain modes of training and modification of individuals, not only in the obvious sense of acquiring certain skills but also in the sense of acquiring certain attitudes'.[5] That is why institutions are always enabling and constraining at the same time.

In more specific and historically concrete terms, this means that the 'structures', to which human beings appear to be exposed and to draw on in their actions, are the effects of earlier human action, of the modes of habitualization and conventionalization, and the material results of such action. Habits and conventions define the applicability of social rules. One may then distinguish two key sets of analytical questions, those pertaining to the construction of such conventions and those pertaining to their effects on individual human action once they exist.[6] These questions will generate a set of terms and concepts, presented in this chapter in rudimentary form, that can be used and developed for a historical sociology of modernity, to be elaborated in the remainder of this book.

With regard to the *creation* of social conventions, the social actors who promote change, their guiding ideas and their interests will be the focus of the analysis. If, as will be the case throughout most of this study, their guiding ideas are framed by the imaginary signification of modernity, and if the interests can be understood as the enhancement of autonomy and rational mastery, then we can call the agents of change *modernizers.* Since they will often be a small group in any given society, situated mostly in influential social locations, we may speak of modernizing elites, and of their project as *modernizing offensives*, in which they use their *power* to spread modernity into society.

The key analytical questions as to the *workings* of social conventions are then: over which realms do these conventions extend (*extension* and *boundaries*)? How completely do they cover the social space over which they extend (*coverage*)? How deeply do they reach into the practices of human beings (*social permeation*)? How strongly and rigidly do they define the capabilities of a living human being who draws on them (*discipline* and *formalization*)? How are the various kinds of practices related to each other and to a common social space (*coherence*)?

Before presenting these concepts more fully, a way of talking about the various kinds of human activities in the world must be introduced. In very broad terms, views on such a basic social ontology seem to be converging on distinguishing – in various ways, though – several basic aspects of human activity and in relating this distinction to different modes of habitualizing practices. Throughout his life-work, Ernest Gellner, for instance, has distinguished 'power, wealth, and belief' as the three kinds of human ties to the world, or has metaphorically termed the three major means with which human beings work on the world as 'plough, sword, and book'.[7] Michael Mann speaks similarly of 'ideological, economic and political' and additionally of 'military power' as the four forms in which human beings organize societies as networks of power.[8]

Drawing on these and other conceptual and classificatory considerations, the following account of modernity will focus on three types of *practices*, practices of material allocation, practices of authoritative power (or domination), and practices of signification (or symbolic representation).[9] When particular practices in these realms become habitualized and rules become set societywide, we can speak of *institutions* of material allocation, of authoritative power and of signification respectively. And when referring to the means by which human beings interact with, and work on, nature and matter, society and other human beings, and on themselves, we may speak of *technologies* of material allocation, of authoritative power and of signification.

The formalized modes of production and exchange in society are referred to as *institutions of material allocation*. They regulate the extraction of goods from nature and the transfer of labour into means of physical and cultural reproduction. Under capitalist conditions this includes significantly the transfer of labour power into income and the transfer of income into (consumer) goods and services. In societies with prevalent capitalist rules of material allocation, then, major – though far from exclusive – means of material allocation are money and markets. *Institutions of authoritative power* in modernity are most importantly, but again not exclusively, bureaucracies and, specifically, the modern state. The crucial problem regarding Western societies – societies under the imaginary signification of autonomy and reason – is to grasp the nature of government at 'the interface between the exercise of power and the exercise of liberty', to analyse the state as 'a mechanism at once of individualization and of totalization'.[10] *Institutions of signification* are the means of providing self-understandings in relation to modes of social organization and to the relation between individuals and society. While a very broad range of such means exists in contemporary society, including religion and technologies of the soul,[11] the focus is here on the discursive representation of society both in 'lay' discourses and in the academic discourses of the social and human sciences.

Though I am quite open with regard to the choice of terminology and exact demarcation of these kinds of practices, three intentions behind my own approach need to be stressed and made explicit. First, I shall try to avoid the terms 'economic', 'political' and 'scientific/ideological', which are used both in the master discourse of modernity and its major critiques. These terms do not only presuppose a fairly strong idea of the separation of social spheres according to different logics, but they also introduce assumptions – affirmative or negative ones – about the normative bases and empirical outcomes of social practices, if they are organized according to these logics. As I tried to explain above, it is very difficult to escape these assumptions, if one does not try to keep a distance from the modern myth. Instead, I shall look at all social practices 'symmetrically', to use a term of the Edinburgh strong programme in the sociology of knowledge.[12] This approach does not entail a denial of the validity of the quest for efficiency, common wealth and truth, but it rejects prejudgements on ways of socially reaching such goals.

Second, this view on social practices does not presuppose that it is proto-typical bourgeois-humanist subjects who engage in them, but it does assume that the human being in her or his bodily existence is a highly relevant ontological unit in social analysis. The condition of human social practices as the interactions of individual human beings is the centre of interest. The organization and transformations of these kinds of social practices are analysed in terms of their impact on human knowledgeability and capability. All three types of institutions are creating and potentially transforming the idea and the reality of the human self over time. Thus, the 'end of the individual' or the 'end of the subject' is a possible, though extreme, finding at the end of the analysis – as, indeed, is also the dominance of the rational and autonomous individual that is hailed in economic and rationalist approaches. But neither one nor the other enters as an assumption into my argument.

Third, at the same time it is difficult to imagine that the absolute predominance of one or the other extreme conception would result from a sociohistorical analysis of modernity. Rather, they mark the space over which the modern condition may be historically traced. In this sense, a delineation of key modes of habitualized social practices at different historical points, and especially of the transformations of these practices, is a means of locating the specific condition of modernity inside this space. The general classification of practices is based on the assumption that the major characteristics of the *social formations* of modernity can thus be identified as historically varying constellations of those institutions of modernity. With these considerations in mind then, the rationales for which will, I hope, become more evident in the historical account, it should be possible to accept this initial typology.

MODERNITY AND POWER: MODERNIZATION OFFENSIVES

In modernity, notions like 'interest', 'control' and 'means' that link ideas of autonomy with ideas of mastery are crucial. Means that are developed and employed, by and for oneself or a self-defined collective, that is, autonomously, in the interest of knowing and controlling nature, social relations or oneself are almost self-justifying; mostly, it is very difficult to argue against them, under modern conditions. This is what Castoriadis tries to capture with the idea of imaginary significations of modernity. These significations provide a common basis of justification for human activities.

It is important to recognize that *all* kinds of 'modern' practices involve both strivings, for increased autonomy and for increased rational mastery, and that both these significations may be embodied in all the habitualizations of such practices, in all modern institutions. Such an approach precludes the kind of – again apriorist, I think – argumentative strategy that has been employed by many critical social theorists (and practitioners of critical involvement). It makes it impossible to posit the mode of socialization of one kind of institution against another one. The most common of such rhetorical moves is to put 'politics' against 'markets', as is done in the socialist tradition. After the critique of bureaucracy had been more widely accepted due to twentieth-century experiences, life-worlds, communities or cultures were placed against both politics and markets. Most recently, the revival of the concept of civil society has been placed in the same intellectual tradition.[13] As close as I may find myself to the problematic that occupies these authors, most of these kinds of reasonings, in my view, combine superficial social analysis and/or overly detached social theorizing with purely wishful thinking.

To put the conceptual problem another way: some of the postmodernist intellectuals, mostly the French ones, have been reproached for conflating a critique of capitalism with an across-the-board critique of modernity. If the dispute is phrased in those terms, I think the postmodernists have the upper hand. 'Capitalism' just refers to some, admittedly important, modern practices which, however, share common features with others. If this is an insight that the post- modernity debate has produced, it was well worth the effort. What is needed is a critique of modernity that comprises a critique of capitalism as one of its major themes.[14]

Many critical social theories, ranging from liberal to Marxian approaches, tend to start from two fundamental normative assumptions. First, the autonomy of the individual, her desire for self-realization and self-fulfilment is hailed; and second, domination, the submission of some human beings to the power of others, is denounced. In analytical terms, their common problem is how to account for the fact that one person's exercise of autonomy may entail domination over another person. Critical theories of capitalism have explained this undeniable fact by sources and mechanisms that lie outside the true desires of human beings, possibly historical residues, or by the erection of the basically modern order on some flawed assumptions or its incompleteness. It is time to recognize, though, after centuries of modern practices, that the problem is inside modernity itself, in the fundamental ambiguity of modern reasoning and modern social practices.

However, there is a tendency in postmodernist writings to link the critique of modernity to its wholesale rejection. It is at this point, I think, that a kind of inverse fallacy is committed, especially because an image of modernity is produced that is rather one-dimensional and poor in terms of modern contradictions. In fact, postmodernists rather fail to provide the needed critique of modernity, the task of which is to grasp the inescapable ambivalence of modernity, in both analytical and normative terms.

In one basic respect, the perspective I try to develop here is close to broadly understood postmodernist conceptions, and crucially different from reifying conceptions in modernist sociological theory: modern institutions are not regarded as autonomous and self-organizing or as occupying specific spheres of life or society, but rather as being structured in and giving structure to an *everyday life*. Taken together, these institutions provide for life forms. Everyday life is not separate from social institutions, but is lived, to varying degrees, in and with such forms of knowledge and habitualized practices. Institutions are built in everyday practices, as much as they provide rules and resources for living one's life.[15]

However, a sociology of modernity needs to go beyond studying the multitude of existing social practices towards identifying the specificities of the institutions of Western societies. The task is to see which of their characteristics causes them to be built and maintained, how they structure life, give opportunities and impose constraints on action. The sum of these enablements and limitations in the everyday practices of individuals in society forms the *condition of modernity*.

If institutions exist only as long as they are recurrently reproduced by living human beings, then it is necessary to focus on their *enabling* effects on at least some individuals or groups. It is quite simply unthinkable that either a transcendental capital subject or any other fully reified institution may continue to exist if it completely dominates all human subjects, as some critical theories tend to argue. However, it may well be possible that by acquiring and using the possibilities that new institutions offer, that is, through their own actions and the effects of these actions, people may subvert certain other avenues of action.

A minimal requirement for developing such an approach is to emphasize the sociohistorical unevenness of modernity. Talk of 'modern society' conceals the fact that orientations and practices in a given social context may be more or less based on the modern imaginary. In the beginning, this imaginary was propagated by elite intellectuals who found some support, partly for quite independent reasons, in society. 'Modernity', so to speak, had very few citizens by 1800, not many by 1900, and still today it is hardly the right word to characterize many current practices. A number of social practices can indeed be better understood as a – partial or radical – rejection of the imaginary signification of modernity, the impact of which gave rise to their development. Exactly what one may call the changing degree of *social permeation* of a 'modern' understanding of individual and social life, *cum* the identification of those actors who promote such an understanding, is a key to the historical transformations of the Northwestern societies over the past two centuries.

Elements of such a reasoning can be found in the works of both Norbert Elias and Michel Foucault. Elias' theory of the civilization of societies of individuals is fundamentally one of *power*, in which the enhancement of control – control over nature, over others, and over oneself – is the key. But it is one that has a full view on the dialectics of power, in which the increase of control by the one may limit the freedom of others. As he never formalizes his tripartite distinction (and in spite of his general evolutionary perspective), he also leaves the possibility of cross-cutting impacts open, for example, that the increase of some people's control over nature may limit the control of others over their social relations or over themselves.[16] Foucault's theorizing has, basically rightly, become known as emphasizing *discipline* and disciplinization. Especially in his later works, however, he was fully aware of special characteristics that the process acquired under modern conditions. In modern societies, such disciplining technologies are developed in and for 'cultures of personal autonomy predicated on a condition of liberty'.[17]

The introduction of the idea of an inevitable dialectics of enablement and constraint in modern institutions and of a power differential as a mover of institutional change shows that the notion of a 'modernization *process*' is inappropriately socially neutralizing. In its stead, one could speak of *modernization offensives*, which are regularly pursued by certain, often small, groups with certain expectations in mind, whereas other groups, often majorities, who are less well informed about the modernization effects, may have little to expect in terms of enablements, at least in the short run, and possibly do object, or would object if they had the necessary information and power.[18]

On a historical level, a major (though admittedly still crude) distinction between two kinds of modernization offensives should be made. *Modernization offensives from above* use the existing power differential to create enabling institutions, in which others will participate only later and often against the interests of the original promoters. *Modernization offensives from below* are counter-moves to defend groups who are the objects of modernizations from above against the constraints and exclusions effected by those modernizations.[19] They normally involve collective action, a mobilization of people who are made equal according to a new classification and subjected to new kinds of rules as such a classificatory group. The modernizing effects reside, then, in the acceptance of the new classification as a 'post-traditional' group, in the collective formation as a 'conceptual community' (Benedict Anderson) or 'class for itself' (Karl Marx) due to the mobilization, and ultimately in the full inclusion of the represented group in the new social arrangement as the result of this action.

Modernization offensives promote new rules for social practices. The introduction of a new set of formal rules will regularly both be based on power and go along with changes in power relations. Most generally, one can see existing *power differentials* as a major moving force of 'modernization'. Generally (and almost trivially), the condition for the introduction of new sets of rules will be optimal, if the expectation of enabling effects is greater than the expectation of accompanying constraints, as weighed by the relative power of the various holders of expectations. The power differential refers to the possibility of making people do and get things done, but it also includes differentials with regard to access to valid knowledge about the effects of rules, and access to the media of communication about rule-setting.

The expectational aspect needs to be stressed, because it is difficult to find any great modern project for which the outcome does not strongly deviate from the identifiable expectations of the promoters. Because of their enabling effects and because modernity's imaginary significations do not permit a general and lasting restriction of the social use of enabling technologies, new institutional arrangements will tend to get generalized throughout society. Once any set of new rules is generalized (and often *because* it gets generalized beyond the group of initial beneficiaries), it may and will involve a more general societal change, often regardless of the intentions of either the promotors or the mass users.

DISCIPLINE AND FORMALIZATION

Is it then possible to talk of a specifically modern mode of structuring the relation of enablement and constraint? A general characteristic of modernity seems to be the wide social and spatial extension of its institutions. Again this feature has been emphasized by Norbert Elias, who speaks of the lengthening of interaction chains in the process of civilization. Georg Simmel had already earlier pointed out, as had Marx in a different way, that money can be regarded as the proto-typical means of lengthening interaction chains.

The most illustrative example of this is the world-market, which has been truly global in respect of a sizeable number of goods for centuries. Also, the depth of permeation of world-market rules into local allocative practices seems to be almost steadily increasing.[20] Another example is the modern state, though this may seem counter-intuitive. Historically, earlier empires were often more widely extended and longer lasting than in more recent times. However, mostly they shaped actual everyday practices only to a very small extent. Only the development of the modern state, from absolutism to the present, is truly marked by the extension of administrative rules far into the everyday life of the subjects and citizens.[21]

The extension of reach, both spatially and into social practices, is clearly related to technical innovations, not least those of transport and communication.[22] Faster and more reliable means of sea travel, and new means of fast long-distance communication would be historical examples relevant to world-market and state expansion respectively. However, the idea of technical advance has to be broadly conceived, it needs to include any formalized modes of operation that do not necessarily involve new technical knowledge or materials. Double book-keeping is an obvious example, not only because its invention happened to coincide with the 'discovery' of America. Census-keeping is a related example for administrative practices.

It is exactly this *formalization* of modes of action that almost all these inventions have in common. Formalization is a way of reinterpreting the world and re-classifying its elements with a view to increasing manageability. The achievements of modern institutions in terms of the extension of reach are regularly based on such kinds of formalization. My understanding of this term is close to Weber's concept of rationalization, provided that the emphasis in Weber's famous sentence is maintained: 'Increasing intellectualization and rationalization do *not*, therefore, indicate an increasing general knowledge of the conditions under which one lives.' They merely mean, Weber continues, a belief in the *knowability* and, following from it, in the *mastery* of the world by means of *calculation*.[23] Re-reading Weber in the light of recent sociology of knowledge and of postmodernism, one may note the explicit disjunction between epistemological validity claims and the sociological observation of spreading techniques of calculation that effectively change the world *and* the outlook of human beings in it. It is not very far from there to Lyotard's (analytical, not normative) emphasis on performativity as the dominant criterion for knowledge evaluation.[24]

Formalization is always based on a *classificatory* procedure. Certain phenomena of reality are ordered and the orders given linguistic expression, thereby a first step of separating them from their context is taken. Classification entails the construction of concepts that *represent* certain aspects of the world rather than merely naming them. Modern practices, not least because of their extension, always involve representations, the presenting of something which is not literally present, that is, money for a good or work, an electronic wave for a sound, a group of human beings selected according to a certain rule for the collective will of the political community, a concept of social science for a part of social life, etc. The rules of formalization are related to the form, rigidity and reach of the representations; a change in those rules will normally involve a restructuring of the social world.

With classification, *boundaries* are also created towards other phenomena in the world that are different, and phenomena of the same class are made equal to each other. To envisage a monetary and market economy, for instance, the first conceptual move is to see certain social phenomena as 'goods' to which monetary values, that is, descriptors in the same unit, can be attached. This move may have been the more important one compared to the derivative notions of self-regulation and enhancement of national wealth.[25]

The lack of any resolution to the debate on the labour theory of value shows the *theoretical* underdetermination (if not arbitrariness) and relative openness of description in unitary terms.[26] *Sociologically*, however, the increasing use of this mode meant a social convention of the formalization of a certain kind of economic expression. The convention was astoundingly 'successful' in increasing the reach of allocative practices generally, and also in enabling individual holders of value access to a wider range of allocative exchange. Formalization, however, to continue on this illustration, also meant that only phenomena that were socially expressible and expressed in money had access to this wider range of exchange. A social valuation process was introduced on the formal basis of this unifying descriptor and regardless of whatever qualities were actually included or excluded by it. The same holds true for the actors in allocative practices, the solely important criterion for which became whether they were holders of money and moneywise valuable qualities or not.[27]

Formalization is a reductive process. By reducing reality to one or a few decisive qualities, it makes it intelligible and manageable. By such effects, it is *enabling*. At the same time, it makes possession of such a quality the decisive access-point to its enabling features. By the very means of classification, it applies strong inclusion–exclusion rules and structures possibilities for action. Its main *constraining* effects reside in the setting of boundaries by excluding certain features from communication and consideration and by excluding certain people under certain circumstances, or with certain intentions, from action possibilities. Such boundaries are always social conventions, created by human beings in identifiable historical circumstances. But at a given point of their existence, they may appear to all or most of the living human beings who draw on them, as *natural*.[28]

There are several ways in which *constraints* may emerge.[29] One is, quite simply, material impossibility. Where a city has been built, farming is impossible. Another one is a restructuring of benefits and advantages that will make one unlikely to pursue certain options. Where one type of rule offering certain opportunities (markets and money, for instance) is widely extended, those who try (possibly for good reasons) to work with a different rule for other opportunities (exchange by barter, for example), may suffer disadvantages. Third, an institution may enable in such a way (regarding the substance of the opportunity and its social distribution) that a change to another arrangement can no longer be effected, given the need for a strong collective expression of will and the structure and stratification of individual wills.[30]

As this description and set of concepts may sound utterly abstract before being used in historical analysis, I shall give another illustration of a quite different kind. The material transformation of land- and city-scape by highway construction during the past half-century is probably unequalled in history on any count one may think of. Nevertheless it has, as far as I can see, never been submitted to a sociological analysis in terms of 'modernization'.

Once their linkages to social rules of action – both enabling and constraining – are recognized, inner-city highways, such as Robert Moses' Cross-Bronx Expressway in New York,[31] can be regarded as an important modern 'institution' structuring parts of the condition of modernity. A new kind of social relations in the public sphere had been created by the transformation of the major cities in the second half of the nineteenth century that had Baron Haussmann, the architect of the Paris boulevards, as one of its promotors, and the rapid growth of urban industrial zones as its social context. The multiplicity of casual encounters, the perpetual fleetingness, the enigma of the many unknown others, the public privacy of the 'family of eyes' has been regarded as the epitome of modernity from Charles Baudelaire to Georg Simmel to Walter Benjamin. It depended on spaces that would invite the display of relatively unguarded bodily presence, such as sitting, walking, talking, looking.

Such ambiences had survived well and even flourished during the growth of many cities between the 1870s and the 1920s. However, the physical presence of such city life came to be an obstacle for new kinds of enablements materialized in the car and the truck. The plans of Robert Moses, New York's twentieth-century Haussmann, were clearly shaped by a modernist view on the enhancement of mastery and of human autonomy. Moses loved the modern city and wanted to improve it. It should be fast, orderly, clean and beautiful; inner-city highways were a major means to that effect. In contrast to some of his followers, who endorsed the new 'space–time feeling' provoked by the 'steady flow' of driving,[32] Moses himself probably did not realize that his conception, driven to perfection, would destroy not only the spatial roots of specific, living human beings, but an entire mode of life. The enabling institution, the highway, literally would be a barrier to many interactions and exchanges. Physically and materially, it constrains those who do not have the means of access (the car) or the desire to profit from its specific achievements (to go fast and far through a city quarter), it prevents them from pursuing activities they may prefer to pursue.

Putting the 'meat axe', as Moses said, to work in a dense urban environment like the Bronx meant literally tearing down many boundaries and liberating traffic to a free flow across the city. But it also entailed the drawing of new boundaries, literally the tracks of the roads. These boundaries have the purpose of securing the formalization of action inside the new institution and of limiting and regulating access to it by excluding those who, for whatever reason, are not fit to apply the rules. In this sense, they disciplined both the users of the institutions and the excluded others.

It would be erroneous to generally model modern institutions after the example of a material technology.[33] But it is important to see that material technologies are used in the building of modern institutions to whose formalization they contribute. When 'in use', they link human activities to formalized rules in a way that also formalizes the 'attached' living human activities, in more or less rigid ways.[34] Rules of highway traffic include prohibitions to stopping or getting out, a fast and steady speed, and unidirectionality, among others. They are not only incompatible with the boulevard, but are more rigid and inflexible. During periods of regular use, it is impossible to communicate about the applicability of its rules, once you are on the highway. Shaping a formalized habitualized practice, boundaries are established that secure rule-following 'inside' and keep those who will not or cannot follow the rules 'outside'.

The restriction of communication to a limited number of officially endorsed signs and the complete exclusion of meta-communication during regular times is indeed a specific feature of the introduction of 'modern' rules more generally, a feature Giddens tries to capture with the term 'abstract systems'.[35] Formalization leads to a reduced concern for particulars of situations and to an increasing rigidity of action. A basic feature of such formalizations of actions and action possibilities is that the more extended and the more rigid an institution is, the more beneficial it is for individuals to comply with its rules than to deviate from them. The institution honours compliance, and the more rigid and extended (or, pervasive) an institution is, the higher are the costs of deviation.

Throughout my argument, I shall employ the imagery of tearing down conventional boundaries and setting up new ones, to make historical processes of liberation and disciplinization understood. When related to concepts of enablement and constraint, of formalization of action and reach of action chains, these terms are more than mere arbitrarily chosen images; they allow one to grasp the historical production of social formations under the significations of modernity. Also, they will allow a view of liberation as more than autonomy, and disciplinization as more than imposition. Historically, liberations may be enforced and not willed by many of those who are exposed to them. And disciplinizations may be a countermove against external impositions by means of establishing capable collective agency.

RULE TRANSFORMATION AND CRISES OF MODERNITY

In such a perspective, historical transformations of modernity will be conceived of as sequences of major rule changes, of institutional innovations, and as changes in configurations of institutions. Promotors of new rule-sets have to be identified, and the enabling and constraining characters of such rule-sets for different groups at different points of their diffusion and application have to be discerned. In spite of possibly lasting unintended effects that appear disconnected from modernizing intentions, 'modernizations' are not self-propelled processes, but modernization offensives, pursued by certain groups of actors for reasons linked to the nature of the institutional changes they promote. To anchor this attempt at a historical sociology of modernity in chronological history will need some sort of periodization. I shall propose a notion of 'crisis of modernity' as a step towards this end.

The term 'crisis' has been too widely diffused in the social sciences to be used innocently any longer. In its Greek origins, the medical term referred to the phase of an illness in which either recovery sets in or death threatens. In its everyday usage, the term lost its neutrality in terms of outcomes, and the connotation of danger and threat, of possibly terminal decline is emphasized. In the social sciences, the term appears to be originally related to organicist thinking, in which a crisis would be exactly equivalent to the critical phase of an illness.[36] It was revived in systemic thinking in the sense that a crisis exists when the reproductive needs of a system are not fulfilled. As in the case of a living body, systemic thinking has to assume a critical level of fulfilment below which reproduction becomes impossible.[37]

Such a strict understanding cannot be upheld, because societies normally cannot be understood as bodies or systems. These concepts presuppose an organic coherence or a functional interrelatedness and self-reference; on such a basis, one may identify illness or crisis as a problem in system maintenance and death or breakdown as a failure of system maintenance. However, conditions of coherence such as may be found in bodies and in purposefully created technical devices are difficult to envisage for the social practices of a multitude of individuals. Sociological thought, as long as it continues along this line, remains trapped in the misconceptions of two of its constitutive phases. The first is the Enlightenment tradition in which coherence and integration were conceived in normative terms as the necessary and inevitable outcome of the use of reason. The second is the classical era of sociological reasoning, about a century later, when the European nation-state empirically seemed to be such a case of an ordered set of social practices, spatially circumscribed and resting in themselves. Also, and maybe equally importantly, intellectual practices themselves were oriented toward the nation and based in national institutions. Since then, sociologists have tended to conflate the general concept of 'society' with the empirical phenomenon of territorially bounded social practices. The *coherence* of social practices, however, cannot be assumed, but its degree has to be made part of the empirical inquiry.

In general terms, it is more appropriate to view societies openly as configurations of institutions, where institutions are seen as habitualized practices. It is the constant reenactment of practices that forms institutions. If we see institutions as relatively stable sets of social conventions, then we may regard the building of such institutions as a process of *conventionalization*, and a crisis as being marked by tendencies towards de-conventionalization, followed by the creation of new sets of conventions. The chains of interaction that link human beings may be reoriented or extended and the kinds of linkages that are used may be altered, and so societies change their shape and extension. Crises will then be understood as periods when individuals and groups change their social practices to such an extent that major social institutions and, with them, the prevailing configuration of institutions undergo a transformation.

Such crises often go along with a sense of decline or rupture or end of an order. Such a sense of 'crisis' (in an everyday meaning) may stem from the fact that many of those people who do not actively change their habits will, during such changes, be exposed to the effects of decisions taken by others. More generally, such periods of transformation are problem-ridden in the view of those who live through it, because it simply is difficult to perceive the collective outcome of many concurrent changes at the time they are enacted. Finally, however, the sense of crisis may also well be limited to those steady observers of society who have come to be called intellectuals from the beginning of the twentieth century onwards. Intellectuals tend to emphasize the need for coherence and to link order strongly with significations. Lack of integration and of signification may often affect many other people quite differently. For instance, the likelihoods for decline or rise of their own position and trade may be reassessed, and one may merely change one's own practices accordingly, often thereby accelerating the change of the configuration.

I shall argue that, in such a perspective, Western societies have experienced two major crises of modernity since its inception.[38] First, attempts to restructure the social order accumulated during the second half of the nineteenth century; and between the closing years of that century and the end of the First World War, the practices of modernity were set on a new social path. Second, from the 1960s onwards, doubts about the adequacy and desirability of the mode of social organization have again increased, and social practices are being restructured. In cultural and intellectual terms, one may say that such reorientations cumulated first in the *fin de siècle* and now in the postmodernity debate. However, in spite of their appearance in some of the self-reflective discourses, such crises are not primarily philosophical or epistemological ones. Most of the philosophical issues are hardly new, they rather recur and gain new attention.

MODERNITY AND CONTINGENCY

The final question that needs to be touched on at this stage, then, is whether the successive crises and transformations of modernity lead in a specific historical direction. This question is not meant to inadvertently let the discussion glide into evolutionism. However, it may be the case that through their recurring attempts at conventionalization and de-conventionalization, human beings may consistently emphasize certain kinds of rules over others, and may make some kinds of rules historically unachievable.

Often, the history of modernity is taken to involve a steady widening of the scope of institutions. The development of the world-market, again, is the prime example. The range of applications of a homogeneous set of social rules is steadily extending, and more and more social practices are guided by these rules. Scope and depth of inclusion increase constantly. Such a globalization of the very few characteristically modern conventions is then seen to entail the dissolution of the historical, locally specific modes of boundary-setting and of rule-making, at least with regard to key sets of social practices. Modernity breaks all boundaries, melts everything into the air.

There is a sense in which this image of the destruction of all boundaries is valid. The acceptance of the idea of individual autonomy as a basic imaginary signification has – in a limited, but important sense – irreversibly transformed the conditions of social development.

> When he is defined as independent, the individual does not . . . acquire a new certainty in place of the old. . . . He is doomed to be tormented by a secret uncertainty. . . . The emergence of the individual does not merely mean that he is destined to control his own destiny; he also has been dispossessed of his assurance as to his identity – of the assurance which he once appeared to derive from his station, from his social condition, or from the possibility of attaching himself to a legitimate authority.[39]

This statement is fully acceptable in terms of a political philosophy of modernity. Thus far, modernity indeed means contingency. Still, if this term were to describe a mode of social life, it probably does not hold for any historical group of actual living human beings. Actual human beings will – and have to – devise means of decreasing contingency. The relevant question for a sociohistorical analysis is whether the conditions for them to do so change.

Though some historical processes can be viewed in terms of increasing contingency, as a general sociological interpretation such a theorem is flawed. It is exactly during periods of crisis that there may be a strong desire to limit the scope of rules by referring to social conditions and invoking authorities. More widely extended institutions are, almost by definition, less amenable to intervention and control by any specific group among those human beings who fall under their range of applicability. But exactly for this reason, we may also find that attempts to decrease sociopolitical (and also individual) contingency are more strongly forthcoming. These institutions invite efforts at limitation and the setting of new boundaries, efforts which are in no way doomed to fail from the start, owing to some inescapable logics of modernity. As I will show later, successful efforts at limiting the scope of modern institutions have strongly shaped the history of modernity – and there is no reason to assume that this will not be the case in the future.

Still, if we survey briefly the history of modernity, anticipating the argument of this book, then we may well find a general increase of contingency. In this context, the current normative political debate on communitarianism is a significant indicator of the present condition of modernity. It is the most recent instance of arguing for boundaries, for limiting the impact of individual liberalism. But compared to earlier political theories with related ambitions, it is the least substantively defined. While it is easy to recognize the problems of individual liberalism, it is extremely difficult, under current conditions, to argue for *any* general norm or rule that sets boundaries to individual autonomy and defines community.[40]

Very little appears as naturally given any longer, and it is difficult to justify a collective rule or outcome when its 'naturalness' cannot be invoked. Current aporias of political theory often emerge because implicit assumptions of earlier thinking have to be withdrawn as norms of social interaction are being de-naturalized. Nation- and culture-specific norms, for example, emerge visibly as set norms when they are questioned by international and intercultural interaction. The increase in social constructedness as well as the awareness of such constructedness, thus make the political issue of justification highly problematic.

In the above terms, a political sociology of modernity must also study the historically changing devices of justification. Modern institutions may vary in the exact degree to which they tend to define moments of social life as situations that have to be treated in common.[41] Historically, the hypothesis is that towards the end of the nineteenth century a greater set of situations was thus defined, and the relevant community was often determined as the nation. Currently, however, the converse seems to be the case, at least in the West. An astonishing feature of many contemporary debates, for instance, is that only deliberately set norms count as being in need of justification, whereas the 'unruly' outcome of many individual practices, such as that of the market or the supremacy of cars as a means of transport, is regarded as 'natural', because it is in line with the fundamental assumption of individual autonomy. Proposals for collective deliberations on substantive matters bear 'the onus of argument', as Charles Taylor formulates it.[42] To see more clearly what arguments have been and can be proposed for what kinds of collective and substantive objectives, we now have to turn to the sociohistorical analysis.

Part II

The first crisis of modernity

Chapter 3

Restricted liberal modernity

The incomplete elaboration of the modern project

The project of a liberal society, focused as it was on the idea of human autonomy, was universal and without boundaries in principle. As such it was truly utopian. A global society, inclusive of all individuals in an egalitarian way, seemed a rather abstract and far-fetched imagery. In historical reality, indeed, the more concrete visions of societal renewal, as they were held by the promotors of the project, were much more limited and very well bounded. A historical sociology of the first century of modernity, so to speak, can rest on the analysis of two main social phenomena of the nineteenth century. First, the socially dangerous openness of modernity was well recognized. As a consequence, the foundations of such a society were only very incompletely elaborated in practice, and means were developed to contain the modern project (Chapter 3).

Second, after the contours of such a contained, restricted liberal society had become visible, a corpus of critical ideas emerged. Its authors tended to claim that the project, in the form in which it had been proposed, was not feasible. Ongoing tensions between the liberation promises and the containment needs seemed to call for new authoritative responses to remedy the problems inherent in the socio-historical realization of the project. By the end of the nineteenth century, the 'post-liberal' compromise that had been reached appeared unstable and unsatisfactory to most of its observers and participants, and – from the end of the First World War onwards, at the latest – new sets of social conventions were being constructed. This extended transformation can be described as the first crisis of modernity (Chapter 4).

My argument on the containment of the modern project will proceed in three steps. Looking at some practices of signification, first, the *intellectual means* of setting boundaries will be discussed in terms of historically varying ways of providing identity for oneself by constructing the other as an inverse image of oneself. Second, focusing on the most important practices of domination, the *institutional form* of enforcing the boundaries towards the other will be analysed by taking a look at the state and law. Third, the *substantive exclusions* will be discussed as ways of externalizing social phenomena that could not be handled in modernist practices of the nineteenth century. After these three steps have been taken, the boundaries can be identified of a social formation that lived up to the universalism and individualism of the liberal project only in a very restricted sense. Ultimately, a brief first excursion will be made into the United States of America which, while not without boundaries of its own making, showed less restrictions than its European counterparts.

BOUNDARY-SETTING (I): MODERNITY AND THE OTHER

As anthropologists maintain, 'cultures' can form only if they define themselves in comparison to something which they are not.[1] The notion of savagery, for instance,

> belongs to a set of culturally self-authenticating devices which includes, among many others, the ideas of 'madness' and 'heresy' as well. . . . They do not so much refer to a specific thing, place, or condition as dictate a particular attitude governing a relationship between a lived reality and some area of problematical existence that cannot be accommodated easily to conventional conceptions of the normal or familiar.[2]

Its sociological or anthropological basis is the 'conception of a divided humanity, and a humanity in which differentness was conceived to reflect a qualitative rather than merely a quantitative variation'.[3]

Similarly, modernist social scientists have often tried to understand their societies in contrast to some other, earlier or distant, counterpart, mostly labelled 'traditional' society. The dichotomy of 'modernity' and 'tradition' has merely succeeded, but not fundamentally altered earlier ones. It is hardly surprising then that only very few social scientists have bothered to give evidence of the existence of such a homogeneous counterpart to 'modernity' nor have they been able to argue for its systematic distinctiveness from their own society. 'Traditional society' is largely a sociological construct that was developed as a tool of comparison when trying to grasp the present.[4]

The discourses of modernity displayed a universalism of reason that provided the basis for its totalizing claims: these were new insights that should basically hold for all humankind. However, not everybody was convinced of the validity of the modernist claims, nor did observations of social reality decisively underpin its validity. Such a situation was clearly a dilemma for a universalist project. It needed to set boundaries in the name of reason. Universality was to be restricted on actual grounds of lacking empirical plausibility as well as political feasibility, and such restrictions were theoretically argued for by making basic distinctions in the realm of universality itself.

Such boundaries were set by the construction and, thereby, the distancing of the other, the removal of the other from the same time-space of humanity. The concept of the barbarian is basically a means of *distancing in space*, barbarians lived elsewhere. The concept of tradition, in contrast, is rather a mode of *distancing in time*. It may seem less radical than the idea of the barbarian, because it allows for a developmental perspective, the mere postponement of full integration of the others into the future. However, it does so only under the condition that the others give up their otherness. As Johannes Fabian has pointed out, the modern perspective is marked by a 'denial of coevalness' to any form of life different from its own. It erected a wall between the other and itself, where 'the very notion of containing walls and boundaries creates order and sense based on discontinuity'.[5] The other is defined 'in a way that *a priori* decides its inferior and, indeed, transient and (until disappearance) illegitimate status. In an age of the forward march of reason-guided progress, describing the Other as outdated, backward, obsolete, primitive, and altogether "pre-", was equivalent to such a decision.'[6]

Enlightenment discourse had developed an encompassing and universal concept of humankind, against the concepts of both king and God. Once the idea of Enlightenment as the exit from self-caused heteronomy was pronounced, it proved uncontrollable and its own dynamics very soon pushed it beyond the initial conceptions. 'Humanity' and 'autonomy' do hardly allow for social limitations, they seem boundary-less, as was recognized at the time. After the French Revolution at the latest, however, it became obvious that the modern project had less secure foundations than it seemed in those self-conscious and optimistic writings. Given the fear, nourished by the *terreur* of the French Revolution, that society could get out of control, a major intellectual struggle was to contain the concept, to close it, to try to set boundaries.[7] The others inside one's own society were identified by their lack of reason and civilization; they comprised most importantly the *lower, working classes*, the *women* and the *mad*.

When the feudal orders disassembled, the lower classes, including farm workers, industrial workers and servants, who were unbound and appeared less controlled, turned into a threat to the social order in the eyes of many observers. Soon the industrial workers were singled out from the paupers. 'Words and notions such as "proletariat," "dangerous classes," haunted the discourse and imagination of the first half of the nineteenth century.'[8] They were seen as inherently more dangerous, because they were easily recognized as a product of the emerging bourgeois society itself. Just like the bourgeoisie they stood at the beginning of their historical existence and could expect to have a future, as, of course, Karl Marx soon recognized and took as a basis for his own philosophy of history. So even if, or precisely because, the lower classes' coevality was hard to deny, clear boundaries had to be set and maintained:

> At the basis of the discussion of the nature of the new 'dangerous classes' of mass society stands a deep and abiding anxiety over the very concept of humanity itself, a concept which, in turn, has its origin in an identification of true humanity with membership in a specific social class.[9]

The exclusion of the lower classes from the liberal order was probably the most prominent topic of political debates and struggles for more than a century after the French Revolution. Many different elements entered into the political theories that were – explicitly or implicitly – applied, ranging from a clinging to feudal conceptions, to linkages between property ownership and the assumption of political responsibility, to issues of moral education and conceptions of representation and representability.

In contrast, the systematic character of the exclusion of women has been much less widely debated and generally been accepted, outside feminist and women's rights circles. Gender in liberal political theory was a silenced issue. From the point of view of many discussants, this restriction was hardly a question of strongly willed exclusion, rather a quite natural extension of a double basic assumption, namely the distinction of a public and a private sphere *cum* the identification of the former with the man and the latter with the woman. Civil society was formed in the public sphere where men represented their property, including wife and children, house and estate, and servants. Only the male, property-owning head of a household, who was capable of sharing the burden as a citizen, could be regarded as a being endowed with full rights.[10]

Only in recent years has the history of the gendering of politics and society been more systematically reworked. It has been shown that the explicit designation of a special status to women is consistently found in the areas of philosophy, the human and social sciences, political theory and actual forms of political participation.[11] Far from liberating women and enabling them to full participation in all social realms, the bourgeois restructuring introduced more formalized rules and formally excluded women from a range of activities, most prominently political participation, to which they could contribute more informally under the Old Regimes, at least under favourable circumstances. In the terms of Joan Landes, 'the collapse of the older patriarchy gave way to a more pervasive *gendering* of the public sphere.' The creation of a realm of collective political self-determination in electoral institutions set boundaries in such a way that women were placed outside. In politics, as in the other discourses, the main argument given was on the natural endowments of women, a specific female anthropology that focused on emotions and lack of control, thus also lack of civilization and amenability to reason. 'The exclusion of women from the bourgeois public was not incidental but central to its incarnation.'[12]

The distinction between reason and unreason is at the roots of all modern attempts at boundary-setting. Its ultimate form hits at the very core of unreason, namely madness. Again, like in the case of the special anthropology of the female sex, very little doubt was voiced until recently about the validity of the discourses on madness and the adequacy of the respective practices of seclusion and control. The extreme shakiness of the ground on which these rested could only be identified when the fundamental affirmative assumption of the need to separate reason and unreason was given up, and detached 'archeological' and 'genealogical' studies into the history of these very discourses were undertaken.[13] I shall not go deeper into this discussion in which others are far more knowledgeable and competent than I am. Rather, I shall draw together some of the strands of this brief outline with a view to its relevance for a sociology of modernity.

Arguably, we can find in every culture sets of classifications which orient everyday activities and structure social institutions. In the modern discourses, the basic classificatory distinction is made between reason and civilization, on the one side, and its inversion on the other: wildness, tradition, disorder, emotion, insanity. A main theme of modern reasoning is the creation of order, by the imposition of order on wildness or, if that is impossible, by the separation of the disorderly from the orderly. This theme is obviously related to the idea of rational mastery; disorder defies prediction and control.

A certain shift in the construction of the other during modernity can be observed, though there is no clear temporal sequence, rather a superimposition of themes with shifting emphases. The mode of distancing became ever more problematic and subtle, in a historical process of *approaching* the other. While the savages could be seen as far away in space and members of traditional social formations as far away in time, workers, women and the mad were indubitably present. And yet, even those were not similarly present. The lower classes were present in one's own society (and firm, possibly), the women in one's own family and intimate relations, and madness in one's own body and mind.

From one perspective, it may be argued that the distancing of the other became more difficult the closer it came. Without doubt, the workers' movement, the women's movement and the debates on psychoanalysis and psychiatry have forced themes on the agenda of the bourgeois revolution that the revolutionaries and their established followers would have preferred to avoid. They were taken by their claim to universality and autonomy, and the unjustified and unjustifiable boundaries they had erected were questioned and, partly at least, dismantled over time. This discourse is, ultimately, one of liberation; it is a specific one, though, because the rhetorical figure under which the observed processes are put is that of the return of the repressed.

From another perspective, one can relate the process of repression and re-thematization to historical changes in the social formation. Then, the argument could be that there was socially threatening otherness in the lower classes, the women and the mad at the outset of the bourgeois project. But throughout its historical development, the social formation was itself transformed, and transformed otherness, in such a way that the danger was reduced. This interpretation is not uncommon for the historical complex of the workers' movement, the 'social question' and the transformation of allocative institutions, and I shall return to it at several points below. Historical transformations of the place of women in society, of the family and of intimacy as well as of modes of constituting self-identity can probably be interpreted along similar lines.[14] The transformations of the social formation can then be read as an actually successful imposition of order on wildness. What was (and had to be) repressed at the outset of modernity, was increasingly controlled and mastered so that it could ultimately be set free.[15]

Both perspectives would accept the historical account as one of the initial setting of boundaries and their gradual, or also less gradual, erosion over time. Later in this chapter, I shall try to show how the substantive terms of some of these boundaries provided the material for a construction of social identity. The modes of construction of social identity themselves changed historically, they became ever more modern, that is self-constituted rather than ascribed or 'natural'. But before going into the substantive analysis, the institutional form, which was used for such purposes and which was to contain the collective identity, needs to be introduced. This form is the state, as a set of rules of domination that was pre-given to the bourgeois movements, but also creatively appropriated and transformed in their struggles.

BOUNDARY-SETTING (II): MODERNITY AND THE STATE

What is at issue in the question of the state is the fencing-in of the new society against its own consequences. In the view of the emancipatory movements, the Old Regime was built on untenable foundations and had to be destroyed. But it proved to be the case that the order of reason would not grow naturally, that instead, to avoid being undermined by the dynamics of its own premises, it had to be defined. Criteria had to be developed for social practices that could then be imposed on an often recalcitrant society.[16]

For the European context, which is at the centre of my argument, it is essential to see that the perceived need for boundary-setting did not come up in a politically de-structured setting. By contrast, the Old Regime had left a very prominent form in, and through, which the new order could be established, namely the modern state that had emerged from feudalism. By the eighteenth century, this order had already been endowed with the notion of *sovereignty*, with a certain degree of formalization of the still personalized power of the ruler by the means of *law*, and with a set of disciplining practices of *governmentality*.[17]

The concept of sovereignty over a territory and the people who lived in it emerged in the conflicts between royal rulers and between the rulers and the estates in Europe during the sixteenth and seventeenth centuries. At the time when the legitimacy of the king was questioned, the conception that everything that was subject to a ruler formed some sort of entity was well established. Rather than abandoning any notion of preconceived entities, as radically liberal thought would have to see it, merely the location of the ultimate source of legitimacy was changed.

> When society can no longer be represented as a body and is no longer embodied in the figure of the prince, it is true that people, state and nation acquire a new force and become the major poles by which social identity and social communality can be signified.[18]

Basically then, the existing and accepted concept of sovereignty had only to be reinterpreted in constitutional and republican ways.[19]

In Europe, this conceptual shift rested most importantly on the existence of the state institutions, and the continuity of these institutions through revolutionary upheavals is evidence of the fact that the shift 'worked' in practical terms. In theoretical terms, however, the tension between individualist and collectivist foundations of the polity, which was characteristic of all social contract theory, had not been alleviated. Rather, it was exaggerated by the experience of 'the people' threatening to indeed exercise its sovereignty during the French Revolution. Hegel, for instance, appreciated both the bourgeois, liberal values and the revolutions, but he strongly recognized the unbounded character of the new society. His understanding of the state as the embodiment of higher reason was a conceptual means of reconciling individual autonomies and particularities with the need for a unifying whole. In those terms, one can put the Hegelian problematic as the reconciliation of the historical achievement of abstract liberties and the need for a reconstitution of collective identity in community.[20]

A similarly paradoxical (or dialectical) development can be observed with regard to policy practices. During the Old Regime, increasingly detailed orders and decrees were issued that tended to regulate ever more aspects of the everyday lives of the ruler's subjects. This was a government invasion into activities hitherto uncontrolled or, at least, not centrally controlled. It had the purpose of enforcing discipline, deepening the hold of state power into society and transforming it into governance. Michel Foucault speaks of the very emergence of 'governance' from a broader and looser concept of rule. It was accompanied by the promotion of the so-called cameral and police sciences at the universities that were supposed to develop systematic knowledge about such policy interventions.[21]

But these changes altered the character of the personalized rule of feudal rulers. While they were not meant to abolish or substitute this rule, they introduced objectified, formalized regulation in the form of public law. In this form, the existence of a set of formally regulated activities provided the space free of public regulation and with it the precondition of the idea of liberty *from* the state. It was in this space, created by the all-pervasive cameralist state practices, that the discourse on liberation could later flourish.[22]

Zygmunt Bauman has put the historical relation between the Enlightenment discourse of liberty and the use of state institutions as follows:

> Harsh realities of politics in the aftermath of . . . the final collapse of the feudal order made the diversity of lives and relativity of truths much less attractive. . . . Enlightened and not-so-enlightened rulers set out to build anew, willfully and by design, the order of things. . . . The new, modern order took off as a desperate search for structure in a world suddenly denuded of structure.[23]

In an impressive range of writings, Bauman has painted a picture of modernity with very sharp contours. In his view, the constitution of modernity should be seen as the monopolistic imposition of a new regime characterized by the will to identify otherness, legislate order and eliminate ambivalence. The monopolistic claim of the modern state to the territory and its people showed close cognitive affinity to the universal claim to truth by philosophy and (social) science. Thus, modern, legislating intellectual practices can be distinguished from postmodern, interpreting ones that emerge later as a response to modern impositions.[24]

This is a powerful portrait, and in an era in which 'actually existing' modernity and modernization are again equated with normative and functional superiority, it is a very timely reminder of quasi-totalitarian domination in the name of the universal idea of reason. But, though he is rarely explicit about historical periods, Bauman shows a peculiar tendency to bracket his main line of argument on the modern imposition of order with two fringe lines. As the quotation above shows, modernity was initially about liberty, diversity and relativity, in his view. This proved untenable, and modernity turned to ordering the chaos, to eliminating ambivalence in the name of reason and by the means of bureaucratic control. Nazism and Stalinism came to be the epitomes of modernity. However, the subflow was never completely suppressed, and liberty, diversity and relativity re-emerged under the sign of postmodernity. Bauman prefers these tendencies, though he recognizes problems of fragmentation and dispersion due to insufficient communication and lack of social consensus and solidarity.[25]

This distinction of main and fringe lines of argument is not very satisfactory. It is conceptually inadequate, since it does not capture the fundamental ambivalence of modernity itself. Also, it distorts the historical occurrences. The quote above suggests that fear of freedom *followed* on the post-revolutionary experience of uncertainty and *led* to the turn towards order. But neither the latter nor the former is true, at least not as the direct and immediate linkage that Bauman suggests. The discourse on modernity included notions of reason, order and control from the beginning, that is, before the revolutions. And, though the idea of a social void has been related to the *terreur* of the French Revolution, the historical experience of diversity and relativity was very limited in post-revolutionary Europe. True, the Revolution heightened the awareness of the need for new boundaries. But the rules provided by the pre-revolutionary states mostly remained (and were often consciously kept) intact, and they were used and transformed for the *bounded* shaping of the new order.

The Enlightenment discourse should not be mistaken for the social practices of the bourgeois revolutionaries. Very soon, the latter were willing to enter into factual coalitions with the more moderate and enlightened of their opponents. Conservative warnings of an inappropriately egalitarian homogenization of society and bourgeois concerns about a containment of the processes set in motion often went hand in hand, in the reasoning of political actors and in the actual reforms and their limitations. The sets of mostly state-organized institutions, like the schools, the prisons and the asylums, which have most penetratingly been analysed by Michel Foucault, showed simultaneously an educational, disciplinary and exclusionary character, as also the respective discourses about them reveal in their more Enlightenment-style or more conservative taint.

On both sides, the conservative and the liberal ones, it also became increasingly clear that the state form might not suffice to maintain social order. Many observers recognized that the containment of the liberal utopia needed to be based on some substantive elements.

THE SOCIAL CONSTRUCTION OF IDENTITY AND THE RETURN OF THE REPRESSED

Modern discourse constructed the human being as capable of teleological action, controlling his body and nature, and as autonomous towards his fellow human beings. These are the essentials of a rational-individualistic theory of human action, which, as the imaginary signification of modernity, is reflected not least in the modernist social sciences.[26] The unreality of this conception did not escape even its promoters and some of their more sceptical contemporaries. Partly, it was seen as a programme, indeed the project of modernity, to liberate human beings from their subjection to nature, from unchosen ties to others, and from the contradictions within themselves. 'After all, modernity is a rebellion against fate and ascription.'[27]

Partly, however, modernizers and their critics were aware of a deep-rooted deficiency in the entire approach. It was suspected that it would create a cold universe, that it would destroy any sense of belonging. In its most optimistic version, the modern discourse regarded the liberations as breaking all unwanted ties, all imposed relations, but freeing human beings to recreate communities of their own choosing. The third item of the French revolutionary slogan, 'brotherhood' (its sexist bias notwithstanding), represents these hopes and expectations.

If not principally, this idea was at least sociologically unrealistic. The modernizing elites themselves based their practices implicitly on the continuity of some 'natural' bonds. And the larger parts of the population who were more exposed to modernity than they had chosen to be, were very open to accepting new collectively binding arrangements without having individually and rationally considered them. Much of the remaining part of this chapter – and actually of the entire book – will be about these two types of bonds, the remaining 'natural' ones, in the process of further dissolution, and the newly created ones, permanently vulnerable to destruction and open to modified recreation.

To some extent, the discussion can be led by taking up again the various othernesses from which modern man tried to distance himself. Modern reasoning emphasized the objective of controlling nature and one's own body. It introduced a strict boundary between the human and the *natural*. This was no short and linear process. From first seeing humankind as an integral part of a harmonious natural order to viewing nature as a source, with the help of which humans can awaken their inner selves, the modern discourse gradually moves towards an instrumental stance towards nature. Rather than being a clear objective, this stand-point was enforced by an intellectual dilemma, namely that of combining the negation of religion with the affirmation of the significance of nature. 'The language that seemed necessary for the first left no place for the second. . . . The problem is denied, the inarticulable remains semi-repressed.'[28] This move did not go fully uncontested. Post-revolutionary romanticism, for instance, tried to reintroduce an idea of natural unity. However, the basic steps for de-deifying nature and for making it amenable to instrumental treatment and exploitation were taken in the modern discourse.[29]

The uncontrolled and unpredictable elements in human behaviour, including madness, were also generally seen as remnants of nature that were to be suppressed. The control of mind and body has, since Freud, been discussed under the rhetorical figure of repression and the 'return of the repressed'. The uncalculated, but nevertheless damaging impact of human activities on nature (after separation, called 'environment') has more recently been debated, as proposed by economists, under the figure of the 'externalization of effects'. Both forms of rhetoric draw on the concept of boundary-setting and exclusion. Once something is defined, a boundary between inside and outside is drawn. Phenomena will structure themselves according to their position towards the boundary, inside or outside. Benefits may be gained from imposing a boundary, but the 'costs' will anyhow occur, though they may be partially (that is, socially, temporarily) invisibilized. Parts of reality are repressed in order to develop other ones. One may argue, though, that the inside ultimately can only be privileged at the cost of a 'return of the repressed'.[30]

Regularly, modern reasoning drew a boundary at places where more open, fluid conceptions prevailed before modernity. The issue of the *genderization* of the public sphere has already briefly been touched upon. While under the Old Regime women of high standing could well contribute to public debate, the French Revolution as well as all later suffrage rules throughout the nineteenth century formally excluded women from institutionalized political participation. Full equality was established in these terms only in the twentieth century, sometimes only after the Second World War.

In contrast to 'the ecological question', 'the woman question' should appear to be 'solvable' on the basis of modern principles, namely by the application of equal rights. Significantly though, the modern way has long been the road not taken in practice. The modern closure seems to consist here in the fact that the social rule for fulfilling the human desire for intimate sociality is written *in ascriptive terms*, namely as an asymmetric bondage through a marriage that subordinates women, confined to the *private realm* of the house. A 'truly modern' focus on the isolated self-centred individual would need to universalize the rules for allocative and authoritative practices and to 'open' the issue of intimate sociality (as well as human procreation). It would let men and women, with all the uncertainties it may entail, self-create these rules in their own practice. So, the genderization of the public sphere and the under-thematization of the issue of gender generally have their systematic place as maintainers of a guarded, bounded realm that is not intended to be exposed to modern liberty.[31]

Gender and nature are clearly two of the key issues of modernity that remain unresolved. Significantly, movements to reconsider both questions, though never completely silent, increased their strength at about the turn to the twentieth century, that is, in the period that I shall label the first crisis of modernity, and after the 1960s, that is, during the second crisis of modernity.

At this point of my argument, I want to stress two other issues that were historically used to settle the contradictions of modernity, at least temporarily. These are the issues of *cultural-linguistic identity* (the national question) and of *social solidarity* (the social question), around which a temporary containment of modernity was achieved. Before discussing these two themes in more detail, the general interlinkage of boundary-setting and identity-building shall be recapitulated. Far from living up to the abstract ideal of isolated individuals set free from all ties and constraints, some boundaries were maintained and others erected in the early history of modernity. Some of the early solutions to the self-created problems of modernity worked with concepts of *natural* givenness. Ethnicity, language and gender provided criteria for how to distribute individuals among social orders and how to place them inside these social orders.[32]

None of these criteria have obviously completely eroded. During the history of modernity, however, even though they have repeatedly been strongly applied, they have tended to become less persuasive. Large-scale migrations made it difficult to allot cultural-linguistic groups to contiguous territories, and attempts at cultural assimilation – though they were often brutally tried – did not always have the intended result. Increasing access to 'public' allocative and authoritative practices as well as the impact of the women's movement have altered the position of women in society. Although complete genderwise contingency of social practices is far from being achieved, a conception of the household as a sociopolitical unit is impossible to maintain. Ascriptive criteria, through which it is completely predetermined whether an individual forms part of a social group or not, are widely seen as inapplicable.

In a first historical step, so to speak, such criteria have been complemented by criteria of interest according to social location. Social identity was then constructed by membership in a class. The class location of an individual was no longer naturally fixed and not completely unalterable. But most of the political discourses between the middle of the nineteenth and the middle of the twentieth century treated it as quasi-natural. An individual was born and socialized into it and would most likely not leave it. As such, it provided a strong social basis for the construction of collective identity.

Most recently, the boundaries of class constructions have tended to erode, too. The likelihood of changing a class position has increased. And, more importantly in terms of identity building, social practices are much less generally organized in parallel terms to an economically determined class location. Current social identity-conveying communities are often also collectively agreed, and not immediately transmitted through socialization. The living individual members themselves participate in the construction and reconstruction of such communities. The feeling of collective identity may be very strong for the individuals concerned, not least because they built it themselves. For the same reason, however, it is open to reflection and often unstable over the life-time of the participating individuals.

This sketch is overly schematic; it will be taken up again and elaborated later. Obviously, at any point in the history of modernity all three forms co-existed, no linear trend through all of a society should be assumed. Still, one can argue for the validity of a more general observation, namely a historical weakening of the assumptions for constructing social identities, from ascriptive and natural to socially acquired and quasi-natural to chosen and socially agreed. Very broadly, and rather as a heuristic guideline for further analysis than as historical fact, the first type can be related to the social formation of restricted liberal modernity (to be further discussed in the following section), the second one to organized modernity, and the third one to extended liberal modernity.

RESTRICTED LIBERAL MODERNITY: THE CONTOURS OF THE CONTAINMENT OF THE LIBERAL UTOPIA

The historical struggles over the feasibility of modernity in Europe focused on the two issues of cultural-linguistic identity and social solidarity which I have already briefly mentioned above. These were struggles about the limitation of the sociohistorical meaning of modernity. While the concept is open and uncontained in principle, attempts were made to contain its impact within collectively controllable limits. The substance of these two limiting criteria is different. Nationhood has been developed as a *constitutive* boundary in terms of social identity. Solidarity, though the idea was already present in the Revolution, is a criterion that rather developed in response to the *impact* of modernity on society. I shall thus deal first with the former, then with the latter issue.

The form that political societies gradually acquired after the modern rupture was not merely a politically liberal and democratic one, but it was the cultural-linguistically based nation-state, at least as an ideal to strive for. The cultural-linguistic basis, as such, has very little to do with the modern notion of autonomy. Erecting a frontier around a territory and defining the inhabitants of the territory in terms of nationality was in contradiction with the idea of the universalism of rights. Also, in terms of its cultural and linguistic substance, it was not an established tradition, rather a new form of boundary. 'The traditional aristocratic elites in pre-modern Europe had found no particular difficulties in governing diverse ethnic or national groups.'[33]

Nevertheless, the idea of the nation-state was soon seized upon as the conceptually appropriate instrument for a workable imposition of modernity. The linkage between liberal ideas and national ideas was the concept of *national* self-determination. 'The fusion of popular sovereignty with the sovereignty and self-determination of the nation – prefigured in the 1789 declaration of human rights – subordinates the modern project of autonomy to a supposedly paradigmatic – but only partly modern – form of collective identity.'[34] The problem then, of course, was who formed part of the collective called nation.

In many European countries, not least Germany and Italy, political intellectuals fused the idea of a liberal polity with the search for a somehow natural collective that should form this polity. The notion was developed that there are such collectives of historical belonging in Europe that are defined by their common, historically transmitted, culture and language. In Germany, Johann Gottfried Herder proposed the concept of *Volk* (people) as an ontological unit, and Friedrich Schleiermacher, in a move that appears now as almost postmodernist, linked the very possibility of knowledge to common linguistic practices and concluded that one should strive to keep the speakers of a common language together. In Italy, the intellectuals of the *risorgimento* were aware that they were not simply arguing for bringing together what belonged together, but indeed constructing a community out of a variety of different cultural orientations and social backgrounds. The basis for belonging then is common history or, at least, the idea of common history.[35] Arguably, the understanding of nation that was prevalent in France was more truly modern, because it merely saw the nation as a necessary frame for individual emancipation (the nation as a collection of individuals), whereas the German ideas were dominated by the concept that the unity of culture and language preceded actual human beings (the nation as a collective individual). But in these two forms, these concepts expressed jointly 'the difficulty that the modern ideology has in providing a sufficient image of social life'.[36]

These intellectual endeavours were far from the aggressive nationalism that became widespread by the end of the nineteenth century, but they clearly intended to set boundaries, to define and contain collective self-determination around the construction of imagined social identities, as, of course, most of the presumed Italians and Germans never had formed an active community in any sense.[37] As such, these efforts were a response to the general opening of social relations that the revolutionary concepts, and increasingly the bourgeois allocative practices, entailed. 'While traditional social lineages and loyalties had lost much of their binding force, the national idea proved to be a substitute for them in as much as it provided a new sort of cohesion among the various social and political groupings.'[38]

Where such an offer for cohesion was accepted and territorially accomplished, external boundaries of the modern polity could be set. During the nineteenth century, however, the question of who should participate in the modern project inside the national society, also became an internally disputed issue. This new dispute was triggered not least by the experience that the dynamics of liberated allocative practices had had an adverse impact on living and working conditions of many compatriots. This is one way of formulating what became known as 'the social question'; its formulation presupposed external boundaries to the polity. The question itself, however, referred to the internal boundaries of early modernity.

Though many of the more moderate revolutionaries in France had not considered the lower classes as fully entitled citizens of modernity, the imaginary of the Revolution was all-inclusive and egalitarian. Among the republicans, furthermore, the expectation was that the establishment of the desired political order, the republic with universal suffrage, would take care of all other problems, since everybody concerned would have a say in collective matters. Later, however, the failure of the Second Republic to satisfy the material needs of its electorate – a failure that entailed the early end of the republic itself – made evident that the social question would remain a key issue even for a democratic polity. 'The social question, thus, appears first as the recognition of a deficiency of social reality with regard to the political imaginary of the Republic.'[39] From then on and especially after the republic had been set on a more secure footing in 1871, much of French political debate centred around the question of how a criterion could be introduced into liberal and democratic reasoning that would allow for dealing with the social question without re-imposing a strong state on the volitions and activities of individuals. Though often put in different terms, the same issue appeared strongly on the political agendas of other countries, too (see Chapter 4).

At this stage of my argument, I merely want to point to two consequences of these historical experiences. First, this early republican problematic showed that the modern polity, all individualism and egalitarianism notwithstanding, showed internal social structures that somehow would have to be taken into account in its social practices. In this sense, the social question can be seen as giving rise to sociology, as the liberal awareness of the persistence of problems of social order. In France, the linkage of the transformation of classical liberalism to the formation of a social group with specific demands becomes crucially evident. In the liberal atmosphere after the July 1830 Revolution the workers turned optimistically to the new regime with their demands, but were rejected. They

> responded by developing a new political and organizational language that met the regime on its chosen terrain: the discourse of liberty. In doing so, the workers embraced, but also modified and elaborated, the liberal language of the French Revolution. Class consciousness, in other words, was a transformed version of liberal revolutionary discourse.[40]

Second, the social question incited the construction of a new, partial collective identity inside modernity. In the late eighteenth century, nobody spoke of workers in the present sense, much less of a *working class*. Working people started to speak of themselves as workers and to generalize their sense of solidarity – gradually and unevenly between trades and countries – between 1780 and 1840 in England, France, the US and Germany.[41] When Marx, not many years later, wrote about the working class, he was featuring what a few years ago had still been a 'taxonomic neologism'.[42] Though partly superseded by the events, his distinction between 'class in itself' and 'class for itself' pointed to the need for constructing a social phenomenon by the mobilization in common activities, discursive and practical. This distinction also shows, in its special way, the very common, if not universal, link between the descriptive and the prescriptive aspect of classifications, 'between addition (rendering equivalent) and coalition (action)'.[43]

The national and the social question were both linked to notions of *collective identity* and of *collective agency*, namely nation-state and class. The handling of these questions by creating organized collective agents should be seen as historical ways and means of containing the unlimited challenges of modernity, of the liberal utopia.[44] Just like nation and nationalism, working class and class struggle have been invented to make collective action possible or to make members of presumed collectives, 'conceptual communities' (Benedict Anderson), really relate to each other, to act together, or to be acted upon.

These identities have, of course, not been invented out of a complete void. In the former case, social elements, like proximity of language and of habits, that existed before the breakthrough of modernity have been used to forge the identity of a territorially defined collective.[45] In the latter case, the consequences of capitalist modernity were assumed to homogenize living conditions and 'class positions', and the socialist writers deemed it necessary to stress this emerging homogeneity discursively to foster the recognition of common interests and enhance solidarity. But in both cases, boundaries were often unclear, people were unwilling to adhere to cultural-linguistically defined states because they felt different, or rejected solidarity because they did not want to see themselves as part of such a working class. And in both cases as well, organizational apparatuses that represented the classificatory convention, the nation-state and working-class organizations, often went far in enforcing the boundaries and repressing dissent.[46]

Regarding the concepts of class and class solidarity, my conceptual considerations have, at this point of the argument, gone too far in historical terms. The class struggle that was fully evolving in the second half of the nineteenth century was rather an attempt to offset the limitations of a regime whose containments the bourgeois elites had considered rather stable by mid-century, at least before the revolts of 1848, and some time later again, after everything had calmed down. This regime was one that we can term *restricted liberal modernity*. It was based on the modern imaginary significations of autonomy and rational mastery, but it also tried to contain their impact by tying actors into restrictive rules.

Restrictions were imposed by means of the state form and the law. States were indeed developed as containers for the building of the modern institutions; their boundaries defined the limits of the reach of the institutions, in territorial terms and otherwise. In economic terms, the 'unbound' Smithian notion of market efficiency was soon countered by the Listian idea of setting protective boundaries to make a national economy prosper.[47] Cultural-linguistic terms, of course, provided the very foundation for the nation-state. Far from remaining in the discursive realm, however, these ideas were also put in institutional forms by the setting up of nationally organized academic institutions, fostering national intellectual traditions, and of national networks of communication and public spheres. In terms of authoritative power, an important limit to autonomy was the restriction of suffrage, which dammed the liberal ideas of modernity against their alleged abuse by the masses.

LIBERAL MODERNITY AND AMERICAN EXCEPTIONALISM (I)

In terms of world history, the fact that, in 1776, a number of far-away and scarcely populated colonies of farmers and tradespeople declared their independence from their mother country, England, itself still rising in power, should have been of little import. As it turned out, it could hardly have mattered more. Almost *immediately*, the American events had an encouraging effect on all those who were striving for democratic reforms in Europe. To the French revolutionaries, in particular, who had been debating the feasibility and specific institutional design of a republic for decades, the constitutions of the American states and the US constitution were examples of the possibility of putting such ideas into practice.

> With the philosophy of the Enlightenment [French reformers] could lift the American Revolution out of its provincial context, and the American Revolution in turn invested their discursive thought with a reality it had not known before. . . . In the eyes of many Frenchmen, here was the first example of popular self-government and free institutions.[48]

Some decades later, when the US had consolidated and developed its own social and economic momentum, it became clear that the North American society was to establish a general, permanent alternative to the European, contained model of modernity. This alternative did not just exist beside European societies, but exerted a continuous influence on them and tended to break up their self-set boundaries. Two aspects may be distinguished. On the one hand, the US could increasingly be seen as an individual alternative, that is, as the locus of emigration. On the other hand, the American mode of organizing allocative practices could gradually alter the European ways by changing the competitive conditions. 'The emergence of the United States as an independent state with an unlimited (in a theoretical sense) supply of land that could be rendered valuable only with a large input of labor altered the basic parameters of the ongoing system' of interrelated societies and nation-states.[49] Both aspects become relevant, of course, only if the US indeed turns out to be more powerful in productive and allocative terms and more attractive in individual terms. In what way then was the US different?

Often, liberal individualism has been mentioned as the foundation of society and politics in the US.[50] While any comparative observation of the US and European societies appears to confirm this view, it fails to provide a sufficient historical explanation. There is no reason for assuming that the early settlers, up to Independence, were more liberal or more individualistic than the people they left behind in Europe. In so far as religious oppression was the background to emigration, one could even expect them to be more 'communitarian' than the average European.[51] In fact, more recent historiography has emphasized that a kind of liberal republicanism, focusing on civic virtue and community, should be seen as the original, early American political tradition. It was only during the first half of the nineteenth century that this republicanism gave way to a much more individualist liberalism.[52]

If these findings are valid, then we may conclude that it was less the political orientations of the founders and the successive generations of Americans than the particular historical conditions under which they tried to build their society that shaped the new order. Superficially it may appear that the American Revolution was very much of the same kind as the French one and other European attempts; indeed, it was basically led for the same principles. However, in contrast to the European struggle against strong adversaries, both in terms of the actual institutions of authoritative power and in terms of the coherence and acceptance of a discourse of societal representation, there were only 'weak competing principles' to the revolutionary ones in North America.[53] Slightly exaggerating the point, one might say that, willing or not, liberal democracy and rights-based individualism remained the only solution the Americans could resort to, after they had done away with the colonial regime. While rules and practices remained habitually in place in France after the Revolution unless they were consciously and radically changed, the Americans really had to build a new order and had to find and *construct* consensual solutions for any social practice. Without any substantive rules to draw on, pluralism and individual rights are all that remain.

In this sense, it was the absence of any self-evident larger political community that furthered the dominance of individualism – or, more precisely, group-mindedness – in the US. In other terms, one may consider the building of the United States as the *construction of modernity without an Old Regime*. The confrontation with the more open, boundless American experience highlights the particularly contained character of historical modernity in Europe. Again with a slight exaggeration, we may say that the key aspects of nineteenth-century European modernity were almost absent in North America. The US knew hardly any state and no restrictions to political participation, no homogeneous cultural-linguistic identity (though a stronger kind of religious one), and no expressible social question.

Americans were (and still are) very reluctant to delegate political powers to centralized, 'far-away' institutions. While factually federal government has become much more powerful, especially after the 1930s, the basic idea is that 'the people' in state and community may reappropriate these powers. Self-determination may apply to any self-formed collective, and may also include, importantly, the right to secede, that is the right to redraw the boundaries of political communities. 'In Hegel's sense, there was no "State" in the United States, no unified, rational will expressed in a political order, but only individual self-interest and a passion for liberty.'[54]

A weak sense of the larger community has an important impact on the understanding of social belonging. Though there was the famous white, Anglo-Saxon, Protestant dominance in the early US, the society was far too plurally composed for any sense of ethnic or religious identity common to all Americans to emerge. With the rise of even more multi-ethnic immigration towards the end of the nineteenth century, any such idea had to be abandoned, and the notion of 'cultural pluralism' came about.[55] As harmonious as this linguistic predecessor of current 'multiculturalism' may sound, there are also adverse impacts of weak substantive identities. Thus, it is often argued, basically rightly I think, that the weakness of the welfare state in the US stems from the impossibility of defining obligations with regard to national citizenship. At least in social terms, there is no strong sense of inclusive boundaries, which would enable one to see the poor as 'our poor', to whom one has moral obligations.

And also more generally, the emphasis on plurality itself does not solve any problem. To find in the belief in a unitarian state, as it was dominant in Europe,

> a sign of pure illusion, as liberal thought encourages us to do, is to deny the very notion of society, to erase both the question of sovereignty and that of the

> meaning of the institution, which are always bound up with the ultimate question of the legitimacy of that which exists. . . . If we adopt this view, we replace the fiction of unity-in-itself with that of diversity-in-itself.[56]

The fallacies of the self-sustaining character of individualism and of the possibility of diversity-in-itself are two of the specific features of American modernity. Both stem from the relatively unbounded origins of American society. What makes them particularly important for my considerations is that they appear to be paradigmatic for the development of modernity in general, a development which then has also been called 'Americanization'. To understand the interdependencies between less and more contained social formations of modernity, it is necessary to analyse the historical development of both. With this in view, I shall repeatedly return to the American society from my European observation-point.

Chapter 4

Crisis and transformation of modernity

The end of the liberal utopia

LIBERTY AND SELF-FULFILMENT: THE IDEAL OF THE SELF AND PRACTICES OF IDENTITY-FORMATION

Broadly speaking we can consider the period from the late eighteenth to the mid-nineteenth century as the time of the building of early, restricted liberal, modernity in the Northwestern quarter of the world. It brought with it the emergence of what we may call modern culture as 'a new moral culture [that] radiates outward and downward from the upper middle classes of England, America, and (for some facets) France'. This modern culture is predicated, not least, on a certain conception of the human self.

> It is a culture which is individualist in . . . three senses . . . : it prizes autonomy; it gives an important place to self-exploration; and its visions of the good life involve personal commitment. As a consequence, in its political language, it formulates the immunities due people in terms of subjective rights. Because of its egalitarian bent, it conceives these rights as universal.[1]

It both enables and obliges individual human beings to create their selves and to self-define their location among other human beings.

By about 1850, such conceptions indeed formed a culture in the sense that they were deeply shared by a substantial number of human beings in this part of the world. They can be found in post-Reformation religious orientations, in the commercial ethos of capitalist entrepreneurs, and they were expressed by the authors of the 'modern novel', focusing on individual development, and the Enlightenment political philosophers. Though the idea of a gradual but inevitable trickling down of high-cultural orientations from the upper to the lower classes (which Taylor's image of out- and downward radiation also conveys) is highly problematic, one can probably say that modern culture spread somewhat through society during the nineteenth century. One very simple reason for this diffusion may well be the fact that the practices of the 'modernist' upper middle classes transformed society and uprooted other cultural orientations to the degree that they became unfeasible.

If this is the case, though, then the social configuration of the nineteenth century is marked by a strong paradox. On the one hand, the rising elites promoted modern, individualist and rationalist, culture and tended to eradicate any alternative to it. On the other hand, there was a feeling – and, often enough, also an awareness – of the impossibility of a self-sustained individualist liberalism. Early modernity resided on the strength of pre-existing boundaries to its application and on the lack of a full social permeation of its concepts, while at the same time the modernizers, intentionally or not, worked at the elimination of those boundaries and at a fuller social permeation. The brief hint at a spatial comparison between North America and Western Europe in the preceding chapter gave a first idea of how distinct varieties of modernity could look if they differed along such lines. A temporal comparison, elements of which I will propose in the remainder of this book, will show the effects of changing boundaries and degrees of social permeation.

One of the guiding assumptions in these considerations is that the very ideal of the modern self may be at stake in these social transformations. At no point during the past two centuries is the idea of the reason-guided, individually self-exploring and self-realizing human being totally discarded. Generally speaking, rather the opposite is true; its diffusion is more and more widely extended. This was no steady process, however. Time and again, alternative conceptualizations of the human being were proposed and, more importantly, socially *practiced.* This occurred not least in reaction to what was perceived as the social impact of modernity. In such a perspective, I shall try to trace conceptions of the self and their transformations through the history of modernity. The starting-point has to be the understanding of the self that was part of the philosophies that stood at the outset of modernity.[2]

Speaking about the self, the term *identity* will be used to refer to the understanding somebody has of her or his life, to the orientations one gives to one's life. In current usage, it conveys the idea of certainty and inner stability, of residing firmly in oneself. A sense of identity may possibly be evolving over one's life-time as part of the process of self-realization, as the bourgeois ideal will have it. Stability or only steady change are not necessary implications of the concept, though, and notions such as fleeting identities or multiple identities will also be used to name specific temporal or situational contexts.[3] If I speak specifically of *self-identity*, I focus on the image an individual person has of herself, in relation to her ideas of self-realization. The term *social identity* will instead refer to the effective rooting of individual identities in collective contexts. Both are of course related, in two senses. First, every process of identity-formation is necessarily a social process. And second, to see oneself as part of a larger group may be the crucial element of one's self-identity.[4]

The sociohistorical assumption that I work with is that larger social transformations tend to uproot generally held social identities, and consequently also self-identities. If that is the case, I shall speak of major processes of *disembedding*, that is, processes through which people are ejected from identity-providing social contexts.[5] In contrast, I shall speak of *reembedding* when new contexts are created such that new social identities may be built. Human beings may be exposed to disembedding processes, such as in forced migration after wars, or they may expose themselves voluntarily to them, that is, 'leaving home' in the literal or the figurative sense. Reembedding, however, can only take place through the active, creative involvement of the concerned human beings, through their development or appropriation of identity options, drawing on the cognitive-cultural material that they find 'offered' in their social contexts.[6]

Moving now back to the historical account, we can probably assume that a basically modern conception of the self, as briefly portrayed above, prevailed among the bourgeois economic and intellectual elites during restricted liberal modernity. The social identity of the members of these groups was shaped by their belief that they belonged to the progressive forces of society, those who would advance humankind from its often-enough miserable fate. We know very little about conceptions of self and the social identity of peasants and workers. For a long time, historians and sociologists have ascribed a very limited – localist and family- and community-oriented – world- and self-view to these groups.[7] More recently, such interpretations have been challenged, not least because it was recognized that they provided a far too convenient mirror image to the progressive views of the modernizers to be true.

Despite this uncertainty, though, we may assume that those conceptions of self and social identity were shaken and stirred up when the effects of the modernization offensives of the bourgeois groups hit the workers and peasants. As a reaction to these effects, and as an attempt to find their own social position under the changing conditions, those who until then had been excluded from modernity defined themselves in their own right and claimed a place in the newly emerging social order. The formation of the workers' movement can be seen as a struggle for social identity in which a collective is formed and social places are created for each individual member of this collective. Again then, as a reaction to these struggles, the bourgeois social identity was shaken, both among the economic and, even more strongly, among the intellectual members of this group. From the combined effect of these collective reorientations emerged what I shall call the first crisis of modernity.

This problematic, though in other terms, had become generally accepted by the late nineteenth century, when the working of a capitalist market economy had drastically changed many aspects of social life and was seen, if uncontrolled, as a major threat to bourgeois values and life-styles themselves. Historically, the main social movement of the time, reaching from conservative academics to working-class radicals, tried to solve the social question by introducing new boundaries that would limit and constrain some kinds of practices while at the same time enabling other ones. This was a process of reconstitution of society in which more of its members were involved than probably ever before and which entailed a major effort at establishing collective agency. In its course, many of the established practices were upset and new institutions built. The process had a first culmination between the turn of the nineteenth century and the end of the First World War. During those years, the – even temporary – outcome was still very open, and the view that no new consolidated order might be establishable was widespread, at least among the elites (and for various reasons).

DISEMBEDDING AND TRANSFORMISM: A POSTLIBERAL COMPROMISE

In the preceding chapter I have tried to show how the emancipatory movements of the bourgeois revolutions, which established the new imaginary signification, recognized that it exceeded their own political ambitions by far. As a consequence, they tried to contain – quite successfully for a while – their own project by drawing on older social resources. However, the dynamics of the newly formed social configuration remained in effect. 'All that is solid melts into air', was Marx's famous description of the effect of bourgeois hegemony on society in the *Communist Manifesto*. Very soon, new tensions emerged in the contained liberal society. Before taking a closer look at the major struggles over the elimination of old containments and the setting of new ones that occurred between the 1880s and the 1960s (through many discontinuities and ruptures) the dynamics that set off the social formation of restricted liberal modernity must be presented.

Liberal theory claimed to have resolved the questions of political expression, economic interest and scientific validity by leaving them to open contest and competition. This was how, in principle, democracy, efficiency and truth were to be achieved. In *practice*, however, from early on most of the nineteenth-century liberals did not trust the conceptions they had themselves proposed. New restrictions were introduced by drawing on established, pre-liberal criteria such as gender, culture, social standing. Much of the force of liberal *theory* had resided in the fact that it did not need to resort to such criteria. One fundamental problem of legitimacy thus arose when liberals did not stand by their own claim.[8] The second problem was that, whether restricted or not, the practices of bourgeois society did not at all appear to fulfil the substantive claim of achieving efficiency, democracy and truth.

The strong claims of liberal theorizing had been its universalism and its assumption of the automatic harmonization of society. Once liberals themselves had abdicated both claims, all questions of political, social and cognitive representation were forcefully brought back to the agenda of social theory and political practice. This was the main feature of the social struggles of the late nineteenth century, a period that, for this reason, I would call the beginning of a postliberal era.[9]

Major conceptual challenges to the restricted liberal version of political order arose with social changes during the second half of the nineteenth century. Bourgeois capitalization had indeed initiated a dynamics that entailed a number of technological innovations, the growth of industry and the growth of cities as new economic-industrial centres. On the part of the working population, these changes in dominant allocative practices provoked strong migration flows from rural into urban areas as well as emigration, often to the Americas. In many respects, this was a major process of disembedding of individuals from the social contexts in which they had grown up.[10] It created widespread uncertainty among those who were disembedded about their individual fate and about their place in society, and among the elites about the order and stability of society as a whole.[11]

As a consequence, a rather radical reconceptualization of society was at stake. In the liberal view, 'the social question' should not have emerged in the first place. Automatic adaptation of individual wills and preferences would have precluded persistent imbalances of this sort. Such a belief, however, had lost most of its plausibility when poverty and hardship spread, when the increase in the wealth of the nation appeared to be too long delayed for too many, when uncertainty prevailed after many people had moved out of the social contexts they were socialized into, and when they had already begun to resort to collective action. Against all classical liberal conceptions, this reaction was an attempt at collectively reappropriating an agential capacity that had been threatened by the dynamics of liberal capitalism.[12]

The major objective of reform movements during the latter half of the nineteenth century was to re-establish some solidity and certainty into the social fabric. Many reformers came from the bourgeois elites, and their idea was, not least, to safeguard order. But the probably more important element was the self-constitution of the working class as a collective capable of defining and representing its own interests. Socialism, trade unions and labour parties spring from this attempt at developing organized responses to social change on the part of a new collective, the working class.[13] Besides their political and economic objectives, the movement also created a new social identity as an industrial worker, fighting for a full place in society or even combining the forces of the future of humankind.[14]

As much of the societal problematic came together in the so-called 'social question', it shall be described here in a bit more detail and with a view to the variations in the ways of reconceptualizing society. All industrializing societies saw themselves as in some fundamental way faced with this question in the latter part of the nineteenth century. They devoted quite some intellectual effort to exploring ways of solving that question, efforts which in many cases came to translate into the constitution of new types of policies such as accident, old age or sickness insurance. 'New forms of social knowledge . . . emerged in tandem with social reform legislation in the earliest phase of European state social policy during the 1880s and 1890s.'[15] However, this apparent parallelism in problem attention cross-nationally should not conceal the fact that both the solutions sought and, indeed, the precise nature of the problems perceived, were premised on significantly different discourses and institutional constellations.

The building of an early welfare state *avant la lettre* was a process whose character as a major societal reorientation by no means escaped the minds of the actors involved. Thus the protagonists of the struggle for poverty relief and for workers' accident insurance were perfectly well aware of the fact that the creation of new collective institutions might involve a major step in a fundamental reorganization of society. A basic form of argument by the proponents of innovation was that society itself had changed and needed institutional adaptation. Industrialization had altered the nature of work and of wealth, what was required were new concepts of risk and of poverty. In Anson Rabinbach's words, 'the idea of social risk was a phenomenon of modernity, a recognition that impersonal forces rather than individual wills were often the determinants of destiny.' Such a discourse, to be found in the words of many contemporary actors, spelled the end of the liberal idea of society.[16]

In the German debates in the *Verein für Socialpolitik* (Association for Social Policy) – founded in 1872–3, shortly after the establishment of the imperial state – the dominant group around Gustav Schmoller adhered basically to a conception of the state as a being with a superior mission standing above class struggles and other particularistic conflicts in society. Its task, to be pursued through a strong bureaucracy in a monarchic system, was to secure a harmonious development of society, to intervene everywhere where conflicts could mount to endanger the well-being of the nation. The founders of the Association saw themselves as being called to contribute to the accomplishment of this new state's task. They stressed the healthy continuity of Prussian stateness which, in their view, was the most important asset Germany could draw on when facing the turmoils of industrialization and organized class dispute.[17] They themselves stood, apart from some minority positions, in the tradition of state-centred thinking, from Hegel onwards, which saw the state as the embodiment of some higher reason.

While there was something of a brief era of liberalism in German states in the mid-nineteenth century, liberal ideas never achieved full societal hegemony in Germany, and liberal institutions flourished only momentarily and only in parts of the territory of the later nation-state. In terms of academic discourse, classical political economy – 'Smithianism' or 'Manchesterism' as it was called somewhat disdainfully by many scholars – never asserted itself strongly, and in the tradition of the state sciences it rather remained an interlude. The work of Robert von Mohl, one of the southwestern liberals, has rightly been characterized as transitory:

> Mohl's policy science as a work of transition looks Janus-faced to two eras. On the one side, there is the old police state, . . . much governing, regulating from above, busy and concerned for everything, but without clear objectives and without understanding the bourgeoisie's striving for autonomy; on the other side, the social movements of the second half of the 19th century announce their appearance from afar, movements which will pose giant tasks to public administration.[18]

French society, by contrast, was shaped by a relatively successful bourgeoisie striving for autonomy, and her state tradition, while extremely strong, was of a different nature to the German one. The continuity of this tradition was important for the struggles on social policy. It gave the proponents the opportunity not to argue for a complete break with earlier principles, but for a rephrasing of a century-old concern in French politics.

> Governments of the Third Republic thought they had the means fully to apply in a methodical way the principles stated in 1789, and they eventually laid down the bases for the modern institutional set of social services in contemporary society.[19]

Among these principles, of course, were both freedom, on the one side, and solidarity, on the other. While under these circumstances it could never be successfully argued that some superior institution could violate freedom of contracts and the equality principle in labour contracts, and shift burdens of responsibility for accidents one-sidedly to the employers, as German insurance laws did, it proved possible to propose substantive state intervention in another way, namely through the solidarity principle.

Many of the republican debates in the 1880s and 1890s were based on solidarism, a political theory which became something like the official social philosophy of the Third Republic. Solidarism introduced into political theory the idea of society as an entity with rights and obligations which co-existed with, and were related to, individual rights. Human beings did not enter into relations with others as isolated individuals, but as already social beings; thus, social rights could be formulated alongside individual rights. The theory of solidarity and the political slogans of solidarism had close links to Durkheimian sociology and its grounding of a theory of society in 'social facts'.

The debates in the United States, in contrast to both France and Germany, show a stronger emphasis on individualist reasoning and related difficulties in justifying social policy institutions. While in France the theory of solidarity was 'a way of synthesizing two different lines of thought: that competition could be the only law of social life, as liberalism claimed, and at the same time that solidarity enhanced contractual relations rather than state authority,' the US debates on social policy 'had remained caught up in an opposition between public and private'.[20] While there were some institutional innovations such as State Boards on Charities, or the US Children's Bureau, national social policy on a scale comparable to European turn-of-the-century measures was undertaken as late as 1935.[21]

A comparison of poverty relief in the US and France shows that a social definition of poverty, instead of an individual one, could be highly contested and ultimately largely rejected in one case and, if not welcomed by general consensus, at least comparatively smoothly accepted in another setting.[22] These outcomes are related to long-standing institutional structures, such as heritages of absolutism and the French Revolution, and intellectual traditions, such as the Comtean one. Both of those saw nation and society essentially as a unit which carried specific characteristics and responsibilities beyond the individual ones. This feature receives even more emphasis in a comparison of two statist, continental European societies, France and Germany. True, there were disputes about the distributional effects of workers' accident insurance, disputes which were underpinned by various conceptions of freedom and responsibility as well as – increasingly – by 'social facts' provided by statistics and social research. But the concepts of a people and a nation as a being superior to individuals – a more typically German argument – or as an aspect of human existence inseparable from individuality – more characteristic of French debates – and of the state as the expression of this social being, were deeply entrenched in public and academic debate alike. Such concepts could relatively easily be drawn upon in policy debates and give rise to expressions such as 'capital of the nation' to describe the labourer's working power. That working power thus became something to be protected by collective action rather than by individual capability and responsibility alone.[23]

In different ways then, the liberal concept of the individual and his autonomy had been eroded in the public debates and policy deliberations until the turn of the century. One conceptual element from which such erosion could start resided with the bourgeois revolution from the beginning, namely the concept of brotherhood in the French Revolution, later to be transformed into solidarity. The revolutionary upheavals of the first half of the nineteenth century, 1830 and 1848, mark further passage points on the way to the undermining of pure liberal-individualist political theory. Only after 1870, however, was the transformation of the restricted liberal societies in full swing. Industrialization and urbanization were more marked, and with the establishment of nation-states in Italy and Germany the national strivings appeared to have ended. The latter point is important, because it entails that boundaries were established, inside which political debate could unfold. Or, in other words, a consolidated political addressee, the state, to which the social question could be posed, was generally available.

By the end of the nineteenth century, economic organization and sociopolitical struggles within the nation-states had developed up to a point where the founding concepts of liberal theory clearly seemed inapplicable.[24] The free and only loosely organized formation of public opinion in political clubs and circles had given way to a range of organized opinion-makers.[25] In the most dynamic sectors of the economy, national monopolies or oligopolies had formed and often the owner had given way to the manager in the direction of firms.[26] In the closing years of the century, workers were on the barricades in many places, making the claim that they marched with history widely believed. The First World War, whatever other causes and meanings it had had, not least showed through its societal mobilization that the organized masses had fully entered history. This did not fail to leave its mark on those who tried to rebuild society after the war's end.

> The 1914–18 War was in Europe as decisive a turning-point as the revolution of 1789. It perhaps marked the clear beginning of the end of pure capitalism. . . . It marked the beginning of the refutation of all the progressive social theories of the nineteenth century.[27]

CRITIQUES: THE MODERN TENDENCY TOWARDS SELF-CANCELLATION

A series of major inquiries into the dynamics of modernity was elaborated successively from after the middle of the nineteenth century up until the 1920s. These analyses may be called the grand critiques of modernity. Their *grandeur*, in my view, resides in the fact that they identified basic problems in the practices of modernity, but that they remained reluctant or unwilling to abandon the imaginary significations of modernity as a consequence. They did not solve the problems, but they achieved a clarity of problem recognition that most other social theories, at the same time or after, could not meet.[28]

Intellectuals in the late nineteenth and early twentieth centuries were generally well aware of the failure of liberal theory, in politics as well as in economics, to either understand the changes in societal practices or to provide criteria for their regulation. All referring to the prevalent liberal mode of societal self-understanding, they developed critical analyses of societal practices, mostly with a view to safeguarding as much as they could of this liberal mode. Four principal types of such critiques can be distinguished. They all problematize, although in very different ways, the tension between the unleashing of the modern dynamics of autonomy and rational mastery, on the one hand, and its, often unintended, collective outcome in the form of major societal institutions. In this context, they all observe deviations from liberal theory in societal practice, and may also question liberal assumptions in their own thinking.[29]

The first was the critique of political *economy* as developed mainly by Karl Marx. In contrast to some of the conservative critics of capitalism, such as the German historical economists who flatly denounced its rationalist individualism, Marx basically adhered to the Enlightenment tradition of individual autonomy. His ideal was 'the free association of free human beings'. In the workings of the 'free' market in capitalism, however, he discovered a societal effect of human economic interaction that asserted itself 'behind the backs' of the actors.

In an economy based on market exchange and the forced sale of labour-power, relations between human beings would turn into relations between things, because they were mediated by commodities. Driven by laws of abstract value, markets would transform phenomena with a use value into commodities, the sole important criterion of which was the money value against which they could be exchanged. The result of such fetishization of products and money and of the reification of social relations would be the alienation of human beings from their own products, from other human beings and from themselves. In such an alienated condition, the possibility for autonomy and sovereignty of the economic actors on either markets of labour, production or consumption would be completely eradicated, though these actors would indeed constantly reproduce these conditions by their own action.

By the end of the nineteenth century, the discourse on political economy had split into two rather neatly distinct parts. The liberal theory of the economy revived inside the academy, when the marginalist revolution seemed to offer a way out of some its theoretical dilemmas. The upshot of this revolution, neoclassical economics, returned to optimism with regard to the collective outcome of individual strivings, if only the individuals could act freely. Marxist discourse, in contrast, consolidated as the political theory of some working-class organizations, most notably German social democracy. In this context of mass organization, not only its economic critique, but also its rudimentary political theory of revolution was taken for granted rather than being further elaborated.

At this point, the critique of modernity tended to shift from the economy to the polity. The second grand critique was the critique of large-scale *organization and bureaucracy*, as analysed most prominently by Robert Michels and Max Weber and, in the context of elite theories of politics and society, by Gaetano Mosca and Vilfredo Pareto. With a view to the enhancement of rational mastery of the world, it postulated the tendency for the formation of stratified bodies with hierarchical chains of command and generalized, abstract rules of action. In the context of a universal-suffrage polity and universalist welfare state (that is, in 'large' societies in which all individuals had to be included on a formal, that is, legally equal, basis in all major regulations), such 'iron cages' had emerged as state apparatuses, big industrial enterprises and mass parties, and would spread further in all realms of social life. While such institutions in fact enhanced the reach of human action generally, they limited it to the application of the rules, inside the cage so to speak, at the same time.

While some 'realist' analyses saw this development as simply inevitable, others, notably Weber's, problematized the construction of iron cages in a more general perspective, as subjecting human beings to the dominance of instrumental rationalities. At this point, we arrive again at the, in my view, most important element of the grand critiques, namely the observation of an undermining of modern principles in and by their application. Weber was particularly torn between the insight in the 'progress' of rationalization, because it enabled the achievement of the hitherto unachievable, and the social loss of criteria, to the use of which the enablement of rationalization could be put. In Karl Löwith's terms, Weber

> attempted to make intelligible this general process of the rationalisation of our whole existence precisely because the rationality which emerges from this process is something specifically irrational and incomprehensible. . . . The elementary and decisive fact is this: every instance of radical rationalisation is inevitably fated to engender irrationality.[30]

Many of the difficulties in reading Weber as a sociologist stem from his desire to search for ways out of such deep contradictions in individual and social life. All that remains, for him, is the personal commitment of the individual and its potential social impact in the form of charismatic leadership.

In these terms, a variant of a critique of conceptions of rationality is that of modern *philosophy and science*, the third grand critique. Weber, too, was aware of the great loss the 'disenchantment of the world' in rational domination entailed. Still, he understood his own social science in rational and value-neutral terms, as he thought no other approach could prevail under conditions of modernity. In contrast, radical and explicit critiques of science were put forward by others in very different forms. The elaboration of a non-scientistic approach to science was attempted in idealist *Lebensphilosophie* as well as, differently, in early twentieth-century 'Western' Marxism, that is, by Max Horkheimer and the early Frankfurt School.[31] In some respects, pragmatism in the US can also be ranged under the critiques of science in as much as a relinkage of philosophy, anthropology and social science was proposed against the unfounded separation of spheres of knowledge in the disciplinary sciences, a relinkage that would also bring the sciences back to a concern for the fundamental issues of the contemporary social world.[32] Notwithstanding all their differences, especially in terms of alternative proposals, these analyses can be summarized as a rejection of positivist, empiricist and determinist science as incapable of reflecting the essentials of human action.

It was in pragmatism in particular – and in Europe in Durkheim's sociology – that a link between moral philosophy, social science and politics was maintained, or rather recreated with a view to responding to the contemporary problems of societal restructuring. Accepting and supporting the basic modern tenets of individual liberty and democracy, these authors recognized that it could only be from the collective endeavours of the human beings themselves that a moral order and 'social control' could be created on such premises.

Thus, we arrive at the fourth critique, that of *morality*.[33] Whereas elements of it can be found very often elsewhere, this theme is most developed in Emile Durkheim's writings. With the emergence of industrial society, Durkheim diagnosed a major transition from mechanic to organic forms of solidarity, in line with a functional division of labour in society. Though traditional religions would hardly be upheld, sociological knowledge about how parts of society related to each other could ground a viable moral education. Functional division of labour, organic solidarity and an adequate social knowledge, thus, were Durkheim's solutions to a problem that was widely diagnosed, in different variants of an alleged transition from community to society.

The problem may be schematically reconstructed as follows. The development of modern society entailed the risk of moral impoverishment, mainly due to two phenomena. The inevitable decline of unquestioned faith eroded a source which could provide foundations for moral behaviour. And if it is true that recurring face-to-face interaction is the basis for the solidarity-supporting insight to the human likeness of the other, such kinds of interaction would be decreasingly relevant in mass societies integrated on the scale of a nation. The two questions that arise are: first, how to ground ethics at all, when no foundational criteria are universally accepted; and second, how to develop adequate standards for morality, when social relations are predominantly 'thin' and at the same time widely extended in space and time, that is to relatively distant others. In such a view, the requirements for ethics have been raised, while the likelihood of agreeing on any ethics at all may have diminished. Again, it is the achievement of reflexively questioning any imposed standards of morality that may subvert the possibility of any standard at all. 'The protestant in search of salvation produces an iron cage incompatible with moral discourse and personal religious status.'[34]

Synthetically, then, an argumentative figure emerges as follows. In the historical development of 'liberal' society, the self-produced emergence of over-arching structures, such as capitalism and the market, organization and bureaucracy, modern philosophy and science, and the division of labour, is identified. These structures work on the individual subjects and their possibilities for self-realization – up to the threat of *self-cancellation* of modernity. The more generalized modern practices become, the more they themselves may undermine the realizability of modernity as a historical project.[35]

In actual fact, the undermining of modernity by its own principles did not mean that modernity became unfeasible. Rather, it acquired a quite different shape. In the words of Max Weber, it is

> as if, knowingly and deliberately, we actually *ought* to become men who require 'order' and nothing but order, who grow nervous and cowardly if this order falters for a moment, and who become helpless if they are uprooted from their exclusive adaptation to this order.[36]

This seemed to be exactly the case between the two great wars of the twentieth century.

TRANSFORMATIONS: STRONGER INSTITUTIONS IN THE NAME OF COLLECTIVE EMANCIPATION

The period between the First and the Second World War with planned (war-time) economy, fascism, national socialism and Soviet socialism seemed to witness the ultimate demise of the liberal notions of politics, economy and science. In the view of many participants and observers of the most diverse political leanings and beliefs, the experience of the (first) war-time economy and social management meant that the full establishment or re-establishment of the liberal institutions was neither possible nor desirable.

Many of the proposals that were made in a protracted struggle over societal reorganization during the inter-war period headed for a greater degree of social organization than any liberal political or economic theory prescribed. Now, the ingenuous idea that atomistic individuals might autonomously achieve a viable organization of society was widely seen as flawed and replaced by notions of more class-, culture- or ethnicity-based collective polities.

The reorganization proposals reached from class-based Soviet socialism, over the French People's Front, the Swedish people's home and the American New Deal to the Vichy regime, Italian fascism and German National Socialism. The Swedish social democratic welfare state and the German National Socialist warfare state, for instance, shared ideological roots. They both relied on notions of new homes and communities that their policies were to provide for the disembedded children of their nations. In the Swedish context, it was the *folkhem*, 'people's home', a concept proposed by Rudolf Kjellén, a conservative political theorist who died in 1923, and used by the social democrats on their way to building a broad political alliance. The concept travelled to Germany via Karl Haushofer, a professor of geopolitics and Nazi theorist, was adapted to German conceptual traditions as *Volksgemeinschaft*, 'people's community', and became a key term of Nazi propaganda.[37] The more ambitious of those approaches in terms of political philosophy may be understood as varieties of 'existential collectivism'. George Lukács, for instance, took great pains to identify the proletariat as a philosophically foundational and politically superior collective that could and would overcome the aporias of capitalist modernity. Martin Heidegger performed a similar manoeuvre in some of his writings with regard to the German people and its opposition to technology-driven mass society.[38]

The consistent position of the US at the individualist edge of the spectrum of societal constellations is also evident here. Michael Walzer has recently pointed out that, unlike in Europe, the term 'home' has never been used in political contexts in the US, that instead it consistently refers to private, personal settings, such as the family or the local background.[39] Still, the Americans, too, felt the need to get together, to define some collective project for themselves as Americans, when they experienced the turmoils of the 1920s and 1930s. The notion of the 'American dream' was coined in the context of the economic crisis to denote the existence and persistence of a specifically American way of life. While this focuses significantly on the freedom of individuals and their pursuit of happiness, Americans nevertheless needed to regain awareness that its vitality lies in having it *in common* and in having to strive together.[40]

It may sound outrageous to relate these political projects to each other in such a direct way.[41] The undeniable argument for such a relation, however, is that it was perceived to exist in the eyes of the contemporary actors. A number of policy intellectuals and economic experts in France, Italy and Germany moved between socialism, fascism and Keynesian economic steering. The 'Roosevelt revolution', as the New Deal was called by Georges Boris, a French socialist, was commonly seen as of a kind with the Italian corporate economy or Stalin's collectivizations. In Italian debates of the 1930s, for instance, fascism is sometimes seen 'as an anticipated response – and, that is, the most serious and advanced one – to the great capitalist crisis', in which the liberal distinctions between individual and universal, between public and private are overcome.[42]

In fact, all these proposals were responses to the perceived instabilities of the postliberal regimes. They were all based on the definition of a, mostly national, collective and on the mobilization of the members of such a collective under the leadership of the state. In their programmes and practices, they all restricted the notion of individual liberty in the name of some collectivity, though of course to highly varying degrees. Often, the political reorientation was seen, and portrayed in propaganda, as some new awakening, a new beginning.[43] As such, it appeared as a collective liberation rather than as the introduction of constraints to individual action.

These discourses are indicative of attempts at a closure of modernity – which was far from being achieved at that point, though maybe it was only the appropriate form of closure that was fought about. The analyses stem from the observation of an exhaustion of the dynamics of liberal modernity. Between the turn of the century and the 1930s, the feeling for the crisis of liberalism seemed to be all-pervasive. It could take the dramatic form of a general conviction that civilized mankind had come to its end, as in the writings of Oswald Spengler and others, and in the mood that has come to be called the *fin de siècle*. But the end of liberalism and of its overly abstract understandings of society could also be desired and seen as overdue, as in the national reawakenings and formations of organically conceived societies in Italy and Germany. Or it could be considered as the historically ripened superseding of an old social formation, as in Marxist-Leninist theorizing. A less fundamental shift occurred in other contexts, such as the American or British ones.

At first sight, our political minds refuse to place these reorientations, some of which were seen as diametrically opposed, under a similar analytical perspective. However, the direction of these reorientations away from a liberal theory of society and towards the formation of collective arrangements which exist prior to any given individual is a common one. And by taking a closer look at the actual modes of organization of social practices, rather than merely at cultural-intellectual statements whose social significance is difficult to assess, some important similarities become visible.[44]

In such terms, *liberal* practices would be based on the free communication and association of a multitude of individual agents, with a view to determining the degree and actual substance of collective arrangements in society. If this is an acceptable description, then it can be argued that such liberal practices were decreasingly important from the 1890s through to the 1960s. They gave way to *organized* practices that relied on the aggregation of groups of individuals according to some social criterion. Communication and decision-making about collective arrangements were made in and between the organizations by leaders who were speaking and acting on behalf of (that is, *representing*) their allegedly homogeneous memberships.

While such socially organizing processes were reaching increasingly higher levels throughout this period of approximately seven-decades, this was no steady course but was characterized by ruptures and discontinuities. Sweepingly applying this perspective across Western Europe, one can say that periods of accelerating organization were the 1890s with the building of national economic monopolies, the growth of socialist (as well as conservative) parties and the decline of electoral political liberalism; the First World War with its concerted war efforts in which employers, trade unions and the state participated under the banner of patriotism; the 1930s with the building of fascism, National Socialism, Stalinism, People's Front (and later Vichy), people's home and New Deal; the Second World War led by such kinds of regimes; and the 1960s with its allegedly de-ideologized post-industrial society. Intermittent breakdowns of organized arrangements and revivals of liberal expectations were witnessed mainly during the 1920s and, at least with regard to allocative practices, the 1950s.

In the following analysis, the unsteady history and comparative dissimilarities will rather be neglected in favour of a, maybe ideal-typical, portrait of a particular social formation that I shall label organized modernity.[45] In such a formation, the setting of boundaries and social production of certainties is generally privileged over and above the liberal assertion of the unlimited autonomy of everybody to create and recreate themselves and their social contexts.

Such a characterization of twentieth-century West European societies is prone to a number of misunderstandings. First, the strategies that were pursued – and to some extent they were conscious strategies indeed – far from intending to halt the dynamics of modernity generally, were meant to channel it into more predictable paths. If brakes were attached to certain social vehicles, then this did not mean that they were to slow down. The existence of brakes indeed allowed an even faster march, to use Schumpeter's apt statement of the time.[46]

Second, if reembedding and increase of certainties were objectives of the organization of practices, the comfort that could be enjoyed varied considerably. Organization means hierarchization and it means exclusion. Those who found themselves at the bottom or outside of the realm of organized practices suffered often more than before. The most terrifying practice of organized modernity was the exclusion of the European Jewry from the right to live under the expansionist and warfaring Nazi regime. With all its dissimilarity to any other occurrence in modern history, I concur with Zygmunt Bauman's portrayal of the Holocaust as an extreme exemplification of organized modernity rather than as a terrible deviation from an otherwise benevolent rule.[47]

The preceding chapters were meant to portray the social configuration of a restricted liberal modernity and its contradictions. Its own dynamics led to a situation in which a number of restrictions could not be upheld any longer. However, a mere loosening of the restrictions seemed to lead to unacceptable uncertainties and actual breakdowns of regimes, such as the Imperial German and Hapsburg ones in the War and its aftermath, and most Central European ones during the 1920s and 1930s with the onset of the various fascisms. It is the task of the following section to spell out the peculiar features of the social formation that can be seen as, through many reversals, succeeding restricted liberal modernity, and is here called organized modernity.

From the preceding argument it should be clear that it is not intended to reify the notion of organized modernity, to prove the existence of such a social formation over extended timespans and areas. Rather, the concept is meant to serve as a designation, in order to grasp certain historical tendencies towards a different organization of social practices. In the following chapters, an analytical description of these organized practices shall be given, first for the social practices of allocation (Chapter 5), then for those of domination (Chapter 6), and finally for those of signification and representation (Chapter 7).

Part III

The closure of modernity

Chapter 5

Networks of power and barriers to entry

The organization of allocative practices

ORGANIZED MODERNITY AS THE RESULT OF LARGE-SCALE CONVENTIONALIZATION

In the preceding chapters I have tried to portray early, nineteenth-century modernity as a societal constellation in which, *initially*, the modern imaginary signification prevails but is restricted to a limited number, and well-defined kind, of people. These boundaries are *then* broken and the limits upset, partly due to the increasing social permeation of the modern imaginary significations, partly in reaction to the disembedding consequences of this increasing permeation. The following chapters are devoted to a systematic analysis of the social configurations that emerged from the attempts to deal with the erosion of boundaries and to re-establish control over social practices.

No metaphysical understanding of a societal need for stability and control is implied here. There probably is a human inclination to prefer some certainty of being able to interpret social situations and predict the actions and reactions of others to a situation of high uncertainty and unpredictability. Lack of certainty or predictability may lead to anxieties and an incapability of acting. In this sense indeed, 'much of the social organization can be interpreted as sedimentation of the systematic effort to reduce the frequency with which hermeneutical problems are encountered and to mitigate the vexation such problems cause once faced.'[1] But there is no reason to assume that 'societies' necessarily 'need' a minimum degree of stability and certainty to subsist, or that human beings always achieve what they may desire in both terms. The sociological imagination has far too often been limited to conceiving very orderly sets of social practices.

However, the historical record of the period between the 1890s and the 1960s shows that, in macro-sociological terms, some degree of stability and certainty was achieved, having been recreated from a situation of uncertainty. Far from being a 'natural' outcome of societal dynamics, this process then should constitute a sociological problematic of high relevance. In the following, I shall try to portray organized modernity as the building of state- and nation-wide conventionalizations of major sets of social practices in a relatively coherent, interlocking form. Conventionalization of practices over widely extended imagined communities is not possible without the representation of such conventions. Classification is the major tool to build representations of social phenomena. But also no representation can be produced, nor can it long be upheld, without being somewhere linked to practices. This mutual dependence of practices and their representations raises a problem for social analysis that I shall briefly discuss before moving to the historical material.

Conventionalization is a process that produces only at its end, if successful, the social reality which was the basis of its imagery. Then, however, when the image is 'finished', it imposes itself on reality, structuring it far beyond what would be detected in detailed observation. Here lies one of the clues to the endless debates about the adequacy of social interpretations. The problem can be illustrated by using some examples that will be cited in the following analysis: Alfred Chandler, for one major aspect, and Michael Piore and Charles Sabel, for another, have produced an image of allocative practices between the end of the nineteenth century and the 1960s that emphasizes the hierarchical organization of the large-scale business enterprise and the industrial mode of mass production of standardized products. In both cases, the analyses were soon followed by a scholarly debate over the adequacy of these historiographies, often showing that many exceptions existed to the allegedly prevailing mode of organization or that even the share of that mode in the overall realm of practice was only minor. As valuable as these objections are for further clarification, they often miss the most important point.[2]

The Chandler and Piore/Sabel portraits were hardly original, generally speaking. They drew on images that were already there for the historical scholars, namely those provided by the contemporary observers of social life, from Marx to Weber to Taylor in this case, but also including the kind of evidence found in archives, journals, state and company documents. Still, it is valid to point out that at Marx's time there were no homogeneous living conditions of the working class and not that much of a 'class for itself' either. At Weber's time there was no predominance of a functioning formal bureaucracy outside Prussia, and very little Taylorization either. These observers and the many others who were actively engaged in such practices cast tendencies of their time into portraits which, due to their existence as imaginations and representations, shaped expectations and orientations, and as such acquired a force in social reality. Even if by 1920 only a tiny share of allocative practices was big-firm, industrial mass production, the view that that would be the mode of organization of the future would shape the orientations of the actors, businessmen and workers alike. Even if one could show that to speak of the homogeneity of the working class and the commonality of interests had never made sense in socioeconomic terms, the existence of this representation and its plausibility for contemporaries had a powerful impact on the structuring of industrial societies.[3] No historical analysis of entire social formations will escape this problem of assessing the relation between actual practices and their representations – neither, by the way, can the actual actors escape it when evaluating their own possibilities for action.

It is exactly this problem that we shall immediately encounter when returning to the historical account. The historical situation which stood at the outset of 'organized modernity' was characterized by specific features which made this project both a feasible and, in the views of many actors, a desirable undertaking. Among these conditions two stand out as particularly important. First, fairly consolidated institutions of material allocation, authoritative power and signification existed that all promised the potential to cohere on the level of the nation-state. Second, one major line of interpretation of these societies' evils had been offered and broadly accepted, even though with wide variations. Liberal society had turned unfeasible because a large group of people existed who did not form part of the bourgeois project but were now strong and important enough to voice their claims. Whether these people were called the working class or, increasingly, the masses was an issue of secondary order. Generally, it was agreed that the fundamental issue of the time was the integration of these people and that this task required new modes of social organization.[4]

The definition of the relevant unit to which social action should refer as the *nation-state*, and the conception of the national society as one structured according to lines of *social classes* provided the basis for the organization of modernity. By the time the restricted liberal concept of society could no longer be upheld, these two concepts were at hand to the actors who were rebuilding modernity. The idea of cultural-linguistic identity had been developed by bourgeois intellectuals from the late eighteenth century onwards and had solid roots in the educated strata. The idea of a working class had been developed alongside the workers' struggles and provided a social identity to large segments of the working population.

Still, even if these discursive resources were available, any solution to social problems was far from evident by the end of the nineteenth century, since these two main concepts, the way they were conceived, did not go along with each other smoothly. To most members of the national elites the existence of an organized, politically active working class was rather a problem than a solution to national policy issues. To many working-class activists, in contrast, who adhered to the idea of international solidarity, the nation-state was a bourgeois relict rather than a container for political action whose contents could be modified. In both respects, the co-operation of both sides during the First World War marked a decisive point of reorientation.

From the doubts and debates that I have labelled the first crisis of modernity, one basic insight was drawn: no natural, automatic way of regulating social affairs would emerge under the imaginary signification of modernity. The hopes and expectations of liberal and Enlightenment thinkers had to be discarded once and for all. Wealth of nations would not automatically arise from free economic initiative. Democracy would not naturally emerge from political freedom. Truth could not be assumed to be best enhanced by full academic autonomy. The restrictions imposed by classical liberalism could not be upheld. Merely relinquishing any restrictions, however, would lead into chaos and disorder. A socially constructed order had to be put in the place of a natural order.[5] To construct order socially meant introducing conventions about how to understand common social phenomena and about how to act in recurring situations.

Conventionalization is a means of reducing uncertainty by limiting the variation of events, actions and interpretations that may take place. It is a collective effort to establish manageability of the social world. One of its general aspects is the attempt to increase intelligibility first by setting up classifications of social phenomena. Another aspect is the reaching of societywide application of these classifications. Manageability cannot be increased as long as relevant groups deviate over definitions of crucial social phenomena.

In analogy to the distinction between modernization offensives from above or from below (as introduced earlier in Chapter 2), one may distinguish conventionalization efforts from above or from below. The most important example for the latter is the workers' movement, which tried to define the workers, their position in society and their interests, all with a view to making a collective that was able to act. Conventionalization is here the product of a problem-induced collective action. The increase of intelligibility proceeds through self-understanding and interpretation of the position of the collective.

If, in contrast, conventionalization is attempted from above with the support of the state apparatuses, quite different means may be used. Apart from compulsory education and the use of the monopoly of violence, the law provides an effective and convenient means of introducing criteria of classification in society. Clearly, there must be some identifiable and interpretable social reality as the basis of a new legal category; lawmakers will not and cannot create law from nothing. But once a legal classification is introduced, social practices will structure themselves with reference to such definition.

Conventionalization from above is also problem-induced action, but the emphasis is on mastery and control. The increase of intelligibility proceeds here through objectivist knowledge, through the imposition of classificatory criteria by a distant observer rather than through the collective action of those who are being classified. The distinction between these two kinds of conventionalization is no neat one in reality. Often the one blurs into the other. Nevertheless it seems worthwhile to introduce it, because one of the important features of the building of organized modernity is the transformation of conventionalization efforts from below into the administration and management of conventionalizations from above. Such a process is usually called institutionalization; the crucial difference it makes for the actual human beings is between being actively involved in the shaping of a collective social identity and being exposed to an existing offer of classifications and routinized forms of collective action. I shall try to point to such transformations with regard to several of the sets of organized social practices to be discussed in this section.

When conventionalizations have been successfully established for a while, their socially constructed character will disappear from the consciousness of the members of a society. The classifications will appear to be representing some natural order of reality. If this is the case, we may speak of the *reification*, or naturalization, of social phenomena. They take on a thinglike character and are seen as having an active, causal impact on human beings.[6] Social phenomena are not things, so reification will not literally occur. What is in view here is rather a situation in which the constructed character of the most fundamental institutions of society has almost completely vanished from the consciousness and in which, thus, the basic setup of society is seen as one that is natural and ideal at the same time.

A state resembling such a description was reached in the 1950s and 1960s. Both the sociological texts and the elite statements of the time exude an air of confidence that what was to be the new natural order of the social world was well known, and had even been reached in some societies. The past decades were read as an uneven, but inevitable movement towards the ideal state. Where phenomena were observed that deviated from the picture, they were regarded as remnants from earlier stages, and societies that were strongly marked by such phenomena were termed backward. This was the heyday of theories of 'modernization' and 'development'. When the consciousness of the construction of existing institutions in human action has disappeared, then alternatives to them and the possibility of change become unthinkable. This is why I shall describe the development towards organized modernity, the end-point of which was reached in the 1960s, as a process resembling reification of social phenomena, as a closure of the modern project.

In contrast to accounts in terms of modernization theory, be it of the 1950s or the 1990s variant, I shall try to emphasize the social *production* of a new societal configuration. Though I shall not be able to sufficiently discuss the breadth of variation between countries, a picture will emerge that shows many conflicts over the restructuring and winners and losers whose fate was not predetermined at the outset. More importantly even, it will show that no 'stable state' was reached with organized modernity, but rather an interim configuration that, while it displayed a certain internal coherence, also bore the seed of its own demise, again through the activities of the human beings living in it.

THE BUILDING OF TECHNICAL-ORGANIZATIONAL SYSTEMS

Key issues in accounts of the social transformations during the later nineteenth century are those restructurings of allocative practices that have come to be labelled (a) the second industrial revolution, (b) the emergence of the oligopolistic, managerial enterprise, and (c) economic protectionism. The former refers to new forms of transportation and communication related to the combustion engine and the telephone and to the applications of scientific insights into electricity and chemistry.[7] Organizational changes went along with material changes. The years before and after the turn of the century witnessed the emergence of the large-scale, increasingly managerial, enterprise and proposals for the planned restructuring of the production process labelled Taylorization.[8] These enterprises operated on markets that were increasingly protected nationally, and sometimes deliberately shared internationally. I shall not reiterate familiar themes of these transformations, but shall focus on certain features of the reorganization of allocative practices which are essential for understanding organized modernity.

(a) Research in the social construction of technology regularly distinguishes between an early phase of development of a technology and a phase of stabilization or 'rigidization'. The former is characterized by great openness and disputes between groups of producers and users of a technology-in-development over its shape and characteristics, while in the latter the basic characteristics are determined and no major changes occur over extended periods. Technologists tended to argue that this pattern reflects the sequence of an original phase of search and experimentation from a later one where the 'one best way' has been found and no fundamental improvements are possible. This view has rightly been challenged by the more recent constructivist perspective on technology, which does not accept technical purism but emphasizes the permanent embeddedness of technical construction in social networks instead.[9]

From such a perspective, the stabilization of a technology can be identified as the social sedimentation of a technical project. Structures of production and of use emerge that are linked to features of the technical artefact but reach far into realms of other social practices. It can be shown, for instance, that innovative activities in the area of transportation were very intense towards the end of the nineteenth century, when the various engine techniques that came to be used for automobiles were invented. A number of these proposals reached the stage of application and entered into the extended organization of car production, almost the epitome of standardized mass production, and of car use, which shaped our societyscapes and organization of private and social lives. By the 1960s, these extended structures of production and use were deeply entrenched in all advanced industrial societies, so that, as is well known, every attempt to change transportation systems faces hitherto insurmountable difficulties. The same even holds true in the realm of technical invention, where not-too-radical proposals to modify engine techniques never accomplished a breakthrough, despite some arguments in their favour in terms of performance.[10]

The social construction of technologies, as of other institutions, is a creative human activity and should not generally be conceived of as merely a response to systemic requirements. It is never a freely floating one, though, but one that is embedded in existing sets of social rules and resources, which it needs to draw on and by which it is limited. Furthermore, it is an activity that is historically located, so an achievement that might be socially accepted in the context of a specific social configuration could face rejection at a later point in time when the configuration has changed and the social space in which it could insert itself is occupied.[11] Indeed, I would like to emphasize the phenomenon that social configurations may show historically varying degrees of openness to the transformation of sets of material practices. Thus, the fact that the late nineteenth century has been described as an era of technical innovation, whereas the first two quarters of the twentieth century were mostly characterized by the permeation of society with the technologies invented before, needs to be interpreted in sociological terms.[12]

The so-called late-nineteenth-century wave of innovations was related to a major transformation of social practices, the one I propose to label the transition from restricted liberal to organized modernity. The social sedimentation of some of these innovations occurred with, and as part of, the stabilization of an entire socioeconomic paradigm. The conventionalization of social practices then entailed the containment of potentially upsetting innovations. Such a process has been labelled 'damming-in', as Dockès and Rosier formulate, or 'locking-in', as Cowan writes; its effects extend from the occupation and defence of markets to the settling of habits and life-styles.[13]

If this is accepted, the question still remains open as to what kinds of material practices would be socially produced and sedimented. The nineteenth, especially the late nineteenth, century marks the beginning of a breakthrough of a number of technical systems that would strongly restructure realms of social reality. The term realm may well be understood in a physical sense, for example, the railroad and – later – the automobile reshaping social space and territory, but it refers also generally to forms of activity, such as business communication via the telegraph and telephone.

The general character of these innovations was that they extended the reach of action, either by establishing a material connection or by strengthening the chains of unambiguous interaction. In principle, interaction chains had assumed global extension since the era of the discoveries. With nineteenth- and twentieth-century means of transportation and communication, however, long interaction chains acquired more of a routine character, and they were much more standardized. Modern institutions often established unambiguity of interaction from the beginning and upheld it all the way along the chain. They did so mainly by two means. First, they brought the information or good that was handled into a shape that was transportable with the technique to be applied. This process meant a work on the good that entailed a reduction to some basic characteristics. Storage and transportation possibilities, for instance, altered food markets and allowed their de-localization. Economies of scale then led to the mass-produced foods that have become typical of this century.[14]

Second, attempts were made to ensure that the way along the interaction chain was closed, that no other, outside interference could occur. An illustrative example, as introduced already earlier (see Chapter 2), is the system of high-velocity roads. A highway system considerably extends the reachable distance. At the same time, however, it rigidly prescribes not only the permissible paths and access-points but also the micro-behaviour of individuals inside the system, and precludes communication and renegotiation about the rules of such behaviour. Further, it erects a boundary between those inside and those outside and, for example, removes the inhabitants of a village without an access-point further from the other members of society than they had been before.[15]

Key features of such material practices are their simplicity and their independence. By the former, I mean that they de-structured more complexly related interactions and recomposed them in preconceived, more orderly and predictable ways, often appearing as uniformity once they had become socially dominant.[16] By the latter, I refer to their de-localized character. Such technologies are conceived of as universally applicable, once certain minimal requirements are met.

With this double character, being simple and independent, they could take the form of 'systems' that could be imposed on a local field of action. In these terms, the second half of the nineteenth and the first half of the twentieth century can be characterized as a period in which social space (literally) was 'perforated' by technical networks, from the railroad to the telephone and electricity networks to car-usable road networks to radio and television broadcasting systems. The growth of these 'primary' technical systems was always based on economies of scale, in one sense or another. The cost of building and/or maintaining a system could be so high that it could only be run cost-efficiently with mass usage. Or a system would only be attractive to users if it had wide coverage like the telephone network, or the broadcasting systems for advertisers. And a wide extension of such networks would provide growth paths for producers of equipment to use them, such as cars or electrical appliances. All these features entailed a move towards standardization of products and homogenization of patterns of behaviour.[17]

A particular example of a social technology showing similar features is the reorganization of production through 'scientific management', later called Taylorism. Two main reasons are usually given for the social attractiveness of Taylorism. The first is that it increases efficiency and productivity. This argument can be traced back to Adam Smith's pin example as evidence for the rationality of the micro-division of labour. The second is that it expropriates not only the workers' skills but also their control over the work process. That is why it can be used to pre-emptively counteract the shop-floor resistance of workers against exploitation. Naturally the first argument tended to be used for the employers' side, the second for the side of the workers' movement. While something can be said in favour of both arguments, I would like to stress another, more general aspect of Taylorism. With its minute decomposition of human movements, scientific management ended up reducing every action into a limited number of component parts. The production process would then be reassembled from these known and measurable parts. In theory, scientific management had complete knowledge of the labour process at its disposal. Such knowledge could then be used for a variety of purposes, be they called efficiency or expropriation of the workers' power. At its basis, however, is the establishment of order and certainty, stability and predictability, on a recalcitrant reality in the factory.[18]

(b) It is a well-known thesis, put forward most prominently by Alfred Chandler, that 'in the last half of the nineteenth century a new form of capitalism appeared in the United States and Europe.'[19] Until then, practices of allocation had been shaped by comparatively small enterprises, which were seen as competing on markets via the prices of their products. Often these companies were directed by the owner who himself possessed the craft or engineering knowledge that was the foundation of the company's production. Towards the end of the nineteenth century, the average size of the firm had grown sharply, partly through direct organizational expansion, partly through mergers. Increasingly, personally owned companies were transformed into or replaced by joint-stock firms, and a new group of economic actors emerged, the salaried managers.[20]

The emergence of the modern, big business enterprises may be related directly to organizational requirements for managing new technical systems, such as railroad and telegraph systems. Subsequently, then, the existence of this new organizational form allowed and stimulated mass production and mass marketing.[21] It will not suffice, however, to point to technical innovations as the main cause of the growth of firms, since some of these techniques showed a long 'maturation' period before they were widely applied. The growth of firms, though, can more precisely be located in time as following on the long depression at the end of the nineteenth century (1873–1895). Organizational expansion can be seen as an escape from the vagaries of the markets under competitive capitalism.

If the share of a firm's product on a market is increased, then the possibility for controlling the market is enhanced. All economic theorizing that concludes on automatic equilibration and maximization via markets has to assume that economic actors are exposed to the workings of the market without being able to strategically shape it. Big firms, however, establish a new kind of economic agency when they are able to influence the conditions of market exchange owing to the size of their own share. Through this kind of organization, companies do not merely benefit from economies of scale, if narrowly understood in technical and economic terms, but they produce a social advantage, namely manageability, on their own field of action.[22]

Late in the twentieth century, when the modern business enterprise acting on oligopolistic markets has become the dominant type of firm, it has repeatedly been argued that the development of advanced capitalism is much less associated with market competition and dynamic entrepreneurship than with increasing organization of production and distribution. The move towards organization should indeed be seen as an attempt to control conditions of action in a general context of fluidity and change. 'Risk avoidance and organizational stability . . . is the usual device of large organizations and firms.'[23]

This reaction on the part of 'capital' is thus not unlike the parallel one on the part of 'labour', namely to organize a share of the market (for products or for labour) as big as possible to control it rather than being exposed to it.[24] It is a move to re-establish certainty under conditions of great uncertainty. Following the principles of bureaucracy, big organizations try to cover as much of the relevant field of action as possible, and to structure their actions in this field according to clear and fixed hierarchical rules.[25]

This transformation of the firm was most pronounced in the most rapidly developing economy of the late nineteenth century, that of the US. The economy that had industrialized earlier, the English one, and those that were industrializing later, like the French, Italian or Scandinavian ones, were less marked by these changes at about that time. But it became clearly evident that 'the first entrepreneurs to create such enterprises acquired powerful competitive advantages.'[26] If these disequilibria did not translate forcefully into other economies at that time (but only after the Second World War), it was owing to the relative 'coherence of national productive systems'[27] and to the existence of boundaries around them.

(c) Like any other practice, the economy should know no boundaries according to the modern imaginary. However, boundary-setting proposals arose very soon to counter the, actual or expected, impact of unlimited freedom on world markets; a nationally organized capitalism took shape. These measures used the nation-state as the container for alternative rules for allocative practices, and they were typically proposed in industrially 'backwards' contexts. In Germany, Friedrich List rejected the free market approach for situations of highly unequal competitiveness. He suggested that a competitive economy needed to be built with the support of the state behind protective tariff borders.[28] Accordingly, most industrializing countries, whose elites tried to follow the English model, actively used boundaries and the state, to achieve their objective. Especially the closing decades of the nineteenth century were 'a period of severe economic crisis throughout the system, to which states responded largely by way of protectionist measures'. Among these were restrictions on the free movement of people, which all major Western states passed with the exception of France where similar proposals kept being defeated.[29]

Allocative practices had shown tendencies towards globalization throughout the nineteenth century. International trade rose strongly, both absolutely and as a share of output, between 1820 and 1870, the heyday of liberal capitalism. However, the trend declined between 1870 and 1913, when protectionist measures were increasingly used. And it was strongly reversed between 1913 and 1950.[30] With its high instabilities, this latter period also witnessed increased attempts to survey and control the economy, and these measures all targeted the national allocative practices. Economic survey institutes were created, Keynesianism and related policy instruments were devised to influence economic indicators, and – mostly after the Second World War – complex and detailed empirical and econometric tools were developed and used.[31]

The space-covering technologies of mass production and mass distribution, the market-covering big firm, and the state-monitored and supported national economy were some key ingredients of the organization of allocative practices, known as 'organized capitalism'. To fully understand the overall set of rules, however, we have to look also at the points where 'the economy' reaches out into social life, at the social conceptions and practices of work and of consumption.

CONVENTIONALIZATION OF WORK

During the late 1970s and 1980s, in Germany at least, the term 'work society' was widely used, mostly in the context of the assertion that work may begin to become scarce in a society based on it. The, often merely implicit, reference was to a social and political order that had promised to provide full-time employment to all adults who wanted it, at an income that would allow them to sustain their life.[32] In those recent debates, the work society appeared as a time-honoured achievement of modernity, even as a natural order. However, it was actually not that long ago that the basic principles of the work society had been fully accepted as social conventions, in some countries as late as the 1960s. And the major social processes of conventionalization also do not date back into pre-history, but can rather precisely be located in the late nineteenth century and the 1930s.[33] They involve most importantly the generalization of wage labour.[34]

(a) Conceptions of *labour and unemployment* were not just there, they had to be invented. Often, the introduction of new classifications of work was parallel to the labour legislation at the end of the nineteenth century. Then, the earlier categories relating to crafts were pushed aside and the notion of 'salaried employee' introduced. This concept did not only homogenize a large part of the working population, it also entailed the creation of its other, namely the unemployed, a category that was inconceivable before.

In France, for instance, an institutionalized category of the unemployed came into existence at the end of the nineteenth century, institutionalized in statistical and legal terms (after the basic idea had been present during the debate about public works in the Second Republic, and the term '*chômeur*' had been coined around 1870). The years after the world economic crisis of 1929 can be regarded as a period in which social norms as to unemployment were established. The volume of work is now counted in terms of work-places and numbers of salaried employees. Between the 1930s and 1950s, not only in France but in most advanced industrial countries, the 'Keynesian convention' of full employment became a policy objective. Since then at the latest, the unemployment figure has become a 'strategic indicator' which all actors involved – employers, unions and government – try to exploit and manipulate according to their interests.[35]

Any such convention is not merely an invention, though, brought about freely at anybody's hands in any desired form. It draws on existing social phenomena, interprets them, and ultimately alters them by enforcing a description on them. The social science perspective to be taken on conventionalization can best be called, following Roy Bhaskar, critical realism:

> Social structures are concept-dependent, but not merely conceptual. Thus a person could not be said to be 'unemployed' or 'out of work' unless she and the other relevant agents possessed some (not necessarily correct or fully adequate) concept of that condition and were able to give some sort of account of it, namely to describe (or redescribe) it. But it *also* involves, for instance, her being physically excluded from certain sites, definite locations in space and time.[36]

From the late nineteenth century, a conception developed that saw society as mainly consisting of two classes; the workers, with the unemployed as a deviant subgroup, and the employers. This view did not at all reflect social reality, but it provided a basic image. For some interests and purposes, however, the two-class society was unsatisfying, and modifications of this image were proposed.

(b) The *differentiated classification of the work force* was a process of social construction that was started at the end of the nineteenth century and concluded by the 1930s – to disappear then from view as construction and reappear as 'natural' reality. Not least in many of the social insurance arrangements, introduced towards the end of the nineteenth century (see Chapter 6), the workers were officially recognized as a distinct social group in society. The mobilization of the workers' movement (being a conventionalization from below) and its increasing strength had led the bourgeois groups to picture a socialist threat to the future of society. From this constellation, the image of society as consisting of two major groups with opposed interests evolved. This picture was quite inaccurate by the turn of the century when a large part of the population was active in agriculture or as small entrepreneurs, craftsmen and shopkeepers, later to be called the 'old middle classes'. But the representation of society in dichotomic terms was powerful in shaping the expectations towards the future.

The classificatory creation of a third position in society was politically often linked to the intention of avoiding the image of a sole alternative between capitalism and socialism. In Germany, such a strategy was obviously already in Bismarck's mind when he proposed the category of employee, basically referring to white-collar workers, as Americans would say, in the social insurance legislation. This category split the camp of salaried workers and diminished the likelihood of all-out solidarity.[37]

A stronger reaction to the two-class representation emerged after the crisis of 1929, which had hit the 'old middle classes' particularly hard. In many variants, a new discourse was proposed which deplored the polarization of society. Often, the forces of both capital and labour were portrayed as destructive to the social fabric, and the healthier elements in society were hailed. These could be the peasants, on the one hand, but also the engineers and professionals, on the other, who worked with knowledge, the substance of progress, and did not submit to the soulless thrivings of the machines, as capitalists and workers did, who were interested solely in profits or subsistence.[38] In France, for instance, where social catholicism had long extended a family image to the sphere of work and had hailed the 'old middle classes', the debate focused explicitly on a 'third way' in the 1930s. During this period, the category was formed that was to be used for the 'new middle classes', the *cadres*, salaried employees with knowledge-based or managing tasks.[39]

(c) Once they were identified and classified (or had built a collective identity and had given themselves a name), it was possible to act on and with the workers (or the workers had enabled themselves to act collectively), to include them in *organized forms of participation.* This capacity reached a new momentum during the First World War when the war needs required the elites to entice the workers to participate fully in the industrial efforts behind the military machine. In exchange, workers' organizations were allowed to participate in industrial relations, the unions were integrated into the administration of production. Thus, the war economy of the First World War saw the beginnings of tripartism: the workers, the firms and the state established collective capability each on their terrain, and then entered into negotiations with each other.[40]

In the aftermath of the First World War, when they had acquired knowledge of their strength and power, the workers also attempted to set themselves in the dominant place of the new economic organizations, via workers' councils and socialization commissions. Except for the Soviet Union, however, all these moves were soon defeated. In fact, even the more moderate and integrative reforms were often withdrawn shortly after the end of the war, though they were maintained to a certain extent in some countries (for example, Germany). Tripartism was a formula that would be fully developed only after the Second World War in most countries, later debated as neo-corporatism. Its character as a model for overall social organization and its relevance in terms of the practices of authoritative power will be discussed in the following chapter.

NORMALIZATION OF CONSUMPTION

Finally, a look shall be taken at the 'output' side of allocative practices. In the late nineteenth century, those workers who were producing consumer goods were generally hardly capable of buying the commodities they were producing – beyond food for which workers' families often spent more than half of their monetary income.[41] One of the major distinctions between the capitalism of the early 1900s and that of the 1960s is that consumption, supported by wage increases, has developed extraordinarily and has taken on a particular mode, usually short-handed mass consumption. Mass consumption is the homogeneous demand for standardized products by a large number of consumers who essentially are simultaneously the producers of these commodities by means of mass-production technologies or, increasingly, their distributors by means of large-scale technological networks. As a result, 'a norm of social consumption' has formed and evolved in capitalist societies as the first 'mode of consumption [that is] specific to capitalism', that is, consumption of capitalistically produced and marketed goods.[42]

Two aspects of this development are important in the present context. First, the social consumption mode created a double tendency towards *individualization and homogenization* for the worker-consumer. Second, once the mode of consumption was socially recognized, it opened a *path of development* for the entire social formation that gave it a certain stability and predictability.

(a) The new mode of consumption entailed a trend towards commodification. For the organization of one's life one would draw less and less on other social resources but would rely on money and markets. I think one may assume that this trend has not yet subsided. It involves the decrease of subsistence agricultural production in workers' families and the decreasing reliance on oneself or family members for as diverse tasks as domestic labour, caring for the sick and elderly, child rearing or even expertise in personal problems. Commodification provides a potential for individualization.[43] As long as a continuous supply of monetary resources is available, there is no need to maintain social ties on grounds of required support.

However, how this potential is socially realized depends on the historical mode of consumption. During the first half of the twentieth century, the commodification of social relations occurred in the context of mass production – especially in the US but increasingly also elsewhere – and that is, as mass consumption of standardized goods. In effect, then, while potentially individualizing, commodification entailed a homogenization of social lives. The American suburb has become the prototype of a normalized style of consumption, in which conformity would reign inside one suburb and where differences of objects between suburbs would clearly mark the social rank order. The phenomenon, though, is not limited to North American society, as Pierre Bourdieu's work on differentiated and at the same time unambiguous modes of distinction in France shows.

We see here the first elements of a shift in the definition of social identity, an issue which shall be discussed in more detail below. With the formation of the practices of organized modernity, social relations that had been de-localized were not in fact individualized but socialized in a very specific way. Organized modernity means the cultural reign of a strong conception of society, 'a laicized world where "society" becomes the general arbiter answerable for the causes of our destiny', in the words of François Ewald.[44] The emergence of a 'consumer society', as it was to be called later, meant in principle that the acquisition of goods could become a means of shaping and displaying one's identity via material objects.[45] However, for most of the original development of this social formation, from the 1920s to the 1960s, the 'available' identities were not only very limited but also rather unambiguously defined.

The way of locating oneself socially in the world was largely shaped by the effective 'nationalization' of social practices. This trend may easily be exaggerated, since it will always be the case that human relations of a particular form and intensity can only be established in face-to-face interaction, that is, the locale of practices will remain of importance.[46] Also a nationally standardized mode of consumption will emerge through the observation of objects that specific others of the local context have acquired, even if such practices are conditioned and mediated by information and incentives provided by the media and advertisements and by the offers of the retail business. However, there is one set of technologies that effectively shifts orientation to the national realm, namely television. By creating the fiction of face-to-face interaction through the audiovisual presence of the other in the living-room, TV provides an idea of proximity that other media could not achieve. At the same time, its national organization provided the background to the homogenization and standardization of orientations, not least, consumer orientations. From its beginning, television may have eroded the 'sense of place',[47] but it recreated a different space of common orientation, the national 'community', or rather, it supported that orientation which was already created by the organization of other practices.

There is one other sense in which the new mode of consumption was socializing. Restricted liberal modernity was essentially a divided society, in which not only formal exclusion rules were valid, but in which life-styles also differed socially according to the material products that were available. In the consumer society of organized modernity, most commodities on offer – such as house, car, durable household goods, also long-distance travel for leisure purposes, etc. – were available for large parts of the population, even if sizes and qualities differed socially. Thus, one might say that full inclusion was reached in this material sense, and the emergence of so-called mass culture is clearly related to this universalization of product-availability. This apparent egalitarianism does not yet say anything about differentials of power and influence. Still, it marks an important shift from the earlier divided society that needs to be further explored below.

(b) The notion of full inclusion already indicates a certain coherence or saturation of the social formation. Such inclusion, however, was approached even in the US only after the Second World War. But the idea that there could be a 'progressive' path of socioeconomic development had emerged already in the 1930s, not least in the context of the rethinking of economic concepts by John Maynard Keynes and others. The notion that the increase of demand, even if debt-financed, could stabilize an economy has to be seen as closely related to the emergence of mass consumption. Instead of seeing wages as merely a drain on profits and investment, their double character as both cost and return was recognized. This concept allowed for the general possibility of reconciling the interests of employers, trade unions and the state.

Mass consumption turned this general possibility into a substantive prospect. High wages, supported by public sector income maintenance measures, would enable workers' families to gradually provide themselves up to the saturation level with all the durable consumer goods that marked modern material culture. This demand, in turn, would entice companies to expand their production up to the same level of continuous supply for instalment and replacement of these goods. To create this general beneficial effect, it was most important to set a wage convention[48] so that the 'rate of money wage increases corresponded to the rate of change of prices plus the rate of change of productivity'[49] as a basic rule of co-ordination. Then demand would sustain accumulation and investment on a stable growth path.

This ingenious circle was behind the fact that growth was mainly centred on the domestic market. Once recognized, as it generally was after the Second World War, this pattern allowed for a high certainty of expectations on allocative practices.

> A fundamentally new development of the post-war period was that the massive growth in production was counterbalanced by an equal growth of consumption – a growth of consumption which, as a result of . . . institutional and policy innovations . . . came to be more or less universally forecast and anticipated, extending to all sectors of the population but first and foremost to wage-earners.[50]

With regard to allocative practices, we may therefore state that by the 1950s a set of rules and conventions had been created that underpinned the expectation of steady and predictable development over the foreseeable future. These rules and conventions had been gradually elaborated, over many struggles and without the end result being in anybody's mind at the beginning, from the late nineteenth century onwards, with the 1890s and the 1930s as two crucial periods of rule-setting. These conventions enabled what has become known as the 'golden age' of capitalism to arise, an era that is now usually fixed as falling broadly between the years 1950 and 1973.[51]

This golden age system of production and its rules of co-ordination sustained an optimism and a certainty over future economic developments that had been unknown earlier in the twentieth century. As late as 1972, a typical authoritative statement reads as follows:

> There is no special reason to doubt that the underlying trends of growth in the early and middle 1970s will continue much as in the 1960s . . . the growth objectives and the capacity of governments broadly to achieve them, have not significantly altered and no special influence can now be foreseen which would at all drastically change the external environment of the European economies.[52]

A year later, however, the future looked much more uncertain, and a decade later it was possible to recognize the extraordinary character of the golden age, to trace it to a unique historical constellation, and to recognize that an era had ended.[53]

Chapter 6

Building iron cages

The organization of authoritative practices

Liberal politics faces a number of foundational questions, many of which can be discussed in terms of the delimitations of the political realms and the justification of boundaries around them. Clearly, the question is not whether boundaries were needed in general. The political has never been, and probably cannot be, thought of without regard to limitations of its scope. But the question of where the boundaries should be set has been a crucial issue in the transformations of modernity. Three aspects may be distinguished: limits to the polity, that is the question of who should be eligible to participate politically; limits to the practice of politics, that is the organization of political representation; and limits to the scope of policy-making, that is the definition of the matters in which collective deliberation may and shall interfere.

THE NATIONALIZATION OF THE MODERN POLITY

First, the issue of *who* is to participate in political deliberation needs to be determined; this is the question of *political citizenship*.[1] On the one hand, the territorial definition of the modern state allows the setting of boundaries to the *outside*, to other states and their populations.[2] On the other hand, limits to who can consider themselves as political beings can also be set *inside* a political entity through the determination of participation rules.

Internally, the tension between a universalist liberal conception and the (more or less) implicit restricted bourgeois reading of it, provided for one of the major political dynamics during the nineteenth century. As Alexis de Tocqueville had predicted, 'once the first step had been taken to reduce the qualifications for the vote it would be impossible to halt the movement at any point short of universal suffrage.'[3] In many states this was introduced after the First World War, though in a number of countries suffrage was extended to women only after the Second World War.[4] There are many ways of playing on the rules of internal citizenship. One may devise voting procedures that discourage selected parts of the population from participation, as the US rules do with regard to Afro-Americans. The distinction between internal and external boundaries may also be blurred by, for instance, granting full social but not political citizenship to immigrant workers, as many states do.[5] Still, with universal suffrage as a widely accepted and unquestioned norm, the internal issue of political citizenship has been fairly settled for most of the later twentieth century. The complete acceptance of the concept of the 'unit citizen' (Rokkan) and of the unmediated linkage of this citizen to authoritative institutions produces the problem of representation which shall be raised in the following section.

Before doing this, however, the external boundaries of political citizenship need to be discussed. Not unlike in the case of other social practices, a sort of coherence on the level of national societies was striven for and achieved in terms of authoritative practices. Whereas inside the state full integration and coverage was provided for, firm boundaries were set to the outside.

These external boundaries reside on the definition of nationality and of authoritative rules deriving from nationality.[6] As mentioned earlier, the idea of national identity had served as a conceptual foundation for political communities through all of the nineteenth century. Only towards the end of the century, however, was such an idea strongly applied to the governance of individuals and populations. The passing and enforcement of immigration restrictions, the introduction of passport obligations, the linkage of social and professional opportunities to citizenship, the emphasis on national attributes in conflicts of all sorts are all phenomena that were introduced or strengthened during the late nineteenth and the early twentieth centuries. It was only then that 'the social construction of national identities' turned fully into the 'nationalization of European societies'.[7]

Paradoxically, the increased acceptance of the peoples' right to self-determination at the beginning of the twentieth century, and especially after the First World War, exacerbated the process of imposing nationalized rules on individuals and, furthermore, of excluding groups of other human beings from this right. In practice, the right to collective self-determination allowed statehood for a small number of cultural-linguistic collectives and turned many more others into officially acknowledged 'minorities' of 'nation-states' dominated by other collectives. The human cost of this 'solution' was enormous, since it entailed strong state efforts to eliminate all ambivalence inside the boundaries, ranging from border adjustments to extermination camps. The very ideal of covering the earth completely with ethnically homogeneous national communities also meant the creation of a new kind of human being, the stateless person, with much less protection than all those who could count on a nation-state to support them in need. Jews became the epitome of this new kind of stranger.[8]

Furthermore, the very foundation of these boundaries was the idea of a population that was not only homogeneous but also rather immobile, partly immobilized by exactly these rules. Through much of the nineteenth century, to try to escape one's fate had meant to move across boundaries. The first two thirds of the twentieth century witnessed both stronger restrictions to voluntary migrations and an unprecedented increase in forced displacements. Nationality came to determine one's fate more strongly.

Normatively, one may argue that only the setting of firm boundaries to the outside will allow a community to develop forms to deal collectively with the issues its members have in common, since otherwise neither a communication over these issues nor a consensus over rules to deal with them can emerge. One may, however, also observe that such 'national closures' have tended to destroy plurality and diversity inside the boundaries and have created a 'truly homogeneous space of political citizenship'.[9] It may also be the case that the latter is a precondition for the former, and that this is one of the dilemmas of political modernity. Even if we suspend judgement for the moment, we will have to note that historically the strengthening of the external boundaries went broadly along with the internal transformation of political citizenship towards the rule of full inclusion.

The universalization of the suffrage, however, was not the only transformation of authoritative practices that needs to be placed in the context of the organization of modernity. As the major expansion of the polity that it was, it must be viewed as a parallel to other redefinitions of the rules of political representation and of the legitimacy of administrative activity, that is, the boundary between public and private spheres.

COLLECTIVE AGENCY AND ELITE CONTROL: MASS-PARTY ELECTORAL POLITICS

In formal-legal terms, the question of political representation enters into the deliberations on electoral systems, where majority vote and proportional representation, for instance, stand for highly different ideas about political collectives and political identities inside a society. Even after the universal, equal and secret vote is established, some sort of 'internal boundaries' are needed, and their setting is more than a purely organizational matter but involves different understandings of the structure of a community.[10]

In societies committed to the imaginary significations of modernity, practices of domination refer to the idea of collective self-rule, labelled democracy. While the label is borrowed from the understanding of politics in the ancient Greek city states, everybody acknowledges that contemporary societies with much more widely extended institutions and practices cannot transfer the idea without alterations. Representation then becomes a key concept, referring to the rules of making 'present' in political deliberations those citizens who cannot directly participate themselves, who are in fact absent. The most general meaning of the concept is that 'in representation something not literally present is considered as present in a nonliteral sense.'[11] There is no major political-legal rule in Western democracies that does not implicitly refer to the idea of representation, though, as I shall argue, there is a tendency to loosen the link between the literally present and what is represented.[12]

The notion of a 'crisis of representation' should not be overused, since, as Umberto Eco once remarked, the concept of representation was in crisis from the very day it was coined.[13] The idea of representation does not solve any question, but opens a number of them. A representation is not the same as the thing it represents since otherwise no representation would be needed. So a minimal set of clarifications is needed as to who are the represented, who are the representatives, and what is their relation. However, liberal theory does not, and probably cannot, provide clear rules in any of these respects.

Liberal theorizing as emphasized during the 'democratic revolutions' was based on a direct counterposition of the individual to a social totality. Emerging from the struggle against feudal structures of privilege, the idea of equality rejected the assumption of politically relevant differences between individuals before entering into political processes. However, the reality of restricted liberal modernity and of capitalism made this assumption soon appear untenable. The consequence drawn was that representation should sensibly be organized according to real or imagined social ties between individuals and according to commonality of interests based on such ties.[14]

The formation of political parties in the modern sense emerged from such a conception of an organization representing a pre-defined segment of social interests. Drawing on but transforming the model of the loosely organized bourgeois groupings of notables, it was pioneered by the workers' movement.[15] By the end of the nineteenth century, these aspirations began to show success. The 1880s marked the beginning of the 'decline of the notables' and the coming of the 'age of the masses' and of mass political organizations.[16] Later, as a reaction to these achievements of the workers' movement, the model was followed and appropriated by other social and political groups; comparatively slowly actually by the conservatives and liberals, the pre-existing political groupings, whose organizations were transformed into full-scale mass parties often only after the Second World War; more rapidly by a new political project, the fascist and National Socialist one, which was also based on the idea of collective identity, though not a social but a racial and national one.[17]

One may speak here of the transformation of a *philosophical* conception of representation, based on the political philosophy of the Enlightenment, into a *sociological* one, based on the sociology of industrial and mass society emerging at the end of the nineteenth century.[18] This conceptual transformation was accompanied by factual 'answers' to questions that liberal theory was unable to pose in terms adequate for a mass society, namely as to (a) the nature of those social ties among individuals that would enable them to be collectively 'represented', and (b) the ways by which actual aggregation of interests and political deliberation would be achieved. These questions were being factually 'closed' during the first two thirds of the twentieth century, but hardly on normatively convincing terms.

(a) Socialist parties, not least German social democracy, provided the model case for modern parties in the new context of representation. They had a programme that was articulating the interests of a certain part of the population. This part was identified by its particular social status, its class location, which defined the common interest of all those who shared it. The party had local chapters, from which participation could rise, but its strength was the nationwide articulation of a basically common interest, which could, furthermore, be objectively determined by scientific study. This party served as a model on which other interests were organized, so that it is not inappropriate to speak of 'the historical importance of class-based politics'[19] in the political organization of modernity.

If polities were clearly organized along class lines, if individuals could identify themselves as members of a class, if members of a class had a common interest, if this interest were expressed by a representative organization, and if this organization were represented in political institutions according to the relevance of the interest it represents, then the class-based party could be the key element of a consistent social theory and practice of political representation. However, this view idealizes the relations between individuals and political projects embodied in parties, making them appear as a, while mediated, still normatively defendable variant of democratic representation.

In contrast, it is important to recognize that insight into class interest was only one kind, and in most cases hardly the most important one, of linkage between individuals and parties. At least two other crucial aspects enter into this relation. Both have to do with the situation of disembedding and uncertainty in which many people found themselves owing to the often drastic changes in the practices of material allocation which we have come to call industrialization.[20] In such a condition when earlier conventions appeared unable to match new requirements, parties offered themselves as holders of also individually appropriate responses. While for most parties some mix of such offers is true, one kind of linkage is known to be more typical of both the political left and the extreme right. With the world-views they propagated, those parties portrayed themselves as capable of establishing new certainties; with the practices they organized in their local chapters they created the possibility of a new social identity and the sense of belonging to a larger group, one ready to face the demands of the time. More towards the centre and the moderate right, linkages of the clientelistic kind are more typical. Party clientelism is basically the transformation of the personal relations between a local, often village-based, population and their protectors, notables or land-owners, into a relation of similarly personal form. In this case, the place of the notable is taken by elected officials and party functionaries, and the exchange is of votes against redistributed taxes in some form or other.[21] Clientelism provides a personal access-point to 'modern' sets of rules that appear bureaucratic and impersonal otherwise. In a broad sense, it is a very widespread practice in our allegedly modern societies.

If this characterization is valid, then the rules of party competition are interpreted in practice not only as the means of social interest aggregation, but also as the means for the creation and local instantiation of 'imagined communities' and as the means for the personalization of 'abstract' rule systems. The social theory of political representation, which is based on the idea of class interest, loses its coherence, unless one is ready to disregard completely the way parties and their vote are constituted.

Writings of political scientists, the supposed specialists of the theory of representation, support this observation. Whenever they try to debate the concept of representation in relation to common practices of domination, they face serious difficulties and tend to conclude that the concept is mysterious or, at best, devoid of content.[22] Consequently, some political theorists conclude that it is a concept one should rather avoid. Still, in the modern context it refuses to go away completely. Others, therefore, have a more sanguine proposal, one that could be termed the de-substantivization of representation. These theorists draw on interpretations of the relationship of the citizen and the party solely in the view of its outcome, the second issue introduced above.

(b) It is important to see that the building of organizations and bureaucracies itself was a *project*, an attempt to build collective agency, that is, social democracy and the organizations of the workers' movement, under the rule of liberal politics.[23] Party organizers recognized that the issue of socialist transformation had to be tackled, at least, at the institutional level of the state (and not the firm or the city), and they tried to build an instrument that would enable the working class to do so. The entire, and very strong, debate on the need for unity, as expressed in terms such as the 'front' or in the communist prohibition of factionalism, goes back to this idea. The obvious reverse side was constraints on the activities of party members and on the permissible discourse in the party.

Under conditions of party competition, the relation of the enabling and constraining features of parties took on a peculiar shape. At a time of expanding suffrage, the promoters of the class interest-based mass party drew on the given rules of representation and at the same time transformed them. They argued that their political stand-point had mass support and that mass support should make a difference in representation. Thus, they promoted the new rule that a political group, to pursue its goals, should have mass support (rather than, say, persuasive arguments or the stronger weaponry). As a consequence, other parties, whether existing or newly forming, became increasingly organized so as to secure a mass following, too.

When a party trying to represent an interest and to act on behalf of a social group meets the rule of competition between parties under mass suffrage, a tension between the objective of truly representing and the objective of success in the competition emerges. It is to the merit of the early sociologists of political elites that they identified this tension, that is, the Italian theorists of the political class, Gaetano Mosca and Vilfredo Pareto, and the German-Italian sociologist of oligopolistic organization, Robert Michels.[24] In the terms introduced earlier, mobilization from below is transformed into mobilization from above, as a result of this tension.

The concept of political class, originating in Mosca, denotes the collective of individuals who participate regularly in state decisions. It is open to empirical analysis – though somewhat assumed to be the case – whether the members of this group regularly show common attitudes and orientations, at least as regards the procedural handling of their activities.[25] The notion of political class allows an understanding of the transformation of concepts of agency and representation into diplomatic top-level bargaining at a great distance from the voters and with an instrumental, strategic attitude. This transformation has almost ideal-typically been portrayed for the Dutch case by Arend Lijphart, who proposed the terms 'politics of accommodation' and 'consociational democracy' for these processes and orders respectively.[26]

The building of such an order was accompanied by what I would term the emergence of an implicit concept of *organized representation*. This order was, for instance, described as follows:

> The current political structure, oriented towards assumptions of social stability, is based upon rather narrow, fixed lines of representation – via the party electoral and interest-group systems. Inasmuch as this structure presupposes order and stability, the leaders bargain and compromise for their respective constituencies. The political outcomes (laws) are refined through compromise decisions which are reached in the process of administrative politics.[27]

On the common ground of elite deliberations, two aspects can be distinguished. First, the organization of the nominally 'political' practices is de-substantivized. Historically, the parties have been built on some sort of conception of special ties between individuals and of common interests, even if that was never unequivocally the dominant reason why voters voted for certain parties. But over time, especially after the Second World War, this foundation was undermined. The concept of the 'catch-all party' supposed that there were no major cleavages in society any longer. In that view, parties merely bundled sections of the elite and proposed them for governing positions. The substance of competitive party democracy was emptied and the accent shifted to its form, namely elite selection.[28] The transformation of the 'original' bureaucratic mass party, which had a class base, into an electoral-professional party signals the erosion of the social substance that went into the organization of representation, even if the form, the party, is maintained.[29]

Second, parts of the practices that could, and should according to an emphatically democratic notion of politics, be handled in universal-suffrage elected bodies are in fact the object of corporate interest mediation. On the basis of industrial and professional 'estate' organization, such processes are often widely recognized by the state nowadays, though they effectively subvert any liberal-democratic idea of representation, which still underlies the concept of interest group pluralism.[30]

In such an order of organized representation it does not matter any longer in terms of the political process and outcome what the relation between the parties and their members and voters is. The political elites may organize it in the way they find most successful (and a strategy close to brand-product advertising has proved the most successful for a while). Relevant for politics is only that they keep their internal relations 'closed', that is, they keep their members and electorate consenting (passively) to their activities. 'Elite cooperation is the primary distinguishing feature of consociational democracy.'[31]

This historical process has recently been neatly summarized as follows:

> The institutionalisation of democracy has been achieved through the *encapsulation* of conflicts rather than through their political pacification as such and, moreover, has necessitated certain crucial preconditions. It is clear, for example, that conflicts can only be encapsulated if the number of actors is either limited or predictable, and if they also prove to be reliable partners, that is, if they can claim to embody the legitimate and efficient representation of their respective socio-political communities.[32]

While it is accepted that the debate about democracy can hardly live without any concept of representation, its meaning was further bent. In the above quotation, representation refers to nothing more than the passive consent, or rather the absence of open dissent, of the voters. Representation is reduced to an empirical criterion of performance, namely of the capacity of a party, or the sum of the established parties, to organize the electorate. On such reduced terms, they succeeded indeed at least until the 1970s. The 'century of mass politics in Western Europe can be seen as a century of electoral stabilisation.'[33] By the 1960s, the most eminent sociologists of elections spoke of a 'freezing' of the party systems,[34] later the term 'closure' was used.[35] Thus, a renowned political theorist could argue that 'the success that parties have had in marrying government action to popular consent has converted the modern doctrine of party government into what is really the most widely accepted normative political theory of representation.'[36]

As a correlate to organized capitalism and a substantial element of organized modernity, I shall call such order of authoritative practices *organized democracy*.[37] By the 1960s, such a concept was dominant in political practice. Parties were not seen to express, but rather to channel the will of the electorate into the representative institutions, thereby transforming it into whatever the organizational elites deemed negotiable and advantageous in the competitive struggle. They were to educate the voters in terms of democracy, directing them to the viable political choices. Rather than expressing, party elites formed and shaped the political discourses and struggles.

REDUCED UNCERTAINTIES AND MONITORED LIVES: THE WELFARE STATE AND SOCIAL POLICY

If authoritative institutions during organized modernity were based on such a 'thin theory of citizenship',[38] an important issue is: what would 'representatives' legitimately be able to decree over the represented? This third question on the organization of authoritative practices points to the *distinction between the public and the private* in modern societies. All liberal and democratic theorizing conceptualized two such distinct realms and relied on fairly strong boundaries between them. However, there have been continuous debates about where the right place for that boundary should be. The restricted liberal state of the mid-nineteenth century was assumed to have a strict notion of the boundary and a strongly constrained political realm. Since then, however, the boundary has not only been more intensely debated and moved again, it has also become much more fuzzy in the political debates and practices of welfare-state, or interventionist, policy-making.

From a viewpoint which regards social citizenship as the historically highest stage of citizenship that can be acquired (a view which T.H. Marshall did not express as much more than a general consensus in the post-Second World War years),[39] Bismarckian social policy always presented a paradox in need of explanation. Apparently, the society that was far behind in terms of political citizenship at the end of the nineteenth century, Imperial Germany, took a leap forward in social citizenship and passed by its otherwise so much more advanced Western neighbours.

At the end of the nineteenth century, in a first wave of welfare-state building, most European societies introduced a number of social policy innovations, such as industrial accident insurance, workers' sickness insurance, old age insurance. A major exception was the US, where measures equivalent to this first European wave were introduced during the 1930s. After the Second World War until the 1960s, a second wave expanded the system of social insurances into an encompassing institutional network, 'from the cradle to the grave', with Beveridge England taking the lead this time.[40] In the words of Abram de Swaan, welfare measures experienced a 'hyperbole of expansion' after 1945.[41]

Earlier, the shift in political discourses underpinning the move from a restricted liberal to a welfare state was outlined (see Chapter 4). Apart from a discourse of justification, the nominally liberal state of the middle of the nineteenth century also lacked the necessary resources for policies of social security. Relying on a night watchman's conception, the state was solely to guarantee internal and external peace and security, and, according to retrospective estimates, had mostly far less than 10 per cent of the domestic product at its disposal, too little to engage in strong redistribution activities.[42]

Already by 1876, though, the German economist Adolph Wagner had a hunch of the process that had begun, and elaborated his 'law of increasing state activity'. Though his reasoning may be doubted, the figures on the rise of the share of the state in the national product confirm his political intuition.[43] Increasingly, the social product, expressed in monetary terms as taxes and state expenditures, was being channelled through one grand standardizing agency, the state. In the context of my argument it is less important to dwell on the political economy of the welfare state, and the focus shall be on another of its key characteristics instead, namely the relation between the individual and the polity that it both presupposes and creates.

The double nature of social policy has long been an issue of political debate. Depending on the historical contexts and the perspectives of the observers, it could either be regarded as an achievement of the working class in struggle or as a paternalistic donation of the state to its subjects. Elements of both a mobilization from below – which, incidentally, also includes charity movements – and of one from above stood, thus, at the origins of social policies. Over time, however, it can almost generally be observed that welfare bureaucracies as well as the professional expertise that goes into their administering of 'cases' get firmly institutionalized. It is this aspect, the solid existence of new knowledge and rules that makes for another important aspect of the organization of modernity.

Certainly, welfare-state measures reduced poverty, lowered inequality and eased the living conditions of many people. This effect is beyond doubt and shall not be questioned here. The form in which this result was achieved was *collectivization*. Both from below and from above, the building of the welfare state was a major collectivizing process. It assigned the members of society to places in well-defined collectives according to age, occupational status, marital status, health status. The status definition was accompanied by expectations about behaviour opportunities and actual behaviour, and an increasing number of welfare bureaucrats and social workers of all kinds were ready to intervene should the reality deviate from the expectations.[45] The effect of the welfare state can without doubt be seen as a standardization of social behaviour and of biographical positions, as, for instance, de Swaan proposes elaborating on Norbert Elias' notion of civilizing process.[46]

The sociological interpretation of this process of collectivization raises a number of questions, a few of which need to be touched on here. The basic idea of social policy was the socialization of risk or, *vice versa*, the enhancement of certainty, for the workers in terms of securing their daily lives, and for the elites in terms of avoiding political unrest. By means of statistical calculation, case assessment and redistributive measures, dangers were transformed into calculable risks, and the event of need was mitigated by, mostly monetary, compensation.[47] Calculation and assessment provided the forms for a rationalization of life that brought standardization about. Following the works of Foucault, these effects on human beings have been described as disciplining impositions. It seems more appropriate, however, to emphasize the interactive nature of such processes, and not to deny *a priori* either the involvement of the human beings in developing the new 'political technologies' or their ability to draw on them actively and interpret and modify them in their application.[48]

Nevertheless the welfare state entailed a drastic transformation of the rules on which individual human beings could draw. Not least, it redefined the social space, its external and internal boundaries, on which assessment of risks was undertaken and over which relative certainties could be spread. The collective and redistributive nature of social policy required the setting of an external boundary. A move away from individualistic reasoning proved not to be very difficult in some European countries, but this move could be undertaken only under the premise that there was some understanding of commonality and community among those over whom the new rules should reign. This is equally evident in the German debates over Bismarck's social policy as in the English ones during the Second World War when 'national unity' was easy to appeal to. Inversely, societies that showed less firm external boundaries and had no solid notion of nation to draw on, such as the

US, continue to 'lag' in welfare-state development and tend to define redistribution, including charity, in more private or groupwise terms.

Internally, the need for assessment required that the space be cleared of ambiguities. Notions such as 'domestic mission' or even 'domestic colonization' point to the desire for the elimination of unsurveillable, uncontrolled spaces. This is where the strong force for standardization and normalization of human activities and expectations stems from; it is inscribed into the political technologies that were used.[49] Stating this is quite different from denying spaces for human interpretation and action, rather it points to the kinds of rules that are interpreted and drawn on. And in a societal perspective it seems to me obvious that, at least temporarily – during the first two post-Second World War decades – an increasing stabilization of social behaviours and an elimination of ambivalences with regard to social positions and expectations were in fact achieved by those means.

This brief discussion of the form and effect of social policy can be underpinned by a look at its major technology. The basic means of social policy was a technology to collectively deal with risk, namely insurance. 'Considered as a technology, insurance is an art of combining various elements of economic and social reality according to a specific set of rules.'[50] Drawing on texts from the 1880s, when societywide insurance arrangements were introduced in France (and elsewhere), François Ewald describes insurance as a way of overcoming individualism while remaining inside a liberal frame of reference:

> It constitutes a mode of association which allows its participants to agree on the rule of justice they will subscribe to. Insurance makes it possible to dream of a contractual justice where an order established by conventions will take the place of a natural order.[51]

Two qualifications need to be added to this apt characterization: first, as Ewald points out, the contract proceeds substantially, of course, via the transformation of risks and destinies into monetary value. As a political technology of conventionalization, it involves, thus, a high degree of formalization and shaping of reality via the translation of a phenomenon into different, more operational terms. Second, at that time, the association was not as free and the contract not as open as it may appear in Ewald's formulation. It was predestined that such arrangements would include exactly defined collectives, such as all working French or all elderly French, to which one either belonged or not. The conventions would be deliberated by the French state in universally applicable terms, that is without variations in the 'rule of justice'. In either respect – adherence to the collective and agreement to the terms – there was less choice than the notion of contractual justice suggests.

This would not be worth pointing out for a historical analysis, because the direction of change was, of course, toward collectivization. But it is significant to note in our context, since the currently ongoing transformations make insurance arrangements look much more like Ewald's characterization than the late-nineteenth-century ones did. Under the impact of deregulation ideas, the definition of the risk collective and the exact terms under which one joins are left much more to individual choice, evidently undermining the idea of societywide collectivization, an issue to which I shall return later (see Chapter 10).

For the moment, it is easy to see that a welfare state, as characterized above, has very little in common with the liberal state as it was envisaged in the mid-nineteenth century. It almost shows more affinities with the 'police state' of the *ancien régime*. What distinguishes it from the latter, though, is its commitment to the idea that the sovereign people are the ultimate arbiter of how, and how intensively, their own activities should be safeguarded and surveilled.

But both the society of late absolutism and the twentieth-century welfare society showed a 'kind of political *a priori*' that allowed the emergence and operation of authorities whose task was 'the calculated supervision, administration and maximization of the forces of each and all'. For such practices Michel Foucault has introduced the notion of *governmentality*. Governmentality refers to technologies that are employed for structuring the space of the practices of domination. It assumes that they can be structured, it is 'programmatic in that it is characterised by an eternal optimism that a domain or a society could be administered better or more effectively, that reality is, in some way or other, programmable.'[52]

What we have seen up to this point appears as a tendency towards an extension of the realm of authoritative practices during the twentieth century. It is not only measurable in terms of the growth of the government share in total revenues but also in increasing and ever more detailed interventions of the state into the social lives of its citizens. This is accompanied by the channelling of the political expressions of these citizens into restricted routes. More commonly, the overpowering weight of the state over the individual used to be emphasized with regard to so-called totalitarian regimes, a concept by which most authors referred to both fascism and (Soviet) socialism. On the one hand, the all-pervasive impact of the collectivist ideology on social lives, and on the other hand an extremely strict and well-guarded conception of representation were seen as pre-empting any open, conflictual understanding of politics. Such analyses have largely been separated from the studies of liberal welfare states – both for valid and for problematic reasons. To define the possibilities of comparison, the final section of this chapter will be devoted to a brief portrait of the modernity of Soviet socialism in the same terms that have been developed before for Western societies.

THE MODERNITY OF SOCIALISM[53]

The debate over the nature of socialism has often split the Western social sciences. True, there were periods in which there was widespread consensus over at least the broad direction of analysis. This was the case, for instance, with the debate about the limits of capitalism and the need for economic planning in the inter-war period, or in the so-called convergence theories of the 1960s that meant to recognize common functional needs in the development of all industrial societies.

In many cases, however, the assumption of radical difference (plus the limited access to first-hand information on socialist societies) has precluded the seeing of similarities between Western and Eastern industrial societies during the twentieth century. This observation holds for approaches that were founded on a strong normative rejection of socialism, such as most theories of totalitarianism after the Second World War, as well as for those that started from some, even if limited, political affinities, such as some strands of the neo-Marxist literature in the 1960s and 1970s. Most such approaches placed socialism unambiguously outside the 'liberal' traditions, turned it into liberal modernity's other.

Instead I shall argue for analysing socialism within the realm of a historical sociology of modernity, though at a very specific, extreme location.[54] The ideas of socialism and of a socialist revolution stand squarely in the history of modernity, of nineteenth-century modernity, its restricted liberal configuration. They are based on central Enlightenment viewpoints such as the possibility of human beings constructing society instead of having to accept it as naturally given, and the directive that such construction should do away with traditions and privileges and should instead be based on reason and knowledge.[55]

The socialist movement and the beginning of the actual building of socialism between the middle of the nineteenth century and 1917 grew from the same roots, and tried to answer the same social questions as the organization of modernity in the West, namely as a collectivist response to the failings of restricted liberal modernity. To put the analysis in the shortest possible form: the social transformations in the West during the first two thirds of the twentieth century and those in the Soviet Union started in the same direction. However, the organization of modernity was much more radical under socialism than in the West, in terms of time-spans, in terms of form (the setting and guarding of strong boundaries),[56] and in terms of substance (the collectivization and the limits to individual autonomy). In all respects, we can see socialism as precisely the epitome of *organized* modernity, rather than as a non-, pre- or even anti-modern social configuration.[57]

In Soviet socialism, social practices became organized substantially around a notion of class (rather than nation *and* class as in Western and Central Europe).[58] They were procedurally based on an interlocking institutional arrangement of state, party and mass organizations, with the single party (rather than competitive parties) at its core. Thus, this extended state apparatus turned into the key organizer of the practices of material allocation. Not least by appropriating what appeared as the high performance of the war-time economies during the First World War and the experience with such uniquely efficient organizations as the famous centralized, hierarchical and state-owned German Post Office, the Soviet economy was soon – and only briefly interrupted by the New Economic Policy – run along the lines of a central plan. The single-party state is also the main organizer of authoritative practices based on a theory of political representation, in which the party is *a priori* defined as the representative of the working class, and the interests of the working class identified with those of the entire people. Thus, a theory of representation, elements of which were present also in Western debates, was developed that was much stronger and more rigid than any Western variant.

This extremely high degree of state organization of social practices was based on a political foundation that can be read as a radical extension of an egalitarian reading of liberal theory. According to such theory nothing should stand between the state as the grand equalizer and victor over old structures of privileges, on the one side, and the single individual, on the other. In the name of control, but also of equality, the socialist state was programmatically an individualizer trying to break all other kinds of social relations, such as cultural identities, religious allegiances or family relations.[59] Since the commonality of class location overarched all other social ties, conflicts could be much more neatly encapsulated – to the degree of extinction – than in the West. Mobilization and association from below were completely replaced by those from above. The (re)building of intra-society relations is what is mainly referred to when the reconstruction of civil society is programmatically claimed now, as some former dissidents in Eastern Europe do.

As radically as socialism appeared to embrace some tenets of modern, revolutionary liberalism, it just as radically rejected the idea of the limitation of the state role as necessary for guaranteeing liberties. It did not subscribe to the liberal distinction of public and private realms, obviously and explicitly not with regard to allocative practices, but neither with regard to other social activities. Where in Western organized modernity a number of private matters had been turned into public policy concerns, socialism blurred the boundaries completely. The parallelism of surveillance and care, of homogenization and reembedding is much more obvious in socialism than in the Western welfare state – especially now that surveillance has been actively destroyed, but practices of care unwillingly dismantled, too. In reaction to the disembedding processes of Western capitalism in the nineteenth century, the socialist movement – but also conservative and rightist political groupings – tried to offer its programme as a new home for the derooted, impoverished individuals. This idea was strongly developed in Soviet socialism and reconstituted in the name of the certainties of scientific socialism. 'The socialist utopia is in fact sustained by a truth which no theory of liberalism narrowly based on the theory of the interdependence of individuals can perceive.'[60]

Ultimately, socialism also exceeded 'actually existing liberalism' by being a more forceful reducer of ambivalence in social life. Building on the certainty of the truth and the strength of the boundaries, the social world was clearly divided into friends and enemies, both internally where Communist parties were striving for power, and externally with a view to the relations between socialist and capitalist countries. Western elites in their fear of communism reciprocated such neat divisions and attempted to establish equally unambivalent perspectives in their societies, especially obviously during the Cold War.

In all these respects, the political class in socialism went in the same direction, but always steps, or rather leaps, beyond the arrangements that were developed in Western societies during the building of organized modernity. Societywide conventionalization and standardization stretched through more social practices and left almost none less regulated; it pervaded them more thoroughly and in more detail, and the safeguarding of conventions was ultimately centralized in one location, not several ones. Saying this, however, does specifically *not* constitute socialism as modernity's co-eval other, embodying the opposite principles, but establishes comparability by focusing on distinctions of degree. If this short characterization is valid on both counts, similarity of direction but difference as to the distance covered, it seems appropriate to regard socialism as the *more organized modernity*, compared to Western societies.

Chapter 7

Discourses on society

Reorganizing the mode of cognitive representation

The changes in the practices of material allocation and of domination, which I portrayed in the two preceding chapters, showed some similar features, namely a movement towards solid forms of organization in which the principle of liberty of the individuals was factually reduced to limited kinds of permissible expression and action. The organization of practices was partly an elite project, partly the result of collective modernizations from below. In both cases it was mainly a reaction to critical results of earlier practices. In socially more neutral terms, that is, hiding the socially uneven participation in them, these responses can schematically be represented as follows: according to the prevailing imaginary signification of modernity, the autonomy of the individual was generally accepted. But it was recognized that the assumption that the interaction of individuals would automatically produce working economies and polities could not be upheld after the right to autonomy had been extended to all human beings inside a given order. Only certain kinds of organization of practices could guarantee such results. To achieve and stabilize such organized practices, individuals will recognize, not least by the experience of crises, that their right to autonomy needs to be restricted and their actions channelled along certain paths.

A cognitive representation of society like that given above would not have been very convincing in, say, 1890 or even 1930, given the degree of organization of allocative and authoritative practices that had been achieved at that time. The objective of this chapter is to show how the mode of cognitive representation of society was also transformed between, broadly, 1890 and 1960. Through many intellectual struggles and by considering a vast variety of alternatives, a mode of representation came to be dominant by about 1960 that 'solved' some problems of the relation of individual and society in ways analogous to those in which related problems were 'solved' by the organization of other social practices.

SOCIAL SCIENCE AS A DISCURSIVE TECHNOLOGY IN THE MODERN STATE

In the preceding chapter I have pointed to an analogy between the 'police state' of the *ancien régime* and the welfare state of the twentieth century in terms of the legitimacy of policy intervention into, and regulation of, the lives of the people. Such interventions and regulations needed not merely to be legitimate, they had also to be adequately possible. To devise means that would secure an adequate behaviour of the population, it was necessary to know about the state of the population and how it would react to decrees and stimuli of various kinds. It can be shown that such 'will to knowledge' as well as the tools of policy knowledge – which may be called discursive technologies – varied historically with changing conceptions of the relation between the individual and the state.

The cameral and policy sciences of the eighteenth century, including the German – descriptive, not numerical – early version of statistics, were mainly an attempt to accumulate as much knowledge as possible about the population as a resource of the principality. The field was broadly ordered according to the concerns of the state, and German academics spent their lives trying to come up with the most appropriate classification of state activities. These sciences decayed with the onset of liberal conceptions of the state. In the Enlightenment tradition of social philosophy, it was assumed that human beings live in a self-regulating, interlocking order as long as they are able or enabled to follow their natural inclinations. Such an understanding decreased the need for policy knowledge, but it stimulated reflections about how such natural harmonies would come about. Such reflections are the basis of the economic and sociological discourses, which emerged from the late eighteenth and early nineteenth century onwards.

I shall return to these discourses shortly. It is important to note, however, that the state apparatus never withered away fully, and that there is some degree of continuity in the production of policy knowledge, a continuity which can be described as the statistical tradition.[1] One of the champions of statistics as the science of society in early nineteenth century was Adolphe Quetelet, who rephrased the use of statistical information in line with the new view of the self-movement of society.

> Given that society was governed naturally by statistical laws, its political government was constrained to an ancillary role. The wise legislator would not try to impose his will on the social system, but would seek first to determine the direction and magnitude of secular social evolution – that is, of the average man.[2]

The discovery of this average man, who was to 'represent' the social totality, stood in the centre of Quetelet's 'social physics', as constructed on the basis of census information via the 'law of large numbers'. Quetelet could not offer much help to those who were interested in variations and distributions; they had to return to the collection of information as exhaustively as possible. When such an interest emerged with regard to the distribution of poverty, researchers turned to the method of the survey, an instrument that was widely used locally between the 1880s and the inter-war period.[3] The appearance of widespread poverty and misery in the context of industrialization, as portrayed earlier (see Chapter 4), was itself seen as a refutation of the optimism of the Enlightenment social philosophies. The need to reconsider social theories in this light also encouraged reflections about tools for gathering information about society.

The period between the end of the nineteenth century and the 1930s witnessed intense debates about a seemingly very specific methodological question. Hidden behind this question, however, was a parallel transformation of a major cognitive and political issue of modernity. The problem was how to generalize observations collected from the study of a part to statements about the whole. Its solution was a number of statistical techniques summarized under the label of representativity. These techniques were developed simultaneously in debates within the statistical profession and about the design of social insurance arrangements. As Alain Desrosières notes, an institutional, a cognitive and a political transformation were closely interlinked, 'the nationalisation of social statistics, . . . the diffusion of the "representative method" and of random selection, and . . . the beginnings of the development of the Welfare State'.[4] The transformation of the conceptually liberal state into a welfare state, or – in broader terms – the transition from liberal to organized modernity, involved the 'substitution of the homogeneous language of statistics and social research for the contradictory language of rights'.[5] Or, as Winston Churchill put it in 1911 on the occasion of the passing of the British National Insurance Act, it meant 'bringing in the magic of average to the aid of the millions'.[6]

From the point that was reached by about 1930, as is well known, the diffusion and application of sampling techniques and survey research increased rapidly. Producers of consumer products, political parties and governments soon recognized the potential of these instruments to estimate the acceptance of what they were offering in terms of products, programmes and policies by the consumers, voters and subjects. It was basically the same approach, then labelled 'empirical social research',[7] which – while initially pursued outside the realms of both statistics proper and sociology proper – was, after the Second World War, integrated into the corps of academic social science. It imposed a very particular notion of the social onto the sociological tradition. Without going into details, I want to raise briefly some implications of such an approach to the observation of society.

Such empirical social research is based on methodological individualism. It thus accepts the one basic tenet of modernity, the primacy of individual autonomy. However, it is a very different kind of individualism from the one assumed in neoclassical economics, where individual rationalities are postulated. In empirical social research, it is from the utterances or behaviours of individuals that social regularities are to be discovered. Neoclassical economics is a post-Enlightenment doctrine – a doctrine of liberal modernity – in the sense that it assumes the self-regulation of a society of reason-endowed (read: rationalistic) individuals. Empirical social research is a postliberal technology – a tool of the organizers of modernity – in the sense that it constructs individuals to make them amenable to policy action. The basic cognitive move that was made was to isolate individuals from each other, ignore whatever social relations they may have and then to counterpose this atomized mass to the state.

> The underlying assumption of social statistics and social research . . . is that singular human beings can be treated as externally related individuals. The State and its individuals are notions from which both social statistics and social research derive.[8]

The ambivalent character of organized modernity is indeed revealed by a look at this instrument. On the one hand, empirical social research accepts individual autonomy. The state does not make an inventory of its resources and then give appropriate orders to its subjects, as the 'police state' of late absolutism did. Rather, policy actors are interested to know what the human beings would do if they were exposed to certain offers, and then they structure their offers in such a way that the outcome is acceptable and order is maintained. The history of such research makes it abundantly clear that the opinions or behaviours of human beings that were initially chosen for inquiry were those that appeared relevant to some policy or commercial actor. While it is true, it is of little relevance to argue that academic social research would later pose all kinds of questions out of other considerations; rather it is important to note that it is impossible to do such research at all without *a priori* considerations. Data can only be treated by imposing some sort of classificatory order on them that does not emerge from the data themselves. As Desrosières points out, all the technical refinements that have been added to quantitative-statistical research between 1930 and the present do not change the basic problem; rather the persistence of such efforts evokes 'the dream of lifting oneself up literally by one's bootstraps from the ground'.[9]

If this is the case, though, then the application of these techniques entails as much the creation of regularities and classes of individuals as it entails their discovery. The important question, then, is: what kinds of entities are constructed so as to make them 'hold together'? The answer to this question leads us back, on the one hand, to the historical studies of conventionalizations, such as socio-professional ones and socioeconomic ones like those on employment and unemployment (as referred to in Chapter 5). On the other hand, we are directed to the structuring interest of the strategic commissioners of research. Then we see how the interest of companies may construct the consumer of standardized goods; the interest of parties may construct the voter; and the interest of governments may construct the usually passive subject who occasionally falls into a state of discontent. These images of human being as consumer, voter and subject are versions of the promise of human beings as the producers of their means, the citizens of their polity and the interpreters of their own lives that liberal modernity hailed. However, they are markedly reduced compared to the original promise.

Taken together, these practices of representation share in producing, and help to reproduce, the order of organized modernity. They construct the image of the institutions of organized modernity and, thus, help to portray them as part of a natural order that need not and cannot be argued about and justified every time its practices are enacted. They also proliferate a view on the limited scope of action more generally, by portraying consumer choice and voter choice as the only rational ways of acting within such orders of practices. In my view, they do not, though, as critics of such research during the 1960s have maintained, quite simply turn human beings into stimulus-dependent, predetermined statistical objects.[10] It seems more appropriate to understand the development of these technologies as arising from a diffuse fear of not knowing what 'the masses' might do rather than from the conception that the masses were incapable of action. The underlying perspective first assumes that one knows too little about how human beings could act, and only in a second step does it try to channel what they might do into controllable paths. Because action threatened to be irregular and disrupting, means were needed to make it, if at all possible, more regular and constant. The commercial and policy elites in a regulatory and interventionist state under full inclusion of the masses saw it as one of their major problems that they had to handle a great number of diverse human beings as subjects. It is exactly this problem perception that is at the root of the breakthrough of statistics and empirical social research as a major instrument of social representation.

EUROPEAN SOCIAL THEORY AND AMERICAN PRAGMATISM: TOWARD A SOCIOLOGY OF MODERNITY

Up to this point, I have developed my argument from a focus on the statistical tradition as one cognitive element that fed into the mode of representation of society that co-emerged with organized modernity. However, the claim on behalf of statistics to become – on its own – the science of modern society was never fully accepted anywhere. The picture becomes more complete only if the view is broadened, and those discourses for which this claim had more legitimately been voiced are included. By the turn of the century, the social sciences – whether under the label of sociology or other names – had taken significant steps towards being accepted as a major interpreter of modernity by the intellectual and political elites.[11]

When in 1920 Leopold von Wiese exclaimed that other academics should work together with sociologists 'to understand and solve the giant enigma which is society',[12] he addressed widely-held expectations which had built up over the preceding three decades now known as the 'classical era' of sociology. In politico-intellectual terms, classical sociologists had started from liberal assumptions, had recognized that societal developments had superseded classical liberalism, but insisted that revisions had to be made in the continuity of that political tradition. They were well aware of the contemporary constellation of a major political restructuring without a clear objective or guiding vision, and they turned this, even if sometimes indirectly, into their major theme. Unable to stick to the idea of a quasi-automatic regulation of social conflicts, but similarly unwilling to move completely away from the tenets of bourgeois liberalism, they devoted their analytical efforts to the search for those phenomena which might provide for a sustainable development of society.[13] Theories of 'organic solidarity' and the relation of religion and morality as in Durkheim, of forms of legitimate domination and 'charisma' in Weber, of the political class and the 'circulation of elites' in Pareto were the products of such searches.

From the turn of the century onwards, however, and increasingly through the inter-war years, such kinds of sociological reappraisals of the liberal tradition lost their persuasiveness. In the larger crisis of the liberal utopia, which I tried to describe earlier (see Chapter 4), both the intelligibility of society by the classical sociological means and the manageability of social order by drawing conclusions from such means were increasingly doubted. The devolution and discontinuity of sociological thought in Europe have also to be seen in this political context – beyond valid observations on academic-institutional inertias and resistances.[14]

One might say the sociological discourse fell apart. On one side, its considerations on a theory of action were taken up by, often highly voluntarist, philosophies of life and the deed. On the other side, what was later to be called empirical social research developed on the fringes or outside academia, or in those European intellectual contexts in which the classical sociological orientation had not prevailed: in the Netherlands as sociography, in Austria in connection with the 'scientific world-view' of neo-positivism.

In Paul F. Lazarsfeld's conception this new sociological approach was initially application-oriented research with a clear orientation to Viennese social democracy in local power positions; later, in American exile, contractor-oriented research without explicit normative preconceptions. His politico-intellectual journey from Austro-marxism and the Research Unit on Economic Psychology at Vienna University to the radio research projects and the Bureau of Applied Social Research at Columbia University is paradigmatic for the interlinked cognitive and political transformations of the period.[15] From the elaboration of new research methods for a political project, that is, the idea of a joint advance of knowledge about, and the condition of, the world, he turned to refining the same methods to sell them to any strategic actor who had both interest in the knowledge and the ability to pay for it. It appears as if even Lazarsfeld, the dynamic methodologist and research organizer, saw these changes in his own life not without regret and a feeling of loss. Discussing the emancipatory claims of critical theorists, he remarked in 1941, apparently referring to himself: 'Some have hit upon the solution of making their social interests their private avocation, and keeping that separate from their research procedures, hoping that one day in the future the two will again merge.'[16]

I want to argue that the falling apart of the sociological discourse into these two parts was related to the construction of organized modernity – and to the specific way in which modernity was temporarily organized in Europe, namely as fascism and its relatives. First, it must be noted that both parts of the broken discourse could well flourish under those regimes. Philosophies of the deed underpinned the idea of a strong man and his will and power to rejuvenate the nation. Empirical social research was often specifically organized to acquire strategically useful knowledge about the state of the population. But both parts flourished only as parts. Taken together, counterfactually, they would have formed an empirically supported social theory of collective action that could have been inscribed into a normative theory of democracy.

Second, it can be argued that at least elements of such latter discourse existed in the social context of the variant of modernity that had perpetually remained less organized, namely the US. This 'underestimated alternative' is pragmatism, if we link the political philosophy of John Dewey with the social theory of George Herbert Mead and the empirical sociology of the Chicago School.[17] Here a body of theoretical and empirical knowledge was elaborated which emphasized the human ability to create and recreate one's own life individually and collectively, but which did not fall into voluntarism and instead studied carefully the enabling and constraining conditions under which such creative action occurred.

That the development and acceptance of such a kind of social knowledge was more easily possible in the US than elsewhere should not be surprising. The ubiquitious, if sometimes latent, dichotomy of the individual and the collective is characteristic of the discourse of modernity in general. In continental Europe, however, the collective tended to take the form of a reason-endowed state, not least because the emancipatory movements ran against the states of the *ancien régime*, the existence of which defined the discursive space of modern reasoning. In the US, in contrast, the founding controversy was rather between individualist liberalism and civic republicanism. The turn away from liberalism, which the society of the US experienced like the European ones in response to the social transformations at the end of the century, thus took the form of a modified renewal of the republican tradition. Dewey's political writings can be seen as an example of this turn, but as in Europe the intellectual turn went beyond strictly political reasoning, including social theory and sociological research efforts, among other elements.

Nevertheless, as even sympathetic readers admit, despite its merits, pragmatism did not in any of its variants become the dominant discourse of American society. Its broader social and political theory remained undeveloped and even its continuation within sociology, symbolic interactionism, no longer provided a strong theoretical impetus after the Second World War, and rather moved to the periphery of the discipline.[18] In terms of the discipline, the shift of hegemony was from the Chicago School in the 1920s and 1930s to Lazarsfeld's Columbia School in the following decades to social policy research in the 1960s. These shifting hegemonies went along with the move of the centre of societal attention from local problems to issues of nationwide markets to those of federal policy, 'a change in the structure of responsibility from private and local to public and national'.[19]

It is here, I think, that the clue to the alleged 'underestimation' of the pragmatist alternative can be found and the deficiencies of this corpus of ideas become evident. If it was the case that social practices were increasingly organized with nationwide extension, then the assets of pragmatism could quickly turn into liabilities, at least in the view of strategic decision-makers – but even beyond their specific knowledge interest.[20] If the focus of authoritative practices shifted to the federation – as during the New Deal and, later, the Great Society – then Dewey's views on the public communicative basis of political deliberation could well look superseded. The theorizing on intersubjectivity and creativity, as fruitful as it generally may have appeared, would be labelled 'micro-sociological' and would be relegated to a corner of the discipline. And research on urban social restructuring touched a, while not irrelevant, very limited part of policy problems, most of which had been redesigned in national terms.

The divide between continental European and North American academics and intellectuals can then be reconsidered. The former were used to thinking in terms of entire societies organized in nation-states and they tried to continue to do so. The cognitive problem which classical sociology failed to solve was to relate the actions of individuals and groups to the level of state-societies, to fully grasp the nature of nationwide organized practices. This is where their project fell apart. The pragmatists, in contrast, have promoted the sounder theorizing, not least because they were able to keep philosophy, social theory and social research together. In as far as they constituted an American alternative, the price to be paid was not posing the problem at all on that level where the Europeans failed.

Ultimately, neither classical European sociology, basically abandoned by the 1920s, nor pragmatist sociology, surviving as a specialty on the periphery of the discipline, became the accepted social discourse of organized modernity. The 'modernization' of the social sciences went a third way, bypassing the problems of either tradition.

COGNITIVE MASTERY OF SOCIETY: SOCIAL SCIENCE MODERNIZED

Classical European sociology was not entirely abandoned. In the US, Talcott Parsons tried to reappropriate the heritage by showing that there were elements in the works of each of the 'classical' authors which did in fact converge. Taken together, they would provide a framework for a social theory that could deal with entire social formations while at the same time being able to account for the rationales of human action. Over time, Parsons developed these ideas into a theory of modern societies as systems, differentiated into functionally related subsystems whose combined workings would safeguard system integration. Empirical social research of increasingly sophisticated methodology resided and flourished somewhat uncomfortably by the side of this grand approach.

Robert Merton's proposal to concentrate on 'middle-range theories' appeared to offer a synthesis between Parsons' and Lazarsfeld's, each in their own way appealing, approaches. Merton argued that the general theory of the social system could impossibly be either supported or falsified by empirical studies. By focusing on institutional subsets of a social system, however, elements of it could be empirically studied applying Lazarsfeldian technology. This synthesis satisfied the interests of both methodologists and theorists to a satisfactory degree, and it underpinned the emergent hegemony in American sociology, a hegemony that quickly extended over the Western world.[21]

Modern sociology, then, by which I mean the dominant approaches during the 'second breakthrough'[22] of this discipline in the 1960s, was basically an incoherent fusion of quantitative-empirical techniques, functionalist and systems theoretical reasoning and an evolutionary social theory of modernization. This peculiar mixture was duplicated in economics where the neoclassical discourse, econometrics *cum* empirical economic research and economic theories of growth lived together in an equally unfounded alliance.[23]

The merits of these syntheses of theoretical discourses and empirical toolkits lay more in enhancing the development of the profession than in clarifying substantive issues. They rather glossed over the theoretical problems that had doomed classical sociology and neoclassical economics to failure earlier in the century. James Coleman, to cite a witness beyond doubt, recently diagnosed a profound inconsistency in sociological practice:

> Concurrently with the emerging dominance in sociology of functional theory at the level of the collectivity came a movement of empirical research that led precisely in the opposite direction. . . . The main body of empirical research was abandoning analysis of the functioning of collectivities to concentrate on the analysis of the behavior of individuals.[24]

Not least from such glaring inconsistencies one may gather that, rather than being a mere response to functional requirements of organized modernity, the shape of the discourses of social science must also be understood in terms of intellectual traditions and institutional locations, an issue I will not dwell on here.[25] It shall just be noted that, by the 1960s, modernized social science had set firm boundaries around itself in organizational as well as in intellectual terms. Disciplines were established at academic institutions, and thus relatively clear criteria on which to judge whether a contribution came from inside the community or not were introduced.

The demarcation of boundaries has cognitive consequences. Knowledge is compartmentalized, and the kind and scope of questions that may be legitimately asked is reduced, with partly drastic effects. The understanding of human action, for instance, is without doubt a key issue for all social science. While an extended debate goes on in philosophy, the social sciences – first economics and then, following the model, sociology – reduced the notion of action to a rationalistic one, which seemed to fit their, equally limited, understanding of modernity.[26] Or the question was even completely relegated from the professional concern, for reasons of methodology. Empirical research, Coleman agrees, is 'lacking a theory of action, replacing "action" with "behavior" and eliminating any recourse to purpose or intention in its causal explanations'.[27]

The demarcation of boundaries also has political consequences with regard to the location and self-understanding of the social scientist in society. By the end of the nineteenth century, as a joint product of the development of the research-oriented university and of the nominally liberal state, intellectual producers had gained some degree of autonomy from immediate state concerns.

Though conditions varied highly between nations, this was broadly the context in which the birth of the universalist 'intellectual' became possible.[28] By the 1960s, the institutional position had become rather more secure in formal terms. But the self-understanding of, at least, the social scientists had begun to change. Increasingly, they opted for putting their allegedly mature knowledge to direct use in society.

If the beginnings of such a new knowledge-policy connection can be traced to the inter-war period, and occasionally earlier, its breakthrough went hand in hand with the great expansion of state activities that has come to be called the Keynesian, or interventionist, welfare state after the Second World War. It entailed outright discourse coalitions for modernization between social scientists and reform-oriented policy-makers and, as such, propagated a profound transformation of the role of the intellectual, from distant and critical observer to activist policy designer and technician.[29] This transformation is based on a conceptualization of the planning of societal development by a scientifically informed elite. In Europe this idea is, in modern times, rooted in humanist reformism and social democracy, but it is obviously ambivalent. There is only a small step from the conception that a reformist elite may act as a transmission belt for the needs of the masses, needs which become known to the elites through social research – a conception which means to retain the emancipatory intention of left-wing politics through 'modernization' – to the idea of ruling elites organized in large-scale bureaucratic apparatuses using knowledge about mass behaviour and about the average citizen to improve control and secure domination.

Either way, this conception rested on fairly strong assumptions about both the state and social science as well as about the entire social formation in which both were embedded. The state had to be regarded as unitary, coherent and capable of action; social science had to be seen as methodologically and epistemologically secure, capable of providing good, objective knowledge; society had to be considered as somehow organized, as characterized by a rather fixed, identifiable structure.

Especially during the 1960s, this interaction acquired features of an outright 'rationalistic revolution'. Western societies witnessed the introduction of a wide array of new governmental technologies. Some of these technologies were based on surveying activities such as economic and social indicators research or opinion research. The data that were produced could be treated according to behavioural assumptions or even more or less elaborated theories of economic development or modernization. Then, steering intervention into the social processes could be effected with a view to harmonization of developments. The proto-typical example is the linkage between Keynesian theory, economic surveys and demand management policies.

Other technologies were more strictly governmental tools, sometimes with fancy technocratic names such as Planning, Programming and Budgeting Systems (PPBS), Programme Analysis Review (PAR) and cost-benefit analysis, or with ambitious labels such as the policy sciences. They all had in common the fact that they provided some formal, often mathematical-quantitative, instrument to measure policy interventions according to their efficiency on the societal segment onto which they were applied.

This period was marked by, as a French research administrator said, a pronounced 'optimism with regard to the completion of the cognitive mastery of society'.[30] And there was no doubt that the way towards cognitive mastery was pursued at the service of the great benefactor, the welfare state, that is, to enhance political mastery of society.[31] In the policy perspective that became dominant throughout much of the social sciences during the 1960s and 1970s, 'the self-perception of society takes the form of a catalogue of problems of government.'[32]

THE TWIN POLITICAL THEORIES OF ADVANCED INDUSTRIAL SOCIETY

Up to this point, this brief characterization of the basic cognitive structure of modernized social science and of the way its practitioners related to state and society has only alluded to the substantive theory of the social order that this kind of social science produced. True, many social scientists worked basically on either specific theoretical or empirical issues with their own, particular justification. Others went into the activity of policy expertise without reflecting much on the broader context of such service. Still, a theory of 'modern' society can be identified that was at the back of such practices. At a closer look, there were indeed two such theories, or two variants of one, of advanced industrial society or 'postindustrial society', an affirmative and a critical one. The basic outlines of these theories are well known, not least because they continue to influence sociological debates. I shall thus not go to great lengths in portraying them, but rather focus on the image of modernity that they provide.

The affirmative variant of this theorizing has generally become known as 'modernization theory'.[33] Modernization theory is a unique combination of an empirical, behaviouralist research approach which produces mass data about individuals' orientations and behaviours; of an evolutionary theory which interprets these data on the basis of assumptions about trends of change; and of a systemic social theory which develops arguments about the factual coherence of mass behaviours and the conditions for attaining such coherence, including the change of social conditions through interventions from a steering position.

The theory works with a foundational distinction between traditional and modern societies. The process of movement from the one to the other state is called development. Once this process is started, it entails modernization and cannot but lead to a modern society, even if delays are possible for various reasons. It is only at the stage of modern society that a new coherence is reached. Then, organism, personality, social and cultural system, as systems of action, interrelate harmonically as much as the subsystems of the social system do, such as the market economy, the democratic polity in the nation-state and autonomous science. The autonomy of science and its consequences, namely technical innovation, provide for the dynamic which, among social systems, is specific to modern society. It is a dynamic inside the system, though, which does not lead to new incoherence.

In more specific terms, works inside the modernization theorem have shown how such coherence is achieved. It did not escape these observers that, to put the issue in my terms, the imaginary signification of modernity as such was neither coherent nor provided for stability. By way of an example, we may take a brief look at the interpretation of authoritative practices in the modernization perspective. In an influential study, Gabriel Almond and Sidney Verba developed the concept of civic culture and portrayed it as a kind of political ideal of organized modernity. On the basis of their findings, as they maintain, the authors dissociate themselves from an activist, participatory ideal of the citizen. Not only do they grant, as did all liberal theory, that citizens might be interested in other things than politics, they also emphasize that a certain degree of passivity and lack of involvement is functionally necessary to secure democratic processes.[34] This is typical of civic culture.

They agree that civic culture is not truly modern, but is drawing on common traditions in a society. They exempt the history of liberal modernity from the long-lasting violations of its own principles and make 'moderated' change, including restrictions to participation, a legitimate objective. Only 'with this civic culture already consolidated, the working classes could enter into politics and, in a process of trial and error, find the language in which to couch their demands and the means to make them effective.'[35] As a desirable result they find that the most highly developed civic cultures have tended to become 'homogeneous'; 'the policy differences have tended to become less sharp, and there is a larger common body of agreement.'[36] Thus what has been described above as a thinning out of the ideal of citizenship is reinterpreted as the progress of political modernity.[37]

The height of this theoretical development had been reached when Talcott Parsons had fully elaborated his systemic account of societies, when David Easton had followed him with similar ambition for the analysis of 'the political system', when Niklas Luhmann and others had followed suit in other countries, and when Karl Deutsch had added cybernetic reasoning to these concepts. These theories envisaged a 'fit' between societal requirements and individual strivings that was seen as characteristic of the modern order and, even if it was not yet attained everywhere, could be achieved if knowledge and politics used their potentials fully.[38]

These types of social theorizing focused on the organized and predictably analysable character of modern society. Starting out from the assumption of the basic overall coherence of society, they identified related substructures or subsystems in it, each of which would have its own logics or mode of operation. The activities of individuals were tied into these social phenomena via behaviour-guiding norms and the learning of these norms or, in some variants, via structural constraints. These theories emphasized the organized, relatively closed nature of overall social relations but tended to see this rather as an achievement.

Parallel to this theorizing an alternative approach was developed which regarded basically the same phenomenon, as I shall argue, namely the closure of modernity, as a threat and a loss.

By now, one can distinguish three consecutive forms which this alternative interpretation took. As its first expression we may regard the writings of the Frankfurt School in exile, specifically those by Theodor W. Adorno, Max Horkheimer and Erich Fromm, but also the contemporaneous works by writers as diverse as Hannah Arendt or José Ortega y Gasset. All these analyses were clearly shaped by the experience that capitalist democracies could turn into what was then called authoritarianism or totalitarianism. There was a strong dose of Marxist reasoning in the Frankfurt contributions, so that the capitalist destruction of social relations was seen as a major cause of these developments. But generally the entire debate went beyond a critique of capitalism and pointed to the emergence of a mass society which impeded the upholding of bourgeois ideals of self-realization and subjected individuals to life as 'cogs in the machine'.

In the 1960s and 1970s, in turn, the second strand of this debate stood, politically, under the impact of the resurgence and stabilization of capitalist democracy and tried to meet, intellectually, the challenge of a theory that claimed to explain this resurgence and stability, namely modernization theory. It is characteristic of this strand that it tended to accept the systemic cast of mainstream theorizing but reoriented it by merging it with Marxist argumentative forms. Thus, subsystems would not, or would only temporarily, be functionally related, rather their workings stood in fundamental contradictions which sooner or later would reassert themselves and lead into open crises. The third, most recent strand in this tradition is formed by some of the poststructuralist writings, in which the structural character of language and discourse and their linkage to power is invoked as a limit and constraint to the action of living human beings.

The common aspect of these critical debates that is most important for my argument here can be read out of a quotation from the author who appears to straddle all three strands of critical thought, Herbert Marcuse. In *One-Dimensional Man* he emphatically denounces 'the closing of the political universe' and 'the closing of the universe of discourse' in advanced industrial society. In his view, the 'containment of social change is perhaps the most singular achievement of advanced industrial society.'[39]

This was a view with which quite a number of modernization theorists would have agreed. The similarity between both images, the affirmative and the critical one, has been described for the US context as early as 1972 as follows:

> The early theories of post-industrial society postulated a static social order marvelously resistant to change. . . . So pervasive was this view that it was shared by structuralists and behaviorists alike, by those who emphasized 'mass society' and those who spoke of 'pluralism', by those who cricized American society from the left and by those who celebrated it from the centre.[40]

Some differences notwithstanding, most of these theories singled out subsystems as effectively activity-ruling structures. Often, they did nothing else but use the distinction of state, economy and society that was one of the corner-stones of societal self-understanding since the Enlightenment. The differentiation of social entities into those relatively autonomous subspheres is an essential element of liberal thinking. And until the present day, this distinction informs most theorizing on society like the neofunctionalist differentiation theories, structuralist or functionalist Marxism, and the Habermasian counterposition of colonizing social systems with an asystemical life-world.

But what has happened conceptually to these subspheres over time? Once, in liberal political philosophy, they were a normative proposal to secure spheres of freedom for the individual in society. Then, in the grand critiques of modernity, they were identified as emerging institutional structures disciplining the individual and endangering the project of modernity. Ultimately, in modern social science, they became reified as some supra-human phenomena to which human beings are subjected, without any action or choice. This is to say that in both of these images of an organized society any conceivable notion of liberal-democratic capitalism is further modified close to being unrecognizable. The notion of autonomous spheres of free human action is abandoned in both major respects: internally, these spheres were not composed of freely competing individuals but of large-scale organizations; and they would not be autonomous either but their workings would, in the affirmative variants, lead to a systemically required convergence of knowledge, production and governance to form a coherent society. In the critical alternatives, the workings of the subspheres would either increase systemic contradiction until the breakdown of the system or, in a more sceptical vein, would further enhance the reification of oppressive superhuman structures and their dominance in society, the 'dark side' of the Enlightenment.

Both types of theorizing shared observations about some basic features of the advanced industrial societies of the 1950s and 1960s: unprecedented growth of production and consumption, that is, a strong dynamic in certain social practices, went along with the relative tranquillity and stability of authoritative practices, while at the same time very limited formal restrictions were imposed on free political expression compared to other times and places. Their core problematic was to explain the co-existence of these features as a specific social configuration. It must have been the extraordinary conjuncture of dynamics, stability and nominal liberty that led them to assume a supra-historical process at work that had arrived at a consolidated path, namely of 'modernization', or even reached its end.

What was largely neglected, though, was that this social configuration had been constructed over intense struggles not so long ago and that its closure was not as complete as they thought. Though the total images prevailed in intellectual discourse, it would be wrong to say that there were no social conflicts. There were quite some – not least, the workers' struggles, in which even the spectre of communism appeared and was used to help contain the political debate. But for the enlightened parts of the elites – the technocrats in the political class as much as the so-called critical intellectuals in the cultural elites – the conflicts could rather easily be embedded in a clear-cut – and basically working – perception of the organization of society. Thus, they were not serious threats, rather, they could be kept discursively under control.

The closure could not be perfect on a terrain of modernity where a commitment to individual autonomy was still maintained. This commitment would preclude habitualized practices turning into commanded orders. While the organization of modernity had made it difficult to break into dominated product markets or into established-party competition, it was not entirely impossible, either. And also, maybe most clearly, not even a forcefully propagated order of representation could turn human beings completely into 'cogs in the machine'. The cultural-intellectual field was not fully closed either.

Still, the analysis of the organization of allocative and authoritative practices (as portrayed in Chapters 5 and 6) shows that the representation of society in these discourses was not completely flawed. With regard to the degree and form of the organization of human practices – and in this sense only – one may speak of a relative closure of modernity. Social practices were organized so that they moderately cohered on the level of national society and formed interlinking sets of institutional rules. At the same time, a discursive image of these interlinking practices was developed that emphasized their coherence and predicted their long-term stability by associating them with a solid developmental perspective. The closure of modernity, the containment of the effectiveness of its imaginary, did occur historically, though it did not prove to be stable over the long run.

At this point, a summary characterization of the order of organized modernity and the basic features of its construction is possible. The achievements of organized modernity were to transform the disembedding and uncertainties of the late nineteenth century into a new coherence of practices and orientations. Nation, class and state were the main conceptual ingredients to this achievement, which provided the substance for the building of collective identities and the setting of boundaries. They were materials that were all at hand, historically, to those who participated in building organized modernity. But they obviously did not cohere naturally. It took half a century of political struggles and of unprecedented violence and oppression to form a social configuration in Western Europe that seemed not only to satisfy major parts of its members but also to develop a dynamic of its own. This was what came to be called the 'long prosperity' or the 'Golden Age of capitalism'; and in some countries, such as Italy and (West) Germany, even the term 'miracle' was used.

Organized modernity was characterized by the integration of all individuals inside certain boundaries into comprehensively organized practices. No definite places in society were ascribed to individual human beings according to pre-given criteria. Social mobility existed and was part of the liberties this society offered. But it was the linkage of such liberties with the organization of practices that provided this social configuration with the assets that may explain its relative stability and 'success' in terms of the, at least tacit, consent of most of its members. Organization meant that each individual was 'offered' a materially secure place,[41] something which had never been the case since the breakthrough of capitalism and was fully achieved only when the Keynesian commitment to full employment became government policy, in some countries as late as the 1960s. It also meant that human beings managed to structure the fields of their action in such a way – by means of formalization, conventionalization and routinization, that is, by the assumption of pre-given 'agreements' about the possible paths of action – that their reach could be widely extended. Thus, new areas of activity were opened and a dynamic set free to cover these areas.

The spatial metaphor of 'covering areas' appropriately highlights both the dynamics of movement and the predictability of direction and scope. In all the kinds of practices analysed here – practices of allocation, domination and signification – the opening of a space by new techniques and its coverage by the application of these techniques was a common image during the 1950s and 1960s, and partly already during the 1930s. A country would be internally colonized by infrastructural means such as electricity networks or highways; durable comsumer goods would be produced and sold until saturation rates – normally at about 100 per cent – were reached; 'wars' were led for the elimination of poverty; and social science would close the last 'knowledge gaps' about society.

This configuration achieved a certain coherence, or closure, at about 1960, in terms of the various institutions, their specific embodiments of collective agency, their interlinkages, and their respective reaches. It appeared as a naturally 'interlocking order'. The 'Keynesian welfare state' was then successfully operating on a national basis, having the population fully integrated and well organized in trade unions and as mass-party voters.[42] It was based on a mass-consumption mode of economic organization, large-scale technological systems connecting all members of society, and regularly recurring mass expressions of political loyalty to the elites. It had also developed a particular kind of reflective self-understanding as conveyed in its social science.

To understand the further occurrences, it is important to recall that this social configuration did not halt or break the dynamics of modernity, but channelled it into historically moderately controllable avenues. To continue on the imagery employed before, as soon as the newly opened spaces are filled, unsettling movements are likely to recur. These movements would touch exactly the boundaries which were established to provide certainty and stability. At that point, the limits to this model proved to be inherent in its construction.

Part IV

The second crisis of modernity

Chapter 8

Pluralization of practices

The crisis of organized modernity

DE-CONVENTIONALIZATION AND THE DEMISE OF ORGANIZED MODERNITY

The preceding portrait of organized modernity could draw on a fairly consolidated knowledge in various fields of the social sciences, even if the reports had to be read with a sociology of knowledge perspective in mind. My main objective was to propose a conceptual perspective that allows an understanding of the construction of social configurations from the interdependent actions of human beings and from the habitualization of forms of action. On the basis of the portrait of organized modernity that has emerged, the task of the remainder of this book is to use such a perspective for grasping the demise of that configuration and to understand the present condition of modernity.

In terms of a major social restructuring, this means trying to advance an understanding of a process which is still very much under way. As far as I can see, nobody can justly claim to have a firm cognitive grip on the present social transformations. The following chapters, thus, should be considered less as an offer for a full explanation, but rather as a proposal of how one can read and interpret current changes in social practices. Much of what follows, then, are also questions for further research and proposals of how to formulate key issues of the modern condition.

In this chapter, I shall try to characterize what I essentially regard as the break-up of the order of organized modernity, analysed in terms of changes of major allocative and authoritative practices. The following chapter is devoted to disorientations regarding the cognitive representation of modernity. While it had seemed possible to provide coherent images of organized modernity, the demise of organized practices has led to an increased awareness of the difficulties of any science of society. One element of the discourse on postmodernity is, of course, exactly the doubt about the very possibility of any cognitive representation of society. At the end of this part, in Chapter 10, I shall return to the issue of the formation of self and social identity, under conditions after the end of organized modernity.

If the building of organized modernity could be analysed in terms of the conventionalization of social practices within set boundaries, much of the more recent changes entail the erosion of boundaries and processes of de-conventionalization. With regard to allocative practices, the coherence of the institutions of organized modernity broke down because the reach of the practices was increasingly extended beyond the controlled boundaries of the national society. The conventionalized practices of domination and signification were upset, partly because their misfit with the allocative practices was experienced as a decreasing performance of these institutions, and partly because the constraining aspects of their own conventions were recognized and fought against.

All of this happened in a context of the erosion of the substantive bases of collective identities. Working-class and national identification had been building blocks for organized modernity. But over time, their relevance appears to have declined, since such boundaries seemed much less important after the full inclusion of the workers into modernity had been achieved and could be materially underpinned. However, the issue of boundaries and identities becomes important again when collective reorientations seem necessary. At that point, the cognitive resources to sustain them, the material from which they were built, may well prove to be exhausted.

With very few exceptions, current analyses of the organization of sets of social practices stress the breaking up of established rules. In some cases, a terminology is chosen that leads to positive associations. Then there may be talk of flexibilization and pluralization. In others, when the emphasis is on disorganization, instability or fragmentation, negative connotations prevail. Regardless of normative aspects, I think many of these analyses can be read as the identification of the upsetting of practice-orienting conventionalizations, or even the breakdown of orders of conventions.

That such processes occur throughout all major fields of social practices should allow us to speak of a crisis of the contemporary social formation, the second crisis of modernity. The main task of the following three chapters is to show what shape this crisis takes. The guiding question is: which of the conventionalizations do still hold, or are even reinforced, and which are breaking up or are reshaped? By a differentiated analysis it should be possible to arrive at the identification of at least the outlines of a new societal configuration.

CHANGES IN THE MODE OF CONTROL: THE RESTRUCTURING OF ALLOCATIVE PRACTICES

The economic crisis of 1974–5, which entailed a decline in real gross national product in most Western countries for the first time in three decades, was the ultimate and unmistakable sign that '*les trente glorieuses*'[1] had come to an end. From the late 1960s onwards, other indications had appeared, but they had either been weaker or limited to only a few countries: increased industrial action and the breakdown of 'concerted action' between employers, unions and government, slackening productivity growth, rising inflation rates, international imbalances with the abandoning of the dollar convertibility into gold and the switch to floating currency exchange rates.[2] By the second half of the 1970s, all these signs added up to a general awareness of the end of an economic era.

The changes in allocative practices, which started at the turn of the 1960s and are still going on, can be described as the breaking of many of the social conventions that had characterized the model of organized modernity. They entail the

> disappearance of the socioeconomic regularities, the reconsideration of the contours of most post-war organizational forms, the bursting of the representations and the expectations and, thus, a major uncertainty as to the looks into the future, the tearing up of solidarities and of constituted interests, etc.[3]

In my brief presentation I shall focus on four major aspects: the 'agreement' to set the terms of industrial relations on the national level was broken; the Keynesian consensus to develop a national consumption-based economy eroded; the organizational rules that fixed and secured position and task for each actor were reshaped; and technical innovations whose applications tended to break existing conventions were no longer upheld.

(a) It was a common feature of many Western economies during the 1950s and 1960s that unemployment tended to decrease, that the wage share in total national income tended to rise, and that profitability of capital diminished. By the early 1970s, this constellation had given rise to an explanation of economic stagnation from the 'lack of profitable production opportunities' due to the wage level or, in other words, from the 'full employment profit squeeze'.[4] The basic idea was that the lack of qualified labour would strengthen the bargaining power of the unions to such an extent that, even if there were still opportunities for market expansion, the return would be 'squeezed' between wage costs on the one side, and market limits to pricing on the other, so that companies would be hesitant to invest. The important point to mark here is that this explanation may apply only under conditions of economies that are *closed* in the sense of restricting migration of labour, or outflow of capital towards labour. It is more likely under *organized* conditions in the sense of successful coalition-building on the part of labour, so that a homogenous labour market exists. Both conditions are generally fulfilled much less now than they were at the beginning of the 1970s.

Domestically, the emergence of a dual labour market can be observed. Due to changes in labour law, (legal or illegal) immigration and/or emerging long-term unemployment after years of economic stagnation, a sizeable part of the working population benefits only in parts, or not at all, from the wage rigidity and fringe regulations that had been introduced during organized modernity. Viewed from the employers' side, the 'choice' between terms of employment reintroduces flexibility. It is a change of conventions whose potential importance far exceeds the share of the less protected segment in the overall labour market: 'the emergence of a fringe of workers outside the central safety-net threatened the comprehensiveness of the system which had been a hallmark of the golden age.'[5]

(b) Furthermore, the strengthening of the bargaining power of the domestic work force during the long boom provided an incentive for companies to internationalize their production.[6] Under relatively liberal terms of world market trade, it was possible to produce in 'newly industrializing countries' (NICs) and import the commodities to the home countries. During the 'golden age' already, world trade had risen again more strongly than production, producing a rapid internationalization of the economies marked by high increases of import penetration rates. From the 1970s onwards, however, this trend turned against some sectors in the industrial countries, which reacted with some protectionist measures even though there was an economists' consensus that such policies needed to be avoided. At the same time, the demise of a manipulable international monetary arrangement such as the Bretton Woods agreement, together with the emergence of speculative currency markets, exposed all countries, particularly smaller ones, more unguardedly to occurrences on the world market. Evidently, such internationalization strongly affected the ability to regulate an economy through national demand management and strategic use of the exchange rate mechanism.

Beginning already after the Second World War, but accelerating after the crisis of the 1970s, one may speak of a 'gradual disappearance of the coherence of national productive systems'.[7] In terms of agency, this is to say that there is no 'fit' any longer between an extended social phenomenon, namely the spatial extension of exchange structures, and a relevant collective actor which would want to observe, control and direct this social phenomenon, namely the state on its territory.[8]

The relevance of the problematic is indicated by the fact that those 'intellectual technologies'[9] that were to re-present the state of the national economy in the offices of the ministries of finance and economic affairs did not work any longer: concepts like the money supply, the foreign balances or the Phillips curve are all focused on the nation. Once the allocative practices no longer cohere in the nation, the phenomena escape the reach of the economic policy-makers and the movements of the indicators for these concepts get out of control. The best-known example is the attempt of the first Mitterrand government in France in 1981 to expand the economy along the lines of Keynesian recipes, only to learn that its interdependence with the neighbouring economies was so strong that adverse international effects outweighed the rise in domestic activities. Having watched this experience of a fairly strong economy, no other government since has even tried to pursue an economic policy against the stream of the majority trend.[10]

The potential of opportunities offered by pursuing certain allocative practices clashed with the limits imposed by the concrete set of arrangements as it existed by the 1960s. For the time being, we witness a gradual demolishing of these arrangements, mostly without them being replaced yet by analogous arrangements that might be more adequate to the situation. The main problem is that no level of collectivity offers itself in the same way as the nation-state did at the end of the nineteenth century, when the first steps on the path to organized modernity were taken. This is a diagnosis that holds not only for allocative, but for authoritative and signifying practices as well, as shall be argued later.

The breakdown of nationally agreed social conventions liberates individual actors – both employers and employees, producers and consumers – from having to follow rules that might not apply well to their specific case, even though they may have been designed as sensible protection rules. In this sense, 'deregulation' indeed provides new opportunities, as the jargon of its promoters will have it. These opportunities are offered to those who benefit from breaking the existing conventions. In terms of economic functions, these are multinational companies which move between nations using differences in conventions; (some) small- and medium-sized companies which could have had greater difficulties following general conventions due to specificities of their activities; and consumers who may benefit from enlarged offers and reduced prices due to internationalized trade.[11]

The opportunities are provided, however, at the cost of existing power differentials having a direct impact on the individual (person or company) instead of being mediated through collective arrangements – a mediation that can be seen as the major argument behind the construction of the arrangements of organized modernity. In the realm of allocative practices, the present restructuring has obvious adverse consequences on the economic steering possibilities of those collective actors who had developed their specific organizational form with regard to the exigencies of (nationally) organized capitalism, namely the state and the unions. The very idea of macro-economic management, which, until as late as the 1960s, was hailed as putting an end to economic crises, had proven to be laden with a complex set of preconditions that could be attained only for a very short period. The Keynesian concepts had bred the universalist idea of an overall and comprehensive guidance of the economic process. As a consequence of the de-nationalization of the economy, it was gradually abandoned, mostly in favour of much more selective intervention and crisis management. More recent economic policy proposals no longer envisage the comprehensive oversight and control of a realm of practices by an entity that is somehow placed in a superior position. Rather, they envisage the actor itself as moving inside the realm of action and trying to enhance its own position by developing the specific strengths and assets that it may have.

The most striking example, indicating indeed a shift in the entire sociopolitical formation, is the abandoning of the commitment to full employment on the part of the national government. Though governments do not explicitly declare that this is the case, their practices since the late 1970s document this clearly. In 1974–5, when unemployment figures rose for the first time again strongly in West Germany after the Second World War, the then chancellor, Helmut Schmidt, explicitly preferred inflation to unemployment. His widely debated statement exemplified in two ways the order of organized modernity. First, he undoubtingly assumed an inverse correlation between the two economic phenomena, the so-called Phillips curve. Indeed, this had been true for the past decades, but ceased to be so at that precise point in time. Second, he implicitly expressed that he saw the political stability of the order based on full employment. Since then, governments have not only accepted the co-existence of both phenomena, but often enough stressed monetary stability even if it were at the price of a higher unemployment level.[12]

If the current transformations involve a loss of agential capacity and of the degree of control which two major organized collectives, the state and the trade unions, have had over a certain realm of practices, then one should trace these institutions back to their guiding ideas – instead of merely either deploring or welcoming these developments. The interventionist state rested on the assumption that there is a common interest of the national collective that has its specific legitimacy and needs a particular organization; similarly, the idea underlying statewide union organization was that there is a common interest of a social class, namely workers and employees.[13] These ideas have given state and union their particular form in the context of the nationwide conventionalization of social practices, and it is first of all this form which is now in question. 'It is the "Fordist-Keynesian" *form* of this state which went into crisis.' What this means for interest organization after organized modernity is very unclear as yet. 'What is at stake is certainly a new synergy between individual interests, social rights, and economic efficacy.'[14] But the outcome in terms of a new temporarily stable synthesis is quite open.

Instead of generally referring to a loss of agency and control, it seems more appropriate to speak of a *change in the locus of agency* and a *change in the mode of control* of social practices. At least two more such transformations need to be discussed with regard to allocative practices.

During recent years, observers have noted changes in the dominant technical mode of production. Whereas mass production of standardized goods had been seen as the model of efficiency at least since Taylorism and Ford's model T, innovations in productive activity now aimed increasingly at enhancing flexibility and specialization instead of merely improving the output–input ratio. A strong variant of such a thesis was proposed about a decade ago by Michael Piore and Charles Sabel, who argued that economic practices were at a second great historical divide, after the one that led from artisanal to industrial production. The new industrial divide was to be of similar dimension but in an inverse direction.[15] I shall distinguish a more organizational (c) from a more technical aspect (d).

(c) The organizational changes may be summarized as a movement towards the loosening of formal hierarchies. The organized modernity approach had emphasized, first, increase in organizational size as a means of 'internalizing' what would otherwise be the environment of the firm and, second, minute definitions of tasks and hierarchies inside the firm as a means of establishing certainty about processes and outcomes. In contrast, the more recent tendencies are towards diminution of the space of total control and more open, less defined relations between the various actors in an interaction chain.[16]

The vertical integration of the production process, long a desired achievement, has been abandoned in favour of relations between a major organizing company and many suppliers, who are formally independent, though they may normally sell most of their product to the one big company. Thus, for instance, FIAT automobile company virtually owned most of the Turin industrial economy in the 1950s, whereas now a great number of suppliers co-operate with FIAT. Major companies in the apparel and fashion business hardly produce at all, but merely put their label into articles of clothing that have been produced according to their specifications by autonomous companies.[17] For decades, the major trend was to incorporate research and development functions into the producing company. Increasingly, more or less stable collaborations are now sought with independent R & D firms or public research laboratories and universities.[18]

Inside the firm a related process occurs, which has programmatically been labelled a move 'from control to commitment'.[19] Instead of fighting the mind and will of the workers, so the argument goes, their capabilities and involvement are encouraged and demanded, by assigning responsibilities for parts of the work process to them. A new concept of human resources is proposed that appears to have a much wider conception of the human actor than the economistic concept of human capital had a few decades ago.[20] Employees are seen not merely as receivers of commands nor as purely economic assets on whom return should be maximized, but as subjects developing their own sense of tasks, responsibilities and satisfaction with regard to the work they are doing.

So far, only very limited parts of the overall economic organization are affected by these changes, and there is no reason not to assume that part of the debate merely serves as rhetoric with the aim of enhancing the commitment of the workers because of the adverse effects of Taylorist organization (such as 'work-to-rule' action, sabotage, absenteeism, inflexibility). Nevertheless, there are reasons of economic viability behind these changes. It had been noted that dense regional networks of small- and medium-sized firms, operating below the level of standardized mass production, had weathered the crises of the 1970s much better than big companies. It was held that they were able to react more flexibly to changing signals from their clients and customers, first because of the greater adaptability of a network of autonomous units compared to one hierarchical unit and, second, because of their lower commitment to a technically rigid organization of production.

If this is the case then, what would be the consequences of such a general relaxing of rigid forms of control? On the one hand, the space for self-employment may increase. On the other, spaces of action may be enlarged for employees, and management may rely more strongly on the self-control of the employees in accordance with company objectives. Both these changes demand a self-understanding of the economic actor – the employee as well as the self-employed – that is different from the one on which Taylorism was built. From the mere acceptance of minute commands and signals, much more self-initiated interpretation of and action on the social world will be expected and required from economic actors. The social effects of such changes on the position and practices of the self will be discussed below (see Chapter 10).

(d) In contrast – but not in contradiction – to organizational sociologists, industrial sociologists stress that recent changes in allocative practices are related to a reassessment of the paradigm of mass production and a turn to 'flexible specialization', that is, the production of smaller series of a greater variety of goods. The existence of another major technological rupture in advanced industrial societies over the past two or three decades is hardly doubted any longer, though it still appears to be difficult to define its exact nature. 'Technologists frequently observe that we are currently undergoing a shift of . . . the technoeconomic paradigm, from one centred around Fordist mass production, to one centred around high technology based on advances in microelectronics.'[21] Against the background of a variety of technical innovations – among which are laser technology, new materials, satellites and possibly soon genetic technologies, besides microelectronics[22] – some have argued that the dominance of the rationality of scale and the pattern of standardization and homogenization have subsided. The types of intervention into materials, living nature and – also – human beings have become finer, more closely directed to the objective of the intervention, and there are more possibilities for informational and communicative control of the effects of an intervention as well as possibilities for correction.

Without wanting (or being able) to analyse this reorientation in depth, I would like to discuss briefly the claim of a trend towards flexibilization, or, *vice versa*, toward the end of standardization. I shall distinguish flexibilization of production from flexibilization of utilization. Generally, the term flexible specialization seems to cover some tendencies of technological potentials in both the production and use of technologies, beyond manufacturing technologies for which it was introduced. Now, a feature of this process is that it does not entail the dismantling of the characteristic technical systems of organized modernity that enhanced the conventionalization of practices (as described in Chapter 5). Instead, it is built on, or hooked up to, them and uses the basic structuring of practices that these systems have provided. Owing to this feature, the technical systems of organized modernity have already been called primary systems, and the more recently added systems secondary ones.[23] Though this terminology is a bit overly schematic, I will stay with it for a moment.

With the recent technical changes, it has been possible to increase speed and precision in the management of information, matter and energy. In so far as the changed practices of allocation allow a greater variety of products to be produced according to more specific demand, this indeed entails de-standardization. However, the same shift involves a strengthening of trends towards the globalization of allocation. Much more often than, say, twenty years ago, production and product markets are effectively or potentially global. The market increase itself enhances standardization. But more importantly, it tends to demand the setting of global standards in cases in which a century ago, quite naturally, national standards would have been sought and established.[24] Often, globally homogeneous component parts will be assembled by means of globally homogeneous manufacturing technology at many different places into a great variety of different products. The notion of secondarization of technical systems captures well this situation of technical flexibility and variety attached onto a generalized pattern.[25]

The emphasis shifts when we begin to look at the utilization of 'new' technologies and the goods that are produced with them. Most of the technical systems of organized modernity involved the standardization of material objects in such a way that their usage led to the standardization of patterns of behaviour and the collectivization of modes of action. The secondary systems, in contrast, often allow diversification of objects and individualization of behaviour patterns. 'Related to the privatization of technology, a tendency towards such systems is evident that enhance the users' freedom to choose.'[26] The flexible specialization of manufacturing, for instance, increases the variety of objects that are affordable to average consumers.

One should not interpret, though, such changes as the foundations of organized modernity being shaken by technical pushes. Indeed, one may argue the other way round: the present societal transformations may have favoured a certain direction of technical development. In the current social restructuring, innovations are applied that were 'hitherto *contained* by the rules of the social game'.[27]

Furthermore, beyond its first heuristic use, the comparison of primary and secondary technologies and their historical location in social configurations has its limits, which may be shown by discussing examples of technologies that appear to deviate from the historical pattern, the car and the telephone. Historically, the diffusion of both techniques falls squarely into the social configuration of organized modernity, the car as a product even being the prime example for the emergence of an 'organized' production and consumption pattern. However, the forms of use both techniques allow are highly individual and private, and were early on recognized as such by the users. In both cases, early restricted patterns of use, such as for military and for business purposes, were soon exceeded, and these techniques became the symbols of independence, autonomy and individuality. The car-and-road system even tended to supersede and replace a transportation system that was much more collectively arranged, the railroad.

So, the broad historical pattern I try to carve out must not be misunderstood as a strong scheme superimposed on diverse and conflict-ridden social realities. In the case of these two techniques, however, a closer look at diffusion patterns reinserts them into a comparative analysis of – more organized or more liberal – modernity. The car received its first diffusion boom in France, a culture known for its individualism, and was an upper-class means of asserting liberty and individuality in an emerging mass society.[28] The full breakthrough of the automobile then occurred obviously in the US, where it seemed to combine the independence drive of the most liberal modernity with the historical path for organized production and consumption. Characteristically, in a culture known for being more collectivist, the German one, the car reached diffusion levels comparable to that of the French one as late as the 1960s. The telephone, analogously, became standard equipment in private households first in the US, whereas in Europe its use remained long limited to military and business purposes, where actually in the army context for some time the one-way, top-down communication was maintained, though two-way communication was technically feasible.[29]

To capture the sum of these recent changes of allocative practices, the notion of the 'disorganization of capitalism' has been proposed by some authors, though it has not really been widely accepted.[30] It conveys the idea that an old, highly organized order is breaking down, but it does not really offer an understanding of the current structure of practices. The transformations do not mark the collapse of all practices, but rather the fact that some of them are extending beyond the boundaries in which they were ordered and which were a precondition for their ordering.

Many of the practices of allocation do indeed work on a more extended scale than ever before. In many regards, effective globalization is happening in realms in which strong barriers had to be surmounted before, when moving from one country to another. Currency and trade unions are a major expression of such extensions; an immediately striking example to any traveller is the working of the banking-machine/credit-card system. Without linguistically-based communication and in practically no time, for hypothetically tens of thousands of users simultaneously, a specific and individual linkage is created between available resources at somebody's place of residence and a distant location, a linkage which is effective in enabling, for instance, consumption acts that may otherwise have been impossible.

The alleged disorganization is in fact accompanied by strong reorganization attempts and, indeed, elements of the emergence of a new, global, order. However, the 'system' lacks the coherence of the old one and does not (yet) provide certainty to a similar extent that the order of organized modernity did.[31]

REOPENING POLITICAL BOUNDARIES: THE CRISIS OF THE WELFARE STATE AND THE BREAKDOWN OF SOCIALISM

Earlier, I described the organization of the practices of authoritative power under organized modernity as a broadly successful range of attempts to limit the scope of the polity, politics and policy relative to the liberal ideal (see Chapter 6). It was, by and large, established that the boundaries of the polity should coincide with those of a nation; that political representation could be practised through competitive parties and political deliberation be reached through top-level bargaining; and that the legitimate activities of the state should extend beyond safeguarding law and order to guaranteeing a decent living to every member of the polity.

These rules were largely created in response to obvious problems in the idea and the history of liberal modernity. Once the relevant actors had recognized their potential for stabilizing the social order, deliberate efforts were devoted to enhancing or maintaining the thus constructed coherence of organized modernity. At the historical point when the greatest coherence was reached – mostly during the 1960s – new strains emerged, and the boundaries were increasingly questioned and began to shake. It is under such a guiding theme that I shall discuss the recent transformations of authoritative practices. Again, I shall proceed by distinguishing the boundaries (a) of policy-making, (b) of politics and (c) of the polity.

(a) At the height of organized modernity, say, by the 1960s, the state was regarded as strong and coherent. In principle, at least, it could acquire all necessary knowledge about society; and it had the ability to intervene into society in a regulating and harmonizing way.[32] Furthermore, the scope of its interventions was consensually defined as vast and was continuously expanding. By the 1990s, the image of the state had changed in all three dimensions.

The call for 'deregulation' is often seen as stemming from the entrepreneurial desire not to be hampered in the pursuit of profitable activities by overdrawn social concern expressed in administrative decrees. While such a view is not entirely wrong, it is based on a counterposition of an economic sphere in which only profitability counts, and a political sphere in which the public good may be defended and the welfare of all be pursued. Such a perspective underestimates the extent to which state regulation may impede liberties in general, and not merely economic liberties. In recent years, all kinds of compulsory arrangements – from public schools to public broadcasting to compulsory insurance schemes – have come under the criticism of citizens who would prefer other substantive arrangements than the state prescribes. In many cases, these demands are raised in the name of plurality and diversity, and have little or nothing to do with commercial considerations – though they may carry an elite bias and may also be directed against the lower quality of publicly provided services. Nevertheless what is visible here is a revival of the liberal idea of limits to state intervention and a renewed emphasis placed on the societal capacity for self-organization.

Beyond the open criticism of entrepreneurs and clients, the planning-oriented, interventionist state also faced internal problems. Ideally, the interventionist state had relied on the idea of a central steering capacity, in which the relation of problem analysis, policy design, policy implementation and policy effects would be unproblematically governed by a hierarchical chain.[33] However, the hierarchical notion of the policy process underestimated the multitude of actors and variety of actor positions that would be involved in any such process. If conceived as an undisturbed top-down process, policies required control and surveillance needs beyond any initial expectations. As a consequence, policy programmes would often be put into effect only in ways which deviated markedly from the intentions, a phenomenon somewhat euphemistically called 'implementation problems', the policy research variant of the sociological notion of unintended consequences. This phenomenon could be called the 'bureaucratic crisis of the welfare state'.[34]

Furthermore, interventionist policy-making had relied far too strongly on the idea of the possible cognitive mastery of society. The definition and analysis of societal issues that could be turned into policy problems seemed relatively unproblematic at the height of social science optimism. For policy-makers and administrators it was often an incomprehensible and painful experience to see that the instruments they offered had been derived from a problem definition which their clients and supposed beneficiaries did not at all share. Beyond implementation problems, policies faced interpretation problems, which were often enough much more persistent.

As a result, the policy-making parts of the political class, including the supporting experts and professionals, have become much more modest with regard to their capabilities than they had been two decades ago. It is observable among these groups how the self-proliferated all-powerful conception of the state is gradually, and sometimes radically, withdrawn. From posing as the omniscient regulator and leader the state is reproposed as a partner and moderator.[35] This withdrawal includes the diffusion of arrangements in which the state disposes of its absolute rights to decree and regulate, and rather delegates these functions to private bodies or performs them in conjunction with such bodies.[36]

In all three respects – the scope, the definition and the execution of policies – the clarity of the model of the all-pervasive interventionist state has disappeared and has given way to a new diffuseness of the boundaries between the spheres of public and private regulation. It would be too simple to state that merely the boundary of public regulation is being pushed back again, a reversal of a hundred-years' historical trend that moved away from the liberal towards the welfarist conception of the state. Rather, the entire relation between public and private spheres is in motion. Due to interpretative and deliberative activities that are pursued in common by public officials and varieties of private groups, the very location of a policy decision in one or the other sphere becomes increasingly problematic.[37] This blurring of boundaries raises issues of legitimacy and sovereignty.

(b) The questioning of the boundaries of organized democracy has taken two main forms, the resort to extra-institutional protest on the one hand, significantly called 'unconventional political action', and the erosion of the electoral institutions on the other.

From the late 1960s onwards, Western societies experienced increased social unrest. Protest movements formed which directed themselves against specific policies, but also expressed a general opposition against forms and substance of politics in 'advanced industrial society'. While the actual dimensions of contestation were not very remarkable in a long-term historical perspective, the common view that '1968' and its aftermaths shook Western societies is nevertheless valid. What was disturbing was that, first, the broad involvement of students showed that potential members of the future elites were ready to violate established rules and, second, that the protest tended to break the widely held imagery of society as a stable and coherent system of rules.[38]

The very notion of unconventional forms of political action, coined by political scientists, reveals this feature.[39] By that time, a consensus was assumed about the regular forms of political participation, namely through elections and – for those who were civic-minded beyond the average citizen – within the organizations of the established parties. To choose not to stay within the realm defined by those conventions meant more than just uttering a deviant opinion. It entailed questioning the very adequacy and legitimacy of those conventions.

Over a short time, unconventional political action transformed from a movement of broad political protests of short duration and small numbers into a great variety of contestations and civic interventions with often greater continuity and more limited, often local, objectives.[40] An example that is often cited is the movement against the use of nuclear energy, which organized nationally and internationally but was also based on continuous activity in local groups working for local objectives.[41] But in many more cases, goals are defined in even more limited terms and of clearly only local relevance. Thus, it is no exaggeration to state that civic involvement has increased across the board, subverting the conventions of organized democracy.

The increased unconventional activity of citizens goes broadly along with a decreased activity in the conventional forms. With regard to elections, the erosion of the party system manifests itself in abstentionism and in decreasing support for the 'established' parties. With regard to party competition, it is visible through the formation of new parties, and the internal restructuring of old parties.[42] Here, a distinction may be made in terms of the attitude to political participation. Some of these activities can be interpreted as attempts to restructure the political institutions so that they may reflect better, and respond more appropriately to, the will of the population. Others, however, must be seen as a turn away from participation in the form in which it is offered.

The distinction is often not very clear in reality, since one attitude may easily shift into the other, provoked by new experiences. However, the difference is evidently great with regard to the consequences. So the formation of some parties may be taken as an example of the former, especially in the case of some environmentalist parties which have emerged from the experience of unconventional participation. In other cases though, such as parties of the New Right, it shows features of an abdication of the idea of participation and of the delegation of civic rights to a leader.

The same ambiguity is characteristic of the attempts at internal restructuring in the old parties. Not least provoked by losses in membership and the concomitant relative successes of 'movement parties' (such as the German Green Party or the Italian Radical Party), some old parties (again most notably the German Social Democratic Party and the former Italian Communist Party) have tried to revive their own heritage by opening up to current social movements and offering themselves as the organized political expression of such movements. Apart from the substantive changes that these manoeuvres entail, they tend to transform the understanding of party organization. What is at stake is exactly the enabling character of an organization with regard to collective action. These openings tend to shift the emphasis from the forceful expression of a common interest to the communicative formation of such an interest. In this sense, they may appear as a reversal of the historical process of party construction and a return to 'mobilization from below'. If they are pursued seriously, the strengthening of will formation is likely to go along with a weakening of the power of the party in party competition – as long as the conventional rules apply in that competition.

The more likely outcome, however, is – without doubting the sincerity of some of the promotors of change – a general de-structuring of the party organization, so that the distribution of influence in the organization becomes less predictable and the durable programmatic profile of the parties withers away. The possibility of the emergence of 'political entrepreneurship' increases also in hitherto tight party systems.[43] It is significant that this kind of entrepreneurship is the common pattern in the US, which again sets this always more liberal modernity apart from more organized ones in Europe.

(c) Since at least the 1960s, it has often been argued that national states, in particular small ones, factually lose their autonomy when allocative practices cross boundaries to a great extent, and when the power of economic actors, often measured in financial resources, far exceeds that of the states on whose territories they are active. Claiming that the reasoning was exaggerated, a counter-argument held that its unique disposal over sovereignty rights would keep crucial power with the state. This is basically where that debate left off.[44]

Granting the validity of both arguments, any assessment would have to rely on the closer examination of interdependencies. Such studies would have to focus on the degree of internationality of practices and the power differentials between actors, on the one hand, and on changes in the distribution of sovereignty rights within the nation-state and between states, on the other.[45] Without anticipating any more detailed studies, two trends over the past two decades are obvious.

First, social practices have tended to become more internationalized at an increasing pace. This is not only true for allocative practices specifically, but has a much broader impact as a consequence of the trend towards globalization of information and communication. Besides the impact of economic interdependence, the 'culture' of a nation is much less of a frame of reference for the minds of the citizens than it used to be, given easier flow of communication and increased cross-boundary travel. It is worth pointing this out since the factual limits to information flow and elite control over it, which were still relevant by the turn to this century, had arguably a strong supportive impact on the formation of a national imagined community. While state sovereignty allows the restriction of both economic and informational internationalism, the use of this power has been made more difficult not only for technical reasons, but also with regard to the threat of losing legitimacy.[46]

In this context, a special aspect is added by an issue which the polities of organized modernity had almost completely neglected, because it had been considered fixed, namely the cultural stability and continuity of the population inside a nationally defined territory. People have immigrated into West European countries for a variety of reasons – as entitled citizens of former colonies, as hired immigrant workers, as political refugees, as refugees from the plight of the Third World, or for reasons of personal preference. In any case, as a result of accumulated immigration hardly any of these countries can consider themselves monocultural – if they ever could. Even beyond the political issues of the day, such as suffrage rights, refugee rights, etc., the plurality and mobility of current populations reopens the issue of the definition of the political entity towards the 'outside'.[47]

Second, many European nation-states have started to dispose of rights of sovereignty and have handed them either internally to regional polities or externally to international regimes. Most of these moves have been taken as a reaction to the changing extension of social practices. Proposals for monetary unions, for instance, are a response to the strengthened business interactions across boundaries and the expected material benefits from such interactions. The granting of regional autonomy, on the other hand, is a response to the criticism that the nationally operating interventionist state disregards the specific organization of practices in regions and communities.

Broadly, any attempt to make polity boundaries correspond to the boundaries of spatially extended habitual practices appears sound, both in terms of expected efficiency of regulations and with regard to normative concerns of democracy. However, one also needs to note that such attempts basically merely ratify the losses of boundary control and abdicate the idea of the unity of the polity. Many of the changes in state organization are basically analogous to those occurring in business organization. The state, though, is not an organization like any other, it carries a universalist reference to representation and legitimation that it cannot really get rid of. Being territorially and population-wise defined, it has to stick to some idea of comprehensive coverage instead of 'groping' in and with a diffuse social realm. I shall return to these issues later (see Chapter 11).

The state of organized modernity could not 'hold', 'contain', as it was designed to do, the transformations of social practices.[48] In the discourse of the Keynesian welfare state, though, it had taken over the responsibility for the orderly continuation of social practices, a promise it was unable to fulfil from the middle of the 1970s onwards. With reference to such strong claims, and with a view of the first signs of strains on the state capacity, a number of social theorists argued at that time that a 'legitimacy crisis' might emerge from the gap between the claim and the reality.[49] In a sense, this came to be the case, though in a different way than was expected.

From the mid-1970s onwards, policy-makers in Western societies were in fact faced with rising and contradictory demands on the part of different social groups. On the one hand, the conditions for reaching socially accepted economic goals, such as full employment, had worsened. On the other hand, in the light of the strong image of the state as the great harmonizer which had been conveyed in earlier years, demands were raised with regard not only to the elimination of poverty but also the enhancement of the quality of life. Instead of trying to reshape authoritative practices with regard to meeting the higher requirements, as some political groups tried, the dominant reaction to this situation came to be the dismissal of the demands as unfulfillable and tendentially illegitimate themselves.[50]

The major discursive means of underpinning this reaction was a renewed emphasis on the liberal foundations of the social order that required that the state do only what other actors could not do. The political classes in Western states withdrew from their earlier claims of strength and will and returned, in line with a liberal ideology, to a more moderate position. For at least a decade, the 1980s, this move precluded any legitimacy crisis to arise in a strong sense. However, the changes in social practices, together with that reinterpretation of the realm of authoritative practices, may have a stronger long-term impact, given that both changes tend to loosen the relation between the individual and the polity (to be discussed in more detail in Chapter 10).

At this point of my argument, I will return to briefly considering Soviet socialism in comparison with Western modernity. For the time being, the life-span of this social order seems to be almost fixed in history. After protracted struggles that brought the organized workers' movements ever closer to power, the first such regime was established in Russia in 1917. Socialism spread to East Central Europe after, and as a result of, the Second World War. It lived through a major crisis in the late 1960s, from which it would never fully recover, and broke down in the late 1980s. Sketched this way, the historical path of socialism coincided very neatly with that of organized modernity. As a way of organizing social practices, this path can be interpreted in the broader historical context of societal development.

If the organization of modernity was much more radical in Soviet socialism than in the West (see Chapter 6), then the same turned out to be true for the demise of socialism as compared to that of organized modernity. It is quicker, leaves less of the old boundaries, and destroys collective arrangements more thoroughly. The political classes in the socialist states were, *mutatis mutandis*, faced with problems similar to those of their counterparts in the West; social practices tended to break out of the conventions in which they were held. However, the marked difference is that socialism had gone much further in the encapsulation of practices than Western organized modernity. After the 1960s, at the latest, the stronger encapsulation became a liability rather than an asset – even from an elite perspective. At that point, the divergence between socialism and the Western societies reemerged, as the ability or inability to respond to the difficulties of an organized-modern social formation became crucial. Elements for an analysis of the demise of socialism can be elaborated from such a perspective.

The organization of allocative practices on the basis of a central plan had developed its own momentum. Other signals from other sources being excluded, the only way to deal with deviations from the envisaged performance was to introduce new performance indicators and monitor the production processes more closely and more often.[51] As long as it could be considered a valid assumption that production technology was fixed and that the only relevant parameter was economies of scale, such a fine-grading of control appeared possible at least in principle, if hardly always in practice. However, some economists recognized early that this would not be the case.

In the 1960s, economic reforms that were to introduce elements of market co-ordination and enhance flexibility were tried in most socialist states. Hungary aside, however, they were all almost completely withdrawn after the suppression of the Prague Spring. It appears as if the economic performance started to decrease then. Even a phenomenon analogous to 'stagflation' emerged when increased unemployment 'on the job' went along with inflation, the latter being measured as an average of subsidized staple goods and expensive new products. If this is correct, it shows a first striking parallel between the restructuring processes in both social formations. Only, the socialist economies did not resort to the techno-organizational instruments that were increasingly employed in the West. One of the reasons may have been that it was suspected that a shift from hierarchical control to self-control in the realm of allocative practices would spread soon to the realm of authoritative practices. The suppression of the Prague Spring was followed by the re-centralization of the production apparatus.

The political classes of socialism were much more obsessed with control and surveillance than their Western counterparts. They had organized authoritative practices in a much more closed form, and proved mostly unable to withdraw to a more flexible position. With variations between countries, proposals outside the established principles and organized channels were regularly not tolerated, no rules to process such proposals were developed, and 'unconventional political action' where it occurred was usually immediately suppressed. At the same time, some sort of loosening of the party organization can be observed. The East German party relaxed the condition that membership must go along with intense political activity. As a consequence, membership figures rose – to gain access to privileges and careers[52] – and political activities declined. Generally, the parties tried to present themselves as the best representatives of the new interests, such as environmentalist ones, whose emergence they recognized as well, though more slowly, as the established Western parties did.

With regard to both allocative and authoritative practices, the socialist political class had to deal with a subversion of the orders of practices, beginning gradually after the end of Stalinism. A certain deal had by then been struck between the political class and the population. With regard to allocation, this deal was known, at least in Poland and the Soviet Union, by the workers' saying: 'They pretend they pay us, we pretend we work.'[53] Such an informal assessment of the state of the economy and its rules legitimated the elaboration of a 'hidden economy'. Though it could never be measured, it can be guessed that the share of exchange that did not follow the plans – as private or inter-firm rechannellings – in the East was greater than the share of exchange that was not reported to the tax authorities in the West.

The equivalent saying in the realm of authority would be (though I never heard it said in explicitly these terms): 'They pretend they govern, we pretend we follow.' The deal entailed that the regime would rule out open repression, as long as the population refrained from open revolt. This rule allowed the hidden distanciation from the foundational political maxims of socialism. While it was struck by the elites to maintain internal stability and manoeuvrability in the world order, it contributed to undermining the regime. Among the people it was by then widely recognized that, as long as the deal was kept, the political class was also in a dependent position with regard to everyday practices, not only the other way round. With the regime strongly committed to providing income maintenance (though at a lower level than in most OECD countries), social security, health care and basic education in universal form and having no disciplinary means at its disposal when 'full employment' was guaranteed and social mobility almost non-existent as a 'career incentive', disciplinary enforcement of obedience as well as work performance was very limited.

It is well known that awareness of crises was not totally absent in the political classes of socialism. One problem was that it could hardly be voiced without sanction from most, except the top, positions in the hierarchy. The other problem was that the classes were caught inside their own, highly conventionalized practices of signification. The way in which the unity of society, state and party had been made a corner-stone for the entire building, there was no conception of other, relatively autonomous spheres in society to which the regulation of some social practices could be handed over and the demand on the political class relieved.[54]

In sum, the political classes of socialism had to defend a very strongly erected system of closed boundaries that proved undefendable as a whole at a time when practices could no longer be kept inside those boundaries. The German Democratic Republic is only the most extreme case of loss of boundary control in this respect. The few years after the end of socialism show more generally that the cognitive and communicative resources needed to re-establish polities on more open principles are very limited in the realm of former socialism. However, the breakdown of the order beyond the old border between West and East should not turn attention away from the fact that the reorientations underway on this side of that border face analogous problems. And the fall of socialism may have exacerbated, rather than eased them. The breakdown of a strongly guarded order of social practices in close vicinity will have a strong impact on the possibilities for safeguarding or restructuring collective arrangements in the West European nation-states or the European community.

Chapter 9

Sociology and contingency

The crisis of the organized mode of representation

CONTESTING ORGANIZED MODERNITY

In the preceding chapter I have tried to characterize what I see as a major societal transformation going on since the 1960s. This transformation entails the breakdown of many of the organized social practices that came to be established over long and partly violent struggles between the beginning of the century and the 1960s. Early on, during these recent transformations, something occurred which soon came to be seen as a major event of high significance, though there was (and is) hardly any agreement regarding in what way it was to be significant. The importance it acquired in the collective memory of the Western societies can be gathered from the fact that the event was given a short designation that is understood by many members of these societies: 1968.

In a sense, what really happened had to seem of minor importance to any sober observer. A couple of thousands of students arrived at political views on current affairs that deviated from those of all major political parties, and when they felt that their sensible opinions were not given due attention, they resorted to direct action at their universities and in their cities. In some countries, these student activities happened to coincide with a wave of industrial action that was stronger than what one had become used to during the preceding decade. Of course, some of the activists on both the students' and the workers' side tried to link the one struggle to the other, but it could sensibly be argued that these struggles had ultimately little in common so that any kind of coalition-building was bound to fail.

While such a characterization does not seem particularly flawed, it had very little appeal to contemporaries. In France, as rumour had it, the President of the Republic was about to flee the country much like the king on the occasion of the French Revolution did. In the US, the National Guard was sent to university campuses where they shot protesting students. In Italy, the country was seen as being on the verge of a social revolution and factions of the political class were secretly preparing a coup and a military dictatorship to put an end to the unrest. From a present viewpoint though, these reactions appear widely exaggerated.

It seems as if not only many of the contestants but also the political elites adhered to political imageries that tended to enlarge the size of the events and failed to see the direction of their likely impact. Both shared a view of social conflict and social revolution that turned out to be invalid for advanced capitalist democracies. Furthermore, both viewed the existing social order in a way that made its complete overturning look possible, as a threat or a hope depending on the stand-point. With such representations still in mind, a mythical image of 'Sixty-Eight' has survived, but only faint ideas about the causes, objectives and impacts of the revolts seem to be alive in the present.[1]

The historical record seems paradoxical and contradictory, therefore. Nowhere did societal institutions change in a way that was clearly and immediately related to the demands of the protesters and the strength of their movements. However, the events are in fact related to some sort of break-up of a social order, a break-up of which they were only one of the most visible elements. I will not add fundamentally new insights to the story, but I would like to offer outlines of an interpretation that sets the events in the context of major societal transformations.

The revolts meant a disruption of established social practices and, even more importantly, a deep questioning of the rationale of some of these practices. With the mode of representation that I sketched above (see Chapter 7), a common means of understanding the social order as stable and coherent had barely been reached when the sons and daughters of the active members of the elite dared to question this image. This disruptive character gave the contestations an important role in dismantling organized modernity – even if hardly any practice was stalled for more than a brief period.

The specific themes of the protest were often provided by the self-satisfied way and unquestioned means through which the elites had developed organized practices as the self-evident natural order. In West Germany, thus, the emergency amendments to the federal constitution were contested as a sign that the control and repression of political articulation should have precedence over civil liberties – and this at a time when National Socialism, as one step on the specifically German path into organized modernity, had hardly been self-critically reflected. In France and Italy, much criticism was directed against the communist parties which were regarded as having accepted the assigned place of institutionalized opposition within organized democracy.

If it was obvious that the protests were directed against the specific ways modern practices were organized, it was largely unclear what alternatives the contestants were heading for. For some of them, one has to say that their own programme was highly contradictory. For others, it appears as if their programme deviated strongly from the effects that the protests had on society.

The threat that issued from the protest in the view of the elites, namely, was that the students and workers were heading towards establishing a new, counter-elitist subject in society, that they appeared willing and able, not only to temporarily upset the organized practices of participation, but to recreate collective political agency on the basis of a new mobilization from below. One may indeed say that such a conception inspired the various socialist and communist parties in the wake of the initial mobilization, and the idea that a strongly willed vanguard elite could actually seize power and transform society was obviously still firmly rooted in the heads of many contestants as well as their opponents.

However, these conceptions can hardly be called characteristic for the broader movement. Furthermore, the early splintering of parts of the movement into mostly small, mostly sectarian groups, each of which developed its own closed orthodoxy and guarded it well, already indicates a significant tension between two aspirations. In substance, the programmes of each of these groups confirmed the emphasis on a collective project, of social revolution and then of societal re-structuring. The practices inside the groups also often demanded from the members a renouncing of individuality and privacy for the sake of the collective. Further, the belief-like resort to time-honoured conceptions of social change and revolution may be interpreted as a search for certainties, for clear-cut guidelines as to what one should devote one's life to.[2]

While each of the groups maintained the claim that they spoke in terms of politics, that is, for an overall societal renewal, in actual practice group identities mostly prevailed over truly political communication. The multiplicity of such projects as well as the lack of a readiness to unite their forces pointed to an actual plurality within the movement. Also, more importantly, the small groups placed an emphasis on maintaining their identity rather than giving it up, or at least loosening control over it, in favour of a greater collective project. If the current situation of 'postmodern sociality' is described as the co-existence of many different 'tribes', within which individual human beings find and create their social identities,[3] this description fits post-1968 groups often better than their self-description as a political project. The main difference to 'postmodern' groups is that the language that was used inside the groups was (still?) a political one.

In other words, the contestation should be seen as consisting of two elements that, while they appeared sequentially related at the time, proved contradictory at a closer look. The first element was the protest against *organized* modernity which demanded interruption of established collective practices. The second element was the project of rebuilding a collective subject, of liberation through 'an essentially new historical Subject'.[4] Of these two elements, the former was undubitably the much stronger one.

With hindsight, the move towards plurality and diversity seems to have been the more significant and lasting impact of 'Sixty-Eight', and not the passing idea of collective renewal. Sometimes 'Sixty-Eight' is dubbed a 'cultural revolution' rather than an attempt at a political one.[5] The cultural revolution was a revolution in the name of individuality, of liberal modernity, against the imposition of any kind of pre-given order. In the radical version, the demand was for autonomy in the strong sense that each individual of a new generation may consider not just ascriptive and natural orders, but even the social conventions of the preceding generation as a heteronomous imposition and a restriction of the possibility for choosing one's own a life-course.[6]

Besides their specific significance in the context of the crisis of organized modernity, there is a more general reason why a look at '*les événements*', as the

French say, of 1968 is enlightening for a sociology of modernity. As I noted at the beginning of my argument (see Chapter 2), the history of modernity is often portrayed as a steady increase of contingency. Tradition, community and unity of the world are destroyed until only isolated individuals are left, or until ultimately even the individual is dissolved into fragments. In most variants of such reasoning an abstract, anonymous, supra-human phenomenon is seen at work in this process. While 'All that is solid melts into air' could be the common heading for all these approaches, it is often neglected that Marx saw the interactions of real human beings, namely the bourgeois, behind these processes – and that he also, at least in 1848, recognized that the bourgeois activities were part of the general Enlightenment project of enabling human beings to realize their selves in their life-projects.

Capitalism, however, could be interpreted as the very specific realization of the life-projects of members of one class in society at the expense of all others. The very restrictions of restricted liberal modernity made this interpretation possible and plausible. Under the conditions of full inclusion and formally equal rights, which characterize organized modernity, such an interpretation cannot easily be upheld. True, inequalities and injustices of many sorts continue to characterize contemporary societies, and often enough social reasons may be invoked that sustain them. A number of the post-1968 social conflicts remain marked by the fight against such inequalities that have been reproduced through both restricted liberal and organized modernity. The 'equal rights' part of the women's movement is a major example.

However, from the 1960s onwards the direction of social criticism in Western societies began to change. As I have tried to show at some length, the achievements of organized modernity were bought at the price of the setting of strict boundaries and conventions. A critique of organized modernity, thus, would be directed at the constraining effects of those boundaries and conventions. Intellectually, the recognition of the social construction of conventions is the major tool of such a critique. It is made visible that there are often no strong grounds for nevertheless universally applied and enforced rules within a polity. Politically, the right to diversity – to be different and to handle things differently – is a claim that stems from such reasoning. Again, the women's movement is a major example, namely where the focus is on gender-identity and difference.

Such claims have proven difficult to deal with under the rules of organized modernity. One may say that the activity of dissolving everything into air, begun in limited form by the bourgeoisie, is being continued on a much broader social basis. From the perspective of those who pursue it, it remains part of the project of self-realization. Such a look at the cultural revolution of the 1960s helps in seeing how the dissolving effects of modernity stem from the activities of human beings rather than abstract forces, and how – under a certain historical condition – dissolution may even be an explicitly formulated, collectively pursued social project in the name of modernity.

Postponing the discussion of the medium-term political effects until later (see

Chapter 11), it may suffice for the moment to state that this cultural revolution introduced a strong, in some respects almost unlimited, attempt at de-conventionalization and recreation of ambivalence in a social order that was regarded as over-conventionalized and closed to any freedom of action beyond pre-established channels. Almost immediately, the questioning of the order of practices extended to a questioning of the order of representation. Very soon, it even led to doubting the very possibility of representation.

AGAINST THE OBJECTIVIST MODE OF REPRESENTATION

In 1961, the Italian Association for the Social Sciences held a congress in Ancona under the general theme 'Sociologists and the centres of power'. The common thrust of most contributions was that sociology had now theoretically and methodologically matured, had produced a safe knowledge base for the understanding of modern society, and was ready to offer this knowledge to policy-makers for the betterment of society. Ten years later, the Italian sociologists met again, in Turin this time, to reflect on their experiences. 'The crisis of sociological method' was now the theme of the congress, and a participant described the contrast between the two meetings as follows:

> The climate of the discussions had entirely changed. During the Ancona congress confidence prevailed in the possibility of sociology to contribute not only to the knowledge, but also to the renewal of the Italian society. . . . The Turin meeting, in contrast, was dominated by doubt, by a diffuse concern about the fate of sociology.[7]

The change was particularly marked in Italy, but basically similar experiences were made by social scientists in most Western countries. The most prominent sociological writings of this period were reflections about the state of the discipline. In most cases, certainties that had prevailed were doubted, in particular the objectivist representation of society as an entity that was fixed in its basic structures and functions. Just for purposes of illustration, I shall mention Alvin W. Gouldner's *Coming Crisis of Sociology*, Jürgen Habermas' controversy with Niklas Luhmann in the aftermath of the dispute on positivism, Alain Touraine's gradually evolving sociology of social movements and Pierre Bourdieu's *Outline of a Theory of Practice*, Franco Ferrarotti's *Alternative Sociology*, and Johan Goudsblom's *Sociology in the Balance*.

In many, though not all, of these theoretical considerations the linkage to the changes in political perceptions are explicitly made. Even more common were statements on the relation of the social sciences to politics and society, in which the interrelatedness of modes of political representation and of cognitive representation were commonly made. An example is the following statement, dated 1971, by prominent American sociologists:

> The United States, as well as various European nations, passed through an era

> of protest during the 1960s. The resultant crisis of authority seems to be paving the way for fundamental changes in the political systems of these nations. It is no longer possible to write uncritically about the basic tenets of the welfare state as did political sociologists such as S.M. Lipset and William Kornhauser, among others, in the 1960s and many political scientists – including Harry Eckstein, Gabriel A. Almond, and Sidney Verba – during the same decade.[8]

In this and many other statements of the time emphasis was laid on the radical questioning of the conceptualization of societal phenomena. The expectation was, politically, that 'fundamental changes' were on the horizon and, analytically, that a re-conceptualization of society would be both necessary and possible in the context of such changes. This historical linkage of crises of political and cognitive representation can be analysed in analogy to the crisis of the preceding turn of the century. The latter provided the context for the emergence of classical sociology as a reasoning on society that was much more self-reflective than earlier evolutionist and determinist social thought.

At that time, the liberal, post-Enlightenment conceptions of society and their sociological and economic offsprings were deemed increasingly inadequate for understanding the ongoing changes in social practice. Even the attempts by scholars like Weber or Durkheim to revise that intellectual tradition did not convince the succeeding generation. As a result, the sociological tradition fell apart (see Chapter 7). From the late 1960s onwards, comprehensive functional or structural models of society lost their persuasiveness in the face of both political contestations and economic downturns, both similarly unforeseen.[9] And again, one might say, sociologists who rightly began to reject those models, failed to come up with any alternative that could compete with the rejected one with regard to comprehensiveness.

A major difference between the two situations is that sociological debate proved to be more continuous and persistent in the more recent one. I would attribute this fact mainly to the firm institutional establishment of social science at universities and other academic institutions. Thus, a minimal precondition for the continuity of a discourse was provided. This continuity meant that much rethinking of theories, concepts and methods could and would take place under the broad assumption of the possibility of a social science. As such, many of these attempts can be seen as exercises in reflexivity, in two senses. First, sociologists re-entered a period in which the reflection of past cognitive practices seemed necessary for a continuation of the project. Second, sociologists recognized (or rediscovered) the reflexive character of their overall enterprise, namely that they were trying to explain a social world in which the inhabitants had already proliferated their own interpretations of it. Those interpretations would inevitably enter into the discourses of sociologists, who are at the same time observers of and participants in this social world.

If we demand that the social sciences provide a single comprehensive cognitive framework to understand the social world, then something like this could be said to have existed during the hegemony of structural-functionalism during the 1950s and 1960s. However, nothing like this could be reproduced after that hegemony had been shaken. And again, one can argue that, after the validity of the existing proposal had been denied, the major problem was to elaborate an ontologically and methodologically convincing theory that would enable us to understand human action and a comprehensive set of extended social practices, usually called society, in their interrelatedness. By the 1980s, it was common to speak of the 'decline of the grand theoretical paradigms' or the 'interregnum' that still reigned in sociology.[10]

SOCIOLOGICAL PRACTICES AFTER THE SECOND CRISIS OF MODERNITY

Nevertheless, sociological practices continued. A brief look at how they were pursued shall be taken, before the more basic question of the possibility of a social science is taken up again. Four main types of practical responses to the post-modernist challenge prevail among practicing social scientists. They are quite distinct in how they view the depth of the crisis and in the aspects of it to which they try to respond.[11]

(a) Perhaps the most common response is what I would call the 'zero reaction', that is, the minimal response to the crisis of representation. It should be recalled that even during the reign of the Mertonian synthesis most of the sociological activities were empirical studies with limited theoretical ambitions of their own, only with a view that they might contribute to a larger edifice. Now these activities may well be continued after the plan for the edifice has been abandoned. If there were no other grounds, then the very existence of a socially established and quite sizeable and, not least, halfway self-governed sociological profession could be cause enough for its persistence.

I do recognize that quite a few sociologists suffer from theoretical and methodological uncertainties. But my hunch is that a larger number feel rather relieved under the present condition, given that the obligation to argue and justify one's procedures is much reduced. In the period of hegemony, the individual work would be valued according to its contribution to the greater body of knowledge. In the period of contestation, a linkage between theory, methodology and the actual social reality would be expected. A researcher would be questioned, for example, on whether multi-country standardized mass questionnaires could really tell us anything about the comparative intensity of political participation. The issue of theoretical evaluation is now much more relaxed, since pluralism of perspectives reigns. And also the methodological question could be easily dismissed by saying that the adequacy of methods is no issue any longer after the farewell to any concept of representation or even 'correspondence' with reality.

(b) If the 'zero reaction' is based on methodological continuity in the face of theoretical uncertainty, the questioning of the foundations of social science has also encouraged new and highly ambitious theoretical efforts. One might call 'hyper-scientization' those approaches that stress intellectual elegance and consistency to the seemingly permissible neglect of 'reality'. Such approaches have been developed in two directions that appeared suitable, namely as an extension of individualist-utilitarian theorizing in the rational choice vein (a kind of economistic invasion of the other social sciences) and as the radicalization of systemic reasoning under the label of self-organization or autopoiesis, in this case revived by infusions from biology and physics.[12] While I may appear to give too short shrift to these two fashionable trends, I have not come across any convincing argument about why the fairly radical theoretical assumptions that both of these approaches take should be more adequate now for a study of human social life than they were in their earlier variants.

(c) A third approach is practised rather with a view to rethinking the relation between theory and practice than with purely theoretical ambitions. It goes back to the strong assumptions on the utilization of social science knowledge for bettering the world that were prevalent during the 1960s. The main assumption in many political, economic and industrial interactions was that the best results would be achieved by the application of superior, that is, objective scientific knowledge. This rationalization trend had reached politics during the 1960s in the form of the alleged and much debated 'scientification of politics'. From the 1970s onwards, however, the use of scientific expertise to legitimate policies provoked contestants to build up their own expertise or to reject the dominant assumption that science produced a superior form of knowledge. The result was a declining belief in science as such and a pluralization of expertise.

More recently, both the scientification and the pluralization model of expertise tend to be overcome and replaced by ideas which refer in more specific forms to the interlinkages between cognitive and political issues. Rather than following either an objectivist or an interest-based epistemology, the newer approaches try to root both knowledge and policy deliberation in discursive interaction. The development has gone so far that often now the label 'post-positivistic' is used even in the midst of the discipline of the policy sciences.[13]

For a typical and very reflective argument for such thinking, one might look at Charles Lindblom's recent *Inquiry and Change*.[14] Lindblom argues that much of mainstream social science has limited the capability of human beings to understand their situation. It has done so by 'professional impairment' (p. 192) due to, in my words, the imposition of an alien perspective, disregard for the knowledge of the observed, overconcern with rigour, operationalization and coherence at the expense of insight into the contexts of action and into the meaning with which actors endow their situations. In many respects, therefore, a 'scientific society' (p. 213), if based on such a conception of science, is a rather negative utopia. Lindblom recommends that one should instead head for a 'self-guiding society', in which the main task of the social scientists is to reduce any impairments in the formation of wants and, thereby, to enable people to find out about their wants. 'In this cold universe, the only blueprint for utopia or any human betterment is what human beings themselves draw, and the path ahead may be longer than the path already walked' (p. 28).

In these three forms, the social sciences, and even more so the various forms of policy sciences, are continued as practices, but they have lost both many of the ambitions that were once held and much of their esteem in wider society. It has occasionally been pointed out that the periods when the social sciences were flourishing were also marked by a strong support for such an undertaking in the broader cultural milieu.[15] This idea entails that interest is shown in the activities from other social realms and that the young generation is more attracted to the field than is usually the case. Both were clearly the case for the social sciences during the 1960s, but this milieu of cultural support has almost completely vanished during the 1980s.

Such a portrait of the current practices of social scientists would force us to recognize the breakdown of the project of social science as it was historically envisaged. There appears to be only a little space which, in the overall field of the social sciences is still occupied by encompassing approaches for analysing the interrelations of social practices. These observations preclude the hailing of either plurality and diversity, as some do, or the continuity and stability of 'normal science', as is also done. However, others may again object, the present situation may just reflect the theoretical and methodological possibilities of a social science in a situation of thorough social transformations which are neither well understood, nor are there possibly even the tools developed to understand them. That is, it may be the only possible shape of a social science after the faith in producing an adequate image of the contemporary social world has subsided. It is in this both intellectual and social context that the discourse on postmodernity emerges, which indeed can be portrayed as the fourth response to the crisis of representation.[16]

(d) The sociology of postmodernity is the legitimate heir of the sociology of postindustrial society – so much so that one could see the promoters of the former as the children revolting against the realism and complacency of their parents, the promoters of the latter. In many respects, postmodernists endorse the theorems of postindustrialists and radicalize them. Where the latter spoke of endless growth of good knowledge to be applied for social betterment, the postmodernists see an arbitrary variety of intervention-oriented concepts evaluated purely according to their performance. Where postindustrialists identified enlightened steering elites in the top positions of an organized society, postmodernists see neither top positions nor any steering worth that name but a diffusion of activities in an ocean of simulation. And the masses are not functionally tied into social subsystems giving readable signals of approval or disapproval, but are an amorphous whole that through its very hyperconformism undermines any quest for legitimacy.[17]

The postmodernity theorists relate to the postindustrial society and the modernization theorem of sociology like the crisis-of-modernity theorists of the turn of the century did to liberal society and liberal political theory. Georg Simmel's sociology of fragmented life can be compared with the resurgent interest in microsociology and in the sociology and anthropology of everyday-life, Weber's iron cage of bureaucracy with Foucault's disciplinary society, and Vilfredo Pareto's transformation of democracy with Jean Baudrillard's mass society in the shadow of silent majorities.[18] In both cases, theorists see that societies are not as they are described in the dominant discourses. They oscillate between two interpretations of this divergence: either the societies have changed, or the discourses were flawed in the first place.

The sociology of postmodernity links a historical claim, the end of a social formation, to a theoretical claim, the inadequacy of the established concepts of social science to account for these recent social transformations. With regard to the historical claim, in my view, postmodernity theorists are likely to be right in identifying a major, real-world, societal restructuring, but their 'end of an era' discourse tends to exaggerate the dimensions of change. This tendency towards exaggeration itself, however, has its own intellectual context and, at least in part, should be appreciated by social theorists. The theoretical claim of postmodernity should largely be seen as a response to reductionist and reified conceptions of the modern in conventional social science and social theory. As in the case of the historical claim, I argue that there is a considerable significance, though often less in the exact terms of such works than in terms of a sensitizing with regard to issues that are neglected or repressed in a social science that often was all too modern.

'THE END OF SOCIAL SCIENCE': CAN THERE BE A POSTMODERNIST SOCIOLOGY?

In its strong variants, the discourse on postmodernity postulates the end of social science, the end of modernity, and the end of the subject.[19] The former assertion refers to the impossibility of obtaining any representation of the world for which valid criteria could be given. It is specifically directed against the narratives by which human beings tend to give order and meaning to their lives and to the communities they live in. As such, this postulate blurs into the second one, since it is modernity in particular that stands behind the master narratives of recent human history. Postmodernists cannot really make up their minds whether modernity has always merely been a human fiction or whether it has now completed its historical path. In either way, the power of its imaginary is supposed to have disappeared. In as far as the modern project was related to the Enlightenment, the second postulate is also linked to the third one. The 'philosophical discourse of modernity' was centred around the subject. Individual autonomy and self-realization were among its main themes. The postmodernist claim now is, again in two variants, that either the autonomy of the self was a mere construction of Enlightenment philosophy or that any social conditions for self-realization have been effectively subverted in the course of human social history over the past two centuries.

It has often enough been observed that the postmodernist claims, in the way they are stated, are exaggerated, self-contradictory, unarguable, or demonstrably wrong. None of these arguments need to be taken up or continued here. The significance of this discourse lies in its contextual validity, in its contribution to an ongoing process of societal reflection, or more precisely, in the way it has achieved a change in the direction of this auto-analysis. That is to say, its contribution does not reside in the rightness of its own positive claims (which, as is well known, many authors like to keep somewhat obscure), but in the critique of social science that it provides. The discourse on postmodernity sees modernist social science as being founded on the assumptions, *a priori*, of the intelligibility of the social world, of the coherence of social practices and of the rationality of action. And for much of social science, one must say, this view is valid.

The significance of this critique can be demonstrated by confronting the three strong claims of postmodernity with conventional wisdom in the modernist social sciences. If the thesis on the end of social science points to the difficulties of cognitive representation of the social world in the social sciences, then it needs to be granted that those difficulties have been very little reflected in most of the social science practices. Much like in the natural sciences, methodological debates were mostly devoted to the improvement of the tools to reveal more features of social reality. Or, as Ralf Dahrendorf reported about the collegial reactions to the German dispute over positivism, neither Karl Popper nor Theodor Adorno were seen as addressing 'the methodological problems of a sociology, which – at least in its everyday business – pursues mainly empirical studies'.[20]

The same can be said about the thesis on the end of modernity. The key features of modernity had become standard assumptions of modernist social science rather than phenomena that can and should be exposed to inquiry. Crucial among these were underproblematized conceptions of the relevant social collective to which human action refers and of the properties of human action itself. The former neglect is evident. Most sociological reasoning – if it was interested in the relation of widely extended practices at all, that is, reasoning with a so-called macro-sociological interest – merely assumed that human action took place within the solid boundaries of 'societies' implicitly or explicitly defined by the existing states. And these societies, consisting of 'peoples' and 'nations', were seen on paths that would lead to, or deviate from, the accomplishment of some final state of history, or at least some perfectly harmonious state. Even if such terminology was mostly out of use after the Second World War, these conceptions of the master narratives of modernity inform even the modernization theories.

The end of the subject, one might argue, was reached within modernist sociology itself, namely in those theories that emphasized the norm-following character of human action to such an extent that individuality disappeared and human beings became cultural 'dopes'. Mostly, the conceptions of human action in the social sciences have either tended toward such a view or, in diametrical opposition, started from the assumption of individual rationality. In both cases, though, the question of the relation of the individual human being to the social world cannot even be posed in empirically and historically open terms, because the answer to it has been turned into a theoretical starting-point.

For all these fundamental issues, the postmodernity discourse has contributed to re-opening questions which modernist social science had closed and kept sealed. The problem with that discourse is that it tends to limit its own impact through the form and language in which its arguments are presented. In other words, it tends to close the issues again before they have really been taken up. The arrogance and, occasionally, thoughtlessness of the postmodernists may, as well as the stubbornness and shortsightedness of the modernists, be blamed for the fact that these questions have not become as open and central to social science and social philosophy as they could be after such provocative views have been voiced.

It appears as if social scientists, even many of those who have recognized the relevance of the questions, have taken them to be unanswerable in the way they are posed. This calls for transforming them into more accessible forms. Proclaiming the end of social science, of modernity and of the subject means, indeed, pretending to have answers to these three key questions rather than inviting debate and inquiry. An interesting proposal that appears to avoid such forgone conclusions has recently been provided by Richard Rorty, whose way of presenting the case can be used even to rephrase the concern. Rorty transforms the claim of the triple end into one of a triple contingency. He sees our present condition as characterized by the insight into the contingency of language, the contingency of community and the contingency of selfhood.[21]

Rorty's discussion of the contingency of language is an epistemological one focused on the possibility of making representations of the world. As everything we say about the world is expressed in some language, and every language itself is social and particular, and relations between languages cannot be specified with regard to validity claims, Rorty argues, we should get rid of the conviction that 'some vocabularies are better representations of the world than others' and 'drop the idea of languages as representations' (p. 21). The consequence is an abdication of philosophy and a turn to poetry. I do not want (and do not feel capable of it) to enter into an epistemological discussion here, but I think that the strong turn Rorty proposes already indicates a main feature of his thinking, namely an under-conceptualization in sociological terms.[22]

While this feature is generally problematic, it becomes crucial when discussion moves from epistemological issues towards genuinely social ones, such as the one of community. There, Rorty claims nothing less than 'to offer a redescription of our current institutions and practices' (p. 45), an objective that sounds remarkably similar to the one which is pursued in this book. However, refusing to even talk about anything that he calls 'foundations', the only insight he has to offer is that 'the citizens of [his] liberal utopia would be people who had a sense of the contingency of their language of moral deliberation, and thus of their consciences, and thus of their community' (p. 61). This view appears, of course, to be fully in line with one aspect of the imaginary signification of modernity, the one of freedom and autonomy. But Rorty does not seem to recognize at all that 'a historical narrative about the rise of liberal institutions and customs' (p. 68) would be the worst of Whiggish historiography if it were done only with that part of the imaginary signification of modernity in mind.

This is so because the ground of the thesis on the contingency of selfhood also becomes slippery as soon as empirical-historical considerations are introduced.

Rorty's lecture on this issue is basically a praise of the strong poet, based on a Nietzschean-Freudian notion of self-creation which sees 'every human being as consciously or unconsciously acting out an idiosyncratic fantasy' (p. 36). From this stand-point, he seems to deplore that there can be no lives 'which are pure action rather than re-action' (p. 42), because they have to deal with others, with matter, with historically set stages.

Here the weakness of his entire approach becomes visible. It resides less in the insistence on contingencies in the philosophical debate on foundations than it does in the unwillingness to accept that there is a structured social and natural world of and around human beings and that this world is the terrain, the only terrain, on which they may create themselves. In this sense, there is no 'pure action' at all, but only 're-action', but re-acting is then exactly the mode, the only available mode, for human self-creation.[23] Occasionally, Rorty appears to grant this generally (pp. 6, 41–2 and 191). But at these points his refusal to even notice historical or sociological statements on the world has a devastating effect. He jumps from general philosophical observations on contingencies to recommendations for practicing political liberalism. Without a sociohistorical account of the condition of contingency, that is, of the modern condition, such a reasoning is either empty or misleading in the search for a 'liberal utopia'.

By appropriating this part of Rorty's philosophizing, I am trying to achieve two things. With him and against modernist social science, I argue for accepting the contingency of all social phenomena as the *a priori* assumptions for social research, and more specifically the contingency of community and selfhood as assumptions for a current study of the condition of modernity. The latter is especially needed now, since this is a historical period in which relatively well-established *social* foundations of both community and self have begun to shake again more strongly. In this sense, we live indeed in a postmodern condition. But against Rorty, and in the continuity of a project which maintains the possibility of a social science, I argue for analysing the specific shapes that community and selfhood do actually take and may possibly take under the present conditions.[24]

As the reader will have recognized, I will claim to have proceeded on the path towards such a sociology on all the preceding pages in this book. The next step will be a discussion of the likely conditions of selfhood during the historical transformations of modernity in the following chapter, to prepare the discussion of the relation of self-identity and community under current conditions in Chapter 11.

Chapter 10

Modernity and self-identity

Liberation and disembedding

ORGANIZED MODERNITY AND SELF-IDENTITY: THE ELIMINATION OF AMBIVALENCE

The question of the historically changing relation of individual selves, social identities and societal configurations accompanied the preceding account of the history of organized modernity – its emergence, temporary consolidation and crisis. This question may now be faced in somewhat more explicit – though hardly conclusive – terms than was possible throughout the analysis. The two major approaches to this question during organized modernity itself have been, first, the mainstream sociological debate on social roles and, second, the view of the fate of the individual in theories of mass society.

The concept of the social role was the main tool by which sociology tried to handle the relation of 'social structure and personality'.[1] In the classical era of sociology very little of that problematic can be found. That discourse was marked by its historical situation, namely that 'modernity' was just being extended to include all members of a society. This meant that the modern ideal of the self was present, but the sociologists were not really able to think that this ideal could reach beyond the bourgeois groups. Many of the sociological theories of the time contained, or were even explicitly based on, elitist elements. Elitism, however, allows an avoidance of the question. To put it schematically, there are some human beings whom one would look at with a focus on personality, and many others to whom the analysis of social structure can be applied.

In twentieth-century social thought, these internal boundaries between entirely different kinds of human beings were visibly eroding, and sociology had to take account of this – not surprisingly in North America first. A conception that allowed one to see both self-identity and society as emerging from the ways human beings actively relate to others was proposed by George Herbert Mead and entered into the works of the Chicago School. For Mead, a 'me' emerges from somebody's perception of the attitude others hold towards her or him.[2] My identity is formed from my way of combining the different 'me's I am confronted with. Mead's conceptualization is a very open one. It allows for identities to emerge or not emerge, depending on the individual's abilities to reconcile different expectations and on the divergence of expectations itself. It also allows for the finding of socially or historically typical forms of social identity. However, much of this openness was soon lost again.

In his attempt to formulate a general theory of society, Talcott Parsons drew on Mead but also on the works of the anthropologist Ralph Linton who proposed seeing individuals as having a determined social status in the structure of a society. The status involved rights and duties and entailed the expectation, on the part of others, of a certain behaviour. Social role, as the dynamic aspect of a status, is the living up to such expectations. In the 1950s and 1960s, Parsons, Robert Merton and others broadened this very deterministic concept without, however, really altering it. Trying to link a theory of action with a theory of order, Parsons stressed the value standards and the 'orientation system' of individuals, and he introduced the idea of functionality of role behaviour for a social order. He writes, 'what the actor does in his relations with others seen in the context of its functional significance for the system ... we shall call his *role*.'[3] Merton emphasized the multitude of roles in any status position and spoke of a 'role-set'. This idea allowed the possibility of role conflicts, and Merton was concerned about the capacity of individuals to master diverse expectations and still perform functionally in their positions. But it also allowed the introduction of individual autonomy, given the need for managing and negotiating expectations to make them compatible.[4]

This latter aspect is important in most recent contributions to the debate, which tend to dissolve the earlier argument on normative and functional integration. The complexity of role-sets is then seen as a difficulty, which may increase the feeling of alienation for the individual and threaten the disruption of functional behaviour. But the very same complexity is also the source of individuation and, consequently, individual autonomy. 'The lack of a basic source of disturbance is also a lack of a basic source for reflection.'[5]

More structurally oriented sociology focused on the social determinants of roles. The basic idea was that diversity of one's social environment would increase the complexity of role-sets. Generally, increasing such diversity would be seen as a feature of modern society. However, no unilinear development to greater complexity would occur, since there were countervailing tendencies. It was observed that class differences often do not promote complex role-sets,

> because they imply that people make invidious social distinctions among strata and discriminate in their role relations on the basis of these class distinctions. Indeed, any ethnic distinctions and ingroup preferences involves discrimination in establishing social relations that counteract the otherwise positive influence of a diverse population structure on complex role-sets.

The same is said to hold for residential segregation, while social and spatial mobility should enhance role-complexity.[6]

Much of this writing is very modernist sociology in the sense that the objectivist view of the detached sociologist sees the limits and determinations of the lives of others in a very clear-cut way, while he only reluctantly grants the sameness of the other to himself. However, it is likely that the observations, while referring to modern society as such, capture something of the organization of modernity. Clearly recognizing that even the lower-class member of society can no longer simply be said to be tied by tradition, the sociologist discovers other determinations that make less of a free individual creating himself and choosing his social identity.

Re-reading this research as a partial self-portrait of organized modernity, we find that, after an initial conceptual openness, the relation of individuals to society is streamlined. The borrowing from anthropology is significant itself, since early anthropology saw 'primitive societies' as ahistoric and static, devoid of conflict and motion. In the Parsonian system, individual self, social role and societal integration are conceptually interlinked to form the 'stable social system',[7] which was how the emerging order of organized modernity was indeed regarded. The more recent emphasis on the capacity of the individual to deal actively with role offers and expectations may then be related to changes in society that mark the end of the very organized form of modernity.[8] I shall return to this question after having briefly discussed the alternative view on modern, mass society.

Off the mainstream of disciplinary debate, the critical theories of mass society, as discussed above, dealt with the question of the relation of the individuals to society more in terms of social philosophy. They tended to stress that opportunities for individuals to define themselves and create their own identity are extremely limited under conditions of a highly organized capitalist society. Daniel Bell's early and exemplary criticism of theorizing about the individual in mass society provides a way of showing into which problems any such reasoning runs.[9]

Some of these approaches, most of which were published between the 1930s and the 1950s, stress the 'disorganization of society', a notion by which they refer to the demise of differentiated social structures, that is, in the form of the estates, and the counterposition of a homogeneous mass of atomized individuals to an all-powerful state. These views deplore the loneliness and powerlessness of the isolated individual, the loss of the variety of possible relations between different people, and often also the loss of cultural values in a general process of downward homogenization. The passive TV spectator, isolated in her suburban home, is a recurrent example. Other approaches, however, focus on the bureaucratization of society, on the establishment of machine-like relations between human beings in a society that is essentially over-organized. While here, too, the destruction of an older social fabric is seen, the bureaucratic over-organization rather leads to a constant mobilization of individuals, but a mobilization merely as 'cogs in the machine' without enabling participation and self-expression.

Bell points out that these approaches, which he identifies – following Edward Shils – as coming from both conservative and neo-Marxist sides, share an 'aristocratic' longing for a less crowded past, and he raises doubts about the desirability of their implicit wishes: 'Mass society is . . . the bringing of the "masses" into society, from which they once were excluded.'[10] But also analytically he sees them as weak. Their 'large-scale abstractions' fail to recognize the degrees to which forms of association, communality, diversity and nonconformism exist in, for instance, American society.[11] All of Bell's critical remarks are well justified: the recourse to a simplistic theoretical dichotomy, the contradictory conceptualization of that dichotomy with regard to the relation of individual and society, and the lack of empirical grounding of the strong claims. Indeed, some of the contributions to the debate on 'postmodernity' today suffer from the same weaknesses.[12]

Given these problems, all of which are still with us, it would be adventurous to offer a full-scale reformulation of the issue of the self in organized modernity. Against the background of my preceding argument and the observations of recent changes in the discourse on self and identity, however, a more fruitful starting-point for further investigation may be proposed. The notion of recurring crises of modernity and the identification of processes of disembedding and reembedding, which are historically distinct as to whom and what kinds of social identities they affect, could be the basis for a socially more specific analysis of the formation and stability of social identities.

Fundamentally modern is exactly 'the idea that we construct our own social identity'.[13] The social existence of this idea is what the societies we look at have in common throughout the entire period of two centuries that is of interest here. As such, thus, it does not give any guidance in defining different configurations. Therefore, I would like to introduce three qualifying criteria.

First, the existence of the idea of identity construction still leaves open the question of whether all human beings living in a given social context share it and are affected by it. The *social permeation* of the idea may be limited. Second, human beings in the process of constructing their social identities may consider this as a matter of *choice*, as a truly modernist perspective would have it. In many circumstances, however, though a knowledge and a sense of the social construction of identities prevails, it may appear to human beings as almost natural, as in a looser sense pre-given or ascribed, which social identity they are going to have. Third, the *stability* of any identity one has chosen may vary. Such a construction of identity may be considered a once-in-a-lifetime occurrence, but may also be regarded as less committing and, for instance, open to reconsideration and change at a later age.

In the order in which they are listed these criteria widen the scope of *constructability* of identities. All conditions of identity-construction have existed for some individuals or groups at any time during the past two centuries in the West. However, I think one can see the width of constructability of identity as a distinguishing feature between the three broad types of modern configurations. To put the thesis the other way round, the widening of the scope of identity construction marks the transitions from one to another social configuration of modernity. These transitions entail social processes of disembedding and provoke transformations of social identities, in the course of which not only other identities are acquired but the possibility of construction is also more widely perceived.

Restricted liberal modernity was a configuration in which the constructability of social identity was hardly accessible to the majority of the population, the peasant and industrial working classes and most women. Exactly for this reason, it may be said that membership in modernity was denied them. This configuration is sharply divided on this issue. Counterposed to the situation of this majority, a small, predominantly male, elite minority hailed the idea of 'making oneself', 'realizing oneself', in terms of social and personal identity, as the advent of true freedom and humanity. This was true for both the intellectual elites and the commercial elites, it was merely the basic understandings of what self-realization meant that differed widely. The predominance of such attitudes among the elites allows one to call the entire configuration one of modernity, though restricted. Historically, their orientations should have decisive impact on the shaping of the social practices and would draw everybody else into modernity, too (see Chapter 4).

The double bourgeois emphasis, intellectually and commercially, on the constructability of social identity introduced the potential for a hitherto unknown openness into social life. In line with a view that emerged around the turn to the nineteenth century, Claude Lefort maintains in emphatic words that

> modern society and the modern individual are constituted by the experience of the dissolution of the ultimate markers of certainty; . . . their dissolution inaugurates an adventure – and it is constantly threatened by the resistance it provokes – in which the foundations of power, the foundations of right and the foundations of knowledge are all called into question – a truly historical adventure in the sense that it can never end, in that the boundaries of the possible and the thinkable constantly recede.[14]

By mid-century, this openness and uncertainty could surely be felt, at least in some realms of social life. From Karl Marx and Friedrich Engels' *Communist Manifesto* and Charles Baudelaire's writings on modern life onwards, this is a view on modernity that has in fact continuously reasserted itself throughout the history of modernity. And the questioning of all foundations was the major feature of the cultural-intellectual crisis of modernity around the turn of the century.

In more specific historico-sociological terms, however, one needs to put more emphasis on the resistance that modernity constantly provokes than Lefort does. This resistance was the energy behind the building of organized modernity, and it came from very different social groups with highly varying interests. When these interests had met for political accommodation, an order could be constructed that could temporarily arrest modernity. At that point, the image could emerge that the boundaries of both the possible and the thinkable had again been firmly set.

The wide extension of market and factory practices, which occurred during the nineteenth century, meant a social process of disembedding for large parts of the population and a questioning of whatever understanding of themselves they had held. The resources to create new social identities would be provided, on the one hand, by the intellectual elites and their discourses on national communities and their boundaries and, on the other hand, by 'the making of the working class', to borrow E.P. Thompson's formulation. These identities were the material on the basis of which a reshaping of social practices could occur to build a new social order in which most inhabitants of a territory could secure a place. The building of this order, which I have described as organized modernity, provided for the conditions of a reembedding.[15]

If one looks at phenomena such as class cultures or class votes, and also at nationalist movements throughout the first half of the twentieth century, I think one can fairly safely assume that such a reembedding indeed took place. Membership in a class or nation was an important marker for orientation.[16] In cases where one orientation was played against the other, as in National Socialism, violent struggles with high participation occurred as well as cruel oppression after the victory of the Nazi movement. In cases where both orientations were joined, such as in Swedish social democracy, an indeed almost homely social atmosphere was created. Though less strongly expressed, the latter became the model of social organization in Western Europe after the defeat of Nazism.

By the 1950s the order of organized modernity was well established. Limited as such expressions are, the high consent of the population to this order in the absence of direct repression may be an indicator for the degree of solid re-embedding of individuals in this social configuration. Through the first half of this century, 'external' national and 'internal' social boundaries had been clearly set. You were German and a white-collar employee, or English and a worker, but whatever you were, it was not by your own choice. Ambivalences had been eliminated by comprehensive classificatory orders and the enforcing of these orders in practice. Mostly, individuals knew where they belonged, but did not have the impression that they had a major part in defining this place. The closure of modernity under the sign of modernization came close to reversing the condition of modernity, as compared to its earlier, restricted liberal, form. The life of the modern human being would no longer be fleeting, contingent and uncertain, but stable, certain and smoothly progressing.

This was the society which many critics, but not only critics, were to label mass society. Daniel Bell was right to dissect inconsistencies in the critical analyses; there was more variety, individuality and sociality than most critics recognized. But their intuition did not really betray them. They saw organized society from the perspective of, not aristocracy but, liberal modernity. That was how they recognized that the bourgeois ideal was indeed abandoned in the sense that, now that people were formally free members of modernity, they did not fully avail themselves of the possibility of constructing their own identities. This was what the theorem of the loss of the individual really referred to – and causes were searched for in the social condition. As insufficient as those social analyses often were, the basic diagnosis was not invalid.

The relative stability and certainty of organized modernity, though, were not to remain. They rested on the organization of social practices in such a way that the practices would join into each other and provide places for (almost) everybody in a society. The process of establishing such practices rested on the existence (and promotion) of organizing criteria that gave them meaning in the eyes of those who would constantly reenact them in their daily lives. Once established and habitualized, such practices may well go on after their (historical-genealogical) organizing criteria have disappeared.

By organizing criteria I refer here to the social identities in terms of nationality and class consciousness. Their disparition, or rather weakening, can indeed be observed during the 1950s and 1960s.[17] While being founded on these identities, the dynamics of organized modernity tended to undermine them by eroding them in more affluent and more homogeneous, 'middle-class', 'mass' culture. It emptied them of their substance, as can be read also from political and sociological terms like 'class compromise' or 'levelled middle-class society' (Schelsky) that were current at that time. All of this may have little impact, as long as the habitualized practices are not affected. But when, in a situation of eroded foundational identities, the order of practices is shaken – for whatever reasons – they cannot be kept up or re-established, since no collective orientations or social identities are at hand to rebuild them.[18] This was the situation that spelt the end of organized modernity and led to the emergence of the phenomenon that came to be known as 'postmodernity'. The transition entailed a further widening of the scope of social-identity construction.

Before I turn to describing the conditions of identity formation after the end of organized modernity, I want to return briefly to the erosion of the organized order of practices (as portrayed in Chapter 8). The relation of the individuals to the institutions changed along with the institutional change. With regard to authoritative practices, the changes entailed a weakening of the linkage between the individual and the polity. With regard to allocative practices, they signalled the return of uncertainty.

THE FLIGHT OF THE CITIZEN

At its height, organized democracy *cum* interventionist welfare state provided a set of well-established routines in which the citizens, in their own best interest, would take their assigned places and fulfil their limited political obligations. The places and obligations, as well as the benefits the citizens could obtain, were originally defined in substantive social or political terms, but with the universalization of policies and the routinization of organized politics they were being de-substantivized.

The organization of authoritative practices was a collective action based on the experience of violent conflicts and of unacceptable dangers and uncertainties in modern life. So, the encapsulation of conflicts – the 'decline of political passions'[19] – and the homogenization of modes of life – expressing them in the language of statistics – cannot be seen as unintended effects, even though the effects went beyond, and outlasted, the intentions. The relative apathy of the citizen and the passivity of the classified welfare recipient and policy object more generally were part of the new order and a requirement to make it work. And so it did, for a while.

It is not really well understood what happened then in the relation between the citizen and the polity. The evidence as given earlier is ambiguous. On the one hand, it points to a re-activation of the political life of the citizenry when people participate unconventionally or even form their own new parties. On the other hand, some observations, such as on abstentionism and declining party memberships, indicate an increasing rejection of politics. In my view, most of the observed phenomena can and need to be interpreted in common as a way of dealing with the experiences of organized modernity.

At first sight it appears contradictory that a trend towards the ever more detailed institutionalization of social relations, which indicates a high degree of mastery and monitoring of those relations, should be accompanied by a kind of 'liberation, a flight of the individuals escaping from the duty to appear as a subject'.[20] But it is exactly the experience of the certainties and routines of political life in the interventionist welfare states that allows individuals to begin to play with the rules on their part, interpret them, use them against the intentions of the rule-makers, and the like.

Media research has given an impetus to rethinking the relations between the political class and the ordinary citizen. Early critical media studies had often assumed that the recipients would be helplessly and passively exposed to whatever messages the media companies wanted to feed them. Later interpretations, however, stressed the active dealing with the signs, which may be played with or composed with regard to specific messages that might only emerge in the relation between the media and the particular individual. A very suggestive, and provocative, transposition of such a perspective on political processes has been offered by Jean Baudrillard in *In the Shadow of the Silent Majorities*,[21] an essay which I shall appropriate here on my own terms.

In organized democracy, the political class has established a very asymmetric, almost a one-way, relation to the citizenry. On the one side, it covers it with opinion polls in forms and on subjects that are processable in party terms. On the other side, it feeds back election platforms and, if in power, policy programmes that are intended to solicit and maintain electoral support. This is practically all the interaction there is, and it is completely structured by the strategic interests of the political class. The citizenry has mostly conformed to this interaction pattern, initially maybe even on the assumption that this instrument enhances political communication. But increasingly it has recognized the strategic reduction of its own role, of 'people's sovereignty', by this means. Given that, thus, the idea of representation was undermined by the political class, the citizenry also came to refuse to be represented and began to use its responses stategically, too.

Drawing implicitly on a social-interest theory of representation, the political class had designed the 'electoral game' as one in which there are (competing) players only on one side, whereas the other side is characterized by determined preferences that merely need to be detected and activated by the players.[22] Such a conception led to the mobilization of the people by and for organizational elites, which was typical of organized modernity. However, the full conventionalization of this mode and its instruments – opinion research and the elections themselves –

allowed the citizens to draw on the rules on their part and to transform the exchange into a more balanced two-way communication, though a very reduced one.

There is no good means of knowing, by empirical research, whether such an inversion or reciprocation indeed takes place, since strategic considerations and 'second thoughts' are not easily revealed by standardized questioning. However, a number of phenomena can sensibly be interpreted in terms of an electoral attitude that is at the same time more active and more distanced toward the political game than the standard view on organized democracy assumes. First, the share of the electorate that exercises a stable party vote tends to decline. Less voters feel they have a quasi-ascriptive relation to a party. Even when they may continue to have stable inclinations, they may play with their vote to effect change in their party. The famous 'Reagan Democrats' are an example of such an attitude as are social democrats who vote occasionally for the Green Party in Germany. Second, voters have recognized that the traditional cleavage parties are not the only ones that may exist. Besides new parties such as environmentalist ones,[23] 'protest' parties or candidates run with increasing success in many countries. Third, voters have noted that established-party governments do indeed respond to their defections and expressions of dissent. They may vote for an anti-tax or xenophobic party expecting – and often rightly so – that governments will no longer dare to raise taxes or will restrict immigration, if they are 'punished' in this way. And, fourth, as a basis of all such considerations, voters assume rightly that party strategists will get to know what the voters try to express via opinion research and media coverage.

In a typically postmodernist gesture, Jean Baudrillard refuses to make up his mind whether he should regard such phenomena as showing resistance or hyperconformism on the part of the masses.[24] But his undecidedness actually captures much of the constellation. The behaviour may be called hyperconformist in that it fully accepts the reduction of politics to the conventions and technologies that have been introduced to encapsulate conflicts. It is resistant, however, in that it turns these tools against the existing political class – and it proves to do so effectively.

The key to understanding the double nature of this transformation is to regard it as the effective undermining of the social-interest based conventions of organized representation. When these conventions are broken, the individual citizens are effectively liberated from the social determination to express their views according to their social location.[25] However, this liberation tends to weaken the linkage between the individuals and the polity even further than the 'thin theory of citizenship' of organized modernity did. Devoid of the substantive underpinning of any social theory, the only connection that exists from the citizenry to the electoral parties is through survey research and media – and the vote. In such a situation, the party elites are as dependent on the electorate as oligopolistic companies are on the consumers.[26] If it is the case (which we do not know with any degree of certainty), that the citizenry from its side has indeed transformed its relation to the polity into one that is analogous to a product market, this is certainly a process of distanciation and a rejection of offers of social identities. It is a liberation from imposed concepts of representation and simultaneously a disembedding, since no other mode of representation takes its place. More specifically, any potential concept of collective agency is abandoned, apart from the mere numerical aggregation of votes analogous to the structuring of a market by accumulated individual consumer preferences.

The combined effects of the two major historical transformations of authoritative practices – the building of organized representation and its destruction – make up for a crucial part of what I will call the historical tendency of the modern project towards self-cancellation. The building of highly organized authoritative institutions was an attempt to create collective agency in the face of disembedding social practices that called for collectivist responses. The building of these institutions, however, also entailed a reduction of the forms of communicative interaction in the realm of authoritative practices. This reduction, in turn, undermined the possibility of politics so that, when the organized rules became inadequate, there were no means left to restore a fuller understanding and a fuller mode of representation of collective action. The second transformation brought the liberation from the constraints of social conventions, but it did so at the cost of a further reduction of political communication. Both transformations signalled an increase of individual autonomy: in the first case with regard to the exposure to social disembedding in the form of collective creativity, in the second case with regard to the constraints by conventions in the form of individual liberation. After the twofold liberations, the prospects for achieving collective self-determination, however, one of the major ambitions of the modern project, are dimmer than at any time before.

Should this partial self-cancellation of modernity be taken light-heartedly? I shall try to give an answer to this question in the following chapter when looking more comprehensively at the present condition of modernity. I think, however, that it is observable that citizens are often aware of it and generally do not take it light-heartedly. It is a common attitude to judge the state of the polity as unsatisfactory and to hope for betterment through an, even if unlikely, collective process of renewal in the realm of politics. This is why new and promising challengers in this realm are likely to be greeted with a degree of interest and sympathy that is at odds with the well-known likelihood of their failure. This interest and sympathy indicate a remaining, very fundamental, ambivalence. Still, it is not (yet?) possible to live completely without the idea of politics. There is a nostalgic yearning for a hero, despite all experience and insight. The way to deal with this real-world ambivalence is to try to regard such political efforts like a spectacle, with sympathies clearly distributed but with the distance retained that is necessary to avoid disappointments. Ultimately, then, such politicians

> are the heroes of a kind of film in real time which, some variants and modifications of the 'casting' apart, tells always more or less the same story, which finishes badly. That story can certainly not be taken for a historical project. But, at least, it allows to keep its scenography functioning of which we retain an irremediable nostalgia.[27]

THE ENTERPRISING SELF AND THE TWO-THIRDS SOCIETY

In the preceding section it was argued that the relation between polity, party and voter in the realm of authoritative practices tends to model itself analogously to the one between market, producer and consumer. At the same time, the relation of the individual to the social order was gradually transformed in the realm of allocative practices, too. During organized modernity the ideal-typical 'economic subject' was the employee/consumer who performed routine tasks in a hierarchical organization for mass production and bought these standardized products, thereby contributing to the mode of mass consumption. This mode of allocative organization allowed most contemporary observers only two ways of interpreting the relation of the individual to the social order, either in terms of obedience and conformity or in terms of resistance and refusal. The break-up of organized modernity, in contrast, has been accompanied by other views which stress creative involvement and self-realization.

In recent years, fuelled by the impact of Thatcherism, a debate on the meaning of 'enterprise culture' has emerged in England.[28] While the term was little more than a political slogan, it meant to underline the need to revitalize British society at the beginning of the Thatcher era, a decade later it appears to have translated into real social transformations. The British situation may even be exemplary for some of the reorientations occurring throughout societies in the Northern hemisphere.

The programme for the enterprise culture consisted of two major, consecutive parts.[29] The initial idea was that privatizations should restore a market economy to make efficiency criteria govern more of economic life. Beyond the actual privatizations, the more general idea was that ' "the commercial enterprise" takes on a paradigmatic status'[30] for other social institutions, too. This extension of the initial idea was marked by the insight that a market economy would only deliver the desired results if it was run by enterprising individuals. Consequently, the political programme also meant to encourage the qualities of the 'enterprising self', namely self-reliance, goal orientation, activism and reward expectation. The perfect member of this society would be 'running [his] own life as a small business'.[31]

This shift is supposed to occur with regard to both the producer aspect and the consumer aspect of the individual. But – against the hopes of Thatcherism – it is clearly more prononunced as a transformation of consumer culture. As such it has caught much attention, not least in postmodernist readings of social change. The possibility of creating multiple worlds of objects is seen as a basis for a very distanced sense of both the world, appearing as simulated or hyperreal, and of one's own identity, the 'end of the subject'. The shift in discourse is very clear in this area. Critical analyses during organized modernity tended to see consumer culture as the displacement of desires for self-realization into a world of objects and pointed to the production of standardized social identities through the orientation towards mass-produced goods. More recent interpretations tend to acknowledge that identity-building may indeed occur also via material objects, and hail both the current diversity of products and the diversity of cultural orientations that it supports.[32]

The flexibilization of production may then be seen to enable – if not really the emergence of individual consumption patterns, then at least – a greater leeway for the creation of modes of 'distinction' and small-group standards. The break-up of organized modernity brings a 'shift from socialised to privatised modes of consumption'.[33] Pierre Bourdieu's landmark study in the sociology of culture, *Distinction*, is possibly the last great analysis of culture under conditions of organized modernity. While he shows that consumer choices are not unidimensionally related to class position, he still observes (for France in the 1960s) a clear structure reproducible on two axes. Arguably, this is no longer the case, but there is far greater choice in consumer practices and greater diversity and variability in defining and creating one's social identity.[34]

If, in some way or other, the phenomenon of 'enterprise culture' exists, the problem is to assess its impact on the relation of individual human beings to the social order which they live in and create. Some critical analyses have seen these developments as another turn in the development of capitalism, as the 'cultural logic of late capitalism'.[35] While it would be fallacious to neglect the commodification of human desires in a comprehensive social analysis, it is equally fallacious to reduce the current developments to this aspect and see them as driven by an abstract logic. In contrast, it is easy to point to, first, the fact that the social opening of standardized modes of self-expression through objects was the work, not of a logic but, of contestants and 'counter-cultural' movements, and that the diffusion of such orientations throughout society was seen with concern by conservative, stability-oriented commentators.[36] Second, from a critical perspective that supports the idea of autonomy it is difficult to deny the actual liberating effects of this shift, since it 'might be argued that neither the figure of the sovereign consumer, nor that of the enterprising producer are altogether illusory', even if they have to be heavily qualified.[37]

On the one hand, the shift towards the 'enterprising self' places new demands on the individual human being. Rather than resting on a secured place in a stable social order, individuals are asked to engage themselves actively in shaping their lives and social positions in a constantly moving social context. Such a shift must increase uncertainties and even anxieties. Visibly, the market offer of expertise to cope with any thinkable situation one might enter into has increased over the past two decades – a development which one may see, from the demand side, rather as a helpful new mode of orientation or, from the supply side, as ways to guide individuals to socially compatible behaviour without resorting to command and force.[38] On the other hand, the social shift towards the 'enterprising self' creates opportunities, it enlarges the scope for self-realization. To assess the relevance and impact of the current transformations on the individual more precisely, we have to locate them in their social contexts. The problematic of the transformations of allocative practices lies in potentially misleading assumptions about their social dimensions and depths.

If the term 'enterprise culture' was a political slogan in favour of the dissolution of the organized practices of post-war Western societies and for the freeing of individuals from the ties of regulations and constraints, the term 'two-thirds society' points critically to the differential impact such a programme might have on different groups in society. Basically, it states that the liberations brought about in the enterprise culture are to the benefit of some, even many, but at the high cost to a sizeable minority.

The term two-thirds society was common in Germany at the turn of the 1970s when the social-democratic conception of the welfare state, a conception of comprehensive coverage, still lingered on, but was threatened.[39] It was supposed to mean that up to one third of society would be regarded as not capable of full integration, in terms of secure employment, living standards, etc. While the exact numbers of that 'third' of the population are never analytically determined (but are regularly still below one third, regardless of measure, in all Western societies), the coining of the term has a political implication. It points out that a part of the population which is sizeable, but at the same time below the threshold of electoral-political relevance, unless coalitions can be formed, is excluded from the main spheres of society in which social identities can be formed. The social democratic conception of politics during organized modernity, in contrast, was based on the assumption that a welfare-state/full-employment coalition would always comprise electoral majorities in industrial societies. If this is no longer the case, then the authoritative rules allow the neglect of the third 'third' – and the discourse on the 'enterprise culture' allows the shifting of the blame for that neglect to these people themselves. They were obviously incapable of gaining an acceptable place, to run the business of their own successfully enough.

In the context of my argument, the reference to the two-thirds society serves only the purpose of pointing to the possibility that the social configuration that succeeds organized modernity may produce an inherent unevenness analogous to those that restricted liberal and organized modernity had shown. In the former, a major part of the population in a given territory was formally excluded from modernity. In the latter, full inclusion had been reached at the price of restricting modes of expression and action. The emerging social configuration may restore the width of modes of expression and action, but it may place new requirements on the availability of the means of self-realization. These requirements are *socially* identifiable as the material, cultural, intellectual means needed to appropriate the vast offer of possible forms of self-creation. However, the reason for whether somebody possesses or acquires them or not tends to be located in the *individuals* themselves.

If the discourse of the enterprise culture becomes the dominant mode of social representation and if simultaneously a two-thirds society emerges, then general conditions of social uncertainty will be created under which the individuals may restrict themselves, may choose not to avail themselves of the opportunities of self-realization that are on offer. In such a situation, some may accept the demands of the enterprise culture and will then struggle to secure social locations that they consider acceptable, not least by resorting to the tools of expertise for self-management that are on offer.[40] Others may try to shift the blame and organize collectively to either develop a mode of representation to discharge themselves (any theory of historical suppression of one's own capabilities, such as nationalisms) or to appropriate by other means what could not be gained through the established rules (such as organized crime).

Before drawing such general conclusions, however, actual modes of identity-building under current conditions shall be considered in somewhat more detail. For this look, I shall limit myself to a more general guiding assumption: the changes that are observed, with regard to both authoritative and allocative practices, tend to enlarge the social space in which identity can be formed. They do not always, however, enlarge the capability of the individual human beings to inhabit these larger spaces, or their interest and motivation to do so.

'POSTMODERNITY' AND SELF-IDENTITY: THE RETURN OF AMBIVALENCE

How far the mode of constitution of individual and social identities today differs from the one during organized modernity is a major theme in writings on postmodernity. Sometimes a 'new individualism' is diagnosed, whereas in other views the ultimate fragmentation and dispersion of the individual is assumed. Many such sweeping interpretations of postmodernity do not take the situation of actually living human beings really seriously, human beings who define their lives, act and are constrained from acting, in and by very real social contexts. As Marlis Buchmann writes, the

> *hypostatization of the individual* in the conception of the subject as the main form of social reality marks one extreme [of social theorizing], the *dismissal of the subject as pure fiction* in the notion of random subjectivity, the other. Both ways of looking at the individual are one-sided interpretations of social reality, insofar as they reify one element in the development of advanced industrial society and neglect the other.[41]

A more adequate analysis has to get closer at the social transformations of the past two or three decades – of which the discourse on postmodernity is a part, in the realm of practices of signification, rather than an explanation.

Let us take a look at cultural practices. The distinction between a sincere and heavy (organized) modernity and a playful and light (extended liberal) postmodernity has itself become part of the cultural-intellectual self-representation of the present age. Architecture and literature are the most widely debated examples, but the postmodernist conceptions extend far beyond these realms and reach wide segments of society. And if we are not inclined to see cultural practices as somehow loosely floating on top of the real streams of society, as a superstructure that is disconnected from, or a false representation of, the base, then some first indications of a general social shift can be found in these realms – even though it is very likely that a look at new cultural practices and the imagery they provide of 'eras' exaggerates social changes.

It is striking that a common comparison today is the one between the 1950s and the 1980s.[42] In many respects, the 1950s now appear to embody a solid, somewhat inert modernity. From functionalist modernism in architecture to role distribution in the 'modern' nuclear family to well-integrated economic and political institutions, they are counterposed to the current playfulness, instabilities and disintegration. In terms of the constitution of self and person, a generational change is often marked. It seems deliberate, for instance, that one of the heroes of a TV series that has often been analysed as prototypically postmodernist, *Miami Vice*, has been given the family name of a hero of a TV series from the 1950s. The earlier Crockett, Davey by first name, was a 'stolid bourgeois', whereas Sonny of *Miami Vice*, who could well be Davey's son, 'is portrayed in multiple relationships, relatively unstructured and subject to quick change'.[43]

The same comparison of social configurations and their typical modes of identity-building is used in a recent 'replica' of a popular sociological study of the 1950s. William H. Whyte's *Organization Man* was a text that emphasized the ways human beings integrated themselves into their contexts and subordinated their lives to the goals of the organizations they belonged to. Paul Leinberger and Bruce Tucker's *The New Individualists*, a study of *The Generation after the Organization Man* is based on interviews with the children of 'organization man'.[44] The authors searched Whyte's interviewees and posed their children similar questions about the orientations in their lives and their views of themselves. Not surprisingly, given the context of 'postmodernity', the interviewees (and the authors, one of whom is himself a descendant of organization man) came up with self-images that were strongly opposed to those of their parents.

Often, it is difficult to disentangle the relations between, not least wishful, self-presentations and the actually ongoing social practices, whether such phenomena should be taken as indications for social change or rather as playing with the fashionable cultural code of postmodernity. Nevertheless, at least an attempt to open some of these questions to further inquiry shall be made.

One of the few writers in the realm of the postmodernist discourse who tries to keep analytical distinctions clear is Douglas Kellner. He asserts that 'the modern self is aware of the constructed nature of identity and that one can always change and modify one's identity at will',[45] and does not claim this to be a characteristic of postmodernity. On the basis of media analysis, he continues to argue that 'far from identity disappearing in contemporary society, it is rather reconstructed and redefined.' Still, he sees a major difference between the condition of modernity in the 1960s and that of the 1990s. In the earlier period, 'a stable, substantial identity – albeit self-reflexive and freely chosen – was at least a normative goal for the modern self.' Today, however, identity 'becomes a freely chosen game, a theatrical presentation of the self, in which one is able to present oneself in a variety of roles, images, and activities, relatively unconcerned about shifts, trans- formations, and dramatic changes'.[46]

Or in other, more sociologically readable, terms:

> While the locus of modern identity revolved around one's occupation, one's function in the public sphere (or family), postmodern identity revolves around leisure, centred on looks, images, and consumption. Modern identity was a serious affair involving fundamental choices that defined who one was (profession, family, political identifications, etc.), while postmodern identity is a function of leisure and is grounded in play, in gamesmanship.[47]

Leinberger and Tucker, too, cast their observations in terms of 'changing conception [s] of what constitutes an individual'. Building on David Riesman's work of the 1950s, they distinguish three different relations of identity-conceptions and social configurations, 'historical modes of conformity'. The inner-directed self was typical of the nineteenth century, valued character and expressed itself through productivity. The members of Riesman's *Lonely Crowd* of the first three quarters of the twentieth century were outer-directed, valued personality and expressed themselves through sociability. The 'new individualists', who emerged in recent years, express themselves through creativity, value the self and may be called subject-directed.[48]

Several recent empirical studies of social practices and identity construction broadly confirm such conceptions. In a sociopsychological study of upper middle-class orientations, Kenneth Gergen works with a similar distinction between modernist and postmodernist conceptions of the self. The former emphasizes predictability and sincerity. In social terms,

> modernists believe in educational systems, a stable family life, moral training, and rational choice of marriage partners. . . . Under postmodern conditions, persons exist in a state of continuous construction and reconstruction. . . . Each reality of self gives way to reflexive questioning, irony, and ultimately the playful probing of yet another reality.[49]

The very notion of selfhood is dissolved in the concept of social relations.[50]

Judith Stacey's study of Californian families stresses the steady construction and reconstruction of everyday practices, too. Gergen's analysis of upper middle-class families traced this phenomenon to technologically enhanced saturation with fleeting, place-unspecific social relations. However, Stacey's lower-class 'families' – that is, a postmodern multitude of sustaining co-operative ties – live in a condition of constant material uncertainty and its members, especially the women, create a variety of social activities and relations not least to make ends meet. For them, a turn to religion reconstitutes some certainty in social life.[51] In a recent study of everyday life among contemporary youths, by Philip Wexler and his collaborators, too, a dissolution of former certainties is identified, which is more often regarded as problematic than as liberating.[52]

A bold attempt to relate the breaking of standardized practices to the formation of social identities has been offered by Marlis Buchmann on the basis of studies of life conditions and life experiences of youth between the 1960s and the 1980s. In her analysis, modern society was characterized until recently by a high standardization, even institutionalization, of the life-course due to state regulation in conjunction with economic rationalization. This order, however, had tended to break up in more recent years, when stages in the life-course were de-standardized and biographical perspectives emerged more strongly. Comparing the experiences of high school classes of the 1960s and the 1980s, Buchmann argues conclusively that 'the 1960 cohort's biographical orientations and subsequent transition behaviors are greatly determined by *social status boundaries*, whereas the 1980 cohort's orientations and actions show more *individually stratified* patterns.'[53]

In line with the argument pursued here, her findings allow her to assume that 'over the last two decades, the[se] highly standardized life trajectories have been "shattered" by structural and cultural developments in *all* major social institutions.' Hypothesizing an 'interplay between the standardization of the life course and the shifts in identity patterns', she relates the 'partial transformation of the life course regime' to the emergence of 'the formation of a highly individualistic, transient, and fluid identity'.[54]

These findings do not give much more than hints, but taken all together, they do indicate that the conditions for identity-formation have significantly changed over the past three or four decades. Social identities had been comparatively stable under organized modernity, but they were so no longer on strong substantive grounds; they were only weakly – and decreasingly – grounded in concepts of belonging and strong evaluations about who to become. If they were stable, they were so because of being firmly bound into coherent and integrative social practices.

The (relative) dissolution of these practices frees the construction of identities. Let us look again at the 'golden age' of capitalism. The growth during these thirty years was based on the arrangements of organized modernity, but the very size and dynamics of these developments undermined the order of practices. An extended period of material growth also transforms the social positions and orientations of the individuals and generations who live through it. This seems to be the common finding of the studies on identity-formation. Thus, we may regard this period as another major process of disembedding. In scope it can probably be likened to that of the second half of the nineteenth century.

At least for the time being, however, no major reembedding is recognizable. Those who are able to do so, may now freely combine identities and switch them almost at will; those who are not will suffer more strongly from anxieties or will resort to, escape into, strong identities, such as religious ones or again nationalist ones. Ability here is probably dependent on personality traits, on the one hand, but also on material possibility, on the other, in a society in which identity is often created and displayed via purchasable objects.

And there is also a problem beyond the uneven distribution of abilities to construct identities. Identity-building relies on some sort of social validation. This even holds for 'fluid identities' which, I guess, can only be sustained in a context in which fluidity of identities is socially accepted and appreciated. If a great diversity of forms of identity-construction prevails, then there will be a broadly equivalent diversity of social contexts which may validate these identities. How, though, may such social contexts relate to each other within a wider order of social practices?

Part V

Towards extended liberal modernity?

Chapter 11

Incoherent practices and postmodern selves

The current condition of modernity

MODERNITY AFTER ITS SECOND CRISIS

More than two centuries ago, the modern rupture brought a transformation of the reflexive discourses of society in such a way that the social struggles of the time were cast in new terms (see Chapter 1). Since then the discourse of modernity was effective in shaping social struggles and their outcomes in the form of new rules and institutions, but at no point was something like the project of modernity achieved. In recent times, rather, the opinion has been voiced that the project itself has gradually been used up in the struggles over its realization, that the ideas have been consumed.

The notion of the end of history is nonsensical if it is supposed to mean that there will be no longer be any major struggles over societal reorganizations. The notion of the end of modernity is wrong if it is to denote that our times can no longer be considered as living with the imaginary significations of modernity, that is, with individual autonomy and rational mastery. However, if the former theorem calls for realizing that there is no goal inscribed – nor inscribable – into History, and the latter that the intellectual and social energies that were put into the modern project are exhausted, then these notions do possibly describe an important aspect of our time. Historical processes may continue without the meaning they were once endowed with; habitualized practices that were created with the project of modernity in mind may go on after having lost their legitimacy.[1] Based on the preceding analysis of the historical transformations of modernity, a – limited – argument can be made that this is indeed the case.

The project of modernity rests on two very basic assumptions, those of the intelligibility and the shapeability (or manageability) of the social world. At the origins of modernity, very strong and clear-cut ideas on how a social order worked were combined with general and far-reaching conclusions on the requirements for reaching a desirable order. One may say that, at that point, society was yet unshaped by modernist interventions, at the same time it was deemed well-understood and perfectly shapeable. In those terms, we can now describe the – meandering, not linear – historical process of the disenchantment of the modern project. The history of the discourses of modernity can be read as variations of this theme, as explorations into how the social world can be known and how it can be changed in an orderly manner.

The crises of modernity are periods in which both intelligibility and shapeability are strongly doubted. Then, a peculiar feature of these ideas becomes visible, namely a reliance on a notion of 'legislative reason', or the idea that intelligibility and shapeability are to be linked.[2] These crises and transformations of modernity are 'progressive' in the sense that ever more intellectual efforts have to be put into the rebuilding of a notion of legislative reason.

In the original ideas, social practices were to form an interlocking order, the possibility of social knowledge was not doubted, and a state was conceived above social practices and endowed with higher historical reason and a unitary will. During the first crisis, practices were no longer seen as self-regulating but were to be organized with the help of a social knowledge whose character was disputed, and by a state that was now seen as an apparatus, erected in the name of a nation and/or a class. Instead of building on natural trends toward coherence and certainty, incoherence and uncertainty had to be actively fought against. The transformation of modernity from a restricted liberal to an organized one should not least be understood in such terms.

During the second crisis, the very possibility of social knowledge of entire societies is denied, and social practices are considered as so incoherent and open to multiple interpretation that the consequences of interventions can in no way be anticipated. Furthermore, the space from which such an intervention could be undertaken, previously held by the state, is seen as non-existent or empty. Terms like disorganization or pluralization appear plausible, since highly organized and bounded practices lose coherence and open up. While some practices of allocation and of signification are effectively globalized, others, some authoritative practices in particular, appear to be losing reach and coverage.

Like the preceding crisis of modernity, the current condition is marked by the confluence of the two kinds of doubts, in intelligibility and in shapeability. The more widely diffused awareness of the constructedness and constructability of the social world has strengthened doubts in the possibility of valid, natural knowledge. The awareness of the plurality and diversity of social practices makes it difficult to imagine a collective actor which would intervene in the name and for the sake of universalist ideas.

These doubts tend to strengthen each other. A loosening of the relatively coherent set of practices of organized modernity is accompanied by a new and stronger emphasis on basic issues of a philosophy of contingency. Such an openness of view, in turn, once it is widespread and applied to every social phenomenon, makes visible the shallow foundations on which the practices of organized modernity were built. One of the great achievements of organized modernity was to make practices somewhat coherent. But the other, similarly important, achievement was to make these arrangements appear as quasi-natural. The naturalization of the social order closed the foundational issues and precluded strong doubts about their viability as well as the very thought of an alternative. This naturalization has now been shaken, if not broken. The confluence is one of a factual loosening of the coherence of organized social practices, on the one hand,

and the loss of the very idea of intelligibility and manageability of social practices on the global scale on which this is now required, on the other.

Where the transition from organized modernity leads to is still open. Its outcome depends not least on how it is perceived by the now living human beings and what kinds of action they think they are capable of and would be willing to engage in. In this process, it is very likely that their – our – predominant experience is the dissolution and dismantling of organized modernity. We appear to be more ready than ever – even if forced rather than willingly at times – to accept a social philosophy of contingency as the basic tool of our self-understanding. What such an experience may mean for the possibilities and forms of individual and collective self-determination after the end of organized modernity is to be discussed in the remainder of this chapter – starting with a second explicit look at American exceptionalism.

LIBERAL MODERNITY AND AMERICAN EXCEPTIONALISM (II)

'Americans regarded their own revolution, unlike the French, as a success.'[3] This entailed that no further revolutions were necessary; it was a revolution to end all revolutions. True, there could well be further conflicts of interests. But those conflicts could be handled and solved in a limited discursive space that was marked by a broad consensus moving only between individualist liberalism and civic republicanism, and in the open social space of a society that was only just building itself, with plenty of resources to distribute and few rules that were already set. In continental European societies, in contrast, the social space in which conflicts could be handled was comparatively limited, whereas the discursive space opened by the French Revolution – in which the ideologies of the nineteenth century were to unfold – was wide.

After their revolution, Americans built a less restricted, more liberal modernity than the Europeans, and they never saw a reason to deviate as strongly from that form as the Europeans did at later times. They never decidedly abandoned liberal modernity, one could say – notably not in the forms of fascism or socialism either. If the current transformation entails, broadly, a move from an organized to a more liberal modernity, then it may be worthwhile to study the shape of a society which has always been comparatively more liberal. If the transition from organized modernity is accompanied by a de-substantivization and de-collectivization of rule-setting, then, too, it may be elucidating to take a look at that place where people have consistently refused to recognize the centrality of problems that others had considered as fundamental and divisive.

Modernity was always less restricted in the US, and where it was the restrictions were of a different kind. No clear boundaries were drawn to the lower classes in the nineteenth century, in so far as those were white. The possibility of upward mobility and the lack of formal barriers to it were part of the motivations to emigrate and became an essential element to societal self-understanding, as cast in the so-called 'American dream'.[4] The theorem of the 'frontier society' points to the openness of boundaries in a quite literal sense. The idea of full control over a territory and, by extension, over a society which was a basic feature of European states was very far from realization through most of American history and was often not seen as desirable either.

In the US, the idea of small-scale communities as the basis of society is part of conventional political wisdom. Historically, social projects and collective identities often have their location in the local community. It is no exaggeration to state that the idea of a society as it exists in Europe is not fully developed in the US.[5] The social practices have started as basically communal and highly diverse ones, often in fact going back to joint settlements. In a comparatively short period they were 'perforated' with nationalized allocative practices from railroads to nationwide products and retail chains to highways. Some of them were in fact disintegrating during that time and their individuals reassembled at quite different places.[6] But despite the nationalization of allocative practices, no strong national society emerged – at least if compared to European societies that were more bounded, had longer and stronger traditions of state institutions, and experienced stronger collectivization efforts.

True, there was some degree of organization of social practices also in the US. From the wave of company mergers before the turn of the century and the heyday of American socialism early in the twentieth century to the New Deal and the War on Poverty as the zenith of the American welfare state, a historical narrative can be provided that runs largely parallel to the European one, including also the break-up of organized modernity. Even during its more collectivistically oriented periods, the Progressive Era and the third-of-a-century between the New Deal and the Great Society (including McCarthyism), the American equivalent to organized modernity remained less organized than most European societies.[7]

The evidence for this consistent distinctiveness of the United States is so overwhelming that it needs hardly any illustration. A few examples may suffice. In the realm of authoritative practices, the most striking feature is the persistent difficulty of supporting a strong role of the state. The share of government revenues in the domestic product is drastically lower than in any European country. Every government measure has to face a principled argument over its justification in terms of a political theory that stresses individual liberties as freedom from government. The lack of public revenues for social purposes is partly offset by private donations and charity, but under such arrangements the uncommunicated outcome of many individual decisions decides on social priorities instead of political deliberation.

Political parties are only loosely organized on the state and federal level and are used for temporary mobilization and interest organization rather than steady programmatic activity on the basis of conceptions of national welfare.[8] The right to self-determination is often understood as inclusive of the right to determine the boundaries of the collective. Such a principle enhances segregation and fragmentation and undermines the long-term stability of polities when interests change.[9] Compulsory collectivist arrangements have remained scarce. Insurance, in particular, is mostly practiced on the basis of free contract or adherence to organizations rather than national or state citizenship.

In the realm of practices of signification, the strength of liberal-individualist reasoning is obviously the most consistent comparative characteristics of the American discursive tradition. Currently, though, two other sociopolitical theories stand at the centre of interest, namely postmodernism and communitarianism. The latter is often regarded as a uniquely American approach, whereas the former flourishes particularly strongly in the US, though it appears everywhere in Western societies.

Postmodernism rejects the idea of substantive foundations of human social life, including bases for universalist values, and stresses difference and plurality instead. In political terms, claims to universality and consensuality are then regarded as expressions of the interests of the dominant white, male Anglo-Saxons in society. A focus on multi-culturalism often goes along with the denial of any commonality between cultures and a priority given to the right of politico-cultural expression of the separate groups. Though spokespersons of postmodernist perspectives – under this or other names – would usually see themselves on the political left, their discourse rather seems to provide a mirror image of a highly segregated and fragmented society.

In contrast, the political theory of communitarianism appears at first sight as a counter-image to the present state of North America. It is a severe critique of 'Lockean individualism' as a foundational political philosophy in a twentieth century of widely extended institutions such as markets and bureaucracies.[10] This critique is then linked to a call for morality and community as corner-stones for a different, good society. The idea of a counter-image vanishes, of course, as soon as one recognizes that this theorizing is built on an endorsement of local community life – of small-scale America, so to say – and tries to extend the moral density of that life to a national scale.[11]

Postmodernism and communitarianism show inverse deficiencies as political discourses of our time. These deficiencies mark the major problematics of social organization in the US – or more generally under conditions of what one may call extended liberal modernity. In postmodernism, there is an almost complete neglect of the issue of political communication and deliberation about common matters. It receives its strength and appeal from a posture against conformity and for diversity and in support of suppressed groups. However, it is incapable of developing any argument for practices on the level of the polity as a whole comprising several 'cultures'. Communitarianism, in turn, focuses on the issue of handling matters of common concern in common practices. However, between philosophical analysis and ethical call, communitarian writings are often at a loss to account for the diagnosed lack of community (or the plurality of diverse communities with few relations between each other) in terms of a social analysis and a social theory. In other words, their analyses fail to recognize how the existing rules of practices support present life-forms, on the one hand, and undermine attempts to change them, on the other.

This brief portrait of the current state of American society and its political debates is meant to help in getting the problematics of social organization after the end of organized modernity into focus. Arguments that position the US as the 'lead society' of modernity or as the 'model' of social development exposing Europe and the rest of the world to 'Americanization' have either been too uncritically accepted or prematurely rejected. 'Americanization' is a theorem that assumes that the North American social configuration basically precedes other ones in the world, especially European ones, timewise, and that by some inevitable, and most often unexplained, historical law these other societies will follow the model. The theorem dates back to the time of the American Revolution, and was probably fully expressed for the first time by Alexis de Tocqueville. In modernization theories of the 1950s and 1960s it was developed into a full-scale social theory, of American origin and widely copied throughout the world.[12] Significantly, with all their rejection of meta-narratives, some postmodernists accept the basic comparative proposition. Or how else should one read Jean Baudrillard's ingenious epigraph to *L'Amérique*, borrowed from the writing on the mirror of US cars: 'Caution: Objects in this mirror may be closer than they appear'?[13]

Often, the theorem is voiced by non-Americans, and not rarely with some hesitation as to the desirability of the process.[14] Then it takes the form of 'anti-Americanism'. Paul Hollander has recently offered an immense collection of expressions of 'anti-American sentiments'. In an additional essay, he proposes an interpretation of these sentiments, arguing summarizingly that

> the hostility American culture provokes is in some ways well-founded. Nonetheless, most critics misidentify the problem. It is not American capitalism, imperialism or mass culture. Rather, it is modernity as represented by the United States. Americanization remains the major form and carrier of modernity in the world today. . . . American culture has come to embody certain fundamental human dilemmas that modernity has thrust into sharp relief. How long can people go on living in a society that offers fewer and fewer certainties? Is modernity as experienced in the US compatible with certain basic human needs, including those of a well-defined moral universe, accessible communities and widely accepted guidelines and limitations to personal ambitions?[15]

Sociologically speaking, anti-Americanism is part of the 'resistance that modernity constantly provokes' (Claude Lefort), and Americanization is a term used for the restructuring of social practices according to the ideas of individual autonomy and rational mastery. Concretely, these phenomena have very little to do with the US. The reference to the US indicates nothing other than that the US tends to be seen as a more (liberally) modern society. To say whether modernity diffuses from North American soil would require a theory on intersocietal impacts in which I will not enter here. For my purposes, these two terms point to the usefulness of a comparative view on the history of modernity. More specifically, they indicate that the problematics resulting from the breaking of organized social practices can more easily be identified in the US.

In this sense, the portrait of the US generates three broad problematics. First, if the 'society' that we can consider as the epitome of liberal modernity knows coherent social practices only to a very limited extent, the concept of society itself may need to be rethought in social analysis, both as an entity with boundaries and a significant degree of cohesion and self-reference and in its relation to the 'economy' and the 'polity'. Second, an answer to these questions can only be given by trying to understand how individuals actually do orient themselves in this world and how they define their own identities after the end of organized modernity. Third, in the present social context it will be much less evident that the commitments and obligations of individuals relate, or can be made to relate, to a bounded polity than modernist thought would have it. If they do not, however, the very possibility of politics is questioned.

THE IDEA OF (CIVIL) SOCIETY

The concept of society has two parallel meanings. First, it is meant to denote a set of bounded social practices. As such, it was most often empirically set along with the territorial (nation-) state, which was supposed to set and define the boundaries relevant for practices. Second, it is used to refer to those social relations that are not part of modernist institutions. Society is then foundational, residual or complementary to those institutions, most notably the state (but now also the market). Over the past two centuries, three main, basically consecutive versions of the latter notion of society can be distinguished.[16]

Modern understandings of the term society rely on a distinction between society and state.[17] Society as the association of free and equal individuals may be regarded as the foundation of the state as the contractually agreed means of securing freedom and equality. Or, in a more historical perspective, the modern state may be seen as the institution that provides the space in which society, as the interaction of individuals, can unfold. During much of the nineteenth century, emphasis was placed on the autonomy and dynamics of the interactions of human beings as members of society. Both the liberty of the entrepreneur and the liberty of the citizen should be restricted as little as necessary to safeguard order. More or less dichotomous or dialectical formulae were elaborated to construct a state which is capable of preserving the unity of the whole while not impeding the play of the particularistic forces of society. With the stress on liberties (which, though, were mostly not extended to everybody), this strong view of society can be regarded as characteristic of restricted liberal modernity.

From the middle of the nineteenth century onwards, this view was increasingly challenged, not least because it became more and more evident that the forces of society were much more particularistic than envisaged and endangered the whole, and the liberal state, as it was conceived, was incapable of providing security and order. Society needed to be 'organized', as Heinrich von Treitschke said in

Germany from a conservative viewpoint. And the workers' movement in fact began to organize its part of society as a means of creating collective capabilities. These discourses and practices indicate the transition towards organized modernity.

In such views, both the dynamics and the restrictions of early modernity revealed the deficiencies of predominantly philosophical understandings of society and made the discourses on society focus on the social as something that can and needs to be organized. Now the organizer of this society would be the state, and the major tension would be shifted to the conceptual pair, 'society' and 'economy', a new, relatively separate modern institution. The effect of liberated market practices had been to erode the forms of society. Rather than being the source of civility and morality, society had to be protected itself against its possible colonization.

With increasing attempts at the 'administration of the social' (Hannah Arendt) by the state, the critique of the undermining of free, unregulated and diverse social practices has been extended from the economy to cover also the bureaucratic state, the second major modernist institution. The 'colonization of the life-worlds' by these systems is the major theme of Jürgen Habermas' diagnosis of modernity. While Habermas sees the potential of communicative interaction and its societal renewal as still residing in these life-worlds, theorists of mass society have often assumed that the original liberating power of societal self-organization had been effectively destroyed by the closure of the modern order. Then, it becomes possible to argue that the 'idea of the social' has historically failed, as some French theorists do.[18] The failure would be due to the very attempt at safeguarding the social. The authoritative organization of society by national bureaucratic states would empty it of its diversity and creative potential no less than its permeation by market practices and the commodification of social relations.

In this context, a third view of society emerges after the end of organized modernity. It postulates a resurgence of civil society, or at least potential resurgence, as a civic reaction to the reductions and reifications of the organized institutions. Many of the writings on the 'new' civil society limit themselves to demonstrating the social-theoretical possibility, analytical consistency and/or liberal political necessity of such a renewal, of the emergence of 'post-traditional, post-conventional egalitarian and democratic forms of association, publicity, solidarity and identity'.[19]

The renewed debate about civil society has to be seen in the double context of disappointed hopes of turning the (socialist or social democratic) state into an agent of societal renewal and of the actual experience of disintegration of coherent institutions in which, at least potentially, collective agency and social-identity formation could have their roots.[20] Such a discourse of civil society, though, needs to be rooted in the observation of social practices. Among those, relatively few, contributions to the debate that aim beyond 'normative attractiveness', at a 'plausibility in terms of empirical analysis and diagnosis of our time',[21] I would like to distinguish two forms. Their difference lies in the significance they attach to changes in authoritative practices.

Both Alain Touraine in his theory of social movements and Michel Maffesoli in his writings on 'post-modern sociality' argue for the need to abandon notions of society which are based on foundations and coherence, and adopt instead more processual, fluid, action-oriented notions. However, they reject theories of individualization that are held by other authors who continue to work in the perspective of modernization theory. Instead they observe the building of new collectives and the creation of new, actual or imagined, communities that provide identities and boundaries inside West European societies. Declarations of allegiances of various sorts, such as regionalism, sexual communities, varieties of quasi-organized youth cultures, etc., fall under this as much as goal-oriented social movements.

The two perspectives differ, though, in their attempts at locating these new social phenomena in the broader community. Maffesoli speaks of tribalization and emphasizes the diversity and plurality of these tribes, who do not add up to a wholeness and do not care about this.[22] Touraine instead sees social movements as the potential source and core of a collective renewal of society. They develop a notion and a desire for broader social change; they are built on the creation of identity, precisely where none may exist now, and that creation is intended to foster collective agency.[23] Where it turns empirical the debate on the new forms of 'society' develops widely divergent views on the actual orientation of individuals and groups as well as on the chances for collective deliberation on common matters. More or less explicitly, they call for a need to redefine the very understanding of politics, because the kinds of social identity that are formed in 'tribes' or 'movements' do not relate to a modernist concept of the political. These two issues, the conditions of identity formation and the possibility of politics after the end of organized modernity, remain to be discussed in the concluding sections.

LIBERTY AND DISCIPLINE: SOCIAL IDENTITY BETWEEN GLOBALIZATION AND INDIVIDUALIZATION

Much of modernist social theory, including prominently the classical sociological tradition, was centrally concerned with what was perceived as 'an increasing split between the world of direct interpersonal relationships and that of large-scale collective organization', the assumption being that 'there is a tradeoff between the expansion of cross-cutting relations linking people widely in a population and the density and intensity of in-group relations within specific sub-populations, including local communities.'[24] The proposition is basically valid. However, social science has either tended to take the historical solution of the problematic for granted by postulating the formation of 'society' as the ultimate outcome of the dissolution of *Gemeinschaft*, or by considering the problematic itself as vanishing due to increasing individualization. Both ways are very modernist indeed, and since then 'society' and 'individual' have led an uneasy co-existence in the social sciences.

Rather – one may say with hindsight – in the era of classical sociology the creation of *imagined* communities, such as nation and class, should have been recognized as a *temporary* fixation of the problematic, over which fierce struggles were led at the time of Durkheim and Weber and afterwards. To the contemporaries, however, these communities did not appear as creations and imaginations but as the natural locations of human beings in a post-traditional society. And in fact, a certain reembedding was achieved of the individuals who were disembedded by the modern turmoils of the building of industries, cities and transportation networks.

The achievement of organized modernity was to effectively focus 'modernized' social practices. While this process had a strong elite bias, it can nevertheless be seen as having its roots in collective action involving many members of those societies. Focusing involved a double movement. On the one hand, theoretically global, open-ended practices were reduced to national, bounded ones. On the other hand, the theoretically infinite plurality and diversity of people on a territory was ordered and bound by a relatively coherent set of conventions for action. By drawing on institutional and cultural means that were available in the nineteenth century, the actual structure and extension of social practices (what came to be called *society*) was made to overlap strongly with the rules for collective deliberation (the *polity*) and many of the socially important means of individual orientation (*social identities*). Many of the phenomena that can be observed during the last quarter of a century can be read as a falling apart of this triple coherence.[25]

Accordingly, analyses of our time stress processes of globalization and of individualization. There is no lack of marked statements of either sort. So theorists of globalization may argue that

> the world market . . . has erased the territorial inscriptions of the productive structures. . . . The occidentalization of the world is a broad movement of uniformization of the imaginary involving the loss of cultural identities.[26]

And theorists of individualization may claim that all stable social orientations like class, culture and family break up and leave the individual human beings in much greater uncertainty and risk when shaping their lives. The constitution of social identity is today placed in a context of global interrelations and interdependencies, regardless of whether observable strategies of identity-building embrace this as a chance or try to deny it.[27]

If these two observations are joined together, then a second-crisis-of-modernity equivalent of the theory of the mass society emerges. Theorists of the latter had argued that the nation-state is the grand individualizer that destroys social structures and collective identities, isolates human beings and makes them dependent on its own, anonymous and machine-like organization. Currently, the same is said to occur on a global scale and the nation-state appears as an almost homely, 'intermediary' institution and container for authentic cultural expression. Such ideas are found both in those theories of postmodernity that have an air of the tragic, since they see these developments as losses *and* as inevitable,[28] and by conservatives who try to maintain or reconstruct bounded institutions based on substantive notions of culture.

These theories are flawed in exactly the same sense in which theories of mass society were flawed. They do recognize the main directions of social developments but they overinterpret the tendencies. With regard to globalization they tend to exaggerate the homogenizing effects and neglect the building of new structures below the global level. With regard to individualization they underestimate the agential capacities of human beings. This is because they see them as merely exposed to homogenizing tendencies without recognizing their potential to draw actively on new rules and build social contexts under changed conditions.

Significantly, a normatively opposite interpretation of the same observations is also possible. Then, the trends toward globalization would be seen as enhancing enablements, as widening and easing the human capability of reaching out widely in space and time. And individualization would be regarded as a liberation from social constraints which limited and channelled the ways in which human beings could draw on the historically available enablements. These views can be found in continuations of the modernist perspective in social thought, but also in those strands of postmodernism that hail the new liberations. Clearly, the interpretations are not completely invalid, and I am certain most readers of this book have experienced and appreciated aspects of these new enablements.

Where, though, does this twofold assessment of globalization and individualization leave us with regard to the current condition of modernity? I shall try to work myself towards an answer by reassessing the questions of community and selfhood in view of their contingency under modern conditions.[29]

The concept of the nation was strongly based on an idea of the historical depth of community, of bonds and commonalities created over long periods. Such a concept heads for the naturalization of boundaries: it invites one to draw sharp distinctions to the others outside the historical community and to ask for limitations of cross-boundary exchange. Arguably, the depth of the class concept was lower than that of the nation, and not least for that reason its identity-constituting potential was more short-lived. However, it is probably generally valid to say that the hold of these quasi-natural identities has been loosening over the past quarter of a century in the West. Furthermore, the cultural revolution against organized modernity emphasized the normative unacceptability of such limitations and doubted the persuasiveness of the idea of natural community at all. What is witnessed instead is, not individualization but, the creation of communities on other substantive grounds that are not historical but chosen by the acting human beings themselves. This holds both for Touraine's social movements and Maffesoli's tribes.[30] Significantly, adherence to communities will also be looser and may change several times during the course of life.

The resulting fluidity of community formation is related to the organization of social practices. What I have called the quasi-naturalness of the social identities during organized modernity stemmed from the overlap of social identities with coherent sets of practices and polity boundaries. Under such conditions, there may be very little choice of social identity, even if an awareness prevails that identities are not ascribed but 'only' socially determined. After the end of organized modernity this overlap has ceased to exist, and the formation of social identities is freed from such predetermination.

This liberation is in a sense a precondition for approaching real individual autonomy as the right and ability to choose the others one wants to associate with as well as the substantive and procedural terms of association. However, it also relieves the search for identity of its existential dimensions. If identities can be changed, if there can be multiple and only relatively obliging bonds to others, and if identity formation may even be temporarily suspended without losing one's social position, then the entire concept of identity may undergo a transformation. Elements of such a transformation are revealed by analyses of 'empirical postmodernism' as shown above (see Chapter 10).

In terms of moral philosophy, one may insist that the very concept of identity needs the assumption of relative stability (or, at least, steady development) and could not do without strong evaluations. As Charles Taylor writes, 'the notion of an identity defined by some mere de facto, not strongly valued preference is incoherent.' Put in these terms, one would have to argue sociologically, though, that such a concept of identity may be partially superseded by social developments. As Taylor himself shows, an existentially relaxed idea of identity goes along well with a 'naturalist', that is, scientistic, supposition on the superfluous character of moral frameworks for action. Postmodernism and scientism may agree on a notion

> of human agency where one could answer the question Who? without accepting any qualitative distinctions, just on the basis of desires and aversions, likes and dislikes. On this picture, [moral-evaluative] frameworks are things we invent, not answers to questions which inescapably pre-exist for us, independent of our answer or inability to answer.[31]

This unintentional mutual reinforcement of performance-oriented scientific practices and the proliferation of postmodernist life-worlds was already inherent in Jean-François Lyotard's description of the postmodern condition. While it can be rejected on grounds of moral philosophy, as Taylor does, it appears highly valid as an element of a sociology of modernity.

All this has to do with the workings of the double imaginary signification of modernity – and this itself is the strongest reason to keep talking about our social formation as one of modernity. The liberal conception of modern institutions (restricted or extended, depending on the extent of social permeation) is the one that best reconciles the two significations of autonomy and rational domination. It proliferates extended structures as chains of more or less formalized interaction, which allow impacts to spread widely over time and space. At the same time, it appears to leave to the discretion of the choosing individual whether she wants to avail herself of this power and in what way she wants to do so.

While this sounds like the best of all possible worlds, it is marked by at least three fundamental problems. The first relates to the socially uneven availability of the material, intellectual and cultural means that modernity provides. In a social world that refuses to provide other collective identifications, distributive justice acquires increasing importance as a provider of access to the material of autonomous identity formation.

Second, even if that were the case, such a modernity may demand more in terms of autonomous identity formation than many individuals would want to choose, if the choice of restricting one's choices were still perceivable. In individual terms, the modern condition is characterized by the demand to 'transform contingency into destiny' (Agnes Heller) when designing one's own course of life. And I would agree with Charles Taylor that this demand is inescapable. Even the rejection of the idea of stable identities and of a firm guide for self-realization is a sort of choice.

Third, a great variety of offers will decrease the likelihood for coming to collective arrangements with high substantive implications. If the general condition of contingency (in philosophical terms) factually translates into a great variety of choices, destinies and social practices (in sociological terms), then this fact itself will have an impact on the modes of social life that are 'available', that can be chosen. It raises the question of the very possibility of politics.

THE POSSIBILITY OF POLITICS

'The exact character of our associational life is something that has to be argued about.' While Michael Walzer like many others endorses a normative notion of civil society, he stresses the need for communicative deliberation in common, a need which cannot be assumed to be met in the concept. It is 'the paradox of the civil society argument', Walzer argues, that the question of how and among whom communication should occur remains underdetermined and requires a turn to the state.

> The state itself is unlike all the other associations. It both frames civil society and occupies space within it. It fixes the boundary conditions and the basic rules of all associational activity. . . . It compels association members to think about a common good, beyond their own conceptions of the good life. . . . Civil society requires political agency.[32]

Political agency during organized modernity resided in the sovereign nation-state and its idea of representation, both of which are now strongly challenged. If the present problems are more than a passing historical conjuncture – and there are many indicators that this is the case – then politics faces a radical dilemma. On the one hand, the very idea of political deliberation depends on concepts of boundaries, membership and representation. On the other hand, the social practices to which politics has to refer may become increasingly 'a-topic',[33] not confinable to any space, so that no possible definable membership group could be found for deliberation, far less any community with a significant degree of shared values and, thus, a substantive basis for common deliberation.

Taking the historical experience into account, it has been suggested that the building of imagined communities may again be the appropriate way to deal with the current experiences of disembedding, several generations and one historical social configuration later.[34] But the present situation is different. The split between the organization of social practices, boundaries of polities and modes of identity formation is wider and the social and cognitive resources to bridge it scarcer than in the otherwise analogous situation about a century ago. It appears as if there is a much stronger break with modernist views on social identities and that a bounded community cannot as comparatively easily – and the process was not at all smooth – be restored again, as was possible after the first crisis of modernity.

To formulate the issue positively, the creation of a certain overlap between social identities, political boundaries and social practices is a precondition for (re-)establishing political agency. To assess the potential for achievement of such an overlap, it is necessary to sociologize and historicize the question of the contingency of community and then search for the actual 'relations of association' between human beings.[35]

Such an *analysis of the state of community* has to go beyond a study of the conditions of sociality and morality, as they were hinted at in the preceding section.[36] (a) The community has to be looked at as a potential political community with regard to the extensions and permeations of practices that human beings share with others and therefore should want to regulate in community. (b) Relations of association have to be analysed with regard to the conditions of such a potential political community, that is, the possibility of proceeding with common deliberation in authoritative practices of such a form that they meet the other social practices at their level of extension, reach and impact.[37]

(a) As noted above, the social sciences have tried to grasp what appeared as specific modes of extension and organization of allocative and authoritative practices by separating the analysis of these realms from the study of other social relations. The disciplinary subdivision of the social sciences has further deepened the gulf between the 'economy' and bureaucratic politics on one side and other social relations on the other. More comprehensive theories, such as most prominently Jürgen Habermas' *theory of communicative action*, have tried to reconnect the fragments of the study of society while acknowledging the specificity of relatively autonomous subspheres at the same time. These social theories can summarizingly be called dualistic, since their characteristic is that they make a basic distinction between systemic arrangements and the different sphere of a 'life-world' – by this or any other name.

Most of these theories are – implicitly or explicitly – based on the acknowledgement of some functional superiority of the rationalization of action in markets and bureaucracies. Sometimes this view appears to be based on the argumentative position that what historically prevails must be superior. Sometimes it is more explicitly argued that such modes of rationalization relieve some social functions from the need for communicative interaction. They are highly enabling precisely through this relieving effect. Normative problems – pathologies – result when the formalized spheres invade and colonize the life-world.

This analytical decoupling of systems and life-world has implications for the concept of politics. It grants that the administration of common matters can basically be handled through the formalized bureaucratic mode of action. The only political problem that seems to remain is to limit the social space of rationalized administration so that the life-world is not too far invaded. This view of functional democracy in dualistic theories has been criticized as entailing 'above all the elimination of the very idea of a democratic project and a corresponding reduction in the meaning and scope of democratic institutions'.[38] To remedy this normative problem of a critical theory, the possibility of a structuring impact of the life-world/civil society on the systemic arrangements is maintained (as generally in Habermas' thinking) and re-emphasized (in recent works), such as through 'the acquisition of influence by publics on the state and economy, and the institutionalization of the gains of movements within the life-world'.[39] As the dualism is maintained, however, it is principally unclear how far such a reverse impact may go and what would remain excluded from re-thematization. The assumption of such dualism raises not only normative problems, it is also analytically troubling.[40]

Such theorizing is based on the valid observation that formalization of action is a key characteristic of modernity. It is also evident that formalization occurred unevenly, that some practices underwent earlier, more rapid and more thorough formalizations. However, the construction of a basic dualism is untenable. First, it reifies the systems that emerge from non-linguistic organization by endowing them with a particular, (relatively) inaccessible logic. In contrast, it needs to be emphasized that any institution – even a money-based, effectively globalized world-market – is based on social conventions that may be altered in principle. The very building of organized modernity was a major process of renegotiating the conventions on which social practices should be built. While the result may not have met anybody's expectations, it was clearly successful in transforming the rules of restricted liberal modernity.

Second, social conventions are not only modifiable in principle, their existence requires the continuous reenactment by living human beings in their everyday practices. No market or bureaucracy can continue to 'function' if their rules are not upheld by those who actually offer and buy, command and obey. While this statement may sound trivial, it is of crucial importance for any social theory. Formalization increases the rigidity of rules, but still hardly any action can be regarded as exactly rule-following, given the specificities of time, space and social context. In a broad sense, every action is a specific, potentially rule-transforming behaviour. The breaking up of the conventions of organized modernity shows how allocative and authoritative practices – at the very core of the 'systems' – are themselves transformed in human action, as ambiguous as the outcomes may be.

Third, while it may please theorists of the new civil society, the preceding argument has a reverse side. Although no supposed 'system' is as formalized as dualistic theorists think, no kind of human action is inaccessible to formalization either. By seeing colonization of the life-world as emanating from the systems, Habermas underestimates both the possibility of formalization and the attractiveness it may have for individuals in every walk of life. The channelling of communication into prestructured paths may be a means of increasing certainty and mastery over the individually relevant parts of the world. The spaces of open communicative action – in the emphatic sense that underlies Habermas' critical thinking – are much more reducible and may actually be much more reduced than dualistic theories normally perceive. Moreover, the space for collective processes of communication may be limited through the diversity of ways in which individuals formalize their 'life-worlds'.[41] In fact, the condition of 'postmodernity' may precisely be that practices are formalized in quite different ways over different spaces and times, and that no common space for a relevant group of people and a relevant set of practices exists.

It is with regard to such deficiencies of dualistic theories, whose preconceptions distort the view of the relation between social practices and the polity, that perspectives on the decline of politics and the public sphere as they were offered by Hannah Arendt some decades ago and are currently found in 'postmodernist' views are pertinent.[42] Hannah Arendt's problem is one that one may call the emptiness of the political space. Her concern is for political articulation, for the maintenance or creation of conditions in which the members of a community could together communicate about, and deliberate on, all issues they have in common. A minimal requirement of political practices should be a communicative process about what it is that various social groups, spanning the globe or dwelling in neighbouring villages, have in common under current social practices, and to find out whether they have to commonly regulate the impacts of these practices. How grand this *koiné* – the space of the common – then is, depends on the ongoing practices and the outcome of communication about them. Arendt bases her sceptical assertion of the decline of politics as she understands it on the view that authoritative practices are founded less and less on collective communication and common deliberation. She also points to the lack of a 'match' between the boundaries of real communities and the range of practices.[43]

This diagnosis is built on two key observations, the devaluation of political action as compared to other human activities and the absence of a public space as a precondition for a reassertion of political discourse in this strong sense. This latter observation, in particular, links up closely to postmodernist diagnoses of the multitude of mutually untranslatable languages and the competition for a fragmented space of public attention. 'In the postmodern habitat of diffuse others and free choices, public attention is the scarcest of all commodities. . . . "Reality", and hence also the power and authority of an imagined community, is the function of that attention.'[44]

Still, it may be legitimately asked why such a perspective should be relevant in our condition – especially given that it was mostly regarded as superseded at the time of Arendt's writing. Liberal modernity could be seen as the desirable social formation; the one where it is possible to follow any practice, to set up any form of institution together with those who share the same substantive notions of the good life, and where the diverse practices and institutions that arise could exist side by side, without (negatively) interfering with each other. Then, in fact, would politics indeed not be needed. Modernist political reasoning – including dualistic theorizing that isolates major parts of social practices from political action – often proceeds as if this were the case.[45]

Such a view, however, is inappropriate. The expansion of modernity was always accompanied by the (creative, to use Schumpeter's term) destruction of life forms. That is how the metaphor arose that modernity nourishes itself by consuming 'traditions'. As I have tried to show at length, that idea is misleading since 'post-traditional' conventions are equally prone to be broken again under changed circumstances. There is no element in modern reasoning that would guarantee that a diverse variety of 'modern practices', that is, autonomously set conventions, could co-exist peacefully. Especially the widely extended present institutions, increasingly global ones, have a strong impact on many phenomena and people around them who neither really chose membership nor set the rules. They limit the possibility for choosing one's own set of practices.

It is here that the Arendtian problematic reemerges. The thin theory of citizenship that prevailed during organized modernity had reduced political participation to the process of elite selection, had de-substantivized political communication, and had made politics itself appear as the mere administration of the social. Currently, such practices cannot easily be upheld, either because they are actively contested or because issues resurface that cannot be handled along those lines. The paradoxical situation has emerged that political issues have been re-opened, while at the same time the limited available means of handling political matters are further disabled.

(b) Or are they? Should the de-conventionalization of organized practices not rather be seen as an opportunity to reappropriate politics than as its ultimate retreat? My portrait of the most recent time has focused on the demise of organized institutions and the emergence of new modes of action and of control. While it is indeed generally true that 'the absence of any single organizing centre in modern western societies does not decrease the possibility for action, nor the capacity for changing social relationships', it remains open to investigation whether 'the fact that modern, western societies have lost their organizing centres allows greater possibilities for a project of democratization than would otherwise be the case.'[46]

Indeed, to really break with modernist political thought and conventional social science, it should not be regarded as predetermined that a disciplinary, bureaucratic organization like the state imposing itself on a bounded, well-regulated society is the only form for organizing the care for what we have in common. Analytically as well as politically, one needs to rethink the kinds of interaction chains that exist or may be built. The observed withdrawal of formal controls and renewed emphasis on responsibility demands an internalization of task understanding and willingness to comply and contribute actively and creatively on the part of the individual. There are indeed more actors and there is more space for agency, but in a highly stratified setting and an inescapably global context. The potentiality of political agency is clearly reduced only if a traditional model of collective action and the building of counter-hierarchies (unions, parties) is assumed. The case is different if one assumes that the concept of long, more openly related interaction chains may also work 'inversely', would produce opportunities for open and creative collective agency.

In terms of Michael Walzer's 'critical associationism' we could imagine 'a large number of different and uncoordinated processes' that would build a kind of solidarity that is adequate to the present condition of modernity.[47] The question is whether the relations of association exist, or can be created, that can shape social practices in a commonly desired way without interfering with the liberal principle of individual autonomy.[48] Something like a strong sense of a weak community would be needed. No strong conceptions of a common good can be enforced if societies, as they regularly do today, do not have common history and culture to the degree that they consent about the good. Nor could such a conception be enforced if our understanding of liberty allows for movements between social spaces and precludes very firm boundaries. A strong sense of weak community renounces the idea of a common good except for the permanent obligation to communicate over what people have in common.[49]

While such political conceptions provide a valid general basis, there are many reasons for assuming that the actual conditions lend themselves very little to the rebuilding of a modernity that would be organized in this new – liberal, inclusive and democratic – sense. Most of the usable resources society-builders could draw on a century ago appear rather exhausted. Most obviously, there is much less cultural material to build collective identities with. The only community that seems appropriate, given the extension of social practices, is the global one. A global identity, however, is sociologically difficult to imagine, as identities are boundaries against something else, something considered alien. If it occurs at all, all indications point to a reorganization on a 'semi-continental' level. North America, Western Europe and East Asia may form political communities, each with strong boundaries to the outside, and some, though probably insufficient, degree of co-ordinated, communicative deliberation internally.

Then, there are hardly any agents who could and would effectively pursue such a rebuilding. In contrast to the preceding turn of the century when nation and class were strongly present in many minds, the coming one does not really offer potential speakers and active collectives who could establish such a further transition of modernity while keeping within the realm of the modern imaginary signification. Also the authority of the intellectuals, who played a strong part in the building of both national and class identities, is discredited with the demise of universalist discourse. There are only two major types of 'intellectuals' who, ignoring or disregarding this situation, dare to speak in an authoritative voice. On the one side, neo-liberals strongly object to any collective reorganization and appear to uphold the old idea of an unbounded modernity. On the other side, intellectual boundary construction is undertaken at the expense of the truly universalist ideas of modernity – even though the word may be invoked. These are those writers whose goal it is to prepare the US for 'the coming war with Japan' or Europe for its struggle against Islam.[50]

Furthermore, there is probably not the minimum of already conventionalized practices that one would need to draw on in rebuilding a somewhat more organized modernity. This minimum was provided by the idea and apparatuses of the European states during the first crisis of modernity. Within the state context and oriented towards it, other institutions existed already – like schools and universities – or could be built – like parties and unions. Neither does the necessary means of unrestricted communication, that is, a public sphere in the emphatic sense, exist, in and through which the open communication over new communities could be led.

All this does not at all mean that fragmentation and dissolution will continue endlessly. Our societies are structured and show very uneven distributions of power. And reorganization and new collectivization may well issue from established power positions. In that case though, this transformation will not meet the requirement I would want to insist on, namely to remain with the modern imaginary signification of human autonomy and self-realization. It may be marked by coercion and oppression, exclusion and extermination.

As this may well be the case, there are widespread and perfectly legitimate doubts as to whether one should really want a reorganization of modernity. Ultimately, the record of organized modernity is a very mixed one. Any of its strong institutions and discourses was enabling and constraining, liberating and disciplining at the same time. The same would almost inevitably be true for another attempt at institution-building. In the present intellectual climate, the constraining impact figures so strongly that almost any argument for collective action and deliberation appears discredited from the start. And who indeed could, with a good conscience, neglect twentieth-century experiences of constraints and disciplines? But how else, on the other hand, can we create the conditions to live our diverse views of the good life in liberty?

Notes

PROLOGUE

1 Zygmunt Bauman (*Modernity and Ambivalence*, Cambridge, Polity, 1991, p. 272) has similarly described the ambition of postmodernity – in his conception of the term – as 'the modern mind taking a long, attentive and sober look at itself', as 'modernity looking at itself at a distance rather than from inside, making a full inventory of its gains and issues, psychoanalysing itself'.

2 In line with what has become the most common, or at least the most consistent, use of terminology, I shall refer to modernity and postmodernity as – historical or ideal-typical – social formations, and to modernism and postmodernism as cultural movements and sets of ideas, often normatively embracing or advocating modernity and postmodernity respectively; see now Barry Smart, *Postmodernity*, London, Routledge, 1993, pp. 16 and 23.

3 To say that a linkage should be re-established does not mean that these three perspectives should be merged, and their specifics be lost. Social and historical research could be unduly restricted, if a specific theoretical conception were seen as a limiting frame. Considerations of social theory must not shy away from morally unpleasant insights into social life, should not 'fear their own results', as a moral philosopher of the nineteenth century once said. There are gains from separation, only they should not lead to fragmentation and mutual neglect.

4 See Marshall Berman, *All That Is Solid Melts Into Air. The Experience of Modernity*, New York, Simon & Schuster, 1982, pp. 23–9.

5 This view has been most strongly expressed by Immanuel Kant. For a recent reappraisal of the principles of modern reasoning see John F. Rundell, *Origins of Modernity. The Origins of Modern Social Theory from Kant to Hegel to Marx*, Cambridge, Polity, 1987.

6 Karl Marx, 'Der achtzehnte Brumaire des Louis Bonaparte', in Karl Marx and Friedrich Engels, *Ausgewählte Schriften*, Berlin, Dietz, vol. 1, 1972, p. 226. (Translations from non-English sources are my own.)

7 Anthony Giddens, *The Constitution of Society. Outline of a Theory of Structuration*, Cambridge, Polity, 1984, p. xxi.

8 That modernity should be *judged* (normatively) in differentiated terms for different 'spheres of justice', has rightly been demanded by Michael Walzer recently (*Spheres of Justice. A Defense of Pluralism and Equality*, New York, Basic Books, 1983). It also has to be *analysed* in differentiated, and not normatively preconceptualized, terms for different spheres of practice and their interrelations. This is what I shall propose.

1 MODES OF NARRATING MODERNITY

1 This distinction has a firm root both in the Enlightenment and in the sociological intellectual tradition. As a means of boundary-setting it is briefly discussed in Chapter 3.

2 As a standard account one may consult the entries on the social and political aspects of 'modernization', written by Daniel Lerner and James S. Coleman respectively, in the *International Encyclopedia of the Social Sciences*, ed. by David L. Sills, London and New York, Macmillan and Free Press, 1968, pp. 386–402.

3 For critical discussions at the height of the debate see, for example, Reinhard Bendix, 'Tradition and modernity reconsidered', *Comparative Studies in Society and History*, vol. 9, 1967, pp. 292–346; Hans-Ulrich Wehler, *Modernisierungstheorie und Geschichte*, Göttingen, Vandenhoeck und Ruprecht, 1975; M. Rainer Lepsius, 'Soziologische Theoreme über die Sozialstruktur der "Moderne" und die "Modernisierung" ', in Reinhart Koselleck (ed.), *Studien zum Beginn der modernen Welt*, Stuttgart, Klett, 1977, pp. 10–29.

4 Robert R. Palmer, *The Age of the Democratic Revolution, Vol. 1, The Challenge*, Princeton, Princeton University Press, 1959.

5 The concept of an initial take-off of capitalist development, related to Marx's view on 'primitive accumulation', was comparatively analysed by Walt W. Rostow, *The Stages of Economic Growth*, Cambridge, Cambridge University Press, 1960, who saw a stretched sequence of national take-offs during the nineteenth century. More recently, Angus Maddison, *Dynamic Forces in Capitalist Development. A Long-Run Comparative View*, Oxford, Oxford University Press, 1991, pp. 8 and 27, names 1820 as the historical point when the capitalist economy was in place throughout the West. For a recent, critical reassessment see Rondo Cameron, 'A new view of European industrialization', *The Economic History Review*, vol. 37, no. 1, 1985, pp. 1–23.

6 As is emphasized in some recent works, for example, Anthony Giddens, *Modernity and Self-Identity. Self and Society in the Late Modern Age*, Cambridge, Polity, 1991; Alain Touraine, *Critique de la Modernité*, Paris, Fayard, 1992; Marshall Berman, *All That Is Solid Melts Into Air. The Experience of Modernity*, New York, Simon & Schuster, 1982; David Harvey, *The Condition of Postmodernity*, Oxford, Blackwell, 1989; Agnes Heller and Ferenc Fehér, *The Postmodern Political Condition*, Cambridge, Polity, 1988.

7 This can be read, for example, from works in the 'new historiography'. Furthermore, virtually all 'thick descriptions' of human practices of action and interpretation question the existence and/or the character and rules of modern institutions. To give just two examples here: Judith Stacey, *Brave New Families. Stories of Domestic Upheaval in Late Twentieth Century America*, New York, Basic Books, 1990; Heidrun Friese, *Ordnungen der Zeit. Zur sozialen Konstruktion von Temporalstrukturen in einem sizilianischen Ort*, Ph.D. thesis, University of Amsterdam, 1991.

8 Michel Foucault, *Les mots et les choses. Une archéologie des sciences humaines*, Paris, Gallimard, 1966, pp. 355–6. The key reference to Reinhart Koselleck's work is the encyclopedia on *Geschichtliche Grundbegriffe*, Stuttgart, Klett-Cotta, several volumes, co-edited by him with Otto Brunner and Werner Conze. For the notion of the modern rupture see his own entries 'Geschichte' and 'Fortschritt' among others. Jürgen Habermas, *The Philosophical Discourse of Modernity*, Cambridge, Mass., MIT Press, 1987; Wolf Lepenies, 'Das Ende der Naturgeschichte und der Beginn der Moderne', in Koselleck, *Studien*, pp. 317–51.

9 For a recent presentation of the problematics and the contested nature of statements on breaks in social practices see, for example, Johann P. Arnason, 'Civilization, culture and power: reflections on Norbert Elias' genealogy of the West', *Thesis Eleven*, no. 24, 1989, pp. 44–70.

10 Accordingly, Rolf Reichardt and Reinhart Koselleck emphasize the 'rupture in societal consciousness' which was brought about by the French Revolution; see Reichardt and

Koselleck (eds), *Die Französische Revolution als Bruch des gesellschaftlichen Bewußtseins*, Munich, Oldenbourg, 1988, for example pp. 659 and 663.

11 In an indirect way, this distinction is also the basis for misunderstandings over normative issues, like the one between Habermas and the French postmodernists. In one of his last writings, Michel Foucault made this beautifully clear, when he distinguished the Enlightenment institutions, to which historically his concept of the 'blackmail of the Enlightenment' may apply, and the ethos of the Enlightenment, to which he felt committed; 'Un cours inédit', *Le magazine littéraire*, no. 207, May 1984, pp. 35–9. In my view, there is a premature jump to normativity in most of the contributions to this debate. Not least for this reason, this book heads for a historico-sociological account of modernity, to restart the debate.

12 This notion is, of course, borrowed from Cornelius Castoriadis, see, for example, *The Imaginary Institution of Society*, Cambridge, Mass., MIT Press, 1987, pp. 369–74. Others would talk about a new context of legitimation; see, for example, Jürgen Habermas' discussion of the concept of legitimacy, *Legitimationsprobleme im Spätkapitalismus*, Frankfurt/M., Suhrkamp, 1973, pp. 131–40. See also Johann P. Arnason, 'The imaginary constitution of modernity', *Revue européenne des sciences sociales*, no. 20, 1989, p. 337.

13 See now Orlando Patterson, *Freedom, Vol. I. Freedom in the Making of Western Culture*, New York, Basic Books, 1991, who tries to trace the idea of personal freedom as far as possible. In the tradition of Marcel Mauss, Louis Dumont has portrayed the 'modern ideology' as based on the idea of free and equal individuals, see his *Essais sur l'individualisme. Une perspective anthropologique sur l'idéologie moderne*, Paris, Seuil, 1983; and *Homo aequalis. Genèse et épanouissement de l'idéologie économique*, Paris, Gallimard, 2nd edn 1985.

14 Jürgen Habermas, *The Theory of Communicative Action*, Boston, Beacon, 1984–7; for a different perspective with similar praise for modern institutions, see recently also Alan Wolfe, *Whose Keeper? Social Science and Moral Obligation*, Berkeley, University of California Press, 1989.

15 Most of Hegel's writings can be read as an attempt to reconcile, after the French Revolution, individual liberties and moral unity in the idea of the state, see for recent readings Axel Honneth, 'Atomisierung und Sittlichkeit: Zu Hegels Kritik der Französischen Revolution', in Forum für Philosophie Bad Homburg (ed.), *Die Ideen von 1789 in der Deutschen Rezeption*, Frankfurt/M., Suhrkamp, 1989, pp. 186–204; and Richard Dien Winfield, *Freedom and Modernity*, Albany, State University of New York Press, 1991. Robert Wuthnow, *Communities of Discourse. Ideology and Social Structure in the Reformation, the Enlightenment, and European Socialism*, Cambridge, Mass., Harvard University Press, 1989, part II, tries to contextualize the Enlightenment 'ambivalence toward the state' (p. 315).

16 An impressive treatise of this issue is Charles Taylor's *Sources of the Self. The Making of the Modern Identity*, Cambridge, Mass., Harvard University Press, 1989.

17 Isaiah Berlin, 'Two concepts of liberty', in *Four Essays on Liberty*, Oxford, Oxford University Press, 1969, pp. 118–72. Erich Fromm (*Escape from Freedom*, New York, Holt, Rinehart & Winston, 1941, pp. 31 and 36) saw the history of modernity in terms of imbalances between processes of individuation and those of self-growth, or in other words, between the degrees of realization of negative and positive freedom. 'The understanding of the whole problem of freedom depends on the very ability to see both sides of the process and not to lose track of one side while following the other.' Programmatically he writes: 'A detailed analysis of European and American history of the period between the Reformation and our own day could show how the contradictory trends inherent in the evolution of "freedom from to freedom to" run parallel – or rather, are continuously interwoven' (op. cit., pp. 104 and 121–2).

18 That there are 'genuine dilemmas' in modernity in both these respects is emphasized by such major critical reworkings of our constitutive reasonings as Taylor's (the quotation is from *Sources of the Self*, p. 503) or Castoriadis', by both of which I have been inspired. Most recently – that is, while I was writing – Alain Touraine's related account, *Critique de la modernité*, has appeared.

19 J.L. Talmon sees the primacy given to reason as the intellectual *Origins of Totalitarian Democracy*, which is the title of his book (London, Gollancz, 1952).

20 The former is emphasized in the writings of Zygmunt Bauman, for example, *Legislators and Interpreters. On Modernity, Post-Modernity and Intellectuals*, Cambridge, Polity, 1987; and *Modernity and Ambivalence*, Cambridge, Polity, 1991. Charles E. Lindblom, *Inquiry and Change. The Troubled Attempt to Understand and Shape Society*, New Haven and New York, Yale University Press and Russell Sage Foundation, 1990; tries to advocate a stronger stress on the latter. Alan Wolfe, op. cit., terms them the political and the economic view respectively, and sees both as inversely deficient.

21 Talmon's merit is to have pointed to totalitarian inclinations in modern thought (op. cit.). It is important to note, however, that both versions of solving the modern dilemmas show these inclinations, if pushed to extremes. If totalitarianism means the suppression of politics as the communication of and deliberation about what people in a community have in common, then individualist theories of self-regulation, including most prominently economics, are totalitarian once they are read as political philosophies. For a development of such an argument, see Pierre Rosanvallon, *Le capitalisme utopique. Critique de l'idéologie économique*, Paris, Seuil, 1979. As a political theory, socialism was indeed a (insufficient) response to the one-dimensionality of the economistic interpretation of the modern project.

22 The distinction is actually not exactly temporal, since all views have long been and continue to be held. But other terminological choices, such as moderate, radical and postmodernism, also tend to convey unhelpful connotations.

23 This point is forcefully developed by Taylor, op. cit., see, for example, pp. 85–6, 156 (where he calls procedural reason 'the standard modern view'), and 243.

24 Referring to this 'classical' modern conception, the ambiguity of modernity is often cast specifically as the one of autonomy and rational mastery. Thus, Cornelius Castoriadis (*Le monde morcelé. Les carrefours du labyrinthe III*, Paris, Seuil, 1990, p. 17) puts the co-existence of autonomy and reason as both conflict and mutual contamination of the two imaginary significations of modernity. Also Alain Touraine focuses his analysis of the 'modernist ideology' on the development of a 'duality of *rationalization* and *subjectivization*' (op. cit., pp. 39 and 15).

25 Richard Rorty, *Contingency, Irony, and Solidarity*, Cambridge, Cambridge University Press, 1989.

26 It is this imbalance, I think, that leads Castoriadis to term 'rational mastery' the second imaginary signification of autonomy. Unlike nature, community, or reason, which are more broadly understood, the notion of rational mastery is one that is already de-substantivized and, possibly, de-collectivized.

27 Touraine, op. cit., p. 15; see Taylor, op. cit., Chapters 14 and 16, for a differentiated argument on the place of Deism in the discourse of modernity. See also Hans Blumenberg, *Die Legitimität der Neuzeit*, Frankfurt/M., Suhrkamp, 1966, for a critical review of the notion of 'secularization'. Clearly, there are kinds of such rethinking that leave a place for religion in a 'modern' world-view – unlike the French anti-religious perspective.

28 'The liberals of Europe always had a problem on their hands, which they usually neglected, to be sure, of explaining how principles could be "self-evident" when there were obviously so many people who did not believe them. Circumstance nearly solved this problem for the Americans . . . When one's ultimate values are accepted wherever

one turns, the absolute language of self-evidence comes easily enough.' (Louis Hartz, *The Liberal Tradition in America. An Interpretation of American Political Thought Since the Revolution*, New York, Harcourt, Brace, & World, 1955, pp. 58–9)

29 This argument is developed by Talmon (op. cit.) in his sketch of political reasoning from Rousseau and Robespierre to totalitarianism.

30 Significantly, a recent liberal theory of justice, such as the one proposed by John Rawls (*A Theory of Justice*, Cambridge, Mass., Belknap of Harvard University Press, 1971, pp. 66–7), pays attention to the issue of change, and refers to the Pareto principle of optimality.

31 Marshall Berman, op. cit., pp. 66–71, is reminded of the story of Philemon and Baucis in Goethe's 'Faust' as an early presentation of this issue.

32 Recent, related attempts are Harvey, *Condition*; Scott Lash, *Sociology of Postmodernism*, London, Routledge, 1990; Fredric Jameson, *Postmodernism, or, The Cultural Logic of Late Capitalism*, Durham, N.C., Duke University Press, 1991; Stephen Crook, Jan Pakulski, and Malcolm Waters, *Postmodernization. Change in Advanced Society*, London, Sage, 1992; Touraine, op. cit. There is an overlap of observations between these studies and mine, though some of the former focus more strictly on cultural phenomena. Generally, my major problem with them is that, where they move to statements on the broader social configuration, they tend to analyse both modernity and postmodernity in terms of unfolding processes and logics rather than as, even if unintended, outcomes of manifold and interdependent human action. While this is not true for Touraine, he also makes a problematic distinction between actors and systems. Like mine, the account by Crook *et al.* includes distinctions between US, West European and East European modernities and between different realms of social practices. At one point, they also use the term 'organized modernity' (p. 113, see also p. 228).

2 ENABLEMENT AND CONSTRAINT: UNDERSTANDING MODERN INSTITUTIONS

1 For a related approach, and a related critique of the modernist social sciences, see Luc Boltanski and Laurent Thévenot, *De la justification. Les économies de la grandeur*, Paris, Gallimard, 1991, for example, p. 44.

2 See Anthony Giddens, *The Constitution of Society. Outline of a Theory of Structuration*, Cambridge, Polity, 1984; Pierre Bourdieu, *The Logic of Practice*, Cambridge, Polity, 1990, for such a view on social theory. Beyond Giddens and Bourdieu, Hans Joas has recently provided a systematic theoretical argument for the creative character of human action, see *Die Kreativität des Handelns*, Frankfurt/M., Suhrkamp, 1992 (forthcoming in English with Polity Press).

3 See most recently Randall Collins, 'The romanticism of agency/structure versus the analysis of micro/macro', *Current Sociology*, vol. 40, no. 1, 1992, pp. 77–97.

4 See also Laurent Thévenot, 'L'action qui convient', in Patrick Pharo and Louis Quéré (eds), *Les formes de l'action. Sémantique et sociologie* (*Raisons pratiques*, no. 1, 1990), Paris, Editions de l'EHESS, 1990, pp. 39–69.

5 Michel Foucault, 'Technologies of the self', in Luther H. Martin, Huck Gutman, and Patrick H. Hutton (eds), *Technologies of the Self. A Seminar with Michel Foucault*, Amherst, The University of Massachusetts Press, 1988, p. 18. To grasp durability and solidity, Pierre Bourdieu has developed the concept of 'habitus' that refers to knowledge and attitudes acquired biographically, that is, in the individually specific historical social context. See his *Logic of Practice*.

6 This separation is obviously somewhat artificial, since these conventions are continuously reshaped by human action. Still, the distinction will be needed when

describing the emergence and transformations of particular kinds of conventions, as I shall try to do later. No warning can be exaggerated, however, since this distinction has given rise to a very unfortunate split of sociological theorizing into theories of the constitution of society and those of the differentiation of society, each of which appear to be incapable of grasping social transformations in satisfyingly comprehensive terms on their own (see Joas, op. cit., Chapter 4). In France, a historical sociology and economics of conventions is being developed that tries to overcome this dichotomy both conceptually and empirically. I shall repeatedly draw on such works, by authors such as Boltanski, Thévenot, Robert Salais, Alain Desrosières, Michael Pollak, François Eymard-Duvernay and others.

7 See Ernest Gellner, *Plough, Sword and Book. The Structure of Human History*, London, Collins Harvill, 1988; and the contributions to John A. Hall and I.C. Jarvie (eds), *Transition to Modernity. Essays on Power, Wealth and Belief*, Cambridge, Cambridge University Press, 1991.

8 Michael Mann, *The Sources of Social Power, Vol. I. A History of Power from the Beginning to A.D. 1760*, Cambridge, Cambridge University Press, 1986, Chapter 1.

9 The focus is obviously selective, due above all to limits of my knowledge and my capability to develop the argument. Thus, I will at least mention three realms, the relative neglect of which may make for a systematic incompleteness of this account of modernity. A further important category would be *practices of social reproduction*, involving the organization of intimacy (family, sexuality, procreation) and making the relation of domestic labour to other allocative practices fully open to analysis. Changes in the social rules for these practices are of obviously high importance for an analysis of the condition of modernity. (A fruitful starting-point is Dorothy Smith's perspective on 'A sociology for women', *The Everyday World as Problematic. A Feminist Sociology*, Boston, Northeastern University Press, 1987, pp. 49–104. She herself, though, has not really continued this line of research and reasoning.) Though I am not able to offer any systematic analysis, at several points I will try to point out where and how a fuller integration of these issues could possibly provide a more adequate understanding of the modern condition. Second, while wars, especially the First World War, will appear as events of major importance in my account, no systematic consideration of *military practices* will be offered either. Third, the analysis of the practices of signification will be possibly unduly restricted (see Note 11).

10 Colin Gordon, 'The soul of the citizen: Max Weber and Michel Foucault on rationality and government', in Scott Lash and Sam Whimster (eds), *Max Weber, Rationality and Modernity*, London, Allen & Unwin, 1987, p. 296–7, referring to Foucault.

11 On the former see, for instance, Franz Xaver Kaufmann, *Religion und Modernität. Sozialwissenschaftliche Perspektiven*, Tübingen, Mohr, 1989; on the latter, Nikolas Rose, *Governing the Soul. The Shaping of the Private Self*, London, Routledge, 1989.

12 See for a discussion of sociology of science and knowledge, Peter Wagner and Björn Wittrock, *Social Sciences and Societal Developments. The Missing Perspective*, Berlin, WZB, 1987 (Paper P 87–3). Transferred via Bruno Latour, the term 'symmetry' is also used in the 'French approach' mentioned above, see Nicolas Dodier, 'Agir dans plusieurs mondes', *Critique*, nos. 529–30, 1991, p. 442.

13 I shall discuss the revival of this concept at the end of my analysis, in Chapter 11.

14 Such a perspective denies the possibility of any 'superior' vantage point of the critic, and, strictly speaking, has no claim to the term critique at all. I would rather stress that any such critique implies self-criticism of the critic, who shares in the social practices which are critically analysed.

15 See for such a perspective Smith, op. cit; and for a related critique of mainstream sociology Ruth A. Wallace (ed.), *Feminism and Sociological Theory*, Newbury Park, Sage, 1989.

16 Norbert Elias, *Was ist Soziologie?*, München, Juventa, 1970, pp. 173–4.
17 Gordon, op. cit., p. 296. Gordon also stresses that Foucault's interest here is very similar to Weber's in *Lebensführung*. Nikolas Rose and Peter Miller have proposed to use some of Foucault's writings for an analysis of current liberalism, see their 'Political power beyond the state: problematics of government', *British Journal of Sociology*, vol. 43, no. 2, 1992, pp. 173–205. In Foucault's own words the ambiguity is cast as follows: 'The "Enlightenment", which discovered the liberties, also invented the disciplines.' (*Discipline and Punish. The Birth of the Prison*, New York, Vintage, 1979, p. 222)
18 The notion of 'modernization offensive' draws on recent interpretations of Weber, Elias and Foucault, see Arthur Mitzman, 'The civilizing offensive: mentalities, high culture and individual psyches', *Journal of Social History*, vol. 20, no. 4, 1987, pp. 663–87; and Robert van Krieken, 'Violence, self-discipline and modernity: beyond the "civilizing process" ', *The Sociological Review*, vol. 37, no. 2, 1989, pp. 193–218. The introduction of this term is clearly not meant to downplay the relevance of unintended effects of such offensives, which may well outlast the intentions of the modernizers.
19 Defence against modernizations from above was the historical pattern. More generally (and especially for more recent 'social movements') one should say that contemporaneous modernization offensives may be directed against each other, when the hierarchical location in society is unclear.
20 Historical-anthropological studies show both quite convincingly, see, for example, two classics of different genres: Fernand Braudel, *La Mediterranée et le monde mediterranéen à l'époque de Philippe II*, Paris, Colin, 1949; or Laurence Wylie, *Village in the Vaucluse*, Cambridge, Mass., Harvard University Press, 1957, Chapter 2. But see later, in the discussion of organized modernity, how world-market permeation can be affected and limited by the setting of boundaries.
21 I may just note the works of Mann, Foucault and Giddens on surveillance, in this regard.
22 Under the double impact of poststructuralism and of new technologies, the distinction between transport and communication gets blurred. Every transport, it can rightly be argued, is also a transport of information, be it people who report from social life in the Americas, or goods that 'report' about the conditions of allocative practices elsewhere. See, for example, Paul Virilio, *L'inertie polaire*, Paris, Bourgois, 1990; Mark Poster, *The Mode of Information. Poststructuralism and Social Context*, Cambridge, Polity, 1990; Louis Kaplan, *Telepathic Technologies. A Seance in Fortean Science*, Berlin, WZB, 1991 (WZB Paper FS II 91–504).
23 Max Weber, 'Wissenschaft als Beruf', *Gesammelte Aufsätze zur Wissenschaftslehre*, Tübingen, Mohr, 4th edn 1973, p. 594. (H.H. Gerth and C. Wright Mills (eds), *From Max Weber. Essays in Sociology*, New York, Oxford University Press, 1946, p. 139)
24 By referring to formalization, I try to de-emphasize the almost inevitable normative connotations of rationalization, intellectualization and progress. Also, I want to stress the form this knowledge takes. Some limited intellectual affinity between Weber and Lyotard has been noted by Charles Turner, 'Lyotard and Weber: postmodern rules and neo-Kantian values', in Bryan S. Turner (ed.), *Theories of Modernity and Postmodernity*, London, Sage, 1990, pp. 108–16.
25 Due emphasis is given to this aspect in Marx's *Capital*. And quite obviously, this way of classifying is still (or again) hotly contested, as the debates about domestic labour and monetary values of environmental quality show.
26 The marginalist revolution in academic economic thought, in fact, can be seen as both a theoretical formalization and a de-substantivization of the value question, in the sense the latter term was introduced above.
27 In contrast to neoclassical economics, the French economics of conventions starts out from the assumption that 'the agreement between individuals, even if it is confined to the contract of a market exchange, is impossible without a constitutive convention'

(Jean-Pierre Dupuy *et al.*, 'Introduction', *L'économie des conventions*, special issue of *Revue économique*, vol. 40, no. 2, 1989, p. 142).

28 In anthropological perspective, boundary-setting is a very basic, universal way of orienting oneself in the world, to make communication possible, and to create social identity; see, for example, Anthony P. Cohen, *The Symbolic Construction of Community*, Chichester and London, Harwood and Tavistock, 1985, pp. 11–12; and Mary Douglas, *Purity and Danger. An Analysis of Concepts of Pollution and Taboo*, London, Routledge & Kegan Paul, 1966.

29 For a discussion of kinds of constraints, see Giddens, op. cit., pp. 174–9.

30 This last form is the one to which the notion of self-cancellation refers (see Chapters 1 and 10).

31 See Marshall Berman's account of Robert Moses' perspectives and the urban consequences of his work; *All That Is Solid Melts Into Air. The Experience of Modernity*, New York, Simon & Schuster, 1982, Chapter V.

32 Berman, op. cit., p. 302.

33 One may refer to formalizations generally as technologies, in the sense of intentionally constructed means to certain ends, as Michel Foucault did. Two cautionary remarks have to be made, however. First, actually existing institutional rules and resources are very often shaped by the unintended collective outcome of many individual actions. Second, the term technology in an everyday sense refers largely to material objects; social institutions, however, may be immaterial or, often, characteristic mixes of material and immaterial elements. (On such issues, see Bernward Joerges, 'Soziologie und Maschinerie: Vorschläge zu einer "realistischen" Techniksoziologie', in Peter Weingart (ed.), *Technik als sozialer Prozeß*, Frankfurt/M., Suhrkamp, 1989, pp. 44–89; and 'Technische Normen – soziale Normen?', *Soziale Welt*, vol. 40, nos. 1–2, 1989, pp. 242–58.)

34 Joerges, op. cit., pp. 62–8.

35 Anthony Giddens, *The Consequences of Modernity*, Cambridge, Polity, 1990, pp. 83–4.

36 To give just one example: Wilhelm Röpke introduces his *Die Gesellschaftskrisis der Gegenwart* (Berne, Haupt, 1979 [1942]) programmatically as the thoughts of an economist 'about the state of illness of our civilized world and about the way to its recovery' (p. 7).

37 For a conceptual discussion see also Jürgen Habermas, *Legitimationsprobleme im Spätkapitalismus*, Frankfurt/M., Suhrkamp, 1973, pp. 9–49.

38 One may also argue that there was a first crisis of modernity already around the turn of the nineteenth century, not least in response to the French Revolution. The numbering of major social transformations would lead us then to a second crisis broadly around the following turn of the century, and a third one after 1960. Both Marshall Berman (op. cit., pp. 16–17) and Alain Touraine (*Critique de la Modernité*, Paris, Fayard, 1992) work mainly with a periodization of modernity, which marks a first transition after the 1790s and a second one only after the 1960s – a view which does not convince me, since it breaks down as soon as one looks beyond intellectual history at the rules of social practices. Indeed, Touraine also gives elements of an interpretation which is closer to mine, see, for example, pp. 216, 302, 364.

39 Claude Lefort, 'Reversibility: political freedom and the freedom of the individual', *Democracy and Political Theory*, Cambridge, Polity, 1988, p. 180.

40 'Whilst reason and justice become solemn references which are available to all, they are subject to interpretation by all, and are linked to a discovery which no individual can disassociate from the mobilization of his capacity for knowledge and speech' (Lefort, op. cit.).

41 Boltanski and Thévenot, op. cit., p. 51.

42 Charles Taylor, *Sources of the Self. The Making of the Modern Identity*, Cambridge, Mass., Harvard University Press, 1989, pp. 196 and 514.

3 RESTRICTED LIBERAL MODERNITY: THE INCOMPLETE ELABORATION OF THE MODERN PROJECT

1 This indeed has been a main theme of anthropology from its beginnings, and more specifically of the reflexive anthropology that has been developed over the past decades, see, for example, James A. Boon, *Other Tribes, Other Scribes. Symbolic Anthropology in the Comparative Study of Cultures, Histories, Religions, and Texts*, Cambridge, Cambridge University Press, 1982.

2 Hayden White, 'The forms of wildness: archeology of an idea', *Tropics of Discourse. Essays in Cultural Criticism*, Baltimore, Johns Hopkins University Press, 1978, p. 151. Reinhart Koselleck has placed similar emphasis on asymmetric oppositions, with which boundaries are set, as means of acting on groups of human beings or as means of achieving agential capacity as a collective; see 'Zur historisch-politischen Semantik asym- metrischer Gegenbegriffe', *Vergangene Zukunft. Zur Semantik geschichtlicher Zeiten*, Frankfurt/M., Suhrkamp, 1979, pp. 214–15. Peter Wehling uses the term 'social myth' for his critical intellectual history of 'modernity' and 'modernization'; see *Die Moderne als Sozialmythos*, Frankfurt/M., Campus, 1992, p. 15.

3 White, op. cit., p. 155.

4 'A sociological past has been worked up, a past which is linked to the present not by carefully observed and temporally located social interaction but by inferentially necessary connections between concepts' (Philip Abrams, 'The sense of the past and the origins of sociology', *Past and Present*, no. 55, 1971, p. 20). For an attempt at a systematic reconstruction see now Heidrun Friese, *Geschichtsbilder. Konstruktionen der vergangenen Zeit*, Berlin, Mimeo, 1991.

5 Johannes Fabian, *Time and the Other. How Anthropology Makes its Object*, New York, Columbia University Press, 1983, pp. 31 and 52.

> Tradition and modernity are not 'opposed' (except semiotically), nor are they in 'conflict'. All this is (bad) metaphorical talk. What are opposed, in conflict, in fact, locked in antagonistic struggle, are not the same societies at different stages of development, but different societies facing each other at the same Time.
>
> (Ibid., p. 155)

6 Zygmunt Bauman, *Intimations of Postmodernity*, London, Routledge, 1992, p. xxvi.

7 'Bourgeois individualism recognized barriers that became visible only when they began to fall. Physical individuality as such was not a sufficient condition for granting political and social, not even legal, equality to all individuals' (Panajotis Kondylis, *Der Niedergang der bürgerlichen Denk- und Lebensform. Die liberale Moderne und die massendemokratische Postmoderne*, Weinheim, VCH, Acta humaniora, 1991, p. 169).

8 Michelle Perrot, 'On the formation of the French working class', in Ira Katznelson and Aristide R. Zolberg (eds), *Working-Class Formation. Nineteenth-Century Patterns in Europe and the United States*, Princeton, Princeton University Press, 1986, p. 95.

9 White, 'The noble savage theme as fetish', in *Tropics*, p. 193.

10 See, for example, Manfred Riedel, 'Gesellschaft, bürgerliche', in Otto Brunner, Werner Conze, and Reinhart Koselleck (eds), *Geschichtliche Grundbegriffe. Historisches Lexikon der politisch-sozialen Sprache in Deutschland*, Stuttgart, Klett-Cotta, vol. 2, 1975, pp. 740–1; and most recently Pierre Rosanvallon, *Le sacre du citoyen. Histoire du suffrage universel en France*, Paris, Gallimard, 1992, on the limits and implications of the modern idea of citizenship. In the nineteenth century, the subject of this discourse was the 'bourgeois', or the 'classical liberal'. It can well be argued that he defended a theory and definitions that strengthened his own interests. However, he could do so by drawing on a long tradition of political theory. For a full understanding of 'classical liberalism' at the turn of the nineteenth century, one needs to see it as an appropriation of a body

of ideas in a certain societal constellation, that is, neither in terms of pure intellectual history nor in terms of the determination of ideas by interests.

11 See George Duby and Michelle Perrot, *L'histoire de femmes*, Paris, Plon, several volumes 1991–2; Geneviève Fraisse, *Muse de la raison. La démocratie exclusive et la différence des sexes*, Aix, Alinéa, 1989; Claudia Honegger, *Die Ordnung der Geschlechter. Die Wissenschaften vom Menschen und das Weib, 1750–1850*, Frankfurt/M., Campus, 1991; Carole Pateman, *The Disorder of Woman. Democracy, Feminism and Political Theory*, Cambridge, Polity, 1989; Joan B. Landes, *Women and the Public Sphere in the Age of the French Revolution*, Ithaca, Cornell University Press, 1988.

12 Landes, op. cit., pp. 2 and 7.

13 Michel Foucault, *Folie et déraison. Histoire de la folie à l'âge classique*, Paris, Plon, 1961.

14 In terms of feminist political strategy, Carole Pateman has called the alternative between remaining excluded or conforming to institutional rules 'Wollstonecraft's dilemma', see *Disorder*, pp. 196–7.

15 The former view is compatible with a historical narrative of liberation, the latter one with one of disciplinization. In their pure forms, both tend to be dominated by normative reasoning, and they often take the metaphysical shape of portraying the gradual realization of a necessary principle. My own task, as set out in the two preceding chapters, will be to rethink these accounts after rereading modernity in terms of the orientations and practices of the actual human beings who produce it.

16 In this sense, one may follow Zygmunt Bauman, *Modernity and Ambivalence*, Cambridge, Polity, 1991, in reading the history of modernity as the elimination of ambivalence, as the imposition of order.

17 I do not want to enter here into the long discussion about the origins of the modern (or bourgeois or capitalist) state. Basically, I follow the critical historical rereading of the materialist tradition as put forward by, among others and with strong variations, Michael Mann, *The Sources of Social Power. Vol. 1*, Cambridge, Cambridge University Press, 1986; Anthony Giddens, *The Nation-State and Violence*, Cambridge, Polity, 1985; and most recently, with critical notes on both Giddens and Mann, Heide Gerstenberger, *Die subjektlose Gewalt. Theorie der Entstehung bürgerlicher Staatsgewalt*, Münster, Westfälisches Dampfboot, 1990.

18 Claude Lefort, 'The permanence of the theologico-political?', in *Democracy and Political Theory*, Cambridge, Polity, 1988, p. 232. This triple enumeration conceals part of the problematic: 'people' is undefined, 'state' is defined by its institutional rules, 'nation' is defined by cultural-linguistic practices. My own argument up to this point was on the 'state'. I shall return to Lefort's notions of 'people' and 'nation' later.

19

> Neither the fact of a non-monarchical regime, nor the various theories of republicanism and libertarianism associated with the English Revolution could have come about without the prior establishing of a 'discourse of sovereignty'. . . . Once the idea of sovereignty had effectively been turned into a principle of government, the way was open for it to be connected to that of 'citizenship'.
>
> (Giddens, op. cit., p. 94)

20 See the contributions by Jürgen Habermas ('Ist der Herzschlag der Revolution zum Stillstand gekommen? Volkssouveränität als Verfahren: Ein normativer Begriff von Öffentlichkeit', pp. 7–36) and Axel Honneth ('Atomisierung und Sittlichkeit: Zu Hegels Kritik der Französischen Revolution', pp. 186–204) to Forum für Philosophie (ed.), *Die Ideen von 1789*, Frankfurt/M., Suhrkamp, 1989.

21 Hans Maier, *Die ältere deutsche Staats- und Verwaltungslehre*, Munich, Beck, 1980 [1966]; Gerhard Oestreich, *Neostoicism and the Early Modern State*, Cambridge, Cambridge University Press, 1982; Michel Foucault, 'Governmentality', *Ideology and Consciousness*, no. 6, 1979, pp. 5–21.

22 Gerstenberger, op. cit., p. 516–17.
23 Zygmunt Bauman, *Intimations*, pp. xiii and xv.
24 Beyond *Intimations*, see his earlier *Legislators and Interpreters. On Modernity, Post-modernity and Intellectuals*, Cambridge, Polity, 1987; *Modernity and the Holocaust*, Ithaca, Cornell University Press, 1989; *Modernity and Ambivalence*, Cambridge, Polity, 1991.
25 See the concluding chapters of *Legislators* and *Ambivalence*; also his *Freedom*, Minneapolis, University of Minnesota Press, 1988.
26 An impressive attempt to portray and criticize sociological theories of action in such a way is Hans Joas, *Die Kreativität des Handelns*, Frankfurt/M., Suhrkamp, 1992.
27 Bauman, *Ambivalence*, p. 68.
28 Charles Taylor, *Sources of the Self. The Making of the Modern Identity*, Cambridge, Mass., Harvard University Press, 1989, p. 343.
29 See most recently on this issue: Bruno Latour, *Nous n'avons jamais étés modernes. Essai d'anthropologie symétrique*, Paris, La Découverte, 1991.
30 Arthur Mitzman ('The civilizing offensive: mentalities, high culture and individual psyches', *Journal of Social History*, vol. 20, no. 4, 1987, p. 674), has used this term to characterize post-revolutionary cultural movements in France. The repression and resurgence of difference and diversity is a prominent theme of postmodernism; see Jean-François Lyotard, *Le différend*, Paris, Minuit, 1983. Michel de Certeau focuses on the selectivity of historiography:

> Modern Western history essentially begins with differentiation between the *present* and the *past*. . . . [Historiographical labor] promotes a selection between what can be *understood* and what must be *forgotten* in order to obtain the representation of a present intelligibility. But what ever this new understanding of the past holds to be irrelevant – shards created by the selection of materials, remainders left aside by an explication – comes back, despite everything, on the edges of discourse or in its rifts and crannies: 'resistances', 'survivals', or delays discreetly perturb the pretty order of a line of 'progress' or a system of interpretation. These are lapses in the syntax constructed by the law of a place. Therein they symbolize a return of the repressed, that is, a return of what, at a given moment, has *become* unthinkable in order for a new identity to *become* thinkable.
>
> (*The Writing of History*, New York, Columbia University Press, 1988, pp. 2 and 4)

31 See, for example, Carol C. Gould, 'Private rights and public virtues: women, the family, and democracy', pp. 3–18; and Helen Bequaert Holmes, 'A feminist analysis of the universal declaration of human rights', pp. 250–64, both in Gould (ed.), *Beyond Domination. New Perspectives on Women and Philosophy*, Totowa, N.J., Rowman & Allanheld, 1984; and Ulrich Beck and Elisabeth Beck-Gernsheim, *Das ganz normale Chaos der Liebe*, Frankfurt/M., Suhrkamp, 1990.
32 If we accept the conception that the *oikos* – of which the male head is nothing but the representative of the polity – cares for social well-being, gender relations, sustainable production and cultural belonging, then these issues would not emerge at all. Only the concomitant universalization and atomization create the problem of the social handling of these issues. Such a genealogical look at the sources of the modern reasoning underlines the weight of the implications that any distinction between public and private realms has for the constitution of society.
33 Wolfgang J. Mommsen, 'The varieties of the nation state in modern history: liberal, imperial, fascist and contemporary notions of nation and nationality', in Michael Mann (ed.), *The Rise and Decline of the Nation State*, Oxford, Blackwell, 1990, p. 216.
34 Johann P. Arnason, 'The theory of modernity and the problematic of democracy',

Thesis Eleven, no. 26, 1990, pp. 38–9.

35 Ernest Gellner, *Nations and Nationalism*, Ithaca, Cornell University Press, 1983; Anthony D. Smith, *Nationalism in the Twentieth Century*, Oxford, Robertson, 1979, p. 3.

36 Louis Dumont, 'Une variante nationale: le peuple et la nation chez Herder et Fichte', *Essais sur l'individualisme. Une perspective anthropologique sur l'ideologie moderne*, Paris, Seuil, 1983, pp. 130–1.

37 The imaginary building of nations is discussed in the recent works of Benedict Anderson, *Imagined Communities. Reflections on the Origins and Spread of Nationalism*, London, Verso, 1983; Eric J. Hobsbawm, *Nations and Nationalism since 1780. Programme, Myth, Reality*, Cambridge, Cambridge University Press, 1990; and Eric J. Hobsbawm and Terence Ranger (eds), *The Invention of Tradition*, Cambridge, Cambridge University Press, 1983; see also Nathan Gardels, 'Two concepts of nationalism: an interview with Isaiah Berlin', *New York Review of Books*, 21 November 1991, pp. 19–23.

38 Mommsen, op. cit., p. 222. Mommsen sees a historical 'transition from a liberal to an exclusivist notion of the nation state' during the nineteenth century (ibid.).

39 Jacques Donzelot, *L'invention du social. Essai sur le déclin des passions politiques*, Paris, Fayard, 1984, p. 33.

40 William H. Sewell Jr., 'Artisans, factory workers, and the formation of the French working class, 1789–1848', in Katznelson and Zolberg, op. cit., p. 60.

41 William H. Sewell Jr., *Work and Revolution in France. Language and Labour from the Old Regime to 1848*, Cambridge, Cambridge University Press, 1980. See for England the classic account: Edward P. Thompson, *The Making of the English Working Class*, London, Gollancz, 1963. Ira Katznelson has recently pointed out that in the US, where residence and work-place used to be spatially separated, and political citizenship granted to workers early on, no strong collective political identity of a working class has emerged; 'Working class formation: constructing cases and comparisons', in Katznelson and Zolberg, op. cit., pp. 26–7.

42 Alain Desrosières, 'How to make things which hold together: social science, statistics and the state', in Peter Wagner, Björn Wittrock, and Richard Whitley (eds), *Discourses on Society. The Shaping of the Social Science Disciplines*, Dordrecht, Kluwer, 1991, p. 207.

43 Desrosiéres, op. cit., p. 200.

44 Nation and class, 'the two imagined or imaginary communities arose together, conjoined, in the same process of modernisation.' (Michael Mann, 'The emergence of modern European nationalism', in John A. Hall and I.C. Jarvie (eds), *Transition to Modernity. Essays on Power, Wealth and Belief*, Cambridge, Cambridge University Press, 1991, p. 141)

45 I hesitate to say prior to modernity in general, as the forging of the unified, 'high-culture', languages, by reformers and writers, and their diffusion and enforcement with the help of printing techniques and administrative rules is itself a 'modern' phenomenon. As the most recent intervention into this debate, see Zygmunt Bauman, 'Soil, blood and identity', *The Sociological Review*, vol. 40, no. 4, 1992, pp. 675–701.

46 Though probably needless to say, I would like to stress that variations between Western societies were high on both counts – class formation and nation-building – and that the particular ways of structuring the polity more or less clearly along lines of nationhood and class had a lasting impact on political struggles, up to the present.

47 Adam Smith, *An Inquiry into the Nature and Causes of the Wealth of Nations*, Chicago, University of Chicago Press, 1976 [1776]; Friedrich List, *The National System of Political Economy*, New York, Longmans Green, 1904 [1841].

48 Joyce Oldham Appleby, 'The American model for the French revolutionaries', in her *Liberalism and Republicanism in the Historical Imagination*, Cambridge, Mass.,

Harvard University Press, 1992, pp. 232–3.

49 Aristide R. Zolberg, 'Bounded states in a global market: the uses of international labor migrations', in Pierre Bourdieu and James S. Coleman (eds), *Social Theory for a Changing Society*, Boulder, Col., and New York, Westview and Russell Sage, 1991, p. 311.

50 A strong such portrait is given by Louis Hartz, *The Liberal Tradition in America. An Interpretation of American Political Thought Since the Revolution*, New York, Harcourt, Brace, & World, 1955.

51 I see only one, secondary, reason why the attitude of the individuals to society, their expectations as to what may and should and should not be collectively arranged, should have *become* more individualistic in the US. This is the experience of emigration.

> No one can deny that conscious purpose went into the making of the colonial world, and that the men of the seventeenth century who fled to America from Europe were keenly aware of the oppressions of European life. But they were revolutionaries with a difference, and the fact of their fleeing is no minor fact: for it is one thing to stay at home and fight the 'canon and the feudal law,' and it is another to leave it far behind.
>
> (Hartz, op. cit., pp. 64–5)

(Albert O. Hirschman, *Exit, Voice and Loyalty*, Cambridge, Mass., Harvard University Press, 1970, Chapter 8, has also drawn on Hartz to explain the exit-mindedness of Americans.) Hartz adds a note that is worth quoting, too:

> In a real sense physical flight is the American substitute for the European experience of social revolution. And this, of course, has persisted throughout our national history, although nothing in the subsequent pattern of flight, the 'safety-valve' notwithstanding, has approximated in significance the original escape from Europe. It is interesting how romance has been thrown alike around the European liberals who stayed home to fight and the American liberals who fled their battle. There are two types of excitement here, that of changing familiar things and that of leaving them, which both involve a trip into the unknown. But though one may find a common element of adventure in flight and revolution, it is a profound mistake to confuse the perspectives they engender.

Especially during the nineteenth century, quite a number of would-be Americans were rebels before they turned exiles. So, they were shaped by the experience of the failure to achieve a desirable collective arrangement in society. Though it may seem so, there are not necessarily any normative implications here.

> The exile is as absolute as the rebel in rejecting the way of life of his society, but instead of fighting it he goes away. . . . [Usually,] he will remain an exile, unable to go back to the society that he has rejected or that has rejected him, yet equally unable to form important relationships with the society to which he has gone.
>
> (Raymond Williams, *The Long Revolution*, Harmondsworth, Penguin, 1961, p. 107)

52 See among the more recent publications following up on the 'Pocock debate', Steven Watts, *The Republic Reborn. War and the Making of Liberal America, 1790–1820*, Baltimore, The Johns Hopkins University Press, 1987; Jeffrey C. Isaac, 'Republicanism vs. liberalism? A reconsideration', *History of Political Thought*, vol. 9, no. 2, 1988, pp. 349–77; and Appleby, op. cit.

53 Robert R. Palmer, *The Age of the Democratic Revolution, Vol. 1, The Challenge*, Princeton, Princeton University Press, 1959, p. 189.

54 Daniel Bell, ' "American exceptionalism" revisited: the role of civil society', *The*

Public Interest, no. 95, Spring 1989, p. 49. Of course, the absence of a unitarian representation for the common good was not considered unproblematic, especially not by intellectuals. See, for instance, John G. Gunnell's account of the cognitive development of early American political science from a search for such an entity: 'In search of the state: political science as an emerging discipline in the US', in Wagner *et al.*, op. cit., pp. 123–61. In general, however, the twentieth-century American social sciences have been as stateless as the society they observed.

55 For a recent review of such debates see Michael Walzer, 'What does it mean to be an "American"?', *Social Research*, vol. 57, no. 3, 1990, pp. 591–614.

56 Lefort, 'Permanence', p. 232.

4 CRISIS AND TRANSFORMATION OF MODERNITY: THE END OF THE LIBERAL UTOPIA

1 Charles Taylor, *Sources of The Self. The Making of the Modern Identity*, Cambridge, Mass., Harvard University Press, 1989, p. 305.

2 This is a difficult argument, since, as far as my knowledge extends, not very much is known about how human beings actually oriented their lives in the past – nor can it, since almost everything has to be inferred from sources in which the human beings themselves do not speak. And, while more sociological and psychological research is devoted to such questions in the present, it is plausible to assume that conceptions of the self are so manifold that it is difficult to generalize across groups and societies. Nevertheless, for better or worse, I shall assume that enough can be inferred from the available insights to elaborate an idea as to the historical transformation of the self throughout modernity, an idea that could then serve as a heuristics for further inquiry. All obstacles and objections notwithstanding, such an analysis is necessary, I would insist, because an understanding of the modern condition, of the condition of human social life in modernity, could not do without an understanding of the social self. As Robert van Krieken writes,

> The historical sociology of personality is difficult territory, because it is a complicated enough task to ascertain what people did in everyday life, let alone what they thought and felt, but it is none the less an enterprise crucial to our understanding of social history.
>
> ('Violence, self-discipline and modernity: beyond the "civilizing process" ', *The Sociological Review*, vol. 37, no. 2, 1989, p. 214)

3 For an empirically oriented discussion of the concept see David H. Demo, 'The self-concept over time: research issues and directions', *Annual Review of Sociology*, vol. 18, 1992, pp. 303–26.

4 Thus, the notion of identity used here includes both more autonomous and more relational ideals of identity as historical and personal possibilities. The former are today often considered more typically male, the latter female. As introduced by feminist scholars over the past two decades, the debate about gender-specific conceptions of identity has re-opened issues that were closed by a male-dominated view of the human being as an autonomous rational individual. Sandra Harding has suggested that histories of modernity would look decisively different, depending on whether they consider gender as an important category or not ('Is gender a variable in conceptions of rationality? A survey of issues', in Carol C. Gould (ed.), *Beyond Domination. New Perspectives on Women and Philosophy*, Totowa, N.J., Rowman & Allanheld, 1984, pp. 46–8). While this is generally true, it must also be granted that the 'male' social identities in modernity, as based on nation and class, have decisively shaped our common history – maybe exactly because gender has been excluded.

5 Borrowing from Anthony Giddens, *The Consequences of Modernity*, Cambridge, Polity, 1990, p. 21: 'By disembedding I mean the "lifting out" of social relations from local contexts of interaction and their restructuring across indefinite spans of time-space.' See also Giddens, *Modernity and Self-Identity. Self and Society in the Late Modern Age*, Cambridge, Polity, 1991, pp. 17–18. Giddens overemphasizes, though, the opposition of local and global. In my view, disembedding may also take place when moving from one locale to another. Furthermore, almost any reembedding will recreate (one or more) new social locales of interaction. To avoid misunderstandings, I should also note that the use of 'embeddedness' in recent meta-theoretical debates about the conceptualization of the 'economic sphere' in relation to other social practices is quite different from both Giddens' and mine. (See Mark Granovetter, 'Economic action and social structure: the problem of embeddedness', *American Journal of Sociology*, vol. 91, no. 3, 1985, pp. 481–510, drawing on Karl Polanyi, *The Great Transformation*, New York, Farrar, Straus & Giroux, 1975 [1944]. The social process which is of interest here is called 'social dislocation' by Polanyi; see pp. 98, 129 and passim.)

6 This may appear to be making too strong claims about the actual orientations of human beings in their everyday lives, with little reliable knowledge availabe for a socio-historical analysis. Rather than a conclusive result, my observations on the historically changing relations of individual selves, social identities and societal configurations should be considered as an offer to formulate further questions.

7 For instance, Everett Rogers, with L. Svennig, *Modernization Among Peasants*, New York, Holt, Rinehart & Winston, 1969, pp. 25–38.

8 This, I think, is the valid part of Jürgen Habermas' argument in *Legitimationsprobleme im Spätkapitalismus*, Frankfurt/M., Suhrkamp, 1973.

9 In the terms of Luc Boltanski and Laurent Thévenot, a liberal polity would be based on civic and market-based modes of justification. Then, one may say that during the first half of the nineteenth century this conception was in a struggle with a domestic conception of the polity, as it was characteristic of feudalism and the Old Regime. From the late nineteenth century onwards, the civic/market-based polity began to be turned into a civic/industrial one. See *De la justification. Les économies de grandeur*, Paris, Gallimard, 1991, pp. 347–56.

10 For data see, for example, Theodor Schieder, 'Europa im Zeitalter der Nationalstaaten und europäische Weltpolitik bis zum Ersten Weltkrieg (1870–1918)', in Theodor Schieder (ed.), *Handbuch der europäischen Geschichte*, vol. 6, Stuttgart, Union, 1968, pp. 6–14. Hartmut Kaelble speaks of an 'enforced restlessness'; *Social Mobility in the Nineteenth and Twentieth Centuries. Europe and America in Comparative Perspective*, New York, St. Martin's Press, 1986, p. 125.

11 The classic work on the rethinking of social order and the decline of liberalism is, of course, Karl Polanyi's *The Great Transformation*; see more recently Adalbert Evers and Helga Nowotny, *Über den Umgang mit Unsicherheit. Die Entdeckung der Gestaltbarkeit von Gesellschaft*, Frankfurt/M., Suhrkamp, 1987.

12 Readers in some countries where liberalism had never really become dominant during the nineteenth century, Germany for instance, may have trouble with this interpretation. Of course, there were varieties of modernity also inside Europe. Not least for this reason, I shall introduce some explicitly comparative observations in the following paragraphs. However, a look at German debates about the need to reconstitute society shows a broad similarity of problematic to other Western nations between the 1870s and the First World War. Most generally, one may say that, while restricted liberal modernity was less liberal in Germany than elsewhere, organized modernity became more organized. There is a persistent deviation of Germany from, say, France or Italy in this regard, but not enough of a *Sonderweg* (special path) to exclude Germany from such an analysis.

13 If we see the end of the 1880s as the 'inauguration of class-war' (Norman Stone, *Europe*

Transformed 1878–1919, Glasgow, Fontana, 1983, p. 48), then this worldwide war lasted rather precisely for one century, though it involved regional agreements on peace or, at least, extended ceasefires. This historical trajectory is reflected, for instance, in the papal encyclica of 1991, which clearly 'talks to' and reconsiders the other major social policy statement of the Vatican, *Rerum novarum* of 1891.

14 For Germany, see Ditmar Brock, *Der schwierige Weg in die Moderne*, Frankfurt/M., Campus, 1991.

15 Anson Rabinbach, 'Social knowledge, fatigue, and the politics of industrial accidents', in Dietrich Rueschemeyer and Theda Skocpol (eds), *Social Knowledge and the Origins of Modern Social Policies*, Princeton and New York, Princeton University Press and Russell Sage Foundation (forthcoming).

16 On the changing meaning of poverty and risk in the late nineteenth century see also François Ewald, *L'Etat providence*, Paris, Grasset, 1986.

17 See Dietrich Rueschemeyer and Ronan van Rossem, 'The Fabian Society and the Verein für Sozialpolitik: social knowledge and early social policy', in Rueschemeyer and Skocpol, op. cit.

18 Hans Maier, *Die ältere deutsche Staats- und Verwaltungslehre*, Munich, Beck, 1980, p. 232.

19 Giovanna Procacci, 'Facing poverty: American and French philanthropy between science and reform', in Rueschemeyer and Skocpol, op. cit.

20 Procacci, op. cit.

21 Margaret Weir, Ann Shola Orloff, and Theda Skocpol (eds), *The Politics of Social Policy in the United States*, Princeton, Princeton University Press, 1988.

22 Procacci, op. cit.

23 In this comparison of two, in different ways, state-centred societies the German intellectual heritage of statist thinking in idealist and organicist terms makes the French notions of solidarity and solidarism look like an expression of extreme liberalism.

24 For Central Europe see, for example, Hans Rosenberg, *Große Depression und Bismarckzeit. Wirtschaftsablauf, Gesellschaft und Politik in Mitteleuropa*, Berlin, de Gruyter, 1967, pp. 62–82.

25 The organization of the public articulation of opinions and interests and of their aggregation has been portrayed by Jürgen Habermas as the factual abandonment of the liberal ideal; see *The Structural Transformation of the Public Sphere. An Inquiry into a Category of Bourgeois Society*, Cambridge, Mass., MIT Press, 1989.

26 This aspect will be discussed in more detail in the following chapter.

27 Geoffrey Hawthorn, *Enlightenment and Despair. A History of Sociology*, Cambridge, Cambridge University Press, 1976, p. 164.

28 So, the following argument is not meant to suggest that such critiques came to be the dominant interpretation of the state of modernity. Mostly they were not, and dominant approaches were often much more one-sided. Also, I shall somewhat stylize the reasoning to make visible what I see as an important argumentative figure, namely the inescapably dilemmatic nature of modernity with regard to justifications of social practices and the (unintended) effects of modes of organization of practices.

29 See Steven Seidman, *Liberalism and the Origins of European Social Theory*, Oxford, Blackwell, 1983, for a reading of classical European social theory, including Marx's work, as being centrally concerned with 'the liberal dilemma' (p. 278).

30 Karl Löwith, *Max Weber and Karl Marx*, London, Allen & Unwin, 1982 [1932], p. 41. Löwith has identified the similarities between Marx and Weber in this respect.

31 Indeed, some observers have ranged Marx's work under the same rubrique of philosophy of life. Thus, some resemblance between these two strands should be not too surprising. See Hannah Arendt, *The Human Condition*, Chicago, The University of Chicago Press, 1958, paras. 43 and 44.

32 On the emergence of pragmatism in the American context see recently, James Campbell, *The Community Reconstructs. The Meaning of Pragmatic Social Thought*, Urbana, Ill., University of Illinois Press, 1992; Cornel West, *The American Evasion of Philosophy. A Genealogy of Pragmatism*, Madison, The University of Wisconsin Press, 1989; more specifically on the present relevance (to which generally all these reappraisals are devoted) Giles Gunn, *Thinking Across the American Grain. Ideology, Intellect, and the New Pragmatism*, Chicago, The University of Chicago Press, 1992. See also Dorothy Ross, *The Origins of American Social Science*, Cambridge, Cambridge University Press, 1991, pp. 229–56.

33 As in some current debates, a new concern for morality was often seen as a remedy against the effects of modern institutions. Historically, then, it is more appropriate to speak of a reappraisal, rather than a critique, of morality. On moral debates in English social science see Stefan Collini, *Liberalism and Sociology. L.T. Hobhouse and Political Argument in England 1880–1914*, Cambridge, Cambridge University Press, 1979; Reba N. Soffer, *Ethics and Society in England. The Revolution in the Social Sciences 1870–1914*, Berkeley, University of California Press, 1978. For a related recent argument see Alan Wolfe, *Whose Keeper? Social Science and Moral Obligation*, Berkeley, University of California Press, 1989.

34 Bryan S. Turner, 'The rationalization of the body: reflections on modernity and discipline', in Scott Lash and Sam Whimster (eds), *Max Weber, Rationality and Modernity*, London, Allen & Unwin, 1987, p. 231, referring to both Weber and Nietzsche.

35 It shall just be noted here that the European variants of these critiques tended to be more pessimistic, whereas the American ones, mostly based on pragmatism, showed some activist optimism. The latter worked less with a dichotomy of individual strivings and collective fate than the former, but rather tried to reconcile both conceptually (see also Chapter 7).

36 The remark stems from a meeting of the Association for Social Policy in Vienna in 1909. Weber added that, in his view, instead of praising the efficiency of bureaucracy one should rather ask 'what one could oppose to this machinery in order to preserve a remnant of humanity from this fragmentation of the soul.' (*Gesammelte Aufsätze zur Soziologie und Sozialpolitik*, Tübingen, Mohr, 1924, p. 414) See also Detlev J.K. Peukert, *Max Webers Diagnose der Moderne*, Göttingen, Vandenhoeck & Ruprecht, 1989.

37 See Björn Wittrock and Peter Wagner, 'Policy constitution through discourse', in Douglas E. Ashford (ed.), *History and Context in Public Policy*, Pittsburgh, University of Pittsburgh Press, 1992, pp. 227–46. Though apparently unaware of these roots, Tim Tilton writes of the political ideas of the then-leading Swedish social democrat Ernst Wigforss that his 'vision of an ideal democratic community embodies more than a set of formal relationships; it assumes a distinctive psychological atmosphere which is anticipated at present by the feeling of comradeship within a happy family or among a circle of close friends.' (*The Political Theory of Swedish Social Democracy. Through the Welfare State to Socialism*, Oxford, Clarendon, 1990, p. 57)

38 See now Agnes Heller, 'The concept of the political revisited', in David Held (ed.), *Political Theory Today*, Cambridge, Polity, 1991, pp. 333–4.

39 'What does it mean to be an "American"?', *Social Research*, vol. 57, no. 3, 1990, pp. 592–3.

40 Régine Robin, 'Le dépotoir des rêves', in Régine Robin (ed.), *Masses et culture de masse dans les années 30*, Paris, Editions ouvrières, 1991, pp. 31–2; Warren I. Susman, 'The thirties', in Stanley Cohen and Lorman Ratner (eds), *The Development of an American Culture*, New York, St. Martin's Press, 1983, pp. 221–8. On the emergence and 'crystallization' of the New Deal order see most recently Steve Fraser and Gary Gerstle (eds), *The Rise and Fall of the New Deal Order, 1930–1980*, Princeton,

Princeton University Press, 1989.

41 Reading the recent German 'historians' dispute' as an attempt at comparison of Nazism to other contemporary political regimes, some contributors tended to reject such a procedure on the grounds of Nazism's uncomparability. I think this is the wrong way of looking at the issue (apart from political intentions in the dispute). It is precisely by comparison (one result of which is to place its emergence in historical context) that Nazism's unequalled determination to extinction becomes visible. See, for example, Hans-Ulrich Wehler, *Entsorgung der deutschen Vergangenheit. Ein polemischer Essay zum 'Historikerstreit'*, Munich, Beck, 1988, pp. 167–71.

42 Alberto Asor Rosa, 'La cultura', in *Storia d'Italia*, vol. IV, 2, Turin, Einaudi, 1975, p. 1498.

43 See Roger Griffin, *The Nature of Fascism*, London, Pinter, 1991, who focuses his analysis of fascism on the idea of palingenesis.

44 Drawing on the now common image of the socialist societies as 'frozen' ones and their demise as a process of 'melting', Régine Robin, op. cit., p. 9, proposes viewing the 1930s as the '*temps forts*' of the freezing of societies. To describe the current problematic, the same metaphor has been used by Jean Baudrillard in the form of a question: 'What does liberty look like when it is unfrozen?' (*La transparence du mal*, Paris, Galilée, 1990, p. 100)

45 The notion of 'organized modernity' is obviously coined after 'organized capitalism', a term that the social democratic theorist Rudolf Hilferding used, first in 1915, to describe the national, oligopolistic formation of capitalism as a successor to the small-firm competitive market capitalism. It seems justifiable to borrow this term, not least because Hilferding was describing, for one set of social practices, the same social transformation that I try to analyse here in terms of an entire social formation. Furthermore, the reference to organization captures a number of overlapping features, such as the turn away from a liberal, individualistic reasoning to a collectivist one, the parallelism of the extension of reach and the limitation of width of practices, or the intention to extend the area of safe control in a generally uncertain environment.

46 Claus Offe has recently reminded us of Joseph A. Schumpeter's statement, see 'Fessel und Bremse. Moralische und institutionelle Aspekte "intelligenter Selbstbeschränkung" ', in Axel Honneth *et al.* (eds), *Zwischenbetrachtungen. Im Prozeß der Aufklärung*, Frankfurt/M., Suhrkamp, 1989, p. 752.

47 Zygmunt Bauman, *Modernity and the Holocaust*, Ithaca, Cornell University Press, 1989.

5 NETWORKS OF POWER AND BARRIERS TO ENTRY: THE ORGANIZATION OF ALLOCATIVE PRACTICES

1 Zygmunt Bauman, *Modernity and Ambivalence*, Cambridge, Polity Press, 1991, pp. 56–7.

2 Often, however, one must admit that the critics had not really been invited by the authors to find it. Many accounts are not very interested in problematizing the mode of historical construction itself and, furthermore, tend to hide the traces of their own construction, in line with the rules of the academic game.

3 There was, of course, a struggle between representations, for example, between anarchists and Marxists, or, in somewhat different terms, between crafts unions and industrial unions. See Luc Boltanski, *The Making of a Class. Cadres in French Society*, Cambridge, Cambridge University Press, 1987, pp. 30–3. And the outcome of these struggles varied between different countries.

4 Both conditions may still appear 'natural' and self-evident to some readers. The fact that they provided for a very specific configuration becomes clear as soon as one notices their absence in other parts of the world during the same period, and in the current

restructuring of our societies in the Northwestern sphere as well.

5 The Enlightenment ideas, though they obviously were social constructions, were seen as based on reasonings about human nature and natural reason. Social order would emerge naturally, if only the basic initial conditions were provided.

6 'Social constructivism', especially in science studies, has often been accused of neglecting the 'hard' character of social phenomena and of implicitly assuming that anything could be constructed at the will of whatever kind of alliances may form in society. The most interesting of these approaches, however, have carefully stressed the double character of all 'social facts', namely their being socially made and their structuring of further action, once they have been successfully constructed. See, for example, Bruno Latour, *Science in Action. How to Follow Scientists and Engineers Through Society*, Milton Keynes, Open University Press, 1987; and for social categories Alain Desrosières, 'How to make things which hold together: social science, statistics and the state', in Peter Wagner, Björn Wittrock, and Richard Whitley (eds), *Discourses on Society. The Shaping of the Social Science Disciplines*, Dordrecht, Kluwer, 1991, pp. 195–218.

7 The classical account is David S. Landes, *The Unbound Prometheus. Technological Change and Industrial Development in Western Europe from 1750 to the Present*, Cambridge, Cambridge University Press, 1969. For the US, see Thomas P. Hughes, *American Genesis. A Century of Invention and Technological Enthusiasm 1870–1970*, New York, Viking, 1989; and for Germany, Joachim Radkau, *Technik in Deutschland. Vom 18. Jahrhundert bis zur Gegenwart*, Frankfurt/M., Suhrkamp, 1989.

8 Michael Piore and Charles Sabel (*The Second Industrial Divide. Possibilities for Prosperity*, New York, Basic Books, 1984) argue this point forcefully, though a bit schematically. See further David F. Noble, *America by Design. Science, Technology, and the Rise of Corporate Capitalism*, New York, Knopf, 1977.

9 Wiebe Bijker, Thomas P. Hughes, and Trevor Pinch (eds), *The Social Construction of Technological Systems. New Directions in the Sociology and History of Technology*, Cambridge, Mass., MIT Press, 1987, has become a minor classic in this field. See more recently Meinolf Dierkes and Ute Hoffmann (eds), *New Technology at the Outset. Social Forces in the Shaping of Technological Innovation*, Frankfurt/M. and Boulder, Col., Campus and Westview, 1992.

10 See Andreas Knie, *Diesel – Genese einer Technik*, Berlin, Edition Sigma, 1990.

11 And in this sense, without assuming a single line of technical progress, one may well speak of 'technological trajectories' to describe a limited variability of change over time, once certain 'decisions' have been taken. See Giovanni Dosi, 'Technological paradigms and technological trajectories: a suggested interpretation of the determinants of technological change', *Research Policy*, vol. 11, 1982, pp. 147–62.

12 The major exceptions are television, though preceded by radio, and nuclear energy. A few years ago, the late economist Kenneth Boulding, born 1910, remarked that he had not witnessed much technical change during his life-time. As surprising as such a statement may sound in an era that is obsessed by the idea that it is driven by technological advance, it rings basically true – though Boulding had to admit that recent computer technology made for a notable change. See also Radkau, op. cit., pp. 222–39.

13 Pierre Dockès and Bernard Rosier, *L'histoire ambiguë. Croissance et développement en question*, Paris, PUF, 1988, p. 191; Robin Cowan, 'Nuclear power reactors: a study in technological lock-in', *Journal of Economic History*, vol. 50, no. 3, 1990, pp. 541–67. See also Robert Boyer, *Technical Change and the Theory of 'Regulation'*, Paris, CEPREMAP papers no. 8707, 1987.

14 One may also compare face-to-face and phone conversation. The loss of the sight of the other and his or her gestures, or the restriction of conversation to two persons, entails reductions as compared to face-to-face interaction. No loss, obviously, is unequivocal.

Human beings will use the possibilities at hand creatively and will establish specific forms of phone communication that are impossible without this technical support. Such reactions to (or actions on) technology may even become considered an art form, as has been acknowledged for letter-writing. Interestingly, phone conversation has not reached this rank. The reason for this may be that letter-writing fell historically in the era of (aristocratic-bourgeois) high culture and 'autonomization' of art, whereas the diffusion of the phone went along with the emergence of so-called mass culture. (From movies one could extract an art of phone conversation.)

15 A strong conception of these instruments of modernity would, of course, always remain illusory. Their application would face, at some point, the 'return of the repressed', the reemergence of characteristics of social and natural phenomena that had been suppressed in the process of reduction for handling purposes. In the realm of policy-making, this feature has been termed '*effets pervers*' (Raymond Boudon) or 'unintended consequences'. The demise of organized modernity should be discussed precisely in those terms (see Part IV below). However, in contrast to some fashionable assertions, the observation of such reactions should not lead to the fallacious view that the working of modern institutions did not have any effect on social (and natural) reality. It has had considerable transformative power on the world, and the present discussion over the limits and perversities of modernity should be seen in the context of its historical power rather than its powerlessness.

16 Joachim Radkau, *Zum ewigen Wachstum verdammt? Historisches über Jugend und Alter großer technischer Systeme*, Berlin, WZB, 1992 (WZB Papers FS II 92–505), pp. 13–14.

17 Certain features made some of these technologies almost compulsory: once a society was restructured with a view to the availability of a technology, a right to technology emerged with the 'socialization' of infrastructural demands, such as the obligation of the utilities to connect everybody with the electricity network. A stronger version of this came with the full employment regimes after the Second World War when the idea of 'equal living conditions' entailed, for instance, that everybody should have access to car-usable, or even high-velocity, roads. At that time, the concept of comprehensive coverage of a social space by a technology was clearly dominant.

18 For recent discussions of Taylorism, see Frank Fischer, *Technocracy and the Politics of Expertise*, Newbury Park, Sage, 1990, pp. 124–8 and 301–7; and Nikolas Rose, *Governing the Soul. The Shaping of the Private Self*, London, Routledge, 1989, pp. 55–60.

19 Alfred D. Chandler, Jr., *Scale and Scope. The Dynamics of Industrial Capitalism*, Cambridge, Mass., Belknap of Harvard University Press, 1990, p. 1.

20 See also on the US Alfred D. Chandler, Jr. and Richard S. Tedlow, *The Coming of Managerial Capitalism. A Casebook on the History of American Economic Institutions*, Homewood, Ill., Irwin, 1985; on Germany Hartmut Kaelble, 'The rise of the managerial enterprise in Germany, c. 1870 to c. 1930', in Kesaji Kobayashi and Hidemasa Morikawa (eds), *Development of Managerial Enterprise*, Tokyo, University of Tokyo Press, 1986, pp. 71–97.

21 Chandler, *Scale*, pp. 51–70.

22 Dockès and Rosier, op. cit., for example, pp. 172 and 318; Kaelble, op. cit., p. 90.

23 Franz Lehner, 'The vanishing of spontaneity: socio-economic conditions of the welfare state', *European Journal of Political Research*, vol. 11, 1983, pp. 439–40, referring to Joseph A. Schumpeter, *Capitalism, Socialism and Democracy*, Kenneth J. Galbraith, *New Industrial State* and J.Q. Wilson, *Political Organizations*.

24 Claus Offe and Helmut Wiesenthal, 'Two logics of collective action', *Political Power and Social Theory*, vol. 1, 1980, pp. 67–115, who also deal with the problem, which I shall discuss with regard to political parties (see Chapter 6), to maintain both unity and

representation in such organizations.

25 The relation of hierarchical to market organization has been at the centre of institutional economics as proposed by Oliver Williamson and others. See for a recent overview Williamson, 'The firm as a nexus of treaties: an introduction', in Masahiko Aoki, Bo Gustafsson, and Oliver E. Williamson (eds), *The Firm as a Nexus of Treaties*, London, Sage, 1990, pp. 1–25.

26 Chandler, op. cit., p. 8. A comparative assessment, with many qualifications, of Chandler's thesis is provided by Kobayashi and Morikawa, op. cit.

27 Dockès and Rosier, op. cit., p. 182.

28 A short, perceptive treatment of List's approach is Keith Tribe's, 'Friedrich List and the critique of "cosmopolitical economy" ', *The Manchester School*, vol. 56, no. 1, 1988, pp. 17–36. Significantly, the German economics profession never fully accepted the terminological shift from 'political economy' to 'economics', suggested by Alfred Marshall, and kept referring to itself as 'national economics' or 'people's economics' (as strange as this may sound in the English language).

29 Aristide R. Zolberg, 'Bounded states in a global market: the uses of international labor migrations', in Pierre Bourdieu and James S. Coleman (eds), *Social Theory for a Changing Society*, Boulder, Col., and New York, Westview and Russell Sage, 1991, p. 312. On the more moderate 'nationalization of France', see Gérard Noiriel, *La tyrannie du national. Le droit d'asile en Europe 1793–1993*, Paris, Calmann-Lévy, 1991.

30 Angus Maddison, *Dynamic Forces in Capitalist Development. A Long-run Comparative View*, Oxford, Oxford University Press, 1991, pp. 74–6. In the inter-war period, the building of a coherent national economy was not at all a 'success story', rather an outright failure in many cases. The decline of exports could not (yet) be matched by domestic mass demand; high instability was the result. See for such a perspective Burkart Lutz, 'Die Singularität der europäischen Prosperität nach dem Zweiten Weltkrieg', in Hartmut Kaelble (ed.), *Der Boom 1948–1973*, Opladen, Westdeutscher Verlag, 1992, p. 43.

31 An extremely perceptive account of the French developments is François Fourquet, *Les comptes de la puissance*, Paris, Encres, 1980. See recently Peter Miller and Nikolas Rose, 'Governing economic life', *Economy and Society*, vol. 19, no. 1, 1990, pp. 1–31. Grahame Thompson, 'The evolution of the managed economy in Europe', *Economy and Society*, vol. 21, no. 2, 1992, pp. 129–51, gives a just reminder of the varieties of national macro-economic management in Europe.

32 This is, so to speak, the latest version of the concept. More generally known, and much more widely accepted, is the version that granted this right to one in a family, the man, at a family income. I cannot treat the variations of this concept in comparative detail here.

33 Maybe the last critical account of the emergence of the work society before its full establishment was given by Hannah Arendt in *The Human Condition*, Chicago, The University of Chicago Press, 1958, in terms of political philosophy.

34 See, for instance, Dockès and Rosier, op. cit., p. 183.

35 Robert Salais, Nicolas Baverez, and Bénédicte Reynaud, *L'invention du chômage. Histoire et transformations d'une catégorie en France des années 1890 aux années 1980*, Paris, PUF, 1986. As can be easily seen, my reflections on allocative practices are broadly committed to the historical and institutional approaches around the economics of conventions and the regulation school, both of French origins, but now being widened into a broader international discussion. For the former see *L'économie des conventions*, special issue of *Revue économique*, vol. 40, no. 2, 1989; for the latter, Robert Boyer, *The Regulation School. A Critical Introduction*, New York, Columbia University Press, 1990. For a comparative discussion of more institutionalist and more systemic reason-

ings in this field, see Paul Hirst and Jonathan Zeitlin, 'Flexible specialization versus post-Fordism: theory, evidence and policy implications', *Economy and Society*, vol. 20, no. 1, 1991, pp. 1–56.

36 Roy Bhaskar, *Reclaiming Reality. A Critical Introduction to Contemporary Philosophy*, London, Verso, 1989, p. 174. See also Desrosières, op. cit., p. 214.

37 Jürgen Kocka, 'Class formation, interest articulation and public policy: the origins of the German white-collar class in the late nineteenth and early twentieth centuries', in Suzanne Berger (ed.), *Organizing Interests in Western Europe. Pluralism, Corporatism, and the Transformation of Politics*, Cambridge, Cambridge University Press, 1981, pp. 63–81; and in German-American comparison, Jürgen Kocka, *White Collar Workers in America 1890–1940. A Social-Political History in International Perspective*, London, Sage, 1980.

38 See, for example, Jeffrey Herf, *Reactionary Modernism. Technology, Culture and Politics in Weimar and the Third Reich*, Cambridge, Cambridge University Press, 1984.

39 Luc Boltanski, *Making of a Class*. For the UK see Simon Szreter, 'The genesis of the Registrar General's classification of occupations', *British Journal of Sociology*, vol. 35, no. 4, 1984, pp. 522–46. For professionals in the US see Eliott Freidson, *Professional Powers. A Study of the Institutionalization of Formal Knowledge*, Chicago, The University of Chicago Press, 1988.

40 Gerald D. Feldman, 'German interest group alliances in war and inflation, 1914–1923', in Berger, *Organizing Interests*, p. 167.

41 See, for example, for Germany, Ditmar Brock, *Der schwierige Weg in die Moderne*, Frankfurt/M., Campus, 1991, pp. 115–17.

42 Michel Aglietta, *A Theory of Capitalist Regulation. The US Experience*, London, New Left Books, 1979 (1976), p. 152. Aglietta, whose work initiated the so-called 'regulation school', has also pioneered the use of the term 'Fordism' for this historical mode of capitalist regulation, a term that, I think, gives far too much honour to the man. I prefer to speak of organized capitalism for the general allocative arrangement, and of mass-consumption capitalism for this specific aspect.

43 In economic and social analysis, the *actual* commodification of social relations has long been overestimated and the extent of remaining non-commodified production and services undervalued. On the other hand, the extent of *possible* commodification of social relations seems to have often been underestimated. Both misconceptions are related to the question as to the boundary of the 'economic sphere' in society, which involves the issue of domestic labour, among others.

44 'Insurance and risk', in Graham Burchell, Colin Gordon, and Peter Miller (eds), *The Foucault Effect. Studies in Governmentality*, Chicago, The University of Chicago Press, 1991, p. 208.

45 For a recent discussion of consumer society and culture, including a literature survey, see Mike Featherstone, *Consumer Culture and Postmodernism*, London, Sage, 1991.

46 The spatiality of human life has in recent years found increasing interest in sociological analysis, probably starting with the works of the human geographer Torsten Hägerstrand. See Allan Pred, *Making Histories and Constructing Human Geographies. The Local Transformation of Practice, Power Relations, and Consciousness*, Boulder, Col., Westview, 1990.

47 Joshua Meyrowitz, *No Sense of Place. The Impact of Electronic Media on Social Behaviour*, New York, Oxford University Press, 1985.

48 Robert Salais and Laurent Thévnot (eds), *Le travail. Marchés, règles, conventions*, Paris, Economica, 1986; on the history of this wage convention see now Robert Boyer and André Orléan, 'Les transformations des conventions salariales entre théorie et histoire: d'Henry Ford au fordisme', *Revue économique*, vol. 42, no. 2, 1991, pp. 233–72. See also Stephen Marglin, 'Lessons of the golden age: an overview', in Stephen A. Marglin and Juliet B. Schor (eds), *The Golden Age of Capitalism.*

Reinterpreting the Postwar Experience, Oxford, Clarendon, 1990, p. 28.

49 Andrew Glyn, Alan Hughes, Alan Lipietz, and Ajit Singh, 'The rise and fall of the golden age', in Marglin and Schor, op. cit., p. 58.

50 Glyn *et al.*, op. cit., pp. 49–50.

51 Maddison, op. cit., p. 121 and passim; Marglin and Schor, op. cit.

52 United Nations, *Economic Survey of Europe in 1971, Part 1. The European Economy from the 1950s to the 1970s*, New York, United Nations, 1972, quoted after Glyn *et al.*, 'The rise and fall of the golden age', op. cit., p. 39.

53 See, for instance, Burkart Lutz, *Der kurze Traum immerwährender Prosperität*, Frankfurt/M., Campus, 1984.

6 BUILDING IRON CAGES: THE ORGANIZATION OF AUTHORITATIVE PRACTICES

1 T.H. Marshall's distinction of civil, political and social citizenship is useful, though it should not be considered as a universal evolutionary sequence, as has often been pointed out ('Citizenship and social class', in *Class, Citizenship, and Social Development*, Garden City, N.Y., Doubleday, 1964, pp. 71–2).

2 For a discussion in terms of political theory, see Michael Walzer, 'Membership', in *Spheres of Justice. A Defense of Pluralism and Equality*, New York, Basic Books, 1983, pp. 31–63.

3 Stein Rokkan gives a reminder of Tocqueville's statement in 'Mass suffrage, secret voting and political participation', *Archives européennes de sociologie*, vol. 11, 1961, p. 137.

4 Most revisions of suffrage coverage after that referred to the minimum age of voters. The importance of this question should not be downplayed, since the idea of the representation of the young may well change with changing life-styles.

5 On the relation of political and social citizenship, see Joseph H. Carens, 'Immigration and the welfare state', and Robert K. Fullinwider, 'Citizenship and welfare', both in Amy Gutmann (ed.), *Democracy and the Welfare State*, Princeton, Princeton University Press, 1988, pp. 207–30 and 261–78 respectively.

6 The interpretive, conventionlike character of this move needs to be stressed since very different ways of determining the nationality of an individual human being can be devised by emphasizing genealogy, birth-place, marital ties or residence to various degrees and giving greater or smaller choice to the individual as to which political community she would want to belong to.

7 Gérard Noiriel, *La tyrannie du national. Le droit d'asile en Europe 1793–1993*, Paris, Calmann-Lévy, 1991, pp. 83–100.

8 For an early discussion of this problematic, see Hannah Arendt, *The Origins of Totalitarianism*, Cleveland, World Publishing Company, 2nd edn 1958, Chapter 9. More recently, see Zygmunt Bauman, *Modernity and the Holocaust*, Ithaca, Cornell University Press, 1989, Chapter 2.

9 The former argument is made by Walzer, op. cit.; the latter observations stem from Noiriel's work, op. cit., p. 92.

10 Nancy L. Schwartz, *The Blue Guitar. Political Representation and Community*, Chicago, The University of Chicago Press, 1988, p. 6.

11 Hannah F. Pitkin, *The Concept of Representation*, Berkeley, University of California Press, 1967, p. 9.

12 See also Russell J. Dalton, 'Political parties and political representation: party supporters and party elites in nine nations', *Comparative Political Studies*, vol. 18, no. 3, 1985, pp. 267–99; Theodor J. Lowi, *The End of Liberalism. Ideology, Policy, and the Crisis of Public Authority*, New York, Norton, 1969, pp. 93–7; Dietrich Herzog,

'Was heißt und zu welchem Ende studiert man Repräsentation?', in Dietrich Herzog and Bernhard Weßels (eds), *Konfliktpotentiale und Konsensstrategien*, Opladen, Westdeutscher Verlag, 1989, pp. 309–11. Lack of space prohibits me from tracing here the problematic back to the age of the democratic revolutions, to the height of the revolutionary activities in France or the US. During these periods the very intensity of political activity and the relative openness of the public space of political communication could lead one to think that, while some representation was necessary, a sufficiently close linkage between representative and represented could be maintained. I shall directly move to the late nineteenth century, when the political space was much more structured and organized and when parties of notables, clientelist parties and mass parties were facing each other in electoral contests.

13 Umberto Eco, 'On the crisis of the crisis of reason', *Travels in Hyperreality*, Orlando, Fla., Harcourt, Brace, Jovanovich, 1990, pp. 126–7.

14 It shall only briefly be noted that the, let us call it, late-Aristotelian conception of the household and the polis, which implicitly ruled restricted liberal modernity, does provide a fairly consistent social theory of political representation. It includes notions of responsiveness and responsibility of the head of the household both to the members of the *oikos* and to the polis. Obviously, though, by excluding women, the propertyless and slaves, it did not abide by universalist ideas of either equality or autonomy, and, thus, proved unacceptable very soon.

15 'The birth of socialist parties gives to the proletariat its first stable representation' (François d'Arcy and Guy Saez, 'De la représentation', in François d'Arcy (ed.), *La représentation*, Paris, Economica, 1985, p. 18).

16 Norman Stone, *Europe Transformed 1878–1919*, Glasgow, Fontana, 1983, pp. 42–73.

17 'The communitarian exaltation nourishes itself equally from the affirmation of the national and the racial collective.' (D'Arcy and Saez, op. cit.)

18 Ibid., p. 9.

19 Russell J. Dalton, 'Responsiveness of parties and party systems to the new politics', in Hans-Dieter Klingemann, Richard Stöss, and Bernhard Weßels (eds), *Politische Klasse und politische Institutionen*, Opladen, Westdeutscher Verlag, 1991, p. 41; the classic study is Seymour Lipset and Stein Rokkan (eds), *Party Systems and Voter Alignments*, New York, Free Press, 1967.

20 In this regard, it is still instructive to read Erich Fromm's *Escape from Freedom*, New York, Holt, Rinehart & Winston, 1941.

21 Sydel Silverman, 'Patronage and community-nation relationships in central Italy', in Steffen W. Schmidt *et al.* (eds), *Friends, Followers and Factions*, Berkeley, University of California Press, 1977, pp. 293–304; Luigi Graziani, *Clientelismo e sistema politico. Il caso dell'Italia*, Milan, Angeli, 1984.

22 See, for example, Sören Holmberg, 'Political representation in Sweden', in Klingemann *et al.*, op. cit., p. 290, with further references to the debate. One may also refer to the beautiful, if slightly sarcastic, description by Eric Voegelin, *The New Science of Politics. An Introduction*, Chicago, The University of Chicago Press, 1952, pp. 27–52.

23 'The term "closure"... indicates at first the achievement of a programme *and* the constraints of a programmation,' as Philippe Lacoue-Labarthe and Jean-Luc Nancy term this double nature ('Le "retrait" du politique', in *Le retrait du politique*, Paris, Galilée, 1983, p. 187).

24 See, for example, Angelo Panebianco, *Political Parties. Organization and Power*, Cambridge, Cambridge University Press, 1988 [1982]; and Alan Ware, *Citizens, Parties and the State. A Reappraisal*, Princeton, Princeton University Press, 1988, for analyses that try to link up to the early sociology of parties and elites.

25 Hans-Dieter Klingemann, Richard Stöss, and Bernhard Weßels, 'Politische Klasse und politische Institutionen', in Klingemann *et al.*, op. cit., pp. 33–4.

26 Arend Lijphart, *The Politics of Accommodation. Pluralism and Democracy in the*

Netherlands, Berkeley, University of California Press, 1975.

27 Orion White, Jr., and Gideon Sjoberg, 'The emerging "New Politics" in America', in M. Donald Hancock and Gideon Sjoberg (eds), *Politics in the Post-Welfare State. Responses to the New Individualism*, New York, Columbia University Press, 1972, pp. 25–6.

28 So that Arend Lijphart, *Democracy in Plural Societies. A Comparative Exploration*, New Haven, Yale University Press, 1977, p. 2, could write about the decline of consociational democracy from the 1960s in that 'consociationalism by its very success has begun to make itself superfluous.'

29 Panebianco, op. cit., p. 264.

30 Pierre Muller and Guy Saez, 'Neo-corporatisme et crise de la représentation', in d'Arcy, op. cit., pp. 121–40. Philippe C. Schmitter (ed.), *Corporatism and Policy-Making in Contemporary Western Europe*, special issue of *Comparative Political Studies*, vol. 10, no. 1, 1977.

31 Lijphart, op. cit., p. 1.

32 Stefano Bartolini and Peter Mair, *Identity, Competition and Electoral Availability. The Stabilisation of European Electorates 1885–1985*, Cambridge, Cambridge University Press, 1990, p. 2 (my emphasis).

33 Ibid., p. 287.

34 Seymour M. Lipset and Stein Rokkan, 'Cleavage structures, party systems, and voter alignments: an introduction', in Lipset and Rokkan, op. cit., p. 50.

35 Bartolini and Mair, op. cit., p. 291.

36 Donald E. Stokes, 'Political parties in the normative theory of representation', in J. Roland Pennock and John W. Chapman (eds), *Representation*, New York, Atherton Press, 1968, p. 152. (Watch the proto-Lyotardian form of argument, in which 'success' validates 'theory'.)

37 Johan Per Olsen has used the term 'organized democracy' in a slightly different way, emphasizing organizational structures of policy-making, in his analysis of Norwegian politics. His starting-point is the question whether unorganized participation during the 1970s, namely through citizen initiatives, should be regarded as a sign of a legitimation crisis of organized democracy. See his *Organized Democracy. Political Institutions in a Welfare State – the Case of Norway*, Bergen, Universitetsforlaget, 1983, esp. pp. 13–38. In their reassessment of the claim that there is a linkage between capitalism and democracy, Dietrich Rueschemeyer, Evelyne Huber Stephens and John D. Stephens observe 'the dilemma that stabilization of formal democracy appears to require serious restrictions on substantive democracy because of the need for protection of elite interests' (*Capitalist Development and Democracy*, Cambridge, Polity, 1992, p. 269).

38 Schwartz, op. cit., p. 57.

39 On the Whiggish elements in this consensus see Asa Briggs, 'The welfare state in historical perspective', *Archives européennes de sociologie*, vol. 2, 1961, p. 222.

40 For data on Europe see Peter Flora *et al.*, *State, Economy, and Society in Western Europe 1815–1975. A Data Handbook, Vol. 1. The Growth of Mass Democracies and Welfare States*, Frankfurt/M., Campus, 1983, pp. 453–551; for the special case of the US now, Margaret Weir, Ann Shola Orloff, and Theda Skocpol (eds), *The Politics of Social Policy in the United States*, Princeton, Princeton University Press, 1988.

41 Abram de Swaan, *In Care of The State*, Cambridge, Polity, 1988, p. 223.

42 Thomas R. Cusack, *The Changing Contours of Government*, Berlin, WZB, 1991 (WZB Paper P 91–304), p. 35; Flora *et al.*, op. cit., pp. 264–5.

43 Government expenditure as a percentage of the net domestic product ranges now from an average of 45 per cent among OECD countries to far exceeding 50 per cent in countries like Sweden, see Cusack, op. cit., p. 35; Flora *et al.*, op. cit., pp. 262–3.

44 An impressively comprehensive treatment of social policy as 'social idea and social movement' in the context of liberalism and capitalism, first published in 1929, is the book by Eduard Heimann, a social democratic theorist, *Soziale Theorie des Kapitalismus. Theorie der Sozialpolitik*, Frankfurt/M., Suhrkamp, 1980.

45 Again, the double nature of social policy can often be observed in the practices, and probably the personalities, of the welfare workers, being gentle help and norm-guided observation at the same time.

46 De Swaan, op. cit., pp. 244–52.

47 François Ewald, 'Insurance and risk', in Graham Burchell, Colin Gordon, and Peter Miller (eds), *The Foucault Effect. Studies in Governmentality*, Chicago, The University of Chicago Press, 1991, pp. 197–210.

48 For contributions to such a debate in German social historiography see Alf Lüdtke, '"Kolonisierung der Lebenswelten" – oder: Geschichte als Einbahnstraße?', *Das Argument*, no. 140, 1986, pp. 536–41; Detlev J.K. Peukert, 'Die Unordnung der Dinge. Michel Foucault und die deutsche Geschichtswissenschaft', in François Ewald and Bernhard Waldenfels (eds), *Michel Foucaults Denken. Spiele der Wahrheit*, Frankfurt/M., Suhrkamp, 1991, pp. 320–33.

49 For a detailed study of the professionalization and public invasion of a practice that was hitherto private see Stephan Leibfried, 'Nutritional minima: on the institutionalization of professional knowledge in national social policy in the US and Germany', in Dietrich Rueschemeyer and Theda Skocpol (eds), *Social Knowledge and the Origins of Social Policies*, Princeton and New York, Princeton University Press and Russell Sage Foundation (forthcoming). This interpretation is not at all meant to deny that the promoters of such technologies were often inspired by a humanist desire for social betterment. The development and application of expert knowledge of the human body and related transformations of the bodily constituted self is in the focus of Jonathan Crary and Sanford Kwinter (eds), *Incorporations*, New York, Zone, 1992.

50 Ewald, op. cit., p. 197. This article draws on Ewald's major work on the construction of the welfare state: *L'Etat providence*, Paris, Grasset, 1986. The French notion of 'providential state' conveys the idea of the secularization of life-destinies (or, the re-deification of the liberal state). William Beveridge, the alleged architect of the British version of the welfare state, disliked the term, because of its 'Santa Claus' and 'brave new world' connotations, and preferred the more sober 'social services state'; see Peter Flora and Arnold J. Heidenheimer, 'The historical core and changing boundaries of the welfare state', in Peter Flora and Arnold J. Heidenheimer (eds), *The Development of Welfare States in Europe and America*, New Brunswick, N.J., Transaction, 1981, p. 20.

51 Ewald, 'Insurance', p. 207.

52 Peter Miller and Nikolas Rose, 'Governing economic life', *Economy and Society*, vol. 19, no. 1, 1990, pp. 3 and 5.

53 By the term 'socialism', I refer to the social practices under the regime of communist or socialist parties that existed in Eastern and, later, Central Europe until 1989–91. It has rightly been argued that a distinction should be made between these actually existing societies and the set of ideas more broadly known under the same name. The solution that I used to prefer, though, 'actually existing socialism', has become very clumsy since these regimes have ceased to exist. So, the shorthand use of 'socialism' may be accepted. As regards my understanding of socialism, I have benefited from extended discussions with Jacek Kochanowicz (mainly about Poland) and Lutz Marz (mainly about the German Democratic Republic).

54 Discussions of the following argument have made me aware of what deeply-felt negative responses this claim may receive. East European scholars in particular have expressed their strong opinion that the movements *against* socialism in the late 1980s were movements *for* the values of modernity and, especially, for the revival of a civil

society that was suppressed during socialism. This experience leads me to state explicitly – though I hope it has become evident by now – that the analytical approach does not imply any normative endorsement. The link to normativity is elsewhere: if we fail to recognize the key characteristics of socialism and of modernity in general, the efforts to build (or rebuild) a more liberal and more humane society in the East (and maybe in the West) will miss their objectives.

55 Here I find myself in agreement with John Gray, 'Totalitarianism, reform, and civil society', in Ellen Frankel Paul (ed.), *Totalitarianism at the Crossroads*, New Brunswick, N.J., Transaction, 1990, pp. 99 and 137, though I disagree on other points (see my remarks on civil society in Chapter 11). Vladimir Iljitch Lenin's *Drei Quellen und drei Bestandteile des Marxismus* (Berlin, Dietz, 1966, pp. 3–10) makes these traditions evident. This is a text that remained in use for the representation of Soviet socialism.

56 On the necessity of boundaries for socialism, see Paul Hollander, 'Border controls: an integral part of the Soviet social-political system', *The Many Faces of Socialism*, New Brunswick, N.J., Transaction, 1983, pp. 79–103.

57 This view resembles the one Zygmunt Bauman takes in *Modernity and Ambivalence*, Cambridge, Polity, 1991, though he tends to generalize for modernity phenomena that I would see as characteristic of a one-sided expression of modernity, namely its organized form. The split in the socialist movement after the Russian Revolution can then be read as a dispute over the degree of organization and over the legitimacy of countervailing principles. Western social democracy and Western Marxism are attempts to rework socialism as idea and practice (the term here being used in the broader sense) by taking the ambivalence of modernity much more openly into account than Soviet socialism and Marxism-Leninism ever did. Related attempts to draw conclusions from twentieth-century experiences with the organization of social practices were mostly short-lived and soon suppressed in Soviet socialism. See also Alain Touraine, *Critique de la Modernité*, Paris, Fayard, 1992, pp. 359–60, for a related interpretation.

58 True, Russian nationalism constituted a relevant aspect of stability in the Soviet Union. As can be seen now at the moment of breakdown at the latest, however, the idea of nation as a practically effective 'imagined community' held statewise only in the core territory, and had, thus, rather imperialist features in the overall Union. An analysis beyond this brief excursus would have to include prominently, of course, a comparative social history of these societies, not least in terms of social structures and of histories of industrialization.

59 See the remarks by modernization theorist Alex Inkeles (*Exploring Individual Modernity*, New York, Columbia University Press, 1983, pp. 299–300) on the 'modern' requirement of the individual to cut ties with 'primordial associations' and the 'continuing preoccupation of the Soviet regime' to accomplish exactly this. Many East Germans, particularly women, were surprised to learn that West German law (under whose application they now fall, too) limits the autonomy of the individual in matters such as marriage, inheritance and abortion much more than East German law did. If modernity were mainly about individuality, as some thought, the (German) West clearly was less modern than the East in these matters.

60 Claude Lefort, 'Reversibility: political freedom and the freedom of the individual', in *Democracy and Political Theory*, Cambridge, Polity, 1988, p. 175. See more generally on totalitarianism, Lefort, *The Political Forms of Modern Society*, Cambridge, Polity, 1986.

7 DISCOURSES ON SOCIETY: REORGANIZING THE MODE OF COGNITIVE REPRESENTATION

1 The 1980s have witnessed a surge of scholarly interest in the history of statistics. My brief presentation is based mainly on the following recent works, in which more references can be found: Alain Desrosières, 'How to make things which hold together: social science, statistics and the state', in Peter Wagner *et al.* (eds), *Discourses on Society. The Shaping of the Social Science Disciplines*, Dordrecht, Kluwer, 1991, pp. 195–218; Ian Hacking, *The Taming of Chance*, Cambridge, Cambridge University Press, 1990; Theodore M. Porter, *The Rise of Statistical Thinking, 1820–1900*, Princeton, Princeton University Press, 1986; Stephen M. Stigler, *The History of Statistics. The Measurement of Uncertainty Before 1900*, Cambridge, Mass., Belknap of Harvard University Press, 1986; Donald MacKenzie, *Statistics in Britain, 1865–1930. The Social Construction of Scientific Knowledge*, Edinburgh, Edinburgh University Press, 1981; Lorenz Krüger, Lorraine Daston, and Michael Heidelberger (eds), *The Probabilistic Revolution, Vol. 1. Ideas in History*; and Krüger, Gerd Gigerenzer, and Mary S. Morgan (eds), *The Probabilistic Revolution, Vol. 2. Ideas in the Sciences*, both Cambridge, Mass., MIT Press, 1987. See also the attempt to relate social science approaches, including statistics, to political theory: Dag Österberg, *Meta-Sociology. An Inquiry into the Origins and Validity of Social Thought*, Oslo, Norwegian University Press, 1988.

2 Porter, op. cit., p. 56; see also Stigler, op. cit., pp. 169–74.

3 As now amply documented in Martin Bulmer, Kevin Bales, and Kathryn Kish Sklar (eds), *The Social Survey in Historical Perspective 1880–1940*, Cambridge, Cambridge University Press, 1991.

4 Alain Desrosières, 'The part in relation to the whole: how to generalise? The prehistory of representative sampling', in Bulmer *et al.*, op. cit., p. 228. This essay and Desrosières, 'Social science', give the best account of the issue.

5 Jacques Donzelot, 'The mobilization of society', in Graham Burchell, Colin Gordon, and Peter Miller (eds), *The Foucault Effect. Studies in Governmentality*, Chicago, The University of Chicago Press, 1991, p. 171.

6 As quoted by Peter Flora and Arnold J. Heidenheimer, 'The historical core and changing boundaries of the welfare state', in Flora and Heidenheimer (eds), *The Development of Welfare States in Europe and America*, New Brunswick, N.J., Transaction, 1981, p. 19.

7 Against the literal meaning, I use the term 'empirical social research' here to denote only the quantitative and methodologically individualist approach that has grown out of survey and opinion research and that can be considered, with some qualifications, as a major element of mainstream social science of the 1950s and 1960s. In more general terms, there has been a great variety of approaches to empirical research on social phenomena, including highly different methodologies and epistemologies. For an attempt to write the history of social research as an essentially bifurcated one between the former understanding and a largely undeveloped alternative to it, see Wolfgang Bonß, *Die Einübung des Tatsachenblicks*, Frankfurt/M., Suhrkamp, 1982.

8 Österberg, op. cit., p. 44.

9 Desrosières, 'The part in relation to the whole', p. 241.

10 Maintaining such a 'critical' stand-point would preclude an understanding of the developments during the second crisis of modernity, as I shall try to show later (see Chapter 9).

11 The following two sections draw partly on my *Sozialwissenschaften und Staat. Frankreich, Italien, Deutschland 1870–1980*, Frankfurt/M., Campus, 1990; and 'Science of society lost: the failure to establish sociology in Europe during its "classical" period', in Wagner *et al.*, *Discourses*, pp. 219–45, which may be consulted for a more differentiated view than can be given here.

12 Leopold von Wiese, 'Die Soziologie als Einzelwissenschaft', *Jahrbuch für Gesetzgebung, Verwaltung und volkswirtschaft*, vol. 44, 1920, p. 44.
13 See also Pietro Rossi, 'La sociologia nella seconda metà del'ottocento: dall'impiego di schemi storico-evolutivi alla formulazione di modelli analitici', *Il pensiero politico*, vol. 15, no. 1, 1982, p. 199.
14 On the latter, see Edward Shils, 'Tradition, ecology, and institution in the history of sociology', *Daedalus*, no. 99, 1970, pp. 760–825.
15 See Michael Pollak, 'Paul F. Lazarsfeld – fondateur d'une multinationale scientifique', *Actes de la recherche en sciences sociales*, no. 25, 1979, pp. 45–59, for a socio-intellectual biography of Lazarsfeld which points to the relation between Lazarsfeld's intellectual course and the transformation of the political views of Austrian (as well as German) social democracy.
16 Paul F. Lazarsfeld, 'Remarks on administrative and critical communications research', *Studies in Philosophy and Social Science*, vol. 9, 1941, p. 14.
17 This argument has forcefully been made by Hans Joas, 'An underestimated alternative: America and the limits of "Critical Theory",' *Pragmatism and Social Theory*, Chicago, University of Chicago Press, 1993, pp. 79–93; on the political inclinations of the Chicago School, see also Dennis Smith, *The Chicago School. A Liberal Critique of Capitalism*, London, Macmillan, 1988; further Martin Bulmer, *The Chicago School of Sociology. Institutionalization, Diversity and the Rise of Sociological Research*, Chicago, The University of Chicago Press, 1984; and on Dewey now, Robert B. Westbrook, *John Dewey and American Democracy*, Ithaca, Cornell University Press, 1991.
18 Hans Joas, 'Symbolic interactionism', in Anthony Giddens and Jonathan H. Turner (eds), *Social Theory Today*, Cambridge, Polity, 1987, pp. 82–116 (now reprinted as 'Pragmatism in American Sociology', in Joas, *Pragmatism*, pp. 14–51). This view is shared by, for example, Peter Manicas, *A History and Philosophy of the Social Sciences*, Oxford, Blackwell, 1987, pp. 214 and 275. (My primary knowledge of pragmatist writings is limited and I rely on the accounts given by, as far as I can see, the most knowledgeable authors in this field, not least those by Hans Joas.)
19 James S. Coleman, 'The structure of society and the nature of social research', *Knowledge*, vol. 1, 1980, p. 340.
20 See also Joas, 'Interactionism', pp. 109 and 111.
21 Shils, op. cit., pp. 74–5; more recently Norbert Wiley, 'The current interregnum in American sociology', *Social Research*, vol. 52, no. 1, 1985, pp. 179–207.
22 Johan Heilbron, *Sociologie in Frankrijk*, Amsterdam, SISWO, 1983.
23 See Richard Whitley, 'The structure and context of economics as a scientific field', *Research in the History of Economic Thought and Methodology*, vol. 4, 1986.
24 James S. Coleman, 'Social theory, social research and a theory of action', *American Journal of Sociology*, vol. 91, 1986, pp. 1313–15.
25 See the collection *Discourses on Society*.
26 A brilliant portrait of this process, as well as a proposal to reverse it, is offered by Hans Joas, *Die Kreativität des Handelns*, Frankfurt/M., Suhrkamp, 1992.
27 Coleman, 'Social theory', p. 1316.
28 Christophe Charle, *Naissance des 'intellectuels' 1880–1900*, Paris, Minuit, 1990.
29 See Ira Katznelson, 'Knowledge about what? Policy intellectuals within the state and capitalism', in Dietrich Rueschemeyer and Theda Skocpol (eds), *Social Knowledge and the Origins of Social Policies*, Princeton and New York, Princeton University Press and Russell Sage Foundation (forthcoming). See also Peter Wagner, 'Reform coalitions between social scientists and policy-makers', in Stuart Blume *et al.* (eds), *The Social Direction of the Public Sciences*, Dordrecht, Reidel, 1987, pp. 277–306; on the location of the intellectual in social space, Heidrun Friese and Peter Wagner, *Der Raum des*

Gelehrten. Eine Topographie wissenschaftlicher Praxis, Berlin, in preparation, both with further references.

30 Robert Fraisse, 'Les sciences sociales et l'Etat', *Esprit*, no. 50, February 1981, p. 372. Fraisse goes on:

> The functional utilization that the administration intended to make of the (research) results as well as, without doubt, also the optimism to which the responsible administrators were induced by the idea of a strong and continuous growth, makes this research bathe . . . in a perspective of completeness. At that time, one reasons in terms of knowledge gaps that are to be closed. The general objective is some sort of exhaustion of the real, as especially the texts of the requests for proposals of that era testify.

31 For an analysis of the Swedish example, see Katrin Fridjonsdottir, 'Social science and the "Swedish model": sociology at the service of the welfare state', in Wagner *et al.*, *Discourses*, pp. 247–70.

32 Colin Gordon, 'Governmental rationality: an introduction', in Burchell *et al.*, op. cit., p. 35.

33 Classics are Cyril E. Black, *The Dynamics of Modernization*, New York, Harper & Row, 1966; and Shmuel N. Eisenstadt, *Tradition, Change and Modernity*, New York, Wiley, 1973; more recent works in that tradition are, with a focus on the individual, Alex Inkeles, *Exploring Individual Modernity*, New York, Columbia University Press, 1983; and in societal terms, Shmuel N. Eisenstadt (ed.), *Patterns of Modernity, Vol. I. The West*, London, Pinter, 1987; for an early critique see Reinhard Bendix, 'Tradition and modernity reconsidered', *Comparative Studies in Society and History*, vol. 9, 1967, pp. 292–346.

34 Gabriel A. Almond and Sidney Verba, *The Civic Culture. Political Attitudes and Democracy in Five Nations*, Princeton, Princeton University Press, 1963, pp. 478–9, 487 and 494. 'The civic culture is appropriate for maintaining a stable and effective democratic political process' (p. 493).

35 Ibid., p. 8. That the culture needs to be 'congruent' with democracy is the key term.

36 Ibid., p. 29.

37 A similar argument could be developed for the reconsideration of the role of the intellectual.

38 'Seldom has social change been interpreted in so managerial a fashion, while all contingencies of action are treated as mere historical variations which cannot alter the "logic of industrialism"' (Reinhard Bendix, op. cit., p. 312, on the book *Industrialism and Industrial Man*, by Clark Kerr and his associates [1960]).

39 Herbert Marcuse, *One-Dimensional Man. Studies in the Ideology of Advanced Industrial Society*, Boston, Beacon, 1964, pp. 19, 84 and xii.

40 Christopher Lasch, 'Toward a theory of post-industrial society', in M. Donald Hancock and Gideon Sjoberg (eds), *Politics in the Post-Welfare State. Responses to the New Individualism*, New York, Columbia University Press, 1972, p. 45.

41 In summarizing sections like this I use quotation marks to avoid mechanistic or organicistic readings of my statements. In this case, society obviously did not offer anything, but trade unions and workers' parties, as well as groups adhering to Christian social thought, fought successfully for a basic acknowledgement of solidarity, as comparative research on the building of the welfare state has made sufficiently clear.

42 Claus Offe, 'Competitive party democracy and the Keynesian welfare state', *Policy Sciences*, vol. 15, 1983, pp. 225–46.

8 PLURALIZATION OF PRACTICES: THE CRISIS OF ORGANIZED MODERNITY

1 Jean Fourastié, *Les trentes glorieuses ou la révolution invisible de 1946 à 1975*, Paris, Fayard, 1979; Robert Boyer, Bernard Chavance, and Olivier Godard, 'La dialectique réversibilité-irréversibilité: une mise en perspective', in Boyer *et al.* (eds), *Les figures de l'irréversibilité en économie*, Paris, EHESS, 1991, p. 15.

2 In 1973 and 1979, the oil price rises demanded by the Organization of Petroleum Exporting Countries (OPEC) brought major resource transfers from the 'Western' industrialized countries, the members of OECD, to the OPEC countries. Among economists it is still disputed whether the economic difficulties that have persisted since the early 1970s were *mainly* caused by the shocklike deterioration of terms of trade for a major import commodity or whether endogenic shifts inside and between the OECD economies were responsible. Either way, though, nobody denies the relevance of the phenomena that I outline in the following. Among some other minor sources, the account is mainly based on Angus Maddison, *Dynamic Forces in Capitalist Development*, Oxford, Oxford University Press, 1991, see, for example, pp. 177–81; Stephen B. Marglin and Juliet B. Schor (eds), *The Goldɩn Age of Capitalism. Reinterpreting the Postwar Experience*, Oxford, Clarendon Press, 1990, partly objecting to Maddison's 'mainstream' account, for example, p. 114; Pierre Dockès and Bernard Rosier, *L'histoire ambiguë. Croissance et développement en question*, Paris, PUF, 1988.

3 Robert Boyer, 'Conclusion: capitalismes fin de siècle', in Boyer (ed.), *Capitalismes fin de siècle*, Paris, PUF, 1986, p. 226.

4 The first statement is the jargon of the West German Council of Economic Advisors at the time, the second notion goes back to Andrew Glyn and Bob Sutcliffe, *British Capitalism, Workers and the Profit Squeeze* (1972); see for a recent reassessment Andrew Glyn *et al.*, 'The rise and fall of the golden age', pp. 76–83; and Stephen Marglin, 'Lessons of the golden age: an overview', p. 19, both in Marglin and Schor, op. cit.

5 Glyn *et al.*, op. cit., p. 95.

6 Folker Fröbel, Jürgen Heinrichs, and Otto Kreye, *The New International Division of Labour*, Cambridge and Paris, Cambridge University Press and Éditions de la Maison des Sciences de l'Homme, 1980; Lars Anell, *Recession, the Western Economies and the Changing World Order*, London, Pinter, 1981, where on pp. 60–1 a comparison to the period before the First World War is offered.

7 Dockès and Rosier, op. cit., p. 182.

8 Gerold Ambrosius and Hartmut Kaelble, 'Einleitung: Gesellschaftliche und wirtschaftliche Folgen des Booms der 1950er und 1960er Jahre', in Kaelble (ed.), *Der Boom 1948–1973*, Opladen, Westdeutscher Verlag, 1992, pp. 15–16.

9 Peter Miller and Nikolas Rose, 'Governing economic life', *Economy and Society*, vol. 19, no. 1, 1990, p. 7.

10 See on France, Peter A. Hall, 'The evolution of economic policy under Mitterrand', in George Ross, Stanley Hoffmann, and Sylvia Malzacher (eds), *The Mitterrand Experiment*, Cambridge, Polity, 1987, pp. 54–72; on the problems facing social democratic governments after the onset of economic difficulties, see Fritz W. Scharpf, *Crisis and Choice in European Social Democracy*, Ithaca, Cornell University Press, 1991.

11 However, it is also arguable

> that the true beneficiaries of economic changes in the 1980s have not been small businesses, but rather multinational companies which have exploited deregulated markets, falling real wages, constrained unions and free currency movements to combine and extend their increasingly global concerns.

(Malcolm Gross and Geoff Payne, 'Introduction: work and the enterprise culture', in Gross and Payne (eds), *Work and the Enterprise Culture*, London, Falmer, 1991, p. 3)

12 For an interesting perspective on this issue, see John Keane and John Owens, *After Full Employment*, London, Hutchinson, 1986, who argue that a return to full employment is neither viable nor desirable. In this context, Robert Reich's recent proposal goes probably farthest in adapting national economy-related (rather than economic in the traditional sense) policies to a reality of strongly de-nationalized economic practices. He abandons the idea of the promotion of national companies and products completely, given the multinational production networks of all major companies, and relies instead on the education and qualification of the domestic workforce to secure them the searched-for and best-paid jobs in an economy that otherwise can only be understood as a global one. (*The Work of Nations. Preparing Ourselves for Twenty-first Century Capitalism*, New York, Knopf, 1991)

13 See, for example, Horst Kern and Charles F. Sabel, 'Trade unions and decentralized production: a sketch of strategic problems in the West German labor movement', *Politics and Society*, vol. 19, no. 4, 1991, pp. 373–402, who propose to rethink the relation of local and national organization of the unions.

14 Boyer, 'Conclusion', pp. 233 and 236.

15 Michael J. Piore and Charles F. Sabel, *The Second Industrial Divide. Possibilities for Prosperity*, New York, Basic Books, 1984. Sabel has restated, and somewhat differentiated, his claim most recently in 'Moebius-strip organizations and open labor markets: some consequences of the reintegration of conception and execution in a volatile economy', in Pierre Bourdieu and James S. Coleman (eds), *Social Theory for a Changing Society*, Boulder, Col., and New York, Westview and Russell Sage, 1991, pp. 23–54. See also the critical comments by Richard Biernacki and by Paul Stark, pp. 54–61. Nigel Gilbert, Roger Burrows, and Anna Pollert speak of the flexibilization theorem as the 'new orthodoxy of economic sociology', in the 'Introduction: Fordism, post-Fordism and economic flexibility', to their (eds), *Fordism and Flexibility. Divisions and Change*, Basingstoke, Macmillan, 1992, p. 2. Stephen Crook, Jan Pakulski, and Malcolm Waters (*Postmodernization. Change in Advanced Society*, London Sage, 1992, pp. 167–96) summarize their own account of these changes as 'disalienation and debureaucratization'. Another recent reassessment of the techno-economic restructurings, including their relation to sociopolitical restructurings, is Bob Jessop, Hans Kastendiek, Klaus Nielsen, and Ove K. Pedersen (eds), *The Politics of Flexibility. Restructuring State and Industry in Britain, Germany and Scandinavia*, Aldershot, Elgar, 1991.

16 From a business administration perspective, an overview over developments in the US is given by Rosabeth Moss Kanter, *When Giants Learn to Dance. Mastering the Challenges of Strategy, Management, and Careers in the 1990s*, New York, Simon & Schuster, 1989. She has reiterated her argument in 'The future of bureaucracy and hierarchy in organizational theory: a report from the field', in Bourdieu and Coleman, op. cit, p. 63–87, where it has been commented upon by Peter Hedström and by Edward O. Laumann, pp. 87–93. The main line of criticism of both 'paradigm shift' arguments, on organization and on production processes, is not that the changes do not occur but that the portrait of the preceding phase, that is, of hierarchical organizations and standardized production, may be overdrawn and, consequently, the extent of change, too. As far as I can see, though, no research seriously doubts the relevance of both types of practices as shaping considerable parts of social practices and as serving as a model for organization and production during organized modernity.

17 See, for example, Kanter, 'Future', p. 68.

18 See, for example, Michel Quéré, 'The technopolis as a response to industrial crisis: observations on the French case', *Industrial Crisis Quarterly*, vol. 4, no. 4, 1990, pp. 311–20.

19 Richard E. Walton, 'From control to commitment in the workplace', *Harvard Business Review*, March/April, no. 2, 1985, pp. 76–84.

20 Michel Crozier, 'Entsteht eine neue Managementlogik?', *Journal für Sozialforschung*, vol. 32, no. 2, 1992, pp. 131–40. Postmodernism has rapidly entered into organization research in recent years; for a critical overview see Martin Parker, 'Post-modern organizations or postmodern organization theory?', *Organization Studies*, vol. 13, no. 1, 1992, pp. 1–17.
21 Robin Cowan, 'High technology and the economics of standardization', in Meinolf Dierkes and Ute Hoffmann (eds), *New Technology at the Outset. Social Forces in the Shaping of Technological Innovations*, Frankfurt/M. and Boulder, Col., Campus and Westview, 1992, p. 287.
22 See, for example, Walt W. Rostow, 'The world economy since 1945: a stylized historical analysis', *Economic History Review*, vol. 38, 1985, p. 253.
23 Joachim Radkau, *Zum ewigen Wachstum verdammt? Historisches über Jugend und Alter großer technischer Systeme*, Berlin, WZB, 1992 (WZB Paper FS II 92–505), pp. 5 and 35–6.
24 See Cowan, op. cit., pp. 295–6, on globalization and standardization. See also the following contributions in the same volume.
25 'In our view, the introduction of greater product variety would represent a new phase of mass production, not its abandonment.' (Robert Boyer, *The Regulation School. A Critical Introduction*, New York, Columbia University Press, 1990, p. xxi)
26 Radkau, *Wachstum*, p. 33; Ithiel de Sola Pool, *Technologies Without Boundaries. On Telecommunications in a Global Age* (ed. by Eli M. Noam), Cambridge, Mass., Harvard University Press, 1990, pp. 15–16.
27 Dockès and Rosier, op. cit., p. 196.
28 Joachim Radkau, *Technik in Deutschland*, Frankfurt/M., Suhrkamp, 1989, p. 146.
29 Richard Rogers, *Visions Dancing in Engineers' Heads. AT&T's Quest to Fulfil the Leitbild of a Universal Telephone Service*, Berlin, WZB, 1990 (WZB Paper FS II 90–102), pp. 45–6.
30 Claus Offe, *Disorganized Capitalism*, Cambridge, Mass., MIT Press, 1987; Scott Lash and John Urry, *The End of Organized Capitalism*, Cambridge, Polity, 1987.
31 Temporary disorder weakens the standardizing effect of accepted conventions. Thus, it allows for greater profits for those who do the right thing in the right place at the right time, as the recent currency turbulences in Europe showed, for instance.
32 Claus Offe, 'Die Staatstheorie auf der Suche nach ihrem Gegenstand: Beobachtungen zur aktuellen Diskussion', in Thomas Ellwein *et al.* (eds), *Jahrbuch zur Staats- und Verwaltungswissenschaft*, vol. 1, Baden-Baden, Nomos, 1987, p. 309.
33 Renate Mayntz, 'Politische Steuerung und gesellschaftliche Steuerungsprobleme – Anmerkungen zu einem theoretischen Paradigma', in Ellwein *et al.*, op. cit..pp. 89–110.
34 I shall actually not discuss in detail here the 'fiscal crisis of the welfare state' (see OECD, *The Welfare State in Crisis*, Paris, OECD, 1981; Pierre Rosanvallon, *La crise de l'Etat-providence*, Paris, Seuil, 1981), which – beyond the problem of the control of external boundaries to be discussed later – seems less relevant for rethinking state and government. See also Thomas R. Cusack, *The Changing Contours of Government*, Berlin, WZB, 1991 (WZB Paper P 91–304).
35 For a recent study, focused on technology policy, see Jeanette Hofmann, 'Implizite Theorien: Interpretationsprobleme regionaler Technologiepolitik', doctoral dissertation, Free University of Berlin, 1992, and the references there.
36 See, for example, Claus Offe, 'The attribution of public status to interest groups: observations on the West German case', in Suzanne Berger (ed.), *Organizing Interests in Western Europe*, Cambridge, Cambridge University Press, 1981, pp. 123–58; Sabino Cassese, 'The rise and decline of the notion of the state', *International Political Science Review*, vol. 7, no. 2, 1986, pp. 120–30.
37 Of course, such interactive processes have a long tradition in most states. Historically,

however, they can mostly be analysed as intra-elite interactions under restricted liberal conditions. Now they tend not only to be universalized throughout society, but are also programmatically hailed as the solution to governance problems that appeared during the 'interventionist' era. For a variety of analyses of this issue, see Charles E. Maier (ed.), *The Changing Boundaries of the Political*, Cambridge, Cambridge University Press, 1987.

38 For this latter reason, I shall take up '1968' again in the following chapter on changing modes of representation.

39 Samuel H. Barnes, Max Kaase *et al.*, *Political Action. Mass Participation in Five Western Democracies*, Beverley Hills, Sage, 1979, see, for example, pp. 13–14 and 45.

40 The notions of 'mobilization politics' and of 'crisis of party allegiance', the latter to be discussed as the complement of the former in the following paragraphs, can already be found in Orion White, Jr., and Gideon Sjoberg (eds), *Politics in the Post-Welfare State*, New York, Columbia University Press, 1972, pp. 23 and 26. See more recently Russell J. Dalton and Manfred Kuechler (eds), *Challenging the Political Order. New Social and Political Movements in Western Democracies*, Cambridge, Polity, 1990.

41 For a comparative study see now Helena Flam (ed.), *Anti-Nuclear Movements and the State*, Edinburgh, Edinburgh University Press, 1993.

42 None of these phenomena shows a steady, or even internationally generalizable, trend. Nevertheless, the 'destructuring of the institutional systems' is the core hypothesis of current research on elections and party systems (Hans-Dieter Klingemann, Richard Stöss, and Bernhard Weßels, 'Politische Klasse und politische Institutionen', in Klingemann et al. (eds), *Politische Klasse und politische Institutionen*, Opladen, Westdeutscher Verlag, 1991, p. 34). See also Herbert Kitschelt, 'New social movements and the decline of party organization', in Dalton and Kuechler, op. cit., pp. 179–208; as a US case study that emphasizes intra-organizational strains see Alan Ware, *The Breakdown of Democratic Party Organization, 1940–1980*, Oxford, Clarendon Press, 1985. Some works are more reluctant to conclude on a major restructuring; to name a few examples: Stefano Bartolini and Peter Mair, *Identity, Competition and Electoral Availability. The Stabilisation of European Electorates 1885–1985*, Cambridge, Cambridge University Press, 1990, do so, but cannot capture the changes in the relation between parties and voters, apart from – of course – not yet noting the events of 1990–1992; Russell J. Dalton, 'Political parties and political representation: party supporters and party elites in nine nations', *Comparative Political Studies*, vol. 18, no. 3, 1985, pp. 267–99, finds linkages between voters' views and party programmes; Bradley M. Richardson, 'European party loyalties revisited', *American Political Science Review*, vol. 85, no. 3, 1985, pp. 751–75, qualifies that 'change and volatility have occurred in a much more inert attitudinal environment than has been thought to exist' (p. 768).

43 'The parties with ideologically rigid programmes and well-integrated electorates tend to disappear in favour of structures with more fluid discourses and electorates.' (François d'Arcy and Guy Saez, 'De la représentation', in François d'Arcy (ed.), *La représentation*, Paris, Economica, 1985, p. 28)

44 For a presentation of the arguments see Thomas J. Biersteker, 'The limits of state power in the contemporary world economy', in Peter G. Brown and Henry Shue (eds), *Boundaries. National Autonomy and Its Limits*, Totowa, N.J., Romwan & Littlefield, 1981, pp. 147–76.

45 A lucid discussion of both theory development and the current transformations of the state is provided by David Held, 'Democracy, the nation-state and the global system', in David Held (ed.), *Political Theory Today*, Cambridge, Polity, 1991, pp. 197–235. See also Evan Luard, *The Globalization of Politics. The Changed Focus of Political Action in the Modern World*, Basingstoke, Macmillan, 1990.

46 In terms of a broad-brush critique of business domination of an arising new world information order, this issue is raised in Herbert I. Schiller, 'The erosion of national sovereignty by the world business system', in Michael Traber (ed.), *The Myth of the Information Revolution. Social and Ethical Implications of Communication Technology*, London, Sage, 1986, pp. 21–34. Arguably, the increased flow of information and the creation of multinational information rights regimes, such as the agreement of the Conference on Security and Co-operation in Europe (CSCE), had a part in the erosion of legitimacy of the socialist regimes. Unlimitable access by the East German population to West German broadcasting media was a perennial problem for the political class in the GDR.
47 The possible impact on political communication and deliberation is foreshadowed in the current US debates about multiculturalism and the claims that are associated with the idea of cultural difference. For the French version of the debate see William Safran, 'State, nation, national identity, and citizenship: France as a test case', *International Political Science Review*, vol. 12, no. 3, 1991, pp. 219–38.
48 A policy analyst used a famous quotation from William Butler Yeats' *The Second Coming* (1921) as the title for his overview over policy effects. See Peter deLeon, 'Things fall apart; the center cannot hold: the crisis in governing', *Policy Sciences*, vol. 15, 1983, pp. 289–304.
49 Jürgen Habermas, *Legitimationsprobleme des Spätkapitalismus*, Frankfurt/M., Suhrkamp, 1973; Alan Wolfe, *The Limits of Legitimacy. Political Contradictions of Contemporary Capitalism*, New York, Free Press, 1977.
50 A crisis report for an elite perspective was provided by Michel Crozier, Samuel P. Huntington, and Joji Watanuki, *The Crisis of Democracy. Report on the Governability of Democracies to the Trilateral Commission*, New York, New York University Press, 1975.
51 Lutz Marz, 'System-Zeit und Entökonomisierung: Zu Zeit/Macht-Dispositionen und mentalen Dispositionen in realsozialistischen Wirtschaften', in Rudi Schmidt (ed.), *Zwischenbilanz-Analysen Zum Transformationsprozeß der ostdeutschen Industrie*, Berlin, Akademie Verlag, 1993, pp. 73–112.
52 See Wolfgang Engler, 'Vom Öffnen und Schließen der Aufstiegskanäle', in *Die zivilisatorische Lücke. Versuche über den Staatssozialismus*, Frankfurt/M., Suhrkamp, 1992, pp. 93–9.
53 Jokes have to be read carefully. This one rather hides the ambiguous relation the socialist workers (and citizens) had to their work (and polity). Regularly insight into the need for allocative and authoritative organization, as well as pride in achievements, went along with such disdain and distanciation. Arguably, exactly such a double orientation – of acceptance and refusal, of identification and distanciation – was characteristic of the situation. See Lutz Marz, 'Geständnisse und Erkenntnisse: Zum Quellenproblem empirischer Transformationsforschung', in Martin Heidenreich (ed.), *Krisen, Kader, Kombinate. Kontinuität und Wandel in ostdeutschen Betrieben*, Berlin, Sigma, 1992, pp. 215–37.
54 As Claude Lefort had envisaged, see 'Pushing back the limits of the possible', *The Political Forms of Modern Society*, Cambridge, Polity, 1986, p. 317.

9 SOCIOLOGY AND CONTINGENCY: THE CRISIS OF THE ORGANIZED MODE OF REPRESENTATION

1 Among the accounts of the developments, I may just cite an elucidating collection of participants' recollections: Ronald Fraser *et al.*, *1968. A Student Generation in Revolt*, London, Chatto & Windus, 1988; and for a study of the social background and world-view of the protesters: Cyril Levitt, *Children of Privilege. Student Revolt in the*

Sixties. A Study of Student Movements in Canada, the United States, and West Germany, Toronto, University of Toronto Press, 1984.

2 Beyond all this – but not unrelated to the more openly political issues – the formation of such small and closed groups also indicated many students' search for a new home away from home. See also Jean-François Lyotard, 'A l'insu (unbeknownst)', in Miami Theory Collective (ed.), *Community at Loose Ends*, Minneapolis, University of Minnesota Press, 1991, p. 47.

3 Michel Maffesoli, *Le temps des tribus. Le déclin de l'individualisme dans les sociétés de masse*, Paris, Méridiens Klincksieck, 1988.

4 Herbert Marcuse, *One-Dimensional Man. Studies in the Ideology of Advanced Industrial Society*, Boston, Beacon, 1964, p. 252.

5 By Panajotis Kondylis, for instance, who writes: 'Structure meant boundary and limitation; ipso facto its destruction was equal to the production of a space in which spontaneity and creativity could grow.' (*Der Niedergang der bürgerlichen Denk- und Lebensform. Die liberale Moderne und die massendemokratische Postmoderne*, Weinheim, VCH, Acta humaniora, 1991, p. 232)

6 In this sense, the movement of 1968 indeed set the path for the 1980s, for whose socio-psychological characterization terms like new individualism, hedonism, narcissism, the greedy years etc. have been used.

7 Pietro Rossi, 'Presentazione', in Rossi (ed.), *Ricerca sociologica e ruolo del sociologo*, Bologna, Il Mulino, 1972, p. 13.

8 Preface by the editors to M. Donald Hancock and Gideon Sjoberg (eds), *Politics in the Post-Welfare State. Responses to the New Individualism*, New York, Columbia University Press, 1972, p. vii.

9 Neo-Marxist structuralism is a partial exception in so far as it appeared capable of understanding rigidities and frictions in society and politics and, thus, limits to reformism. It lost appeal, though, even with opposition movements during the 1970s, not least owing to its own rigidity.

10 Michael Pollak, 'Historisation des sciences sociales et sollicitation sociale de l'histoire', *Bulletin de l'Institut de l'histoire du temps présent*, no. 13, 1983, p. 9; Norbert Wiley, 'The current interregnum in American sociology', *Social Research*, vol. 52, no. 1, 1985, pp. 179–207.

11 This typology is based on nothing other than my own observations of the field and with no other purpose in mind than opening a space of debate in the search for an adequate response.

12 A recent overview over the latter is Wolfgang Krohn, Günter Küppers, and Helga Nowotny (eds), *Selforganization. Portrait of a Scientific Revolution*, Dordrecht, Kluwer, 1990.

13 See for models of knowledge–policy interaction Björn Wittrock, 'Social knowledge and public policy: eight models of interaction', in Peter Wagner *et al.* (eds), *Social Sciences and Modern States. National Experiences and Theoretical Crossroads*, Cambridge, Cambridge University Press, 1991, pp. 333–53; for a general discussion of the legitimacy of post-positivistic reasonings, Carol H. Weiss, 'Policy research: data, ideas, or arguments', pp. 307–32 in the same volume; for explications of specific approaches, John S. Dryzek, *Discursive Democracy*, Cambridge, Cambridge University Press, 1990; Frank Fischer, *Evaluating Public Policy*, Chicago, Nelson-Hall (forthcoming).

14 Charles E. Lindblom, *Inquiry and Change. The Troubled Attempt to Understand and Shape Society*, New Haven and New York, Yale University Press and Russell Sage Foundation, 1990.

15 Eugenio Garin, *La cultura italiana tra '800 e '900*, Bari, Laterza, 1961, and Alberto Asor Rosa, 'La cultura', in *Storia d'Italia*, vol. IV, 2, Turin, Einaudi, 1975, pp. 879–80, for Italian positivism in the last century; Diana Pinto, 'Sociology, politics and society

in post-war Italy', *Theory and Society*, vol. 10, 1981, pp. 671–705, for Italy after the Second World War; Pierre Bourdieu and Jean-Claude Passeron, 'Sociology and philosophy in France since 1945: death and resurrection of a philosophy without subject', *Social Research*, vol. 34, no. 1, 1967, pp. 162–212.

16 In the broad discursive field that could go under the label of postmodernism, I am here only interested in sociological arguments, which I shall try to distil out of the literature. For references, I may point to my first attempt to do so: 'Liberty and discipline: making sense of postmodernity, or, once again, towards a sociohistorical understanding of modernity', *Theory and Society*, vol. 22, 1992, pp. 467–92. See also Wolfgang Welsch, *Unsere postmoderne Moderne*, Weinheim, VCH, Acta humaniora, 1988.

17 These observations can either be cast in terms of a loss of both intelligibility and/or manageability of the world or in terms of an achievement, a recovery of what had been repressed by the imposition of homogenizing modernist discourses and institutions on a heterogeneous social world.

18 A continuity from Weber to Foucault is seen by John O'Neill, 'The disciplinary society: from Weber to Foucault', *The British Journal of Sociology*, vol. 37, no. 1, 1986, pp. 42–60; and by Stefan Breuer, 'Die Evolution der Disziplin', *Kölner Zeitschrift für Soziologie und Sozialpsychologie*, vol. 30, 1978, pp. 409–37; as well as in several contributions to Scott Lash and Sam Whimster (eds), *Max Weber, Rationality and Modernity*, London, Allen & Unwin, 1987, see Bryan S. Turner, 'The rationalization of the body: reflections on modernity and discipline', pp. 222–41, Colin Gordon, 'The soul of the citizen: Max Weber and Michel Foucault on rationality and government', pp. 293–316, and Scott Lash, 'Modernity or modernism? Weber and contemporary social theory', pp. 355–77. On the relation of Simmel's work to contemporary sociology, see Michael Kaern, Bernard S. Phillips, and Robert S. Cohen (eds), *Georg Simmel and Contemporary Sociology*, Dordrecht, Kluwer, 1990. Vilfredo Pareto, *The Transformation of Democracy*, New Brunswick, N.J., Transaction, 1984.

19 Significantly, there is not as yet a corollary sub-discourse on the end of capitalism.

20 Ralf Dahrendorf, 'Anmerkungen zur Diskussion der Referate von Karl R. Popper und Theodor W. Adorno', in Adorno *et al.*, *Der Positivismusstreit in der deutschen Soziologie*, Neuwied, Luchterhand, 1969, p. 148.

21 Richard Rorty, *Contingency, Irony, and Solidarity*, Cambridge, Cambridge University Press, 1989.

22 Rorty would have to respond that the project of a social science does indeed not make any sense from his perspective and needs to dissolve into poetry, too. But he himself relies – pretty naively – on sociological notions, when he argues for his key political concept of solidarity, for instance, see op. cit., p. 191. A strong criticism of Rorty's views is provided by Roy Bhaskar, see his *Reclaiming Reality. A Critical Introduction to Contemporary Philosophy*, London, Verso, 1989 (Chapter 8 on 'Rorty, realism, and the idea of freedom'); and more recently *Philosophy and the Idea of Freedom*, Oxford, Blackwell, 1991 (Section 1: 'Anti-Rorty'). In the former he points to the issue just discussed and affirms that 'there is more to normative social science than creative redescription' (p. 175).

23 If I get it right, this is also the 'main post-Rortian point' which Bhaskar makes when he demands that the world be construed 'as structured, differentiated and changing'; *Philosophy*, p. viii.

24 In Zygmunt Bauman's terms, this is a call for 'a sociology of postmodernity, rather than a postmodern sociology' ('Is there a postmodern sociology?', in *Intimations of Postmodernity*, London, Routledge, 1992, p. 111). See also Albert Scherr, 'Postmoderne Soziologie – Soziologie der Postmoderne?', *Zeitschrift für Soziologie*, vol. 19, no.1, 1990, pp. 3–12.

10 MODERNITY AND SELF-IDENTITY: LIBERATION AND DISEMBEDDING

1 To quote a title of one of Talcott Parsons' books, *Social Structure and Personality*, Glencoe, Ill., The Free Press, 1964; see also Hans Joas, 'Role theory and socialization research', in *Pragmatism and Social Theory*, Chicago, University of Chicago Press, 1993, p. 215.
2 George Herbert Mead, *Mind, Self, and Society from the Standpoint of a Social Behaviorist*, Chicago, University of Chicago Press, 1934, p. 175.
3 Talcott Parsons, *The Social System*, Glencoe, Ill., The Free Press, 1951, p. 25.
4 See, for a recent discussion, Helena Znaniecka Lopata, 'Role theory' and Lewis A. Coser, 'Role-set theory and individual autonomy', both in Judith R. Blau and Norman Goodman (eds), *Social Roles and Social Institutions. Essays in Honor of Rose Laub Coser*, Boulder, Col., Westview, 1991, pp. 1–11 and 13–20 respectively.
5 Rose Laub Coser, *In Defense of Modernity. Role Complexity and Individual Autonomy*, Stanford, Stanford University Press, 1991, p. 25.
6 Peter M. Blau, 'Multigroup affiliations and complex role-sets', in Judith Blau and Goodman, op. cit., p. 38; see also Peter L. Berger, Brigitte Berger, and Hansfried Kellner, *The Homeless Mind. Modernization and Consciousness*, New York, Random House, 1973, Chapter 3. It is thus significant that Georg Simmel, who was interested in urban life and witnessed obviously more mobility than on the societal average, stressed multiple kinds of activity and fleeting identities. This is what makes his work so fascinating for a reconsideration in terms of postmodernity; see David Frisby, *Fragments of Modernity. Theories of Modernity in the Works of Simmel, Kracauer and Benjamin*, Cambridge, Polity, 1985.
7 B.J. Biddle, 'Recent developments in role theory', *American Review of Sociology*, vol. 12, 1986, p. 70.
8 Feminist sociology has had a major part in opening this issue by introducing notions of gender identity and of 'individualization' as a recent social trend; see, for example, Elisabeth Beck-Gernsheim, 'Vom "Dasein für andere" zum Anspruch auf ein Stück "eigenes Leben" – Individualisierungsprozesse im weiblichen Lebenszusammenhang', *Soziale Welt*, vol. 34, no. 3, 1983, pp. 307–41.
9 Daniel Bell, 'America as a mass society: a critique', contribution to a conference on 'The future of freedom' in 1955, now in Bell, *The End of Ideology. On the Exhaustion of Political Ideas in the Fifties*, New York, Free Press, 1960, pp. 21–38.
10 Ibid., p. 38. Bell fails to explicitly note that there is an affirmative variant of this theorizing, too.
11 Bell is a sophisticated intellectual of organized modernity. (He calls Paul F. Lazarsfeld's conceptualization of 'mass' 'neutral' and thus shows more unguardedly than in any of his writings on the theme how much he believes in the idea of 'the end of ideology'.) It is striking to see how many of the themes he touches upon should become prominent in the context of the postmodernity debate a quarter of a century later. The same holds, as mentioned above, for sophisticated critics of organized modernity, such as Marcuse.
12 In and beyond the tradition of the critique of mass society, Jürgen Habermas has tried to develop an evolutionary theory of both self- and societal identity, drawing not least on psychological research; see *Zur Rekonstruktion des Historischen Materialismus*, Frankfurt/M., Suhrkamp, 1976, pp. 63–126. This part of his work marks the transition from organized-modernity intellectual discourse in a similar sense in which the theorem of individualization does the same for more mainstream sociology.
13 Martin Hollis, 'Of masks and men', in Michael Carrithers, Steven Collins, and Steven Lukes (eds), *The Category of the Person. Anthropology, Philosophy, History*, Cambridge, Cambridge University Press, 1985, p. 230.

14 Claude Lefort, 'Reversibility: political freedom and the freedom of the individual', *Democracy and Political Theory*, Cambridge, Polity, 1988, p. 179.

15 The drastic enlargement of the citizenship of modernity that this process also entailed meant a disembedding for the small groups who had occupied places of high standing under restricted liberal modernity and were about to lose them, or at least to lose their automatic claim to these positions. Besides aristocratic groups that had safeguarded some privileges into the bourgeois times, officers and large land-owners for instance, established intellectuals were a group that was hit by this process. In European societies, academics and professors had enjoyed considerable prestige as mandarin intellectuals and advisors. Their concern or even despair about the loss of status they envisaged found expressions in their thinking and writing about history and society. This was particularly the case in Germany, where the standing of the mandarins had been especially high and the evolution of mass society very rapid during Imperial and Weimar times. A portrait of this group is given by Fritz Ringer's *The Decline of the German Mandarins*, Cambridge, Mass., Harvard University Press, 1969.

16 On 'standardized markers' as symbols for social identity see Anthony Giddens, *The Constitution of Society*, Cambridge, Polity, 1984, pp. 282–3.

17 Klaus Megerle, 'Die Radikalisierung blieb aus: Zur Integration gesellschaftlicher Gruppen in der Bundesrepublik während des Nachkriegsbooms', pp. 107–26; and Hartmut Kaelble, 'Boom und gesellschaftlicher Wandel 1948–1973: Frankreich und die Bundesrepublik Deutschland im Vergleich', both in Kaelble (ed.), *Der Boom 1948–1973. Gesellschaftliche und wirtschaftliche Folgen in der Bundesrepublik Deutschland und in Europa*, Opladen, Westdeutscher Verlag, 1992. Also Ditmar Brock, *Der schwierige Weg in die Moderne*, Frankfurt/M., Campus, 1991, pp. 243–6.

18 One such likely reason is mere generational change, as in the case of the student revolt, when young people raised on the ideas of liberty and self-realization refused to re-enact practices for which good justifications were lacking.

19 Jacques Donzelot, *L'invention du social. Essai sur le déclin des passions politiques*, Paris, Fayard, 1984.

20 Claude Gilbert, 'Fin de contrat', *Traverses*, nos. 33–4, 1985, p. 20. Gilbert calls the 1950s and 1960s, in line with my view on organized modernity, the 'classical era' of modernity.

21 New York, Semiotext(e), 1983 (first in French in 1978). On media studies, see, for instance, Deborah Cook, 'Ruses de guerre: Baudrillard and Fiske on media reception', *Journal for the Theory of Social Behaviour*, vol. 22, no. 2, 1992, pp. 227–38.

22 I use the language of game and rational-choice theory here deliberately, not because I think it is generally an appropriate way of looking at the social world, but because it has been increasingly imputed to electoral behaviour. This change in language indeed marks real-world transformations.

23 Which are mostly regarded as transforming the cleavage structure – though it may soon be difficult to use the term cleavage structure at all any longer, if the tendencies that are described here prevail.

24 In a more recent text, he uses the formula that the mass 'does not speak any longer, but it causes' (Jean Baudrillard, *La transparence du mal*, Paris, Galilée, 1990, p. 85). I share the view of many of Baudrillard's critics that his writings are often confused and his thoughts obscenely cynical. There is thus no point in searching for his stand-point, either in analytic or in normative terms. But the flash-like insights of some of his texts are worth taking up and reinterpreting, since much of more modernist social science is incapable of arriving at such points.

25 See Claude Gilbert and Marc Guillaume, 'L'acharnement politique ou l'effort de représentation', in François d'Arcy (ed.), *La représentation*, Paris, Economica, 1985, p. 95; and Gilbert, op. cit., p. 23.

26 François d'Arcy and Guy Saez, 'De la représentation', in d'Arcy, op. cit., p. 29. The analogy raises the question whether and how far authoritative issues can be transformed into allocative issues.
27 Marc Guillaume, 'La stratégie du lézard', *Traverses*, nos. 33/4, 1985, p. 32.
28 Among the recent contributions I note Russel Keat and Nicholas Abercrombie (eds), *Enterprise Culture*, London, Routledge, 1991; Roger Burrows (ed.), *Deciphering the Enterprise Culture. Entrepreneurship, Petty Capitalism and the Restructuring of Britain*, London, Routledge, 1991; Paul Heelas and Paul Morris (eds), *The Values of the Enterprise Culture. The Moral Debate*, London, Routledge, 1992; Malcolm Gross and Geoff Payne (eds), *Work and the Enterprise Culture*, London, Falmer, 1991.
29 On the history of the concept in the English context see Paul Morris, 'Freeing the spirit of enterprise: the genesis and development of the concept of enterprise culture', in Keat and Abercrombie, op. cit., pp. 21–37.
30 Russel Keat, 'Introduction: starship Britain or universal enterprise', in Keat and Abercrombie, op. cit., p. 3.
31 Ibid. p. 6. See also Paul Heelas, 'Reforming the self: enterprise and the characters of Thatcherism', in the same volume, pp. 72–90; and Nikolas Rose, 'Governing the enterprising self', in Heelas and Morris, op. cit., pp. 141–64.
32 As a transitional text, see Jean Baudrillard, *La société de consommation, ses mythes, ses structures*, Paris, Denoël, 1970; more recently Mike Featherstone, 'Lifestyle and consumer culture', *Consumer Culture and Postmodernism*, London, Sage, 1991, pp. 83–94; Daniel Miller, *Material Culture and Mass Consumption*, Oxford, Blackwell, 1987.
33 Roger Burrows and Catherine Marsh, 'Consumption, class and contemporary sociology', in Burrows and Marsh (eds), *Consumption and Class. Divisions and Change*, London, Macmillan, 1992, pp. 1–14 for a general discussion of these issues.
34 Pierre Bourdieu, *Distinction. A Social Critique of the Judgment of Taste*, London, Routledge & Kegan Paul, 1984. This observation is also made, though not elaborated, by Bryan S. Turner, 'Periodization and politics in the postmodern', in Turner (ed.), *Theories of Modernity and Postmodernity*, London, Sage, 1990, p. 4; and now by Gerhard Schulze, *Die Erlebnisgesellschaft. Kultursoziologie der Gegenwart*, Frankfurt/M., Campus, 1992, p. 20.
35 Fredric Jameson, *Postmodernism, or, The Cultural Logic of Late Capitalism*, Durham, N.C., Duke University Press, 1991.
36 Daniel Bell, *The Cultural Contradictions of Capitalism*, London, Heinemann, 1976.
37 Keat, op. cit., p. 9.
38 The former view is made strongly in Anthony Giddens, *Modernity and Self-Identity*, Cambridge, Polity, 1991; the latter in Nikolas Rose, *Governing the Soul*, London, Routledge, 1990; and Peter Miller and Nikolas Rose, 'Governing economic life', *Economy and Society*, vol. 19, no. 1, 1990, pp. 1–31.
39 The German term, which I am not really sure translates well into English, is *Zweidrittelgesellschaft.* Göran Therborn speaks similarly of 'The two-thirds, one-third society', in Stuart Hall and Martin Jacques (eds), *New Times. The Changing Face of Politics in the 1990s*, London, Lawrence & Wishart, 1989, pp. 103–15. In the text, he even invokes the 'Brazilianisation of advanced capitalism' (p. 111). Elsewhere the term 'dual society' has been used (Burrows and Marsh, op. cit., p. 3, referring to Peter Saunders). Americans would probably speak of the third 'third' as the underclass; see Fred Siegel (ed.), 'Social breakdown', a thematic issue of *Dissent*, Spring 1991, pp. 163–292.
40 Which, in sum, clearly convey the message that nobody has to fail in one's profession, social milieu, intimate life, psycho-physical controls, etc., since there are recipes to deal with anything.

41 Marlis Buchmann, *The Script of Life in Modern Society. Entry into Adulthood in a Changing World*, Chicago, The University of Chicago Press, 1989, p. 75 (original emphasis).

42 A brief analysis of the change in social science discourse over that period is offered by Ronald Dore, 'Sovereign individuals', in John A. Hall and I.C. Jarvie (eds), *Transition to Modernity. Essay on Power, Wealth and Belief*, Cambridge, Cambridge University Press, 1991, pp. 178–84. He refers to the portraits of organized modernity as given by Riesman, Whyte and others and compares them to the resurgent more individualist ones. His interest is in the structural conditions of 'individuation' as measured by

> the answer to the following question: how much of the things people do and say is the result of individual conscious choice, as opposed to being the unthinking repetition of habit, or the performance without question of 'the proper thing to do', or the acceptance of the decision of some state authority or of some group to which one belongs, or . . . the following, possibly against inclination, of what seem unassailably prescribed social norms?
>
> (p. 178)

43 Douglas Kellner, 'Popular culture and the construction of postmodern identities', in Scott Lash and Jonathan Friedman (eds), *Modernity and Identity*, Oxford, Blackwell, 1992, p. 151.

44 Bruce Leinberger and Paul Tucker, *The New Individualists. The Generation After Organization Man*, New York, Harper & Collins, 1991.

45 Kellner, op. cit., p. 142.

46 Ibid., pp. 157–8.

47 Ibid., p. 153.

48 Leinberger and Tucker, op. cit., pp. 17–18, 233, 236 and 363. The latter is a somewhat awkward term that is meant to refer both to the value of subjectivity and to being subjected, in an open-ended way, to a plurality of social stimulations. A related study on German youth is Rainer Zoll *et al.*, *Nicht so wie unsere Eltern! Ein neues kulturelles Modell?*, Opladen, Westdeutscher Verlag, 1989. The authors point to a broader validity of their findings in Western societies (pp. 9–10).

49 Kenneth J. Gergen, *The Saturated Self. Dilemmas of Identity in Contemporary Life*, New York, Basic Books, 1991, pp. 6–7. In his view, the modernist conception is preceded by a romantic one that focuses on personal depth.

50 Ibid., pp. 139–170, drawing not least on the work of Carol Gilligan.

51 Judith Stacey, *Brave New Families. Stories of Domestic Upheaval in Late Twentieth Century America*, New York, Basic Books, 1990.

52 Philip Wexler, Warren Crichlow, June Kern, Rebecca Martusewicz, *Becoming Somebody: Toward a Social Psychology of School*, Falmer Press, 1992. A recent study has suggested that the capacity to maintain networks of social relations on which one may rely in case of need may itself be structured according to social locations. When institutionalized supports are withdrawn, a 'two-thirds society' may emerge also in social terms; see Martin Diewald, *Soziale Beziehungen. Verlust oder Liberalisierung?*, Berlin, Sigma, 1991, p. 252.

53 Buchmann, op. cit., pp. 183–4 (my emphasis).

54 Ibid., pp. 188 and 187. On the social organization and modern standardization of the life course see generally Martin Kohli, 'Social organization and subjective construction of the life course', pp. 271–92; and John W. Meyer, 'The self and the life course: institutionalization and its effects', pp. 199–216, both in Aage B. Sorensen, Franz E. Weinert, and Lonnie R. Sherrod (eds), *Human Development and the Life Course*, Hillsdale, N.J., Lawrence Erlbaum, 1986.

11 INCOHERENT PRACTICES AND POSTMODERN SELVES: THE CURRENT CONDITION OF MODERNITY

1 On the former see Lutz Niethammer, *Posthistoire. Ist die Geschichte zu Ende?*, Reinbek, Rowohlt, 1989; on the latter, in a political science perspective, Thomas Mirbach, *Überholte Legitimität? Oder: Auf dem Weg zu einem neuen Politikbegriff*, Darmstadt, Wissenschaftliche Buchgesellschaft, 1990. Significantly, modernization theory is currently being revived, but the assumption of the functional coherence of the practices of modernity is relaxed. In 'neo-modernization theory' or 'Modernization II', the sectors of a modern society

> *may or may not* constitute a comprehensive set of fundamental sectors or dimensions. One task of Modernization II would be to critically examine antecedent work on societal differentiation to evaluate the logical and empirical adequacy of the Parsonian legacy.'
>
> (Edward A. Tiryakian, 'Modernization: exhumetur in pace (rethinking macrosociology in the 1990s)', *International Sociology*, vol. 6, no. 2, 1991, p. 173, my emphasis)

The processual noun 'modernization' had indeed already opened the way for a conception of modern practices that could continue without the modern project being still alive. See also Wolfgang Zapf, 'Modernisierung und Modernisierungstheorien', pp. 23–39, and Erwin K. Scheuch, 'Schwierigkeiten der Soziologie mit dem Prozeß der Modernisierung', pp. 109–39, both in Zapf (ed.), *Modernisierung moderner Gesellschaften*, Frankfurt/M., Campus, 1991.

2 See Zygmunt Bauman, 'Philosophical affinities of postmodern sociology', *The Sociological Review*, vol. 38, no. 3, 1990, pp. 411–44; and Bauman, *Legislators and Interpreters*, Cambridge, Polity, 1987.

3 Dorothy Ross, *The Origins of American Social Science*, Cambridge, Cambridge University Press, 1991, p. 25. Ultimately, this seems to me to be the very basic reason why the discourse on postmodernity tends to take a playful, liberating form in America, and a tragic, nostalgic form in France.

4 Exclusion worked towards the black (slave) population; and the struggle over this question, from the Civil War to the civil rights movement and the urban riots, remains an issue that neither American ideology nor policy can handle. It is amazing (and shocking, I must say) to see how little impact the experience of the relation of Euro-Americans to Afro-Americans has had on work in sociology and political theory in the US. For a critical discussion of exclusion and inclusion in American citizenship see now Judith N. Shklar, *American Citizenship. The Quest for Inclusion*, Cambridge, Mass., Harvard University Press, 1991.

5 A recent collection of essays on the state of the US emphasizes, in the summarizing words of a reviewer, that ' "American society" in fact effectively no longer exists. The United States remains an integral nation-state ... but internally it has become decentered' (Anthony Giddens, 'Is the American Dream over?', *Contemporary Sociology*, vol. 21, no. 4, 1992, p. 431; review essay on Alan Wolfe (ed.), *America at Century's End*, Berkeley, University of California Press, 1992).

6 The Southern blacks are the most striking case of a fate that also befell many Americans of other ethnic origins, not least as a consequence of the Great Depression (and also the wars).

7 For the equivalent to what I call organized modernity the term 'corporate liberalism' has been used for the US, though in a number of different ways. James Weinstein, *The Corporate Ideal in the Liberal State*, Boston, Beacon Press, 1968, describes the political programme for an organized social formation; R. Jeffrey Lustig, *Corporate Liberalism.*

The Origins of Modern American Political Theory, Berkeley, University of California Press, 1982, writes more broadly about an 'organized' societal self-understanding emerging from the 'fracture of liberalism' at the turn of the nineteenth century.

8 Seymour Martin Lipset, 'No third way: a comparative perspective on the Left', in Hans-Dieter Klingemann *et al.* (eds), *Politische Klasse und politische Institutionen*, Opladen, Westdeutscher Verlag, 1991, pp. 93–5.

9 As a striking case study for the segregating and fragmenting impact of very liberal political rules on urban politics, see Daniel Lazare, 'Collapse of a city', in *Dissent*, Spring 1991, pp. 267–75.

10 See in particular Robert N. Bellah, Richard Madsen, William M. Sullivan, Ann Swidler, and Steven M. Tipton, *Habits of the Heart. Individualism and Commitment in American Life*, Berkeley, University of California Press, 1985; and more recently by the same group, *The Good Society*, New York, Knopf, 1991.

11 This is exactly its peculiarly American feature. More broadly understood, communitarian theories comprise also nationalism, socialism and political Catholicism – kinds of political thought that have flourished in Europe much more than in North America. The current European interest in communitarianism should be understood not least as a response to the demise of the home-grown communitarian theories. This demise, in turn, follows on the insight in the absence of the communities that were at their base: the nation, the working class, and a religion that is shared polity-wide. These absences have long characterized the US.

12 See Theda Skocpol's remark on the 'lead society', in 'Bringing the state back in: strategies of analysis in current research', in Peter B. Evans, Dietrich Rueschemeyer, and Theda Skocpol (eds), *Bringing the State Back In*, Cambridge, Cambridge University Press, 1985, p. 6.

13 Paris, Grasset, 1986.

14 For Germany see Frank Trommler, 'Aufstieg und Fall des Amerikanismus in Deutschland', in Trommler (ed.), *Amerika und die Deutschen*, Opladen, Westdeutscher Verlag, 1986, pp. 666–76. For a collection of French essays on both the fascination with and rejection of America see Denis Lacorne, Jacques Rupnik, and Marie-France Toinet (eds), *The Rise and Fall of Anti-Americanism. A Century of French Perception*, Basingstoke, Macmillan, 1990.

15 From the *New York Times*, as reprinted in the *International Herald Tribune*, 4–5 July 1992. The underlying analysis is *Anti-Americanism. Critiques at Home and Abroad 1965–1990*, New York, Oxford University Press, 1992.

16 A fourth one, the one referring to the order of social practices preceding restricted liberal modernity, need not be discussed here, since it was used as the asymmetrical opposition to society, namely community (*Gemeinschaft*).

17 For more detail see Manfred Riedel, 'Gesellschaft, bürgerliche', in Otto Brunner, Werner Conze, and Reinhart Koselleck (eds), *Geschichtliche Grundbegriffe*, Stuttgart, Klett, vol. 2, 1975, pp. 719–800; John Keane, 'Despotism and democracy', in Keane (ed.), *Civil Society and the State. New European Perspectives*, London, Verso, 1988, pp. 35–71.

18 Jacques Donzelot, *L'invention du social*, Paris, Fayard, 1984; Jean Baudrillard, *A l'ombre des majorités silencieuses ou la fin du social*, Paris, Denoël/Gonthier, 1982, p. 70: 'The social regresses in the same proportion as its institutions develop.'

19 Andrew Arato and Jean Cohen, 'Civil society and social theory', *Thesis Eleven*, no. 21, 1988, p. 45.

20 See, for example, Daniel Bell, ' "American exceptionalism" revisited: the role of civil society', *The Public Interest*, no. 95, Spring 1989, p. 56.

21 Volker Heins, 'Ambivalenzen der Zivilgesellschaft', *Politische Vierteljahresschrift*, vol. 33, no. 2, 1992, p. 240.

22 Michel Maffesoli, *Le temps des tribus. Le déclin de l'individualisme dans les sociétés de masse*, Paris, Méridiens Klincksieck, 1988; 'Post-modern sociality', *Telos*, no. 85, 1990, pp. 89–92; see also Alberto Melucci, 'Social movements and the democratization of everyday life', in Keane, op. cit., pp. 245–60.
23 Alain Touraine, 'An introduction to the study of social movements', *Social Research*, vol. 52, no. 4, 1985, pp. 749–87; and *Le retour de l'acteur. Essai de sociologie*, Paris, Fayard, 1984, pp. 177–80. In his latest book, *Critique de la Modernité*, Paris, Fayard, 1992, the concept of the 'Subject' entails a double emphasis on personal liberty and collective action against the 'apparatuses of power', for example, p. 369.
24 Craig Calhoun, 'Indirect relationships and imagined communities: large-scale social integration and the transformation of everyday life', in Pierre Bourdieu and James S. Coleman (eds), *Social Theory for a Changing Society*, Boulder, Col., and New York, Westview and Russell Sage, 1991, pp. 95 and 96.
25 Alain Touraine's notion of the 'dissociation' of a former 'correspondence' of modernity and the social actors seems to stem from a similar observation – which he, though, casts in terms of actors and systems, see *Critique*, pp. 164–5, 225 and 409.
26 Serge Latouche, 'La fin de la société des nations', *Traverses*, nos. 33–4, 1985, pp. 39–40.
27 Jonathan Friedman, 'Narcissism, roots and postmodernity: the constitution of selfhood in the global crisis', in Scott Lash and Friedman (eds), *Modernity and Identity*, Oxford, Blackwell, 1992, pp. 333 and 360–2.
28 Jean François Lyotard makes this connection himself in 'Une ligne de résistance', *Traverses*, nos. 33–4, 1985, pp. 63–4.
29 A similar argument can be made, I think, for the contingency of language drawing on semiotic analyses and relating the diffusion of certain languages to the possibilities of communication that they offer. I will refrain from trying this here, however.
30 Even if the substantive idea is related to an ascriptive criterion, such as being black or being a woman, there is today a strong element of choice in whether one would make this criterion important for one's own self-realization, that is, by making belonging to the respective community a part of one's self-understanding.
31 *Sources of the Self. The Making of the Modern Identity*, Cambridge, Mass., Harvard University Press, 1989, p. 30.
32 Michael Walzer, 'The idea of civil society', *Dissent*, Spring 1991, pp. 293–304, quotations from pp. 300–2. This lecture was published in an issue of *Dissent* that was otherwise devoted to the 'social breakdown' in the US, edited by Fred Siegel, pp. 163–292.
33 Claude Gilbert and Marc Guillaume, 'L'acharnement politique ou l'effort de représentation', in François d'Arcy (ed.), *La représentation*, Paris, Economica, 1985, p. 92.
34 See, for example, Calhoun, 'Indirect relationships', op. cit. pp. 110–13; and Zygmunt Bauman, *Intimations of Postmodernity*, London, Routledge, 1992, p. xvii.
35 Claus Offe, 'Fessel und Bremse: Moralische und institutionelle Aspekte "intelligenter Selbstbeschränkung" ', in Axel Honneth *et al.* (eds), *Zwischenbetrachtungen. Im Prozeß der Aufklärung*, Frankfurt/M., Suhrkamp, 1989, p. 755.
36 'It is quite possible to be strongly in favour of a morality based on a notion of the good but lean to some procedural formula when it comes to the principles of politics. . . . The political issue is . . . quite distinct from that of the nature of moral theory' (Taylor, op. cit., p. 532).
37 The idea that the concept of self-governing needs to be related to the organization of practices is found in Barry Hindess, 'Imaginary presuppositions of democracy', *Economy and Society*, vol. 20, no. 2, 1991, pp. 173–95.
38 Johann P. Arnason, 'The theory of modernity and the problematic of democracy', *Thesis Eleven*, no. 26, 1990, p. 39. The same observation must be at the basis of Claus

Offe's invocation of the image of the car without brakes. The running car stands for functional efficacy, the lack of a brake for the impossibility of re-thematizing the mode of running, see Offe, op. cit., pp. 752–3.

39 Arato and Cohen, op. cit., p. 55. By commenting on the recent debate, Jürgen Habermas restates his understanding of public sphere and civil society in *Faktizität und Geltung. Beiträge zur Diskurstheorie des Rechts und des Demokratischen Rechtsstaats*, Frankfurt/M., Suhrkamp, 1992, pp. 429–67.

40 Stephen Crook, Jan Pakulski, and Malcolm Waters (*Postmodernization. Change in Advanced Society*, London, Sage, 1992) remain unclear about the conceptual status they give to the processes of differentiation and de-differentiation of systems that they emphasize. Their concluding disclaimer notwithstanding, they appear to work with some duality of abstract logics and collective action. Hans Joas, in contrast, has argued for the reconstruction of the notion of differentiation itself, see 'The democratization of differentiation: on the creativity of collective action', in Jeffrey Alexander and Piotr Sztompka (eds), *Rethinking Progress. Movements, Forces and Ideas at the End of the Twentieth Century*, Boston, Unwin Hyman, 1990, pp. 182–201.

41 To point briefly back to earlier discussions: the literature giving advice for self-realization, which Giddens has studied, may be one of the means through which communicative forms are 'de-traditionalized' but at the same time conventionalized in a new way. The issue of an open collective communicative space is what distinguishes Touraine's theory from Maffesoli's. The former tends to see social movements creating such a space and thus recreating politics, whereas the latter focuses on the reemergence of creative social action disregarding the question of politics – or leading to a new understanding of politics, see his latest *La transfiguration du politique. La tribalisation du monde*, Paris, Grasset, 1992. While I think that Maffesoli's view is more valid, I remain – in contrast to him – very sceptical about the consequences.

42 Seyla Benhabib's comparison of Arendt's and Habermas' views on the public sphere is more generous to Habermas, but also identifies tensions in his conceptualization resulting from 'overly rigid boundaries', see 'Models of public space: Hannah Arendt, the liberal tradition and Jürgen Habermas', *Situating the Self. Gender, Community and Postmodernism in Contemporary Ethics*, Cambridge, Polity, 1992, esp. p. 111.

43 In both respects, the loss of a political language and the loss of a linkage between political agency and the appropriate realm of politics, it is taken up and emphasized by a number of, mostly French, theorists, such as Jean-François Lyotard, Claude Lefort, Marc Guillaume, Claude Gilbert and Jean-Luc Nancy. See, for instance, the collection in *Traverses*, nos. 33–4, 1985. Philippe Lacoue-Labarthe and Jean-Luc Nancy have gone as far as comparing the de-substantivization of authoritative practices with totalitarianism. While classical totalitarianism was emptying the political space by imposing a transcendental perspective resorting to nation or class, the new, 'un-published' totalitarianism proceeds via the dissolution of transcendence at all, the factual prohibition of bringing substantive issues up as issues of common deliberation. ('Le "retrait" du politique', in Philippe Lacoue-Labarthe and Jean-Luc Nancy (eds), *Le retrait du politique*, Paris, Galilée, 1983, p. 192)

44 Zygmunt Bauman, *Intimations*, op. cit., p. xx, on the postmodernist transformation of the public sphere and the subsequent further limitation of the possibility of politics.

45 As Zygmunt Bauman has pointed out (*Freedom*, Minneapolis, University of Minnesota Press, 1988, p. 96), the modernist way of dealing with politics has most often preferred the 'exit' to the 'voice' option, in Albert Hirschman's apt terms. Rather than trying to deal together with common issues, people elaborated ways of shifting the emphasis on the good life elsewhere, in other 'non-political' realms of practice or, literally, to other spaces. In a global society, though, most such practices return as political ones.

46 Agnes Heller and Ferenc Fehér, 'On being dissatisfied in a satisfied society II', *The*

Postmodern Political Condition, Cambridge, Polity, 1988, pp. 33 and 35.

47 Walzer, op. cit., pp. 303 and 302. But see in historical perspective the related call:

> The magic word 'association', which, imported from France, spread since the thirties and gave expression to the desire for a new structure of a society in the process of dissolution, captured many people. It was used for the solution of 'the social question' in the corporatist-conservative, the liberal-societal and in the socialist-revolutionary sense.
>
> (Werner Conze, 'Vom "Pöbel" zum "Proletariat": Sozialgeschichtliche Voraussetzungen für den Sozialismus in Deutschland', in Hans-Ulrich Wehler (ed.), *Moderne deutsche Sozialgeschichte*, Köln, Kiepenheuer und Witsch, 1966 [1954], p. 129. Conze writes about Germany in the 1830s.)

48 The issue could also be phrased as the impossibility of relying on a purely negative concept of liberty, in Isaiah Berlin's terms. See 'Two concepts of liberty', *Four Essays on Liberty*, Oxford, Oxford University Press, 1969, pp. 118–72.

49 As Chantal Mouffe puts it,

> we need to conceive of a mode of political association that, although it does not postulate the existence of a substantive common good, nevertheless implies the idea of commonality, of an ethico-political bond that creates a linkage among the participants in the association.
>
> ('Democratic citizenship and the political community', in Miami Theory Collective (ed.), *Community at Loose Ends*, Minneapolis, University of Minnesota Press, 1991, pp. 75–6)

50 George Friedman and Meredith Lebard, *The Coming War with Japan*, New York, St. Martin's Press, 1991; Karl-Otto Hondrich, *Lehrmeister Krieg*, Reinbek, Rowohlt, 1992; for an attempt to provide alternative foundations for thinking about European identity see Jacques Derrida, *The Other Heading*, Bloomington, Ind., Indiana University Press, 1992.

Bibliography

Abrams, Philip, 'The sense of the past and the origins of sociology', *Past and Present*, no. 55, 1971, pp. 18–32.

Aglietta, Michel, *A Theory of Capitalist Regulation. The US Experience*, London, New Left Books, 1979 [1976].

Almond, Gabriel A., and Sidney Verba, *The Civic Culture. Political Attitudes and Democracy in Five Nations*, Princeton, Princeton University Press, 1963.

Ambrosius, Gerold, and Hartmut Kaelble, 'Einleitung: Gesellschaftliche und wirtschaftliche Folgen des Booms der 1950er und 1960er Jahre', in Hartmut Kaelble (ed.), *Der Boom 1948–1973*, Opladen, Westdeutscher Verlag, 1992, pp. 7–32.

Anderson, Benedict, *Imagined Communities. Reflections on the Origins and Spread of Nationalism*, London, Verso, 1983.

Anell, Lars, *Recession, the Western Economies and the Changing World Order*, London, Pinter, 1981.

Appleby, Joyce Oldham, 'The American model for the French revolutionaries', *Liberalism and Republicanism in the Historical Imagination*, Cambridge, Mass., Harvard University Press, 1992.

Arato, Andrew, and Jean Cohen, 'Civil society and social theory', *Thesis Eleven*, no. 21, 1988, pp. 40–64.

Arendt, Hannah, *The Human Condition*, Chicago, The University of Chicago Press, 1958.

—— *The Origins of Totalitarianism*, Cleveland, World Publishing Company, 2nd edn 1958.

Arnason, Johann P., 'The theory of modernity and the problematic of democracy', *Thesis Eleven*, 1990, no. 26, pp. 20–45.

—— 'Civilization, culture and power: reflections on Norbert Elias' genealogy of the West', *Thesis Eleven*, no. 24, 1989, pp. 44–70.

—— 'The imaginary constitution of modernity', *Revue européenne des sciences sociales*, 1989, no. 20, pp. 323–37.

Asor Rosa, Alberto, 'La cultura', in *Storia d'Italia*, vol. IV, 2, Turin, Einaudi, 1975.

Barnes, Samuel H., Max Kaase *et al.*, *Political Action. Mass Participation in Five Western Democracies*, Beverly Hills, Sage, 1979.

Bartolini, Stefano, and Peter Mair, *Identity, Competition and Electoral Availability. The Stabilisation of European Electorates 1885–1985*, Cambridge, Cambridge University Press, 1990.

Baudrillard, Jean, *La transparence du mal*, Paris, Galilée, 1990.

—— *L'Amérique*, Paris, Grasset, 1986.

—— *In the Shadow of the Silent Majorities*, New York, Semiotext(e), 1983 (first published in French in 1978).

—— *La société de consommation, ses mythes, ses structures*, Paris, Denoël, 1970.

Bauman, Zygmunt, *Intimations of Postmodernity*, London, Routledge, 1992.

—— 'Soil, blood and identity', *The Sociological Review*, vol. 40, no. 4, 1992, pp. 675–701.
—— *Modernity and Ambivalence*, Cambridge, Polity, 1991.
—— 'Philosophical affinities of postmodern sociology', *The Sociological Review*, vol. 38, no. 3, 1990, pp. 411–44.
—— *Modernity and the Holocaust*, Ithaca, Cornell University Press, 1989.
—— *Freedom*, Minneapolis, University of Minnesota Press, 1988.
—— *Legislators and Interpreters. On Modernity, Post-Modernity and Intellectuals*, Cambridge, Polity, 1987.
Beck, Ulrich, and Elisabeth Beck-Gernsheim, *Das ganz normale Chaos der Liebe*, Frankfurt/M., Suhrkamp, 1990.
Beck-Gernsheim, Elisabeth, 'Vom "Dasein für andere" zum Anspruch auf ein Stück "eigenes Leben" – Individualisierungsprozesse im weiblichen Lebenszusammenhang', *Soziale Welt*, vol. 34, no. 3, 1983, pp. 307–41.
Bell, Daniel, ' "American exceptionalism" revisited: the role of civil society', *The Public Interest*, no. 95, Spring 1989, pp. 38–56.
—— *The Cultural Contradictions of Capitalism*, London, Heinemann, 1976.
—— 'America as a mass society: a critique', in *The End of Ideology. On the Exhaustion of Political Ideas in the Fifties*, New York, Free Press, 1960, pp. 21–38.
Bellah, Robert N., Richard Madsen, William M. Sullivan, Ann Swidler, and Steven M. Tipton, *The Good Society*, New York, Knopf, 1991.
—— *Habits of the Heart. Individualism and Commitment in American Life*, Berkeley, University of California Press, 1985.
Bendix, Reinhard, 'Tradition and modernity reconsidered', *Comparative Studies in Society and History*, vol. 9, 1967, pp. 292–346.
Benhabib, Seyla, 'Models of public space: Hannah Arendt, the liberal tradition and Jürgen Habermas', *Situating the Self. Gender, Community and Postmodernism in Contemporary Ethics*, Cambridge, Polity, 1992.
Berger, Peter L., Brigitte Berger, and Hansfried Kellner, *The Homeless Mind. Modernization and Consciousness*, New York, Random House, 1973.
Berlin, Isaiah, 'Two concepts of liberty', in *Four Essays on Liberty*, Oxford, Oxford University Press, 1969, pp. 118–72.
Berman, Marshall, *All That Is Solid Melts Into Air. The Experience of Modernity*, New York, Simon & Schuster, 1982.
Bhaskar, Roy, *Philosophy and the Idea of Freedom*, Oxford, Blackwell, 1991.
—— *Reclaiming Reality. A Critical Introduction to Contemporary Philosophy*, London, Verso, 1989.
Biddle, B.J., 'Recent developments in role theory', *American Review of Sociology*, vol. 12, 1986, pp. 67–92.
Biersteker, Thomas J., 'The limits of state power in the contemporary world economy', in Peter G. Brown and Henry Shue (eds), *Boundaries. National Autonomy and Its Limits*, Totowa, N.J., Rowman & Littlefield, 1981, pp. 147–76.
Bijker, Wiebe, Thomas P. Hughes, and Trevor Pinch (eds), *The Social Construction of Technological Systems. New Directions in the Sociology and History of Technology*, Cambridge, Mass., MIT Press, 1987.
Black, Cyril E., *The Dynamics of Modernization*, New York, Harper & Row, 1966.
Blau, Peter M., 'Multigroup affiliations and complex role-sets', in Judith R. Blau and Norman Goodman (eds), *Social Roles and Social Institutions. Essays in Honor of Rose Laub Coser*, Boulder, Col., Westview, 1991, pp. 37–51.
Blumenberg, Hans, *Die Legitimität der Neuzeit*, Frankfurt/M., Suhrkamp, 1966.
Boltanski, Luc, *The Making of a Class. Cadres in French Society*, Cambridge, Cambridge University Press, 1987.

Boltanski, Luc, and Laurent Thévenot, *De la justification. Les économies de la grandeur*, Paris, Gallimard, 1991.

Bonß, Wolfgang, *Die Einübung des Tatsachenblicks*, Frankfurt/M., Suhrkamp, 1982.

Boon, James A., *Other Tribes, Other Scribes. Symbolic Anthropology in the Comparative Study of Cultures, Histories, Religions, and Texts*, Cambridge, Cambridge University Press, 1982.

Bourdieu, Pierre, *The Logic of Practice*, Cambridge, Polity, 1990.

—— *Distinction. A Social Critique of the Judgement of Taste*, London, Routledge & Kegan Paul, 1984.

Bourdieu, Pierre, and Jean-Claude Passeron, 'Sociology and philosophy in France since 1945: death and resurrection of a philosophy without subject', *Social Research*, vol. 34, no. 1, 1967, pp. 162–212.

Boyer, Robert, *The Regulation School. A Critical Introduction*, New York, Columbia University Press, 1990.

—— *Technical Change and the Theory of 'Regulation'*, Paris, CEPREMAP papers no. 8707, 1987.

—— 'Conclusion: capitalismes fin de siècle', in Robert Boyer (ed.), *Capitalismes fin de siècle*, Paris, PUF, 1986.

Boyer, Robert and André Orléan, 'Les transformations des conventions salariales entre théorie et histoire: d'Henry Ford au fordisme', *Revue économique*, vol. 42, no. 2, 1991, pp. 233–72.

Boyer, Robert, Bernard Chavance, and Olivier Godard, 'La dialectique réversibilité-irréversibilité: une mise en perspective', in Robert Boyer, Bernard Chavance, and Olivier Godard (eds), *Les figures de l'irréversibilité en économie*, Paris, EHESS, 1991, pp. 11–33.

Braudel, Fernand, *La Mediterranée et le monde mediterranéen à l'époque de Philippe II*, Paris, Colin, 1949.

Breuer, Stefan, 'Die Evolution der Disziplin', *Kölner Zeitschrift für Soziologie und Sozialpsychologie*, vol. 30, 1978, pp. 409–37.

Briggs, Asa, 'The welfare state in historical perspective', *Archives européennes de sociologie*, vol. 2, 1961, pp. 221–58.

Brock, Ditmar, *Der schwierige Weg in die Moderne*, Frankfurt/M., Campus, 1991.

Buchmann, Marlis, *The Script of Life in Modern Society. Entry into Adulthood in a Changing World*, Chicago, The University of Chicago Press, 1989.

Bulmer, Martin, *The Chicago School of Sociology. Institutionalization, Diversity and the Rise of Sociological Research*, Chicago, The University of Chicago Press, 1984.

Bulmer, Martin, Kevin Bales, and Kathryn Kish Sklar (eds), *The Social Survey in Historical Perspective 1880–1940*, Cambridge, Cambridge University Press, 1991.

Burrows, Roger (ed.), *Deciphering the Enterprise Culture. Entrepreneurship, Petty Capitalism and the Restructuring of Britain*, London, Routledge, 1991.

Burrows, Roger, and Catherine Marsh, 'Consumption, class and contemporary sociology', in Roger Burrows and Catherine Marsh (eds), *Consumption and Class. Divisions and Change*, London, Macmillan, 1992, pp. 1–14.

Calhoun, Craig, 'Indirect relationships and imagined communities: large-scale social integration and the transformation of everyday life', in Pierre Bourdieu and James S. Coleman (eds), *Social Theory for a Changing Society*, Boulder, Col., and New York, Westview and Russell Sage, 1991, pp. 95–121.

Cameron, Rondo, 'A new view of European industrialization', *The Economic History Review*, vol. 37, no. 1, 1985, pp. 1–23.

Campbell, James, *The Community Reconstructs. The Meaning of Pragmatic Social Thought*, Urbana, Ill., University of Illinois Press, 1992.

Carens, Joseph H., 'Immigration and the welfare state', in Amy Gutmann (ed.), *Democracy and the Welfare State*, Princeton, Princeton University Press, 1988, pp. 207–30.

Cassese, Sabino, 'The rise and decline of the notion of the state', *International Political Science Review*, vol. 7, no. 2, 1986, pp. 120–30.
Castoriadis, Cornelius, *Le monde morcelé. Les carrefours du labyrinthe III*, Paris, Seuil, 1990.
—— *The Imaginary Institution of Society*, Cambridge, Mass., MIT Press, 1987.
Certeau, Michel de, *The Writing of History*, New York, Columbia University Press, 1988.
Chandler, Alfred D. Jr., *Scale and Scope. The Dynamics of Industrial Capitalism*, Cambridge, Mass., Belknap of Harvard University Press, 1990.
Chandler, Alfred D. Jr., and Richard S. Tedlow, *The Coming of Managerial Capitalism. A Casebook on the History of American Economic Institutions*, Homewood, Ill., Irwin, 1985.
Charle, Christophe, *Naissance des 'intellectuels' 1880–1900*, Paris, Minuit, 1990.
Cohen, Anthony P., *The Symbolic Construction of Community*, Chichester and London, Harwood and Tavistock, 1985.
Coleman, James S., 'Social theory, social research and a theory of action', *American Journal of Sociology*, vol. 91, 1986, pp. 1309–35.
—— 'The structure of society and the nature of social research', *Knowledge*, vol. 1, 1980, pp. 333–50.
—— 'Modernization: political aspects', in David L. Sills (ed.), *International Encyclopedia of the Social Sciences*, London and New York, Macmillan and Free Press, 1968, pp. 395–402.
Collini, Stefan, *Liberalism and Sociology. L.T. Hobhouse and Political Argument in England 1880–1914*, Cambridge, Cambridge University Press, 1979.
Collins, Randall, 'The romanticism of agency/structure versus the analysis of micro/macro', *Current Sociology*, vol. 40, no. 1, 1992, pp. 77–97.
Conze, Werner, 'Vom "Pöbel" zum "Proletariat": Sozialgeschichtliche Voraussetzungen für den Sozialismus in Deutschland', in Hans-Ulrich Wehler (ed.), *Moderne deutsche Sozialgeschichte*, Köln, Kiepenheuer und Witsch, 1966, pp. 111–36.
Cook, Deborah, 'Ruses de guerre: Baudrillard and Fiske on media reception', *Journal for the Theory of Social Behaviour*, vol. 22, no. 2, 1992, pp. 227–38.
Coser, Lewis A., 'Role-set theory and individual autonomy', in Judith R. Blau and Norman Goodman (eds), *Social Roles and Social Institutions. Essays in Honor of Rose Laub Coser*, Boulder, Col., Westview, 1991, pp. 13–20.
Cowan, Robin, 'Nuclear power reactors: a study in technological lock-in', *Journal of Economic History*, vol. 50, no. 3, 1990, pp. 541–67.
—— 'High technology and the economics of standardization', in Meinolf Dierkes and Ute Hoffmann (eds), *New Technology at the Outset. Social Forces in the Shaping of Technological Innovations*, Frankfurt/M. and Boulder, Col., Campus and Westview, 1992, pp. 279–300.
Crary, Jonathan, and Sanford Kwinter (eds), *Incorporations*, New York, Zone, 1992.
Crook, Stephen, Jan Pakulski, and Malcolm Waters, *Postmodernization. Change in Advanced Society*, London, Sage, 1992.
Crozier, Michel, 'Entsteht eine neue Managementlogik?', *Journal für Sozialforschung*, vol. 32, no. 2, 1992, pp. 131–40.
Crozier, Michel, Samuel P. Huntington, and Joji Watanuki, *The Crisis of Democracy. Report on the Governability of Democracies to the Trilateral Commission*, New York, New York University Press, 1975.
Cusack, Thomas R., *The Changing Contours of Government*, Berlin, WZB, 1991 (WZB paper P 91–304).
d'Arcy, François, and Guy Saez, 'De la représentation', in François d'Arcy (ed.), *La représentation*, Paris, Economica, 1985, pp. 7–31.
Dahrendorf, Ralf, 'Anmerkungen zur Diskussion der Referate von Karl R. Popper und

Theodor W. Adorno', in Adorno *et al., Der Positivismusstreit in der deutschen Soziologie*, Neuwied, Luchterhand, 1969.
Dalton, Russell J., 'Political parties and political representation: party supporters and party elites in nine nations', *Comparative Political Studies*, vol. 18, no. 3, 1985, pp. 267–99.
—— 'Responsiveness of parties and party systems to the new politics', in Hans-Dieter Klingemann, Richard Stöss, and Bernhard Weßels (eds), *Politische Klasse und politische Institutionen*, Opladen, Westdeutscher Verlag, 1991, pp. 39–56.
Dalton, Russell J., and Manfred Kuechler (eds), *Challenging the Political Order. New Social and Political Movements in Western Democracies*, Cambridge, Polity, 1990.
deLeon, Peter, 'Things fall apart; the center cannot hold: the crisis in governing', *Policy Sciences*, vol. 15, 1983, pp. 289–304.
Demo, David H., 'The self-concept over time: research issues and directions', *Annual Review of Sociology*, vol. 18, 1992, pp. 303–26.
Derrida, Jacques, *The Other Heading*, Bloomington, Ind., Indiana University Press, 1992.
Desrosières, Alain, 'How to make things which hold together: social science, statistics and the state', in Peter Wagner, Björn Wittrock, and Richard Whitley (eds), *Discourses on Society. The Shaping of the Social Science Disciplines*, Dordrecht, Kluwer, 1991, pp. 195–218.
—— 'The part in relation to the whole: how to generalise? The prehistory of representative sampling', in Martin Bulmer, Kevin Bales, and Kathryn Kish Sklar (eds), *The Social Survey in Historical Perspective 1880–1940*, Cambridge, Cambridge University Press, 1991, pp. 217–44.
Dierkes, Meinolf, and Ute Hoffmann (eds), *New Technology at the Outset. Social Forces in the Shaping of Technological Innovations*, Frankfurt/M. and Boulder, Col., Campus and Westview, 1992.
Diewald, Martin, *Soziale Beziehungen. Verlust oder Liberalisierung?*, Berlin, Sigma, 1991.
Dockès, Pierre, and Bernard Rosier, *L'histoire ambiguë. Croissance et développement en question*, Paris, PUF, 1988.
Dodier, Nicolas, 'Agir dans plusieurs mondes', *Critique*, nos. 529–30, 1991, pp. 427–58.
Donzelot, Jacques, 'The mobilization of society', in Graham Burchell, Colin Gordon, and Peter Miller (eds), *The Foucault Effect. Studies in Governmentality*, Chicago, The University of Chicago Press, 1991, pp. 169–79.
—— *L'invention du social. Essai sur le déclin des passions politiques*, Paris, Fayard, 1984.
Dore, Ronald, 'Sovereign individuals', in John A. Hall and I.C. Jarvie (eds), *Transition to Modernity. Essays on Power, Wealth and Belief*, Cambridge, Cambridge University Press, 1991, pp. 167–84.
Dosi, Giovanni, 'Technological paradigms and technological trajectories: a suggested interpretation of the determinants of technological change', *Research Policy*, vol. 11, 1982, pp. 147–62.
Douglas, Mary, *Purity and Danger. An Analysis of Concepts of Pollution and Taboo*, London, Routledge & Kegan Paul, 1966.
Dryzek, John S., *Discursive Democracy*, Cambridge, Cambridge University Press, 1990.
Duby, George, and Michelle Perrot (eds), *L'histoire de femmes*, Paris, Plon, several volumes 1991–2.
Dumont, Louis, *Essais sur l'individualisme. Une perspective anthropologique sur l'idéologie moderne*, Paris, Seuil, 1983.
—— *Homo aequalis. Genèse et épanouissement de l'idéologie économique*, Paris, Gallimard, 1985.
Dupuy, Jean-Pierre *et al.*, 'Introduction', *L'économie des conventions*, special issue of *Revue économique*, vol. 40, no. 2, 1989, pp. 141–5.
Eco, Umberto, 'On the crisis of the crisis of reason', *Travels in Hyperreality*, Orlando, Fla., Harcourt, Brace, Jovanovich, 1990.

Eisenstadt, Shmuel N. (ed.), *Patterns of Modernity, Vol. I. The West*, London, Pinter, 1987.
—— *Tradition, Change and Modernity*, New York, Wiley, 1973.
Elias, Norbert, *The Society of Individuals*, Oxford, Blackwell, 1991.
—— *Was ist Soziologie?*, München, Juventa, 1970.
Engler, Wolfgang, 'Vom Öffnen und Schließen der Aufstiegskanäle', in *Die zivilisatorische Lücke. Versuche über den Staatssozialismus*, Frankfurt/M., Suhrkamp, 1992, pp. 88–99.
Evers, Adalbert, and Helga Nowotny, *Über den Umgang mit Unsicherheit. Die Entdeckung der Gestaltbarkeit von Gesellschaft*, Frankfurt/M., Suhrkamp, 1987.
Ewald, François, 'Insurance and risk', in Graham Burchell, Colin Gordon, and Peter Miller (eds), *The Foucault Effect. Studies in Governmentality*, Chicago, The University of Chicago Press, 1991, pp. 197–210.
—— *L'Etat providence*, Paris, Grasset, 1986.
Fabian, Johannes, *Time and the Other. How Anthropology Makes its Object*, New York, Columbia University Press, 1983.
Featherstone, Mike, *Consumer Culture and Postmodernism*, London, Sage, 1991.
Feldman, Gerald D., 'German interest group alliances in war and inflation, 1914–1923', in Suzanne Berger (ed.), *Organizing Interests in Western Europe. Pluralism, Corporatism, and the Transformation of Politics*, Cambridge, Cambridge University Press, 1981, pp. 159–84.
Fischer, Frank, *Evaluating Public Policy*, Chicago, Nelson-Hall (forthcoming).
—— *Technocracy and the Politics of Expertise*, Newbury Park, Sage, 1990.
Flam, Helena (ed.), *Anti-Nuclear Movements and the State*, Edinburgh, Edinburgh University Press, 1993.
Flora, Peter, and Arnold J. Heidenheimer, 'The historical core and changing boundaries of the welfare state', in Peter Flora and Arnold J. Heidenheimer (eds), *The Development of Welfare States in Europe and America*, New Brunswick, N.J., Transaction, 1981, pp. 17–34.
Flora, Peter *et al.*, *State, Economy, and Society in Western Europe 1815–1975. A Data Handbook, Vol. 1. The Growth of Mass Democracies and Welfare States*, Frankfurt/M., Campus, 1983.
Foucault, Michel, 'Technologies of the self', in Luther H. Martin, Huck Gutman, and Patrick H. Hutton (eds), *Technologies of the Self. A Seminar with Michel Foucault*, Amherst, The University of Massachusetts Press, 1988.
—— 'Un cours inédit', *Le magazine littéraire*, no. 207, May 1984, pp. 35–9.
—— 'Governmentality', *Ideology and Consciousness*, no. 6, 1979, pp. 5–21.
—— *Discipline and Punish. The Birth of the Prison*, New York, Vintage, 1979.
—— *Les mots et les choses. Une archéologie des sciences humaines*, Paris, Gallimard, 1966.
—— *Folie et déraison. Histoire de la folie à l'âge classique*, Paris, Plon, 1961.
Fourastié, Jean, *Les trentes glorieuses ou la révolution invisible de 1946 à 1975*, Paris, Fayard, 1979.
Fourquet, François, *Les comptes de la puissance*, Paris, Encres, 1980.
Fraisse, Geneviève, *Muse de la raison. La démocratie exclusive et la différence des sexes*, Aix, Alinéa, 1989.
Fraisse, Robert, 'Les sciences sociales et l'Etat', *Esprit*, no. 50, February 1981, pp. 21–7.
Fraser, Ronald *et al.*, *1968. A Student Generation in Revolt*, London, Chatto & Windus, 1988.
Fraser, Steve, and Gary Gerstle (eds), *The Rise and Fall of the New Deal Order, 1930–1980*, Princeton, Princeton University Press, 1989.
Freidson, Eliott, *Professional Powers. A Study of the Institutionalization of Formal Knowledge*, Chicago, The University of Chicago Press, 1988.
Fridjonsdottir, Katrin, 'Social science and the "Swedish model": sociology at the service of

the welfare state', in Peter Wagner, Björn Wittrock, and Richard Whitley (eds), *Discourses on Society. The Shaping of the Social Science Disciplines*, Dordrecht, Kluwer, 1991, pp. 247–70.

Friedman, George, and Meredith Lebard, *The Coming War with Japan*, New York, St. Martin's Press, 1991.

Friedman, Jonathan, 'Narcissism, roots and postmodernity: the constitution of selfhood in the global crisis', in Scott Lash and Jonathan Friedman (eds), *Modernity and Identity*, Oxford, Blackwell, 1992, pp. 331–66.

Friese, Heidrun, *Geschichtsbilder. Konstruktionen der vergangenen Zeit*, Berlin, Mimeo, 1991.

—— *Ordnungen der Zeit. Zur sozialen Konstruktion von Temporalstrukturen in einem sizilianischen Ort*, Ph.D. thesis, University of Amsterdam, 1991.

Friese, Heidrun, and Peter Wagner, *Der Raum des Gelehrten. Eine Topographie wissenschaftlicher Praxis*, Berlin, in preparation.

Frisby, David, *Fragments of Modernity. Theories of Modernity in the Works of Simmel, Kracauer and Benjamin*, Cambridge, Polity, 1985.

Fröbel, Folker, Jürgen Heinrichs, and Otto Kreye, *The New International Division of Labour*, Cambridge and Paris, Cambridge University Press and Editions de la Maison des Sciences de l'Homme, 1980.

Fromm, Erich, *Escape from Freedom*, New York, Holt, Rinehart & Winston, 1941.

Fullinwider, Robert K., 'Citizenship and welfare', in Amy Gutmann (ed.), *Democracy and the Welfare State*, Princeton, Princeton University Press, 1988, pp. 261–78.

Gardels, Nathan, 'Two concepts of nationalism: an interview with Isaiah Berlin', *New York Review of Books*, 21 November 1991, pp. 19–23.

Garin, Eugenio, *La cultura italiana tra '800 e '900*, Bari, Laterza, 1961.

Gellner, Ernest, *Plough, Sword and Book. The Structure of Human History*, London, Collins Harvill, 1988.

—— *Nations and Nationalism*, Ithaca, Cornell University Press, 1983.

Gergen, Kenneth J., *The Saturated Self. Dilemmas of Identity in Contemporary Life*, New York, Basic Books, 1991.

Gerstenberger, Heide, *Die subjektlose Gewalt. Theorie der Entstehung bürgerlicher Staatsgewalt*, Münster, Westfälisches Dampfboot, 1990.

Gerth, H.H., and C. Wright Mills (eds), *From Max Weber. Essays in Sociology*, New York, Oxford University Press, 1946.

Giddens, Anthony, 'Is the American Dream over?', *Contemporary Sociology*, vol. 21, no. 4, 1992; review essay on Alan Wolfe (ed.), *America at Century's End*, Berkeley, University of California Press, 1992, pp. 430–2.

—— *Modernity and Self-Identity. Self and Society in the Late Modern Age*, Cambridge, Polity, 1991.

—— *The Consequences of Modernity*, Cambridge, Polity, 1990.

—— *The Nation-State and Violence*, Cambridge, Polity, 1985.

—— *The Constitution of Society. Outline of a Theory of Structuration*, Cambridge, Polity, 1984.

Gilbert, Claude, 'Fin de contrat', *Traverses*, nos. 33–4, 1985, pp. 20–5.

Gilbert, Claude, and Marc Guillaume, 'L'acharnement politique ou l'effort de représentation', in François d'Arcy (ed.), *La représentation*, Paris, Economica, 1985, pp. 89–97.

Gilbert, Nigel, Roger Burrows, and Anna Pollert, 'Introduction: Fordism, post-Fordism and economic flexibility', in Nigel Gilbert, Roger Burrows, and Anna Pollert (eds), *Fordism and Flexibility. Divisions and Change*, Basingstoke, Macmillan, 1992, pp. 1–9.

Glyn, Andrew, Alan Hughes, Alain Lipietz, and Ajit Singh, 'The rise and fall of the golden age', in Stephen A. Marglin and Juliet B. Schor (eds), *The Golden Age of Capitalism. Reinterpreting the Postwar Experience*, Oxford, Clarendon, 1990, pp. 39–125.

Glyn, Andrew, and Bob Sutcliffe, *British Capitalism, Workers and the Profit Squeeze*, Harmondsworth, Penguin, 1972.
Gordon, Colin, 'Governmental rationality: an introduction', in Graham Burchell, Colin Gordon, and Peter Miller (eds), *The Foucault Effect. Studies in Governmentality*, Chicago, The University of Chicago Press, 1991, pp. 1–51.
—— 'The soul of the citizen: Max Weber and Michel Foucault on rationality and government', in Scott Lash and Sam Whimster (eds), *Max Weber, Rationality and Modernity*, London, Allen & Unwin, 1987, pp. 293–316.
Gould, Carol C., 'Private rights and public virtues: women, the family, and democracy', in Carol C. Gould (ed.), *Beyond Domination. New Perspectives on Women and Philosophy*, Totowa, N.J., Rowman & Allanheld, 1984, pp. 3–18.
Granovetter, Mark, 'Economic action and social structure: the problem of embeddedness', *American Journal of Sociology*, vol. 91, no. 3, 1985, pp. 481–510.
Gray, John, 'Totalitarianism, reform, and civil society', in Ellen Frankel Paul (ed.), *Totalitarianism at the Crossroads*, New Brunswick, N.J., Transaction, 1990, pp. 97–142.
Graziani, Luigi, *Clientelismo e sistema politico. Il caso dell'Italia*, Milan, Angeli, 1984.
Griffin, Roger, *The Nature of Fascism*, London, Pinter, 1991.
Gross, Malcolm, and Geoff Payne (eds), *Work and the Enterprise Culture*, London, Falmer, 1991.
Gross, Malcolm, and Geoff Payne, 'Introduction: work and the enterprise culture', in Malcolm Gross and Geoff Payne (eds), *Work and the Enterprise Culture*, London, Falmer, 1991, pp. 1–8.
Guillaume, Marc, 'La stratégie du lézard', *Traverses*, nos. 33–4, 1985, pp. 29–32.
Gunn, Giles, *Thinking Across the American Grain. Ideology, Intellect, and the New Pragmatism*, Chicago, The University of Chicago Press, 1992.
Gunnell, John G., 'In search of the state: political science as an emerging discipline in the US', in Peter Wagner, Björn Wittrock, and Richard Whitley (eds), *Discourses on Society. The Shaping of the Social Science Disciplines*, Dordrecht, Kluwer, 1991, pp. 123–61.
Habermas, Jürgen, *Faktizität und Geltung. Beiträge zur Diskurstheorie des Rechts und des demokratischen Rechtsstaats*, Frankfurt/M., Suhrkamp, 1992.
—— 'Ist der Herzschlag der Revolution zum Stillstand gekommen? Volkssouveränität als Verfahren: Ein normativer Begriff von Öffentlichkeit', in Forum für Philosophie Bad Hamburg (ed.), *Die Ideen von 1789 in der deutschen Rezeption*, Frankfurt/M., Suhrkamp, 1989, pp. 7–36.
—— *The Structural Transformation of the Public Sphere. An Inquiry into a Category of Bourgeois Society*, Cambridge, Mass., MIT Press, 1989.
—— *The Philosophical Discourse of Modernity*, Cambridge, Mass., MIT Press, 1987.
—— *The Theory of Communicative Action*, Boston, Beacon, 1984–7.
—— *Zur Rekonstruktion des Historischen Materialismus*, Frankfurt/M., Suhrkamp, 1976.
—— *Legitimationsprobleme im Spätkapitalismus*, Frankfurt/M., Suhrkamp, 1973.
Hacking, Ian, *The Taming of Chance*, Cambridge, Cambridge University Press, 1990.
Hall, John A., and I.C. Jarvie (eds), *Transition to Modernity. Essays on Power, Wealth and Belief*, Cambridge, Cambridge University Press, 1991.
Hall, Peter A., 'The evolution of economic policy under Mitterrand', in George Ross, Stanley Hoffmann, and Sylvia Malzacher (eds), *The Mitterrand Experiment*, Cambridge, Polity, 1987, pp. 54–72.
Hancock, M. Donald, and Gideon Sjoberg (eds), *Politics in the Post-Welfare State. Responses to the New Individualism*, New York, Columbia University Press, 1972.
Harding, Sandra, 'Is gender a variable in conceptions of rationality? A survey of issues', in Carol C. Gould (ed.), *Beyond Domination. New Perspectives on Women and Philosophy*,

Totowa, N.J., Rowman & Allanheld, 1984, pp. 43–63.

Hartz, Louis, *The Liberal Tradition in America. An Interpretation of American Political Thought Since the Revolution*, New York, Harcourt, Brace, & World, 1955.

Harvey, David, *The Condition of Postmodernity*, Oxford, Blackwell, 1989.

Hawthorn, Geoffrey, *Enlightenment and Despair. A History of Sociology*, Cambridge, Cambridge University Press, 1976.

Heelas, Paul, 'Reforming the self: enterprise and the characters of Thatcherism', in Russel Keat and Nicholas Abercrombie (eds), *Enterprise Culture*, London, Routledge, 1991, pp. 72–90.

Heelas, Paul, and Paul Morris (eds), *The Values of the Enterprise Culture. The Moral Debate*, London, Routledge, 1992.

Heilbron, Johan, *Sociologie in Frankrijk*, Amsterdam, SISWO, 1983.

Heimann, Eduard, *Soziale Theorie des Kapitalismus. Theorie der Sozialpolitik*, Frankfurt/M., Suhrkamp, 1980.

Heins, Volker, 'Ambivalenzen der Zivilgesellschaft', *Politische Vierteljahresschrift*, vol. 33, no. 2, 1992, pp. 235–42.

Held, David, 'Democracy, the nation-state and the global system', in David Held (ed.), *Political Theory Today*, Cambridge, Polity, 1991, pp. 197–235.

Heller, Agnes, 'The concept of the political revisited', in David Held (ed.), *Political Theory Today*, Cambridge, Polity, 1991, pp. 330–43.

Heller, Agnes, and Ferenc Fehér, *The Postmodern Political Condition*, Cambridge, Polity, 1988.

Herf, Jeffrey, *Reactionary Modernism. Technology, Culture and Politics in Weimar and the Third Reich*, Cambridge, Cambridge University Press, 1984.

Herzog, Dietrich, 'Was heißt und zu welchem Ende studiert man Repräsentation?', in Dietrich Herzog and Bernhard Weßels (eds), *Konfliktpotentiale und Konsensstrategien*, Opladen, Westdeutscher Verlag, 1989, pp. 307–35.

Hindess, Barry, 'Imaginary presuppositions of democracy', *Economy and Society*, vol. 20, no. 2, 1991, pp. 173–95.

Hirschman, Albert O., *Exit, Voice and Loyalty*, Cambridge, Mass., Harvard University Press, 1970.

Hirst, Paul, and Jonathan Zeitlin, 'Flexible specialization versus post-Fordism: theory, evidence and policy implications', *Economy and Society*, vol. 20, no. 1, 1991, pp. 1–56.

Hobsbawm, Eric J., *Nations and Nationalism since 1780. Programme, Myth, Reality*, Cambridge, Cambridge University Press, 1990.

Hobsbawm, Eric J., and Terence Ranger (eds), *The Invention of Tradition*, Cambridge, Cambridge University Press, 1983.

Hofmann, Jeanette, 'Implizite Theorien: Interpretationsprobleme regionaler Technologiepolitik', doctoral dissertation, Free University of Berlin, 1992.

Hollander, Paul, *Anti-Americanism. Critiques at Home and Abroad 1965–1990*, New York, Oxford University Press, 1992.

—— 'Border controls: an integral part of the Soviet social-political system', *The Many Faces of Socialism*, New Brunswick, N.J., Transaction, 1983, pp. 79–103.

Hollis, Martin, 'Of masks and men', in Michael Carrithers, Steven Collins, and Steven Lukes (eds), *The Category of the Person. Anthropology, Philosophy, History*, Cambridge, Cambridge University Press, 1985.

Holmberg, Sören, 'Political representation in Sweden', in Hans-Dieter Klingemann, Richard Stöss, and Bernhard Weßels (eds), *Politische Klasse und politische Institutionen*, Opladen, Westdeutscher Verlag, 1991, pp. 290–324.

Holmes, Helen Bequaert, 'A feminist analysis of the universal declaration of human rights', in Carol C. Gould (ed.), *Beyond Domination. New Perspectives on Women and Philosophy*, Totowa, N.J., Rowman & Allanheld, 1984, pp. 250–64.

Hondrich, Karl-Otto, *Lehrmeister Krieg*, Reinbek, Rowohlt, 1992.
Honegger, Claudia, *Die Ordnung der Geschlechter. Die Wissenschaften vom Menschen und das Weib, 1750–1850*, Frankfurt/M., Campus, 1991.
Honneth, Axel, 'Atomisierung und Sittlichkeit: Zu Hegels Kritik der Französischen Revolution', in Forum für Philosophie Bad Homburg (ed.), *Die Ideen von 1789 in der deutschen Rezeption*, Frankfurt/M., Suhrkamp, 1989, pp. 186–204.
Hughes, Thomas P., *American Genesis. A Century of Invention and Technological Enthusiasm 1870–1970*, New York, Viking, 1989.
Inkeles, Alex, *Exploring Individual Modernity*, New York, Columbia University Press, 1983.
Isaac, Jeffrey C., 'Republicanism vs. liberalism? A reconsideration', *History of Political Thought*, vol. 9, no. 2, 1988, pp. 349–77.
Jameson, Fredric, *Postmodernism, or, The Cultural Logic of Late Capitalism*, Durham, N.C., Duke University Press, 1991.
Jessop, Bob, Hans Kastendiek, Klaus Nielsen, and Ove K. Pedersen (eds), *The Politics of Flexibility. Restructuring State and Industry in Britain, Germany and Scandinavia*, Aldershot, Elgar, 1991.
Joas, Hans, *Pragmatism and Social Theory*, Chicago, University of Chicago Press, 1993.
—— 'Symbolic Interactionism', in Anthony Giddens and Jonathan H. Turner (eds), *Social Theory Today*, Cambridge, Polity, 1987, pp. 82–116 (now reprinted as 'Pragmatism in American sociology', in Joas, *Pragmatism*, pp. 14–51).
—— 'The democratization of differentiation: on the creativity of collective action', in Jeffrey Alexander and Piotr Sztompka (eds), *Rethinking Progress. Movements, Forces and Ideas at the End of the Twentieth Century*, Boston, Unwin Hyman, 1990, pp. 182–201.
—— *Die Kreativität des Handelns*, Frankfurt/M., Suhrkamp, 1992 (English translation forthcoming).
Joerges, Bernward, 'Soziologie und Maschinerie: Vorschläge zu einer "realistischen" Techniksoziologie', in Peter Weingart (ed.), *Technik als sozialer Prozeß*, Frankfurt/M., Suhrkamp, 1989, pp. 44–86.
—— 'Technische Normen – soziale Normen?', *Soziale Welt*, vol. 40, nos. 1–2, pp. 1989, 242–58.
Kaelble, Hartmut, 'Boom und gesellschaftlicher Wandel 1948–1973: Frankreich und die Bundesrepublik Deutschland im Vergleich', in Hartmut Kaelble (ed.), *Der Boom 1948–1973. Gesellschaftliche und wirtschaftliche Folgen in der Bundesrepublik Deutschland und in Europa*, Opladen, Westdeutscher Verlag, 1992, pp. 219–47.
—— 'The rise of the managerial enterprise in Germany, c. 1870 to c. 1930', in Kesaji Kobayashi and Hidemasa Morikawa (eds), *Development of Managerial Enterprise*, Tokyo, University of Tokyo Press, 1986, pp. 71–97.
—— *Social Mobility in the Nineteenth and Twentieth Centuries. Europe and America in Comparative Perspective*, New York, St. Martin's Press, 1986.
Kaern, Michael, Bernard S. Phillips, and Robert S. Cohen (eds), *Georg Simmel and Contemporary Sociology*, Dordrecht, Kluwer, 1990.
Kanter, Rosabeth Moss, 'The future of bureaucracy and hierarchy in organizational theory: a report from the field', in Pierre Bourdieu and James S. Coleman (eds), *Social Theory for a Changing Society*, Boulder, Col., and New York, Westview and Russell Sage, 1991, pp. 63–87.
—— *When Giants Learn to Dance. Mastering the Challenges of Strategy, Management, and Careers in the 1990s*, New York, Simon & Schuster, 1989.
Kaplan, Louis, *Telepathic Technologies. A Seance in Fortean Science*, Berlin, WZB, 1991 (WZB Paper FS II 91–504).
Katznelson, Ira, 'Knowledge about what? Policy intellectuals within the state and

capitalism', in Dietrich Rueschemeyer and Theda Skocpol (eds), *Social Knowledge and the Origins of Social Policies*, Princeton and New York, Princeton University Press and Russell Sage Foundation (forthcoming).

—— 'Working-class formation: constructing cases and comparisons', in Ira Katznelson and Aristide R. Zolberg (eds), *Working-Class Formation. Nineteenth-Century Patterns in Europe and the United States*, Princeton, Princeton University Press, 1986, pp. 3–41.

Kaufmann, Franz Xaver, *Religion und Modernität. Sozialwissenschaftliche Perspektiven*, Tübingen, Mohr, 1989.

Keane, John, 'Despotism and democracy', in John Keane (ed.), *Civil Society and the State. New European Perspectives*, London, Verso, 1988, pp. 35–71.

Keane, John, and John Owens, *After Full Employment*, London, Hutchinson, 1986.

Keat, Russel, 'Introduction: starship Britain or universal enterprise', in Russel Keat and Nicholas Abercrombie (eds), *Enterprise Culture*, London, Routledge, 1991, pp. 1–17.

Keat, Russel, and Nicholas Abercrombie (eds), *Enterprise Culture*, London, Routledge, 1991.

Kellner, Douglas, 'Popular culture and the construction of postmodern identities', in Scott Lash and Jonathan Friedman (eds), *Modernity and Identity*, Oxford, Blackwell, 1992, pp. 141–77.

Kern, Horst, and Charles F. Sabel, 'Trade unions and decentralized production: a sketch of strategic problems in the West German labor movement', *Politics and Society*, vol. 19, no. 4, 1991, pp. 373–402.

Kitschelt, Herbert, 'New social movements and the decline of party organization', in Russell J. Dalton and Manfred Kuechler (eds), *Challenging the Political Order. New Social and Political Movements in Western Democracies*, Cambridge, Polity, 1990, pp. 179–208.

Klingemann, Hans-Dieter, Richard Stöss, and Bernhard Weßels, 'Politische Klasse und politische Institutionen', in Hans-Dieter Klingemann, Richard Stöss, and Bernhard Weßels (eds), *Politische Klasse und politische Institutionen*, Opladen, Westdeutscher Verlag, 1991, pp. 9–36.

Knie, Andreas, *Diesel – Genese einer Technik*, Berlin, Edition Sigma, 1990.

Kocka, Jürgen, 'Class formation, interest articulation and public policy: the origins of the German white-collar class in the late nineteenth and early twentieth centuries', in Suzanne Berger (ed.), *Organizing Interests in Western Europe. Pluralism, Corporatism, and the Transformation of Politics*, Cambridge, Cambridge University Press, 1981, pp. 63–81.

—— *White Collar Workers in America 1890–1940. A Social-Political History in International Perspective*, London, Sage, 1980.

Kohli, Martin, 'Social organization and subjective construction of the life course', in Aage B. Sorensen, Franz E. Weinert, and Lonnie R. Sherrod (eds), *Human Development and the Life Course*, Hillsdale, N.J., Lawrence Erlbaum, 1986, pp. 271–92.

Kondylis, Panajotis, *Der Niedergang der bürgerlichen Denk- und Lebensform. Die liberale Moderne und die massendemokratische Postmoderne*, Weinheim, VCH, Acta humaniora, 1991.

Koselleck, Reinhart, 'Zur historisch-politischen Semantik asymmetrischer Gegenbegriffe', *Vergangene Zukunft. Zur Semantik geschichtlicher Zeiten*, Frankfurt/M., Suhrkamp, 1979.

—— entries 'Fortschritt' and 'Geschichte, Historie', in Otto Brunner, Werner Conze, and Reinhart Koselleck (eds), *Geschichtliche Grundbegriffe*, Stuttgart, Klett-Cotta, vol. 2, 1975, pp. 351–423 and 593–717.

Krieken, Robert van, 'Violence, self-discipline and modernity: beyond the "civilizing process" ', *The Sociological Review*, vol. 37, no. 2, 1982, pp. 193–218.

Krohn, Wolfgang, Günter Küppers, and Helga Nowotny (eds), *Selforganization. Portrait of a Scientific Revolution*, Dordrecht, Kluwer, 1990.

Krüger, Lorenz, Lorraine Daston, and Michael Heidelberger (eds), *The Probabilistic Revolution, Vol. 1. Ideas in History*, Cambridge, Mass., MIT Press, 1987.

Krüger, Lorenz, Gerd Gigerenzer, and Mary S. Morgan (eds), *The Probabilistic Revolution, Vol. 2. Ideas in the Sciences*, Cambridge, Mass., MIT Press, 1987.
Lacorne, Denis, Jacques Rupnik, and Marie-France Toinet (eds), *The Rise and Fall of Anti-Americanism. A Century of French Perception*, Basingstoke, Macmillan, 1990.
Lacoue-Labarthe, Philippe, and Jean-Luc Nancy, 'Le "retrait" du politique', in Philippe Lacoue-Labarthe and Jean-Luc Nancy (eds), *Le retrait du politique*, Paris, Galilée, 1983, pp. 183–98.
Landes, David S., *The Unbound Prometheus. Technological Change and Industrial Development in Western Europe from 1750 to the Present*, Cambridge, Cambridge University Press, 1969.
Landes, Joan B., *Women and the Public Sphere in the Age of the French Revolution*, Ithaca, Cornell University Press, 1988.
Lasch, Christopher, 'Toward a theory of post-industrial society', in M. Donald Hancock and Gideon Sjoberg (eds), *Politics in the Post-Welfare State. Responses to the New Individualism*, New York, Columbia University Press, 1972, pp. 36–50.
Lash, Scott, *Sociology of Postmodernism*, London, Routledge, 1990.
—— 'Modernity or modernism? Weber and contemporary social theory', Scott Lash and Sam Whimster (eds), *Max Weber, Rationality and Modernity*, London, Allen & Unwin, 1987, pp. 355–77.
Lash, Scott, and John Urry, *The End of Organized Capitalism*, Cambridge, Polity, 1987.
Lash, Scott, and Sam Whimster (eds), *Max Weber, Rationality and Modernity*, London, Allen & Unwin, 1987.
Latouche, Serge, 'La fin de la société des nations', *Traverses*, nos. 33–4, 1985, pp. 36–43.
Latour, Bruno, *Nous n'avons jamais étés modernes. Essai d'anthropologie symétrique*, Paris, La Découverte, 1991.
—— *Science in Action. How to Follow Scientists and Engineers Through Society*, Milton Keynes, Open University Press, 1987.
Laub Coser, Rose, *In Defense of Modernity. Role Complexity and Individual Autonomy*, Stanford, Stanford University Press, 1991.
Lazare, Daniel, 'Collapse of a city', in *Dissent*, Spring 1991, pp. 267–75.
Lazarsfeld, Paul F., 'Remarks on administrative and critical communications research', *Studies in Philosophy and Social Science*, vol. 9, 1941, pp. 2–16.
Lefort, Claude, *Democracy and Political Theory*, Cambridge, Polity, 1988.
—— *The Political Forms of Modern Society*, Cambridge, Polity, 1986.
Lehner, Franz, 'The vanishing of spontaneity: socio-economic conditions of the welfare state', *European Journal of Political Research*, vol. 11, 1983, pp. 437–47.
Leibfried, Stephan, 'Nutritional minima: on the institutionalization of professional knowledge in national social policy in the US and Germany', in Dietrich Rueschemeyer and Theda Skocpol (eds), *Social Knowledge and the Origins of Social Policies*, Princeton and New York, Princeton University Press and Russell Sage Foundation (forthcoming).
Leinberger, Bruce, and Paul Tucker, *The New Individualists. The Generation After Organization Man*, New York, Harper & Collins, 1991.
Lenin, Vladimir Iljitch, *Drei Quellen und drei Bestandteile des Marxismus*, Berlin, Dietz, 1966.
Lepenies, Wolf, 'Das Ende der Naturgeschichte und der Beginn der Moderne', in Reinhart Koselleck (ed.), *Studien zum Beginn der modernen Welt*, Stuttgart, Klett, 1977, pp. 317–51.
Lepsius, M. Rainer, 'Soziologische Theoreme über die Sozialstruktur der "Moderne" und die "Modernisierung" ', in Reinhart Koselleck (ed.), *Studien zum Beginn der modernen Welt*, Stuttgart, Klett, 1977, pp. 10–29.
Lerner, Daniel, 'Modernization: social aspects', in David L. Sills (ed.), *International*

Encyclopedia of the Social Sciences, London and New York, Macmillan and Free Press, 1968, pp. 386–95.

Levitt, Cyril, *Children of Privilege. Student Revolt in the Sixties. A Study of Student Movements in Canada, the United States, and West Germany*, Toronto, University of Toronto Press, 1984.

Lijphart, Arend, *Democracy in Plural Societies. A Comparative Exploration*, New Haven, Yale University Press, 1977.

—— *The Politics of Accommodation Pluralism and Democracy in the Netherlands*, Berkeley, University of California Press, 1975.

Lindblom, Charles E., *Inquiry and Change. The Troubled Attempt to Understand and Shape Society*, New Haven and New York, Yale University Press and Russell Sage Foundation, 1990.

Lipset, Seymour Martin, 'No third way: a comparative perspective on the Left', in Hans-Dieter Klingemann, Richard Stöss, and Bernhard Weßels (eds), *Politische Klasse und politische Institutionen*, Opladen, Westdeutscher Verlag, 1991, pp. 57–106.

Lipset, Seymour Martin, and Stein Rokkan, 'Cleavage structures, party systems, and voter alignments: an introduction', in Seymour Lipset and Stein Rokkan (eds), *Party Systems and Voter Alignments*, New York, Free Press, 1967.

Lipset, Seymour Martin, and Stein Rokkan (eds), *Party Systems and Voter Alignments*, New York, Free Press, 1967.

List, Friedrich, *The National System of Political Economy*, New York, Longmans Green, 1904 [1841].

Lowi, Theodor J., *The End of Liberalism. Ideology, Policy, and the Crisis of Public Authority*, New York, Norton, 1969.

Löwith, Karl, *Max Weber and Karl Marx*, London, Allen & Unwin, 1982 [1932].

Luard, Evan, *The Globalization of Politics. The Changed Focus of Political Action in the Modern World*, Basingstoke, Macmillan, 1990.

Lüdtke, Alf, ' "Kolonisierung der Lebenswelten" – oder: Geschichte als Einbahnstraße?', *Das Argument*, no. 140, 1986, pp. 536–41.

Lustig, R. Jeffrey, *Corporate Liberalism. The Origins of Modern American Political Theory*, Berkeley, University of California Press, 1982.

Lutz, Burkart, 'Die Singularität der europäischen Prosperität nach dem Zweiten Weltkrieg', in Hartmut Kaelble (ed.), *Der Boom 1948–1973*, Opladen, Westdeutscher Verlag, 1992, pp. 35–59.

—— *Der kurze Traum immerwährender Prosperität*, Frankfurt/M., Campus, 1984.

Lyotard, Jean-François, 'A l'insu (unbeknownst)', in Miami Theory Collective (ed.), *Community at Loose Ends*, Minneapolis, University of Minnesota Press, 1991.

—— 'Une ligne de résistance', *Traverses*, no. 33–4, 1985, pp. 60–5.

—— *Le différend*, Paris, Minuit, 1983.

MacKenzie, Donald, *Statistics in Britain, 1865–1930. The Social Construction of Scientific Knowledge*, Edinburgh, Edinburgh University Press, 1981.

Maddison, Angus, *Dynamic Forces in Capitalist Development. A Long-Run Comparative View*, Oxford, Oxford University Press, 1991.

Maffesoli, Michel, *La transfiguration du politique. La tribalisation du monde*, Paris, Grasset, 1992.

—— 'Post-modern sociality', *Telos*, no. 85, 1990, pp. 89–92.

—— *Le temps des tribus. Le déclin de l'individualisme dans les sociétés de masse*, Paris, Méridiens Klincksieck, 1988.

Maier, Charles E. (ed.), *The Changing Boundaries of the Political*, Cambridge, Cambridge University Press, 1987.

Maier, Hans, *Die ältere deutsche Staats- und Verwaltungslehre*, München, Beck, 1980 (first published in Neuwied, Luchterhand, 1966).

Manicas, Peter T., *A History and Philosophy of the Social Sciences*, Oxford, Blackwell, 1987.

Mann, Michael, 'The emergence of modern European nationalism', in John A. Hall and I.C. Jarvie (eds), *Transition to Modernity. Essays on Power, Wealth and Belief*, Cambridge, Cambridge University Press, 1991, pp. 137–65.

—— *The Sources of Social Power, Vol. I. A History of Power from the Beginning to A.D. 1760*, Cambridge, Cambridge University Press, 1986.

Marcuse, Herbert, *One-Dimensional Man. Studies in the Ideology of Advanced Industrial Society*, Boston, Beacon, 1964.

Marglin, Stephen, 'Lessons of the golden age: an overview', in Stephen A. Marglin and Juliet B. Schor (eds), *The Golden Age of Capitalism. Reinterpreting the Postwar Experience*, Oxford, Clarendon, 1990, pp. 1–38.

Marglin, Stephen B., and Juliet B. Schor (eds), *The Golden Age of Capitalism. Reinterpreting the Postwar Experience*, Oxford, Clarendon Press, 1990.

Marshall, Thomas Humphrey, 'Citizenship and social class', *Class, Citizenship, and Social Development*, Garden City, N.Y., Doubleday, 1964.

Marx, Karl, 'Der achtzehnte Brumaire des Louis Bonaparte', in Karl Marx and Friedrich Engels, *Ausgewählte Schriften*, vol. 1, Berlin, Dietz, 1972.

Marz, Lutz, 'Geständnisse und Erkenntnisse: Zum Quellenproblem empirischer Transformationsforschung', in Martin Heidenreich (ed.), *Krisen, Kader, Kombinate. Kontinuität und Wandel in ostdeutschen Betrieben*, Berlin, Sigma, 1992, pp. 215–37.

—— 'System-Zeit und Entökonomisierung: Zu Zeit/Macht-Dispositionen und mentalen Dispositionen in realsozialistischen Wirtschaften', in Rudi Schmidt (ed.), *Zwischenbilanz Analysen Zum Transformationsprozeß der ostdeutschen Industrie*, Berlin, Akademie Verlag, 1993, pp. 73–112.

Mayntz, Renate, 'Politische Steuerung und gesellschaftliche Steuerungsprobleme – Anmerkungen zu einem theoretischen Paradigma', in Thomas Ellwein, Joachim Jens Hesse, Renate Mayntz, and Fritz W. Scharpf (eds), *Jahrbuch zur Staats- und Verwaltungswissenschaft*, vol. 1, Baden-Baden, Nomos, 1987, pp. 89–110.

Mead, George Herbert, *Mind, Self, and Society from the Standpoint of a Social Behaviorist*, Chicago, University of Chicago Press, 1934.

Megerle, Klaus, 'Die Radikalisierung blieb aus: Zur Integration gesellschaftlicher Gruppen in der Bundesrepublik während des Nachkriegsbooms', in Hartmut Kaelble (ed.), *Der Boom 1948–1973. Gesellschaftliche und wirtschaftliche Folgen in der Bundesrepublik Deutschland und in Europa*, Opladen, Westdeutscher Verlag, 1992, pp. 107–26

Melucci, Alberto, 'Social movements and the democratization of everyday life', in John Keane (ed.), *Civil Society and the State. New European Perspectives*, London, Verso, 1988, pp. 245–60.

Merton, Robert K., *Social Theory and Social Structure*, New York, Free Press, 1957.

Meyer, John W., 'The self and the life course: institutionalization and its effects', in Aage B. Sorensen, Franz E. Weinert, and Lonnie R. Sherrod (eds), *Human Development and the Life Course*, Hillsdale, N.J., Lawrence Erlbaum, 1986, pp. 199–216.

Meyrowitz, Joshua, *No Sense of Place. The Impact of Electronic Media on Social Behavior*, New York, Oxford University Press, 1985.

Miller, Daniel, *Material Culture and Mass Consumption*, Oxford, Blackwell, 1987.

Miller, Peter, and Nikolas Rose, 'Governing economic life', *Economy and Society*, vol. 19, no. 1, 1990, pp. 1–31.

Mirbach, Thomas, *Überholte Legitimität? Oder: Auf dem Weg zu einem neuen Politikbegriff*, Darmstadt, Wissenschaftliche Buchgesellschaft, 1990.

Mitzman, Arthur, 'The civilizing offensive: mentalities, high culture and individual psyches', *Journal of Social History*, vol. 20, no. 4, 1987, pp. 663–87.

Mommsen, Wolfgang J., 'The varieties of the nation state in modern history: liberal, imperial, fascist and contemporary notions of nation and nationality', in Michael Mann (ed.), *The Rise and Decline of the Nation State*, Oxford, Blackwell, 1990, pp. 210–26.

Morris, Paul, 'Freeing the spirit of enterprise: the genesis and development of the concept of enterprise culture', in Russel Keat and Nicholas Abercrombie (eds), *Enterprise Culture*, London, Routledge, 1991, pp. 21–37.

Mouffe, Chantal, 'Democratic citizenship and the political community', in Miami Theory Collective (ed.), *Community at Loose Ends*, Minneapolis, University of Minnesota Press, 1991.

Muller, Pierre, and Guy Saez, 'Neo-corporatisme et crise de la représentation', in François d'Arcy (ed.), *La représentation*, Paris, Economica, 1985, pp. 121–40.

Niethammer, Lutz, *Posthistoire. Ist die Geschichte zu Ende?*, Reinbek, Rowohlt, 1989.

Noble, David F., *America by Design. Science, Technology, and the Rise of Corporate Capitalism*, New York, Knopf, 1977.

Noiriel, Gérard, *La tyrannie du national. Le droit d'asile en Europe 1793–1993*, Paris, Calmann-Lévy, 1991.

O'Neill, John, 'The disciplinary society: from Weber to Foucault', *The British Journal of Sociology*, vol. 37, no. 1, 1986, pp. 42–60.

OECD, *The Welfare State in Crisis*, Paris, OECD, 1981.

Oestreich, Gerhard, *Neostoicism and the Early Modern State*, Cambridge, Cambridge University Press, 1982.

Offe, Claus, 'Fessel und Bremse: Moralische und institutionelle Aspekte "intelligenter Selbstbeschränkung" ', in Axel Honneth, Thomas McCarthy, Claus Offe, and Albrecht Wellmer (eds), *Zwischenbetrachtungen. Im Prozeß der Aufklärung*, Frankfurt/M., Suhrkamp, 1989, pp. 739–74.

—— *Disorganized Capitalism*, Cambridge, Mass., MIT Press, 1987.

—— 'Die Staatstheorie auf der Suche nach ihrem Gegenstand: Beobachtungen zur aktuellen Diskussion', in Thomas Ellwein, Joachim Jens Hesse, Renate Mayntz, and Fritz W. Scharpf (eds), *Jahrbuch zur Staats- und Verwaltungswissenschaft*, vol. 1, Baden-Baden, Nomos, 1987.

—— 'Competitive party democracy and the Keynesian welfare state', *Policy Sciences*, vol. 15, 1983, pp. 225–46.

—— 'The attribution of public status to interest groups: observations on the West German case', in Suzanne Berger (ed.), *Organizing Interests in Western Europe*, Cambridge, Cambridge University Press, 1981, pp. 123–58.

Offe, Claus, and Helmut Wiesenthal, 'Two logics of collective action', *Political Power and Social Theory*, vol. 1, 1980, pp. 67–115.

Olsen, Johan Per, *Organized Democracy. Political Institutions in a Welfare State – the Case of Norway*, Bergen, Universitetsforlaget, 1983.

Österberg, Dag, *Meta-Sociology. An Inquiry into the Origins and Validity of Social Thought*, Oslo, Norwegian University Press, 1988.

Palmer, Robert R., *The Age of the Democratic Revolution, Vol. 1, The Challenge*, Princeton, Princeton University Press, 1959.

Panebianco, Angelo, *Political Parties. Organization and Power*, Cambridge, Cambridge University Press, 1988 [1982].

Pareto, Vilfredo, *The Transformation of Democracy*, New Brunswick, N.J., Transaction, 1984.

Parker, Martin, 'Post-modern organizations or postmodern organization theory?', *Organization Studies*, vol. 13, no. 1, 1992, pp. 1–17.

Parsons, Talcott, *Social Structure and Personality*, Glencoe, Ill., The Free Press, 1964.

—— *The Social System*, Glencoe, Ill., The Free Press, 1951.

Pateman, Carole, *The Disorder of Woman. Democracy, Feminism and Political Theory*, Cambridge, Polity, 1989.

Patterson, Orlando, *Freedom, Vol. I. Freedom in the Making of Western Culture*, New York, Basic Books, 1991.
Perrot, Michelle, 'On the formation of the French working class', in Ira Katznelson and Aristide R. Zolberg (eds), *Working-Class Formation. Nineteenth-Century Patterns in Europe and the United States*, Princeton, Princeton University Press, 1986, pp. 71–110.
Peukert, Detlev J.K., 'Die Unordnung der Dinge: Michel Foucault und die deutsche Geschichtswissenschaft', in François Ewald and Bernhard Waldenfels (eds), *Michel Foucaults Denken. Spiele der Wahrheit*, Frankfurt/M., Suhrkamp, 1991, pp. 320–33.
—— *Max Webers Diagnose der Moderne*, Göttingen, Vandenhoeck & Ruprecht, 1989.
Pinto, Diana, 'Sociology, politics and society in post-war Italy', *Theory and Society*, vol. 10, 1981, pp. 671–705.
Piore, Michael J., and Charles F. Sabel, *The Second Industrial Divide. Possibilities for Prosperity*, New York, Basic Books, 1984.
Pitkin, Hannah F., *The Concept of Representation*, Berkeley, University of California Press, 1967.
Polanyi, Karl, *The Great Transformation*, New York, Farrar, Straus & Giroux, 1975 [1944].
Pollak, Michael, 'Historisation des sciences sociales et sollicitation sociale de l'histoire', *Bulletin de l'Institut de l'histoire du temps présent*, no. 13, 1983.
—— 'Paul F. Lazarsfeld – fondateur d'une multinationale scientifique', *Actes de la recherche en sciences sociales*, no. 25, 1979, pp. 45–59.
Porter, Theodore M., *The Rise of Statistical Thinking, 1820–1900*, Princeton, Princeton University Press, 1986.
Poster, Mark, *The Mode of Information. Poststructuralism and Social Context*, Cambridge, Polity, 1990.
Pred, Allan, *Making Histories and Constructing Human Geographies. The Local Transformation of Practice, Power Relations, and Consciousness*, Boulder, Col., Westview, 1990.
Procacci, Giovanna, 'Facing poverty: American and French philanthropy between science and reform', in Dietrich Rueschemeyer and Theda Skocpol (eds), *Social Knowledge and the Origins of Modern Social Policies*, Princeton and New York, Princeton University Press and Russell Sage Foundation (forthcoming).
Quéré, Michel, 'The technopolis as a response to industrial crisis: observations on the French case', *Industrial Crisis Quarterly*, vol. 4, no. 4, 1990, pp. 311–20.
Rabinbach, Anson, 'Social knowledge, fatigue, and the politics of industrial accidents', in Dietrich Rueschemeyer and Theda Skocpol (eds), *Social Knowledge and the Origins of Modern Social Policies*, Princeton and New York, Princeton University Press and Russell Sage Foundation, (forthcoming).
Radkau, Joachim, *Technik in Deutschland. Vom 18. Jahrhundert bis zur Gegenwart*, Frankfurt/M., Suhrkamp, 1989.
—— *Zum ewigen Wachstum verdammt? Historisches über Jugend und Alter großer technischer Systeme*, Berlin, WZB, 1992 (WZB Papers FS II 92–505).
Rawls, John, *A Theory of Justice*, Cambridge, Mass., Belknap of Harvard University Press, 1971.
Reich, Robert B., *The Work of Nations. Preparing Ourselves for Twenty-first Century Capitalism*, New York, Knopf, 1991.
Reichardt, Rolf, and Reinhart Koselleck (eds), *Die Französische Revolution als Bruch des gesellschaftlichen Bewußtseins*, Munich, Oldenbourg, 1988.
Revue économique, special issue on *L'économie des conventions*, vol. 40, no. 2, 1989.
Richardson, Bradley M., 'European party loyalties revisited', *American Political Science Review*, vol. 85, no. 3, 1991, pp. 751–75.
Riedel, Manfred, 'Gesellschaft, bürgerliche', in Otto Brunner, Werner Conze, and Reinhart Koselleck (eds), *Geschichtliche Grundbegriffe. Historisches Lexikon der*

politisch-sozialen Sprache in Deutschland, Stuttgart, Klett-Cotta, vol. 2, 1975, pp. 719–800.

Ringer, Fritz, *The Decline of the German Mandarins*, Cambridge, Mass., Harvard University Press, 1969.

Robin, Régine, 'Le dépotoir des rêves', in Régine Robin (ed.), *Masses et culture de masse dans les années 30*, Paris, Editions ouvrières, 1991, pp. 9–41.

Rogers, Everett, with L. Svennig, *Modernization Among Peasants*, New York, Holt, Rinehart & Winston, 1969.

Rogers, Richard, *Visions Dancing in Engineers' Heads. AT&T's Quest to Fulfil the Leitbild of a Universal Telephone Service*, Berlin, WZB, 1990 (WZB Paper FS II 90–102).

Rokkan, Stein, 'Mass suffrage, secret voting and political participation', *Archives européennes de sociologie*, vol. 11, 1961, pp. 132–52.

Röpke, Wilhelm, *Die Gesellschaftskrisis der Gegenwart*, Berne, Haupt, 1979 [1942].

Rorty, Richard, *Contingency, Irony, and Solidarity*, Cambridge, Cambridge University Press, 1989.

Rosanvallon, Pierre, *Le sacre du citoyen. Histoire du suffrage universel en France*, Paris, Gallimard, 1992.

—— *La crise de l'Etat-providence*, Paris, Seuil, 1981.

—— *Le capitalisme utopique. Critique de l'idéologie économique*, Paris, Seuil, 1979.

Rose, Nikolas, 'Governing the enterprising self', in Paul Heelas and Paul Morris (eds), *The Values of the Enterprise Culture. The Moral Debate*, London, Routledge, 1992, pp. 141–64.

—— *Governing the Soul. The Shaping of the Private Self*, London, Routledge, 1989.

Rose, Nikolas, and Peter Miller, 'Political power beyond the state: problematics of government', *British Journal of Sociology*, vol. 43, no. 2, 1992, pp. 173–205.

Rosenberg, Hans, *Große Depression und Bismarckzeit. Wirtschaftsablauf, Gesellschaft und Politik in Mitteleuropa*, Berlin, de Gruyter, 1967.

Ross, Dorothy, *The Origins of American Social Science*, Cambridge, Cambridge University Press, 1991.

Rossi, Pietro, 'La sociologia nella seconda metà del'ottocento: dall'impiego di schemi storico-evolutivi alla formulazione di modelli analitici', *Il pensiero politico*, vol. 15, no. 1, 1982, pp. 188–215.

—— 'Presentazione', in Pietro Rossi (ed.), *Ricerca sociologica e ruolo del sociologo*, Bologna, Il Mulino, 1972.

Rostow, Walt W., 'The world economy since 1945: a stylized historical analysis', *Economic History Review*, vol. 38, 1985, pp. 252–75.

—— *The Stages of Economic Growth*, Cambridge, Cambridge University Press, 1960.

Rueschemeyer, Dietrich, and Ronan van Rossem, 'The Fabian Society and the Verein für Sozialpolitik: social knowledge and early social policy', in Dietrich Rueschemeyer and Theda Skocpol (eds), *Social Knowledge and the Origins of Modern Social Policies*, Princeton and New York, Princeton University Press and Russell Sage Foundation (forthcoming).

Rueschemeyer, Dietrich, Evelyne Huber Stephens, and John D. Stephens, *Capitalist Development and Democracy*, Cambridge, Polity, 1992.

Rundell, John F., *Origins of Modernity. The Origins of Modern Social Theory from Kant to Hegel to Marx*, Cambridge, Polity, 1987.

Sabel, Charles F., 'Moebius-strip organizations and open labor markets: some consequences of the reintegration of conception and execution in a volatile economy', in Pierre Bourdieu and James S. Coleman (eds), *Social Theory for a Changing Society*, Boulder, Col., and New York, Westview and Russell Sage, 1991, pp. 23–54.

Safran, William, 'State, nation, national identity, and citizenship: France as a test case', *International Political Science Review*, vol. 12, no. 3, 1991, pp. 219–38.

Salais, Robert, and Laurent Thévenot (eds), *Le travail. Marchés, règles, conventions*, Paris, Economica, 1986.

Salais, Robert, Nicolas Baverez, and Bénédicte Reynaud, *L'invention du chômage. Histoire et transformations d'une catégorie en France des années 1890 aux années 1980*, Paris, PUF, 1986.

Scharpf, Fritz W., *Crisis and Choice in European Social Democracy*, Ithaca, Cornell University Press, 1991.

Scherr, Albert, 'Postmoderne Soziologie – Soziologie der Postmoderne?', *Zeitschrift für Soziologie*, vol. 19, no. 1, 1990, pp. 3–12.

Scheuch, Erwin K., 'Schwierigkeiten der Soziologie mit dem Prozeß der Modernisierung', in Wolfgang Zapf (ed.), *Modernisierung moderner Gesellschaften*, Frankfurt/M., Campus, 1991, pp. 109–39.

Schieder, Theodor, 'Europa im Zeitalter der Nationalstaaten und europäische Weltpolitik bis zum Ersten Weltkrieg (1870–1918)', in Theodor Schieder (ed.), *Handbuch der Europäischen Geschichte*, vol. 6, Stuttgart, Union, 1968, pp. 1–196.

Schiller, Herbert I., 'The erosion of national sovereignty by the world business system', in Michael Traber (ed.), *The Myth of the Information Revolution. Social and Ethical Implications of Communication Technology*, London, Sage, 1986, pp. 21–34.

Schmitter, Philippe C. (ed.), *Corporatism and Policy-Making in Contemporary Western Europe*, special issue of *Comparative Political Studies*, vol. 10, no. 1, 1977.

Schulze, Gerhard, *Die Erlebnisgesellschaft. Kultursoziologie der Gegenwart*, Frankfurt/M., Campus, 1992.

Schwartz, Nancy L., *The Blue Guitar. Political Representation and Community*, Chicago, The University of Chicago Press, 1988.

Seidman, Steven, *Liberalism and the Origins of European Social Theory*, Oxford, Blackwell, 1983.

Sewell, William H. Jr., 'Artisans, factory workers, and the formation of the French working class, 1789–1848', in Ira Katznelson and Aristide R. Zolberg (eds), *Working-Class Formation. Nineteenth-Century Patterns in Europe and the United States*, Princeton, Princeton University Press, 1986, pp. 45–70.

—— *Work and Revolution in France. Language and Labour from the Old Regime to 1848*, Cambridge, Cambridge University Press, 1980.

Shils, Edward, 'Tradition, ecology, and institution in the history of sociology, *Daedalus*, no. 99, 1970, pp. 760–825.

Shklar, Judith N., *American Citizenship. The Quest for Inclusion*, Cambridge, Mass., Harvard University Press, 1991.

Siegel, Fred (ed.), 'Social breakdown', a thematic issue of *Dissent*, Spring 1991, pp. 163–292.

Silverman, Sydel, 'Patronage and community-nation relationships in central Italy', in Steffen W. Schmidt, Laura Guasti, Carl H. Landé, and James C. Scott (eds), *Friends, Followers and Factions: A Reader in Political Clientelism*, Berkeley, University of California Press, 1977, pp. 293–304.

Skocpol, Theda, 'Bringing the state back in: strategies of analysis in current research', in Peter B. Evans, Dietrich Rueschemeyer, and Theda Skocpol (eds), *Bringing the State Back In*, Cambridge, Cambridge University Press, 1985.

Smart, Barry, *Postmodernity*, London, Routledge, 1993.

Smith, Adam, *An Inquiry into the Nature and Causes of the Wealth of Nations*, Chicago, University of Chicago Press, 1976 [1776].

Smith, Anthony D., *Nationalism in the Twentieth Century*, Oxford, Robertson, 1979.

Smith, Dennis, *The Chicago School. A Liberal Critique of Capitalism*, London, Macmillan, 1988.

Smith, Dorothy, 'A sociology for women', *The Everyday World as Problematic. A Feminist Sociology*, Boston, Northeastern University Press, 1987, pp. 49–104.

Soffer, Reba N., *Ethics and Society in England. The Revolution in the Social Sciences 1870–1914*, Berkeley, University of California Press, 1978.
Sola Pool, Ithiel de, *Technologies Without Boundaries. On Telecommunications in a Global Age* (ed. by Eli M. Noam), Cambridge, Mass., Harvard University Press, 1990.
Stacey, Judith, *Brave New Families. Stories of Domestic Upheaval in Late Twentieth Century America*, New York, Basic Books, 1990.
Stigler, Stephen M., *The History of Statistics. The Measurement of Uncertainty Before 1900*, Cambridge, Mass., Belknap of Harvard University Press, 1986.
Stokes, Donald E., 'Political parties in the normative theory of representation', in J. Roland Pennock and John W. Chapman (eds), *Representation*, New York, Atherton Press, 1968.
Stone, Norman, *Europe Transformed 1878–1919*, Glasgow, Fontana, 1983.
Susman, Warren I., 'The thirties', in Stanley Cohen and Lorman Ratner (eds), *The Development of an American Culture*, New York, St. Martin's Press, 1983, pp. 215–60.
Swaan, Abram de, *In Care of The State*, Cambridge, Polity, 1988.
Szreter, Simon, 'The genesis of the Registrar General's classification of occupations', *British Journal of Sociology*, vol. 35, no. 4, 1984, pp. 522–46.
Talmon, J.L., *Origins of Totalitarian Democracy*, London, Gollancz, 1952.
Taylor, Charles, *Sources of the Self. The Making of the Modern Identity*, Cambridge, Mass., Harvard University Press, 1989.
Therborn, Göran, 'The two-thirds, one-third society', in Stuart Hall and Martin Jacques (eds), *New Times. The Changing Face of Politics in the 1990s*, London, Lawrence & Wishart, 1989, pp. 103–15.
Thévenot, Laurent, 'L'action qui convient', in Patrick Pharo and Louis Quéré (eds), *Les formes de l'action. Sémantique et sociologie* (*Raisons pratiques*, no. 1, 1990), Paris, Editions de l'EHESS, 1990, pp. 39–69.
Thompson, Edward P., *The Making of the English Working Class*, London, Gollancz, 1963.
Thompson, Grahame, 'The evolution of the managed economy in Europe', *Economy and Society*, vol. 21, no. 2, 1992, pp. 129–51.
Tilton, Tim, *The Political Theory of Swedish Social Democracy. Through the Welfare State to Socialism*, Oxford, Clarendon, 1990.
Tiryakian, Edward A., 'Modernization: exhumetur in pace (Rethinking macrosociology in the 1990s)', *International Sociology*, vol. 6, no. 2, 1991, pp. 165–80.
Touraine, Alain, *Critique de la Modernité*, Paris, Fayard, 1992.
—— 'An introduction to the study of social movements', *Social Research*, vol. 52, no. 4, 1985, pp. 749–87.
—— *Le retour de l'acteur. Essai de sociologie*, Paris, Fayard, 1984.
Tribe, Keith, 'Friedrich List and the critique of "cosmopolitical economy" ', *The Manchester School*, vol. 56, no. 1, 1988, pp. 17–36.
Trommler, Frank, 'Aufstieg und Fall des Amerikanismus in Deutschland', in Trommler (ed.), *Amerika und die Deutschen*, Opladen, Westdeutscher Verlag, 1986, pp. 666–76.
Turner, Bryan S., 'Periodization and politics in the postmodern', in Turner (ed.), *Theories of Modernity and Postmodernity*, London, Sage, 1990.
—— 'The rationalization of the body: reflections on modernity and discipline', in Scott Lash and Sam Whimster (eds), *Max Weber, Rationality and Modernity*, London, Allen & Unwin, 1987, pp. 222–41.
Turner, Charles, 'Lyotard and Weber: postmodern rules and neo-Kantian values', in Bryan S. Turner (ed.), *Theories of Modernity and Postmodernity*, London, Sage, 1990, pp. 108–16.
United Nations, *Economic Survey of Europe in 1971, Part 1. The European Economy from the 1950s to the 1970s*, New York, United Nations, 1972.
Virilio, Paul, *L'inertie polaire*, Paris, Bourgois, 1990.
Voegelin, Eric, *The New Science of Politics. An Introduction*, Chicago, The University of Chicago Press, 1952.

Wagner, Peter, 'Liberty and discipline: making sense of postmodernity, or, once again, towards a sociohistorical understanding of modernity', *Theory and Society*, vol. 22, 1992, pp. 467–92.

—— 'Science of society lost: the failure to establish sociology in Europe during its "classical" period', in Peter Wagner, Björn Wittrock, and Richard Whitley (eds), *Discourses on Society. The Shaping of the Social Science Disciplines*, Dordrecht, Kluwer, 1991, pp. 219–45.

—— *Sozialwissenschaften und Staat. Frankreich, Italien, Deutschland 1870–1980*, Frankfurt/M., Campus, 1990.

—— 'Reform coalitions between social scientists and policy-makers', in Stuart Blume, Joske Bunders, Loet Leyderdorff, and Richard D. Whitley (eds), *The Social Direction of the Public Sciences*, Dordrecht, Reidel, 1987, pp. 277–306.

Wagner, Peter, and Björn Wittrock, *Social Sciences and Societal Developments. The Missing Perspective*, Berlin, WZB, 1987 (Paper P 7–3).

Wallace, Ruth A. (ed.), *Feminism and Sociological Theory*, Newbury Park, Sage, 1989.

Walton, Richard E., 'From control to commitment in the workplace', *Harvard Business Review*, March/April, no. 2, 1985, pp. 76–84.

Walzer, Michael, *Spheres of Justice. A Defense of Pluralism and Equality*, New York, Basic Books, 1983.

—— 'The idea of civil society', *Dissent*, Spring 1991, pp. 293–304.

—— 'What does it mean to be an "American"?', *Social Research*, vol. 57, no. 3, 1990, pp. 591–614.

Ware, Alan, *Citizens, Parties and the State. A Reappraisal*, Princeton, Princeton University Press, 1988.

—— *The Breakdown of Democratic Party Organization, 1940–1980*, Oxford, Clarendon Press, 1985.

Watts, Steven, *The Republic Reborn. War and the Making of Liberal America, 1790–1820*, Baltimore, The Johns Hopkins University Press, 1987.

Weber, Max, 'Wissenschaft als Beruf', *Gesammelte Aufsätze zur Wissenschaftslehre*, Tübingen, Mohr, 4th edn 1973.

—— *Gesammelte Aufsätze zur Soziologie und Sozialpolitik*, Tübingen, Mohr, 1924.

Wehler, Hans-Ulrich, *Entsorgung der deutschen Vergangenheit. Ein polemischer Essay zum 'Historikerstreit'*, Munich, Beck, 1988.

—— *Modernisierungstheorie und Geschichte*, Göttingen, Vandenhoeck und Ruprecht, 1975.

Wehling, Peter, *Die Moderne als Sozialmythos*, Frankfurt/M., Campus, 1992.

Weinstein, James, *The Corporate Ideal in the Liberal State*, Boston, Beacon Press, 1968.

Weir, Margaret, Ann Shola Orloff, and Theda Skocpol (eds), *The Politics of Social Policy in the United States*, Princeton, Princeton University Press, 1988.

Weiss, Carol H., 'Policy research: data, ideas, or arguments', in Peter Wagner, Carol H. Weiss, Björn Wittrock, and Hellmut Wollmann (eds), *Social Sciences and Modern States. National Experiences and Theoretical Crossroads*, Cambridge, Cambridge University Press, 1991, pp. 307–32.

Welsch, Wolfgang, *Unsere postmoderne Moderne*, Weinheim, VCH, Acta humaniora, 1988.

West, Cornel, *The American Evasion of Philosophy. A Genealogy of Pragmatism*, Madison, The University of Wisconsin Press, 1989.

Westbrook, Robert B., *John Dewey and American Democracy*, Ithaca, Cornell University Press, 1991.

Wexler, Philip, Warren Crichlow, June Kern, and Rebecca Martusewicz, *Becoming Somebody: Toward a Social Psychology of School*, Falmer Press, 1992.

White, Hayden, *Tropics of Discourse. Essays in Cultural Criticism*, Baltimore, Johns Hopkins University Press, 1978.

White, Orion, Jr., and Gideon Sjoberg, 'The emerging "New Politics" in America', in M. Donald Hancock and Gideon Sjoberg (eds), *Politics in the Post-Welfare State. Responses to the New Individualism*, New York, Columbia University Press, 1972.

Whitley, Richard, 'The structure and context of economics as a scientific field', *Research in the History of Economic Thought and Methodology*, vol. 4, 1986.

Wiese, Leopold von, 'Die Soziologie als Einzelwissenschaft', *Jahrbuch für Gesetzgebung, Verwaltung und Volkswirtschaft*, vol. 44, 1920.

Wiley, Norbert, 'The current interregnum in American sociology', *Social Research*, vol. 52, no. 1, 1985, pp. 179–207.

Williams, Raymond, *The Long Revolution*, Harmondsworth, Penguin, 1961.

Williamson, Oliver, 'The firm as a nexus of treaties: an introduction', in Masahiko Aoki, Bo Gustafsson, and Oliver E. Williamson (eds), *The Firm as a Nexus of Treaties*, London, Sage, 1990, pp. 1–25.

Winfield, Richard Dien, *Freedom and Modernity*, Albany, State University of New York Press, 1991.

Wittrock, Björn, 'Social knowledge and public policy. Eight models of interaction', in Peter Wagner, Carol H. Weiss, Björn Wittrock, and Hellmut Wollmann (eds), *Social Sciences and Modern States. National Experiences and Theoretical Crossroads*, Cambridge, Cambridge University Press, 1991, pp. 333–53.

Wittrock, Björn, and Peter Wagner, 'Policy constitution through discourse', in Douglas E. Ashford (ed.), *History and Context in Public Policy*, Pittsburgh, University of Pittsburgh Press, 1992, pp. 227–46.

Wolfe, Alan, *Whose Keeper? Social Science and Moral Obligation*, Berkeley, University of California Press, 1989.

—— *The Limits of Legitimacy. Political Contradictions of Contemporary Capitalism*, New York, Free Press, 1977.

Wuthnow, Robert, *Communities of Discourse. Ideology and Social Structure in the Reformation, the Enlightenment, and European Socialism*, Cambridge, Mass., Harvard University Press, 1989.

Wylie, Laurence, *Village in the Vaucluse*, Cambridge, Mass., Harvard University Press, 1957.

Zapf, Wolfgang, 'Modernisierung und Modernisierungstheorien', in Wolfgang Zapf (ed.), *Modernisierung moderner Gesellschaften*, Frankfurt/M., Campus, 1991, pp. 23–39.

Znaniecka Lopata, Helena, 'Role theory', in Judith R. Blau and Norman Goodman (eds), *Social Roles and Social Institutions. Essays in Honor of Rose Laub Coser*, Boulder, Col., Westview, 1991, pp. 1–11.

Zolberg, Aristide R., 'Bounded states in a global market: the uses of international labor migrations', in Pierre Bourdieu and James S. Coleman (eds), *Social Theory for a Changing Society*, Boulder, Col., and New York, Westview and Russell Sage, 1991, pp. 301–25.

Zoll, Rainer *et al.*, *Nicht so wie unsere Eltern! Ein neues kulturelles Modell?*, Opladen, Westdeutscher Verlag, 1989.

Index